# THE BILL OF RIGHTS IN MODERN AMERICA

THIRD EDITION, REVISED AND EXPANDED

# The
# Bill of Rights
# in
# MODERN
# AMERICA

EDITED BY

**DAVID J. BODENHAMER** AND **JAMES W. ELY JR.**

INDIANA UNIVERSITY PRESS

This book is a publication of

Indiana University Press
Office of Scholarly Publishing
Herman B Wells Library 350
1320 East 10th Street
Bloomington, Indiana 47405 USA

iupress.org

© 2022 by Indiana University Press

*Manufactured in the United States of America*

First printing 2022

Cataloging information is available from the Library of Congress.

ISBN 978-0-253-06070-9 (hardcover)
ISBN 978-0-253-06071-6 (paperback)
ISBN 978-0-253-06072-3 (e-book)

# CONTENTS

# THE BILL OF RIGHTS IN
# MODERN AMERICA

# INTRODUCTION

### DAVID J. BODENHAMER
### JAMES W. ELY JR.

THE SECOND DECADE OF THE twenty-first century provides a timely opportunity to review the contested place of individual rights in American life and the US constitutional order. There has been a virtual explosion in claims of rights. While some of these can be traced to provisions in the Bill of Rights, others have extratextual roots in the dramatic political and cultural changes of the past several decades. To complicate matters, some claims of rights clash with other claims and raise challenging questions about which have precedence. The partisan divisions that mark contemporary life make this issue even more contentious.

The essays in this volume, written for a general audience, examine the significance of the Bill of Rights in modern American society as well as claims of rights not grounded on specific constitutional provisions. Although informed by a historical perspective, the authors focus on contemporary issues and explore the current understanding of the Bill of Rights as well as rights claims more broadly. First published in 1993, with a second edition in 2008, the essays, all by leading scholars, have been thoroughly revised and expanded to address the impact of current developments. Four new essays—those by Paul Moreno, Adam D. Moore, Kunal M. Parker, and Marie-Amélie George—are included. In addition to offering fresh perspectives on emerging or rapidly evolving rights, these essays and authors bring younger and more diverse voices to the volume.

American thinking about rights has evolved over time. The framers of the Constitution made a conscious decision to omit a bill of rights. They reasoned that it was unnecessary to restrain a federal government of limited powers. The framers also believed that state bills of rights offered adequate protection to individuals. During the ratification debates, however, the Anti-Federalists used the absence of a bill of rights as a powerful weapon to oppose the proposed

Constitution. Supporters of the Constitution found it politically necessary to promise a federal declaration of individual rights in order to win ratification. The Bill of Rights as proposed by Congress in 1791 was a legacy of the Anti-Federalist critique of the Constitution.

The Bill of Rights has not always occupied a central place in US constitutional dialogue. Consistent with the intention of the framers, the Supreme Court concluded in *Barron v. Baltimore* (1833) that the Bill of Rights applied only to the operations of the federal government. Each state was restricted solely by its own bill of rights. This did not change until the end of the nineteenth century, when the Supreme Court in *Chicago, Burlington and Quincy Railroad Company v. Chicago* (1897) concluded that the just compensation principle of the Fifth Amendment's takings clause was an inherent part of due process and thus applicable to the states through the Fourteenth Amendment. In the early twentieth century, the justices began gradually to extend other provisions of the Bill of Rights to state activity. Many provisions of the Bill of Rights pertaining to the rights of criminal defendants were not applied to state proceedings until the 1960s.

Throughout much of US constitutional history, the Bill of Rights played a secondary role in shaping individual liberties. Indeed, many rights that Americans assert today, such as a right to privacy, are not even mentioned in the Constitution explicitly. Historically, rights were typically defined by legislative bodies and popular conventions. As the Bill of Rights was applied to the states, however, the Supreme Court became the major body determining the substantive content of rights. During the Warren Court era (1953–69), the justices expansively interpreted freedom of speech and religion, the rights of criminal defendants, and the rights of racial minorities.

The understanding of rights remains a matter of intense debate. Should the provisions of the Bill of Rights be construed broadly or strictly? Should courts recognize claims of rights beyond those articulated in the Constitution? To what extent should federalism, the balance between federal and state authority, impact the formulation and enforcement of individual rights? Jurists and scholars are sharply divided on these issues, as are legislators and the general public.

One sign of this debate is clearly reflected in thinking about the judicial function. Liberals, who have long been proponents of a "living constitution" that in theory evolved to meet changing circumstances, have increasingly turned to legal formalism. With so many precedents potentially in jeopardy, they now assert that the landmarks of the Warren Court era must be shielded from scrutiny and possible abandonment. Conservatives, on the other hand, have moved away from their announced preference for a deferential judiciary. Many have called for the Supreme Court to resume its historic role of actively protecting economic and religious rights from legislative infringement.

This volume does not predict the course of future developments, nor do the essays express a common view of recent controversies. On the contrary, we believe it is vital to demonstrate the range and variety of attitudes that influence American thinking about rights. The essays provide a fresh and lively dialogue that probes contemporary controversies over the scope and protection of individual rights. Although the essays do not directly address the role of the Tenth Amendment, which reserves to the states or the people any powers not assigned or prohibited by the Constitution, many of them touch on the important question of federalism in the context of liberties.

The volume is divided into five sections. Part 1, "The Nature of Rights," broadly probes the nature of constitutionalism and its relation to individual liberties. The extent to which rights are properly confined to those set forth in written documents has long been an issue in American constitutionalism. Daniel T. Rodgers describes how historically the aspirations of different groups have done much to shape the growth of new rights. According to Rodgers, this open-ended rights consciousness could not be restricted to the specific language of the Bill of Rights.

Part 2, "Modern Rights in Controversy," comprises essays that treat current issues in interpreting the Bill of Rights and related constitutional provisions. The First Amendment contains several important guarantees of personal freedom. The clauses protecting free speech and prohibiting an establishment of religion have figured prominently in recent litigation before the Supreme Court. Suzanna Sherry examines free speech jurisprudence, arguing that the core value of the free speech clause is protection against government censorship. In addition, she considers the applicability of the anti-censorship principle to such contested areas as commercial speech, obscenity, and campaign finance laws. The justices have also been called on to determine the appropriate relationship between religious institutions and the state. Melvin I. Urofsky discusses the current establishment clause and free exercise jurisprudence. He points out the distinctions between those favoring an accommodation of religious belief and state and those adhering to a strict separation between religion and government.

The scope of the Second Amendment, and the allied issue of gun control legislation, has long been a topic of intense scholarly and political debate. Yet for decades this subject did not figure prominently on the docket of the Supreme Court. Then in 2008 the Court determined that the Second Amendment protected the right of an individual to bear arms and that the provision was binding on the states. Robert J. Cottrol and Raymond T. Diamond examine the intent of the framers and discuss this new era of Second Amendment jurisprudence, which assumes even more importance considering the mass shootings that plague modern America.

James Madison's decision to place guarantees of property in the Fifth Amendment next to criminal justice protections underscores the close association of property rights with personal liberty in the mind of the framers of the Constitution. Following the constitutional revolution of 1937, however, the Supreme Court largely abandoned its historic role as a champion of the rights of property owners. James W. Ely Jr., assesses the uncertain place of property in modern constitutional thought, giving particular attention to the takings clause of the Fifth Amendment. He concludes that the Supreme Court, although more protective of economic rights than at any time since the New Deal era, continues to relegate property to a secondary constitutional status.

Although the Fourteenth Amendment was adopted much later than the Bill of Rights, the equal protection clause elevated equality before the law into a cardinal principle of US constitutionalism and profoundly shaped interpretation of the first ten amendments. As demonstrated by decades of legally imposed racial segregation, it proved difficult to achieve the ideal of equality. Paul Moreno explores the contemporary meaning of equality and affirmative action policy in the context of employment and school admissions. Stressing the inherent tension between the traditional conception of individual rights and the more recent notion of collective equality among racial groups, he notes the lack of consensus about the meaning of equal rights.

Part 3, "Individual Rights and Public Safety," probes the often-contentious matters of crime control and the rights of the accused. The Fourth and Fifth Amendments contain significant provisions to safeguard individuals from abuse of the criminal process and deprivation of property. Since the 1960s, the control of crime and Supreme Court decisions interpreting the scope of criminal due process have become heated political issues. Against the background of earlier Court decisions, David J. Bodenhamer examines the due process revolution engineered by the Warren Court and argues that subsequent Courts' trimming of the landmark decisions of the 1960s amounts to a conservative counterrevolution in the understanding of the rights of the accused. Laurence A. Benner and Michal R. Belknap also focus on the rights of the accused, especially in relationship to police practices, which assumes greater significance given the recent spate of police shootings and the rise of the Black Lives Matter movement. These tragic incidents have unfolded among a changing judicial understanding of the Fourth Amendment's prohibition against unreasonable searches and seizures and the Fifth Amendment's privilege against self-incrimination and the controversial *Miranda* rule.

Part 4, "Emerging Rights," considers the protection of individual rights through the invocation of unenumerated rights in essays new to this volume. Adam D. Moore, whose disciplinary roots are in philosophy and information science, explores different definitions of privacy and the history of legal protection of privacy, both constitutional and statutory. He notes that the word *privacy* does not appear in the Constitution and that many scholars view the creation of this right as more a matter of personal autonomy than freedom from governmental intrusion. As immigration policy has again become a topic of sharp political controversy, Kunal M. Parker takes a close look at the constitutional law of immigration and citizenship. He emphasizes that the Supreme Court has affirmed plenary power in the federal government over immigration and exclusion, and hence the gap between the status of citizen and alien widened in the past century. Marie-Amélie George tackles the rapid evolution of LGBTQ rights, attributing greater judicial receptivity to such rights to significant changes in public opinion. She traces jurisprudential shifts with respect to same-sex marriage and employment discrimination and considers unresolved issues pertaining to the status of transgender individuals.

Part 5, "State Constitutional Rights," explores the often-neglected subject of rights under state constitutions. Some commentators have urged increased reliance on state constitutional law to safeguard individual rights. The essay by Randall T. Shepard, chief justice emeritus of the Indiana Supreme Court, who has been a leader in asserting the role of state constitutions in the federal system, addresses this important topic. A former president of the National Conference of Chief Justices (2005–6), he assesses the prospect for libertarian decisions based on state bills of rights.

Today Americans are engaged in a far-ranging debate about the role of the Supreme Court in society. Central to this dialogue is the need to balance the fundamental premise of majority rule with the protection of core values expressed in the Bill of Rights. Another complication is the emergence of terrorism as a major national concern, which places the challenge of defining the rights of the accused in a new context. The following essays speak to this debate and illustrate the wide diversity of opinion that characterizes current constitutional thinking. By design, the essays are annotated sparingly. Aimed at a general audience, we wish to invite discussion, not overwhelm readers with footnotes. The sources relied on by the authors, as well as suggestions for further reading, may be found in the bibliographic essay for each chapter.

*DJB and JWE*
*May 2020*

PART I

*The Nature of Rights*

# ONE

—◆—

## RIGHTS CONSCIOUSNESS IN
## AMERICAN HISTORY

DANIEL T. RODGERS

IT IS A TRUISM OF contemporary American law practice that lawyers spend little time teaching their clients the importance of rights. From the minute seekers of legal aid cross law offices' thresholds, they bring the rights-saturated language of their political culture with them. Anger, outrage, hurt, self-interest, and a vivid sense of injustice all flood into rights talk. Into rights talk, too, flow the opposite impulses: altruism, hope, selflessness, and loyalty. Intervening into the flood of rights talk, the everyday task of lawyers is to nudge their clients toward the pared-down case statements that the courts can be expected to admit.[1] But the language of rights—intense, abstract, expansive, and open-ended—has never been easily corralled.

For well over two centuries, rights consciousness has left an indelible mark on social and political relations in the United States. The consequences have not always been benign. Rights talk has sluiced complex issues of policy into competing rights claims, often at the expense of deliberation and compromise. It has swept key issues of democratic politics into the undemocratic rule of the courts and flooded every aspect of life with legalist argument. And yet rights talk has also been one of the most important ways in which Americans have infused their politics with a dimension beyond mere law or interests. Arguments about rights—essential, inalienable, human rights—have been among the key tools Americans have used to debate what a good society might look like, freed of injustice and the dead hand of the past. In its messiness, power, and contradictions, rights talk is one of the fundamental strands of US history.

Only a fraction of the historic contest over rights has taken place within the confines of the courts or the Constitution. Scholarship on the Bill of Rights has consistently exaggerated the place of that document in the dynamics of rights history in the United States. The courts have never been as imaginative producers of rights as those who have pressed their arguments on the justices or raised them on street corners or in churches or labor union halls. Rights talk in the American past has been the talk of town meetings, political rallies, newspapers, voluntary associations, religious assemblies, workmates, family gatherings, protest crowds, and electoral huckstering. In moments of crisis this broad diffusion of rights consciousness has ignited angry collisions of competing rights, as the rights of enslaved Americans have smashed up against the rights of other Americans to hold property in slaves, the breadline standees' right to a job against the rights of free enterprise, the rights of pregnant women against the rights of the unborn. Popular politics in the United States has been the site of not only extravagant rights assertions but also endemic rights violations, perpetuated in the name of justice, security, patriotism, racial purity, or even in the name of rights themselves. Rights have been invented and repudiated, expanded and violated, striven for and struggled over. The current emotionally charged and politically polarized furor over the rights of asylum seekers, immigrants, and transgender persons is no historical aberration; its dynamics are among the most familiar in US history. Yet it is from this ongoing passionate, democratic debate over rights that the expansion of rights has historically drawn its primary energy.

As deep a feature of American political culture as it has been, rights consciousness has not been static. There are four key phases in its history. Each was marked by a moment of heightened rights consciousness and, by consequence, of fertile, even audacious, rights invention. The first of these phases, extending from the beginning of the struggle over English colonial policy through 1791, witnessed an explosion of popular rights claims, the habit of thinking about rights with the word *natural* as their key modifier, and a passion for rights declarations. That movement collided with a nervous counterreaction against popular rights construction to produce, scarred and circumscribed, a federal bill of rights. The period from the 1820s through the Civil War and Reconstruction saw a second eruption of rights claims, more radical in its focus on the social rights of workers, women, and enslaved people. A quite different dynamic governed the third phase, from the 1880s through the mid-1930s, as the courts moved aggressively into the creation of rights. Their wholesale construction of new property and entrepreneurial rights triggered a sharp reaction among many of those who had historically been key constituents of rights-based politics. Then out of the changed mental landscape of the Second World War and grassroots struggles for racial justice came yet a fourth era of rights invention whose reverberations still dominate contemporary US politics.

Waves of massive rights invention, passionate contests, partial success, and retreat—these have been the core dynamics of rights in America. A messier history than Bill of Rights mythology admits, it contains its own stories of heroism and inspiration.

## UNALIENABLE RIGHTS

In 1776 there was nothing remarkable in the Declaration of Independence's stress on the term *rights*. In a different historical context, colonists' grievances over taxes and trade might have coalesced around other claims: custom, for example, or justice, or (as some of the phrases of the 1770s had it) the people's general "happiness."[2] Several factors combined, however, to press the fears and outrage of rebellious colonists into a language of rights. Most important was the precedent of 1688–89, the Glorious Revolution in which Parliament had deposed a king and forced the Declaration of Rights on his successor. Afterward, with each expansion of Parliament's powers, the American colonial assemblies had been quick to assert "equivalent rights" for themselves. Some of the colonies had won statements of liberties and privileges from their governors, charters that the Americans had begun to imagine as local variations on the Magna Carta. Not surprisingly, then, when resistance to the heavy-handed imperial reforms intensified, the movement's leaders were quick to denounce the new measures as violations of their "most essential rights and liberties."[3] From the Stamp Act Resolutions of 1765 through the Continental Congress's declaration of rights in 1774 and beyond, the patriot leaders and publicists drummed home the point that the new measures endangered their chartered and constitutional rights, the historical rights due to every British subject.

What was striking in Thomas Jefferson's phrase was the adjective *unalienable*—abstract, indistinct, and still novel in the 1770s. At the beginning of the colonial resistance, there had been little in the Anglo-American past to predict that the leaders of the rebellion would so quickly desert the safe ground of history and precedent for rights that were merely imaginary—natural rights, antecedent to law, indeed to history itself. But the move to establish rights not by sorting through the law but by imagining what the human condition must have been at the moment of its birth—or had to be by its very constitution—was quick to gather force. "The sacred rights of mankind are not to be rummaged for among old parchments or musty records," Alexander Hamilton declared in 1775. "They are written, as with a sunbeam, in the whole *volume* of human nature."[4]

The danger of departing from legally established rights to rights grounded in the original design of nature was not lost on the patriot leaders. Not the least of their fears was that such a move might allow the definition of rights to escape the control of lawyers and educated men and throw it open to any colonist with a philosophical bent. To the end of the Revolution, there were individuals who resisted open-ended declarations of rights. But the exigencies of argument pressed hard in the other direction, as escalating cycles of protest, repression, and outrage pushed the patriot demands beyond any sure foundation of precedent and constitution. Rights grounded in nature were rights that by definition constrained every government, even the emergency committees of safety that had begun to move into the revolutionary power vacuum by 1774–75. In practice, the American Revolution, like all revolutions, suppressed a great many rights, as experienced by loyalists whose property was seized, or whose buildings were burned, or who were harried out of their villages. Yet coming on the heels of a decade of petitions and declarations, the same revolutionary fervor that made liberty seem so fragile that rights had to be smashed to preserve it also impelled the patriots to put rights on paper. And, in the now deeply politicized process, risk a flood of new ones.

The first declaration of rights to bind a patriot government was Virginia's, debated at length in May and June 1776. Its philosophical untidiness was witness to the diverse pressures on the revolutionary state. The Virginia Declaration of Rights was a compound of individual rights, legal and procedural rights, and collective rights (the right to a popular militia and the revolutionary right to abolish any government faithless to the "public weal"), together with general statements of political principles and pious statements of morality. In a gesture full of symbolic meaning, the Virginians claimed these rights not as grievances against the Crown but as the "basis and foundation of government" itself.

During the first years of independence, less than half the states followed Virginia's example of rights declaration. How deeply the new rights talk had lodged in popular politics, however, became clear as early as 1778, when the Massachusetts town meetings rejected a constitution drafted without a bill of rights. Nowhere in late eighteenth-century America can one find so close a reading of public opinion as in the returns of the town meetings that discussed the constitution's failings. Some of them bear the marks of bookish lawyers; others have the spelling of little-schooled farmers. What is striking is the breathtaking inventiveness with which people were now talking about rights: the inalienable right to follow the dictates of one's conscience (though it meant disestablishment of the clergy); the right to absolute property in oneself (though it meant the death of slavery); the right to make public officials stand for annual election; the right of even poor or Black men to vote; the right "engraved in human nature" to a fairly apportioned legislature; the "unalienable right" of popular ratification of a constitution.[5] Unhinged from history and formal law, loosed from the monopoly of learned men, the business of imagining rights had grown from an argumentative strategy to a volatile popular movement.

Rights talk of this sort was still alive when the Constitutional Convention met in 1787, and it is in this context that its failure to propose a federal bill of rights must be understood. Prudence, to be sure, was against the project, given how fiercely the clauses of the state bills of rights had been debated and

· with what diverse results. So was the exhaustion of the delegates by the time George Mason, author of the Virginia declaration, raised the issue in Philadelphia. The deeper instinct, however, was more conservative. The drafters had already carefully deleted every instance of the term *rights* from the Constitution in favor of more cautious references to *immunities* and *privileges*. As *The Federalist*'s lame and belated treatment of the issue made clear, the Constitution's drafters were anxious to evade altogether the unpredictable popular talk of rights and focus debate instead on constitutional mechanics and national pride.[6]

When the Constitution came before the state ratifying conventions, however, it quickly became evident that the framers had miscalculated popular sentiment. The Anti-Federalists' objections to the Constitution only began with the omission of a bill of rights. The sticking point was the power and scope of the proposed national government. By the time the ratification debate reached Virginia, however, the Anti-Federalists had made enactment of a bill of rights, prefixed to the Constitution, a condition of their acquiescence.[7]

It fell to James Madison in the First Congress to fulfill the bargain, though he was himself no partisan of bills of rights. When Jefferson wrote from France that "a bill of rights is what the people are entitled to against every government on earth," a skeptical Madison responded that "parchment barriers" like Virginia's rarely made much difference. In his opening remarks to an impatient Congress, Madison stressed not the philosophical value of a bill of rights but the expediency of one in the current moment as "highly politic, for the tranquility of the public mind, and the stability of the Government."[8] Had Madison had his way, the guarantees of the first ten amendments would not have stood out as a separate bill of rights but would have been woven unobtrusively through the body of the Constitution. Several of the rights that had gathered strong support in the ratifying conventions Madison let drop from his proposal altogether: the right of the people to "instruct" their representatives, a prohibition against chartered monopolies, and a constitutional limitation on peacetime armies. Other proposals succumbed to the caution of Madison's colleagues. In response to the demand that the Constitution begin with a clear statement of constitutional principle, Madison proposed prefixing a clause acknowledging the people's constitutional right to reform (though not abolish) their governments, but the proposal did not get past the House of Representatives. Following the language of the ratifying conventions, Madison proposed three substantial paragraphs elaborating the rights of free speech, assembly, and conscience. The House compacted them into two abbreviated clauses; the Senate bundled them into a sentence. The House would have preserved most of the newly articulated rights against both the state and federal governments; the Senate restricted the First Amendment's scope to acts of Congress.[9]

It was no wonder that leaders of the bill of rights movement like William Grayson complained that their amendments had been "so mutilated and gutted that in fact they are good for nothing."[10] That turned out to be an exaggeration colored by disappointment. In time the amendments were to become, as Madison grudgingly admitted they might, "a good ground for an appeal to the sense of the community."[11] Unlike the Constitution, drafted in secret convention, the Bill of Rights was born as a demand from below. Politically, however, its enactment had been a holding action. It was not a speaking of the framers' mind, as partisans of pure "original intent" have imagined. It was a document born in debate, dissension, compromise, and contending power—in short, out of the usual processes of popular politics. The amendments proposed no new rights. Rather, they gathered up the fervor of rights invention that the struggle with Britain had loosed and filtered out a cautious sliver of it.

### EXPANDED RIGHTS

Rights consciousness in the late eighteenth century focused on official oppression: the tyranny of priests and kings, rapacious tax collectors, corrupt judges, and overbearing officeholders. Domination that was rooted in property, class, racial distinctions, or patriarchy, by contrast, had fallen largely outside the purview of the first bills of rights. In the middle years of the nineteenth century, Americans on the margins of politics began to think seriously about socially constructed forms of power and a second eruption of rights invention ensued.

The first hints of change appeared in the artisans' and workingmen's associations of the 1820s and 1830s. Urban artisans had been central to the struggle against Britain; it was their spokesmen who, in the debates over the Pennsylvania bill of rights of 1776, had tried to incorporate a declaration "That an enormous Proportion of Property vested in a few Individuals is dangerous to the Rights, and destructive of the Common Happiness of Mankind."[12] In the early nineteenth century, as new forms of wage labor and capital organization began to erode the traditional props of artisan life, workingmen's groups revived, recasting the Revolution's language of rights to meet the changed economic relations.

The claims of the new labor associations were not for the enforcement of rights already fixed in the law. As in the eighteenth century, the dynamic in rights talk lay in the utopian possibilities of the idea of "natural" rights—the invitation to imagine those inherent rights that must have preceded law, custom, and social convention at the moment of society's birth. John Locke had justified a natural right to property in this way. Now people in radically different social and economic circumstances than Locke seized on conjectures about the original relationship between labor and property and recast them in popular terms: the "natural and unalienable right" of "all who toil . . . to reap the fruits of their own industry," as the Philadelphia journeymen mechanics put it in 1828; the right to "just remuneration" for a day's toil; the laborers' "natural right" to dispose of their own time as they saw fit.[13] Everywhere in the Euro-American world that the new class relations took hold, workers reached into the dominant language of politics to express their sense of injustice. In mid-nineteenth-century America, the result was a dramatic expansion of the domain of rights.

If rights talk could be turned from claims against governments to claims against private oppression, however, there were other potential users. By the 1830s, a burgeoning antislavery movement was spinning off incendiary rights claims, among them the slavery-nullifying natural right of "every man . . . to his own body [and] to the produce of his own labor."[14] A decade later a new women's rights movement was alive with utopian rights claims: a woman's right to property separate from her husband; to a "sphere of action" as broad as her conscience demanded; to the vote; to all the rights "integral" to her moral being.[15] The radical rights challenges of the mid-nineteenth century rarely drew on the language of the Bill of Rights. Much more contagious were the abstract phrases of the Declaration of Independence. The workingmen's petitions were saturated with Jefferson's phrases. The women's rights convention at Seneca Falls in 1848 put its case into an elaborate paraphrase of the Declaration. Four years earlier, the antislavery Liberty Party had incorporated Jefferson's "certain unalienable rights" passage into its platform, as the Republicans would do again in 1860.[16]

The rights innovators of the mid-nineteenth century formed no common movement. In both the abolitionist and women's movement, many preferred talk of duties and Christian obligations to potentially unbounded claims of rights. As for the workingmen's movement, in an era of ugly mob attacks on free northern Blacks and their White allies, it was shot through with the racism of the time. Many of the same political figures who championed the rights of White free labor succeeded in cutting down the civil freedoms of northern Black citizens and forcing them from the voting rolls. What joined the inventors of new rights was not a common cause but a tactical and ideological contagion—a sense, passed from out-group to out-group, that the rhetorical legacy of the Revolution was ripe for reemployment, this time not against the grand tyranny of kings and despots but against the customary, everyday tyrannies of capital, bosses, slave masters, and husbands.

The response to the new wave of rights demands was mixed and ambivalent. Some of slave society's theorists went so far as to deny that governments were required to recognize any fundamental rights at all. Others tried to elaborate a politics grounded in loyalty and obligation.[17] But as long as White southerners clung to the ultimate right of secession, and as long as slave owners felt the need to call their human property something more secure than a mere social convention, any general repudiation of natural rights talk was foreclosed. The upshot at the political center was a rhetoric of circumlocution, compromises, silences, and strident reassertions, until—in a spectacular collision of competing rights claims—the nation broke into pieces in 1861.

The second wave of rights invention came to a more mixed end than the first. The death of slavery was its boldest, most sweeping achievement. With the defeat of the Confederacy, northern Republicans went south to force phrases from the northern states' bills of rights into the Reconstruction constitutions. The radical workingmen's claim that all persons had an inalienable right to "the fruits of their labor" was injected into some of the southern states' bills of rights in an effort to prevent slavery from rising up, phoenix-like, under any other name. By 1868 the right of Black men to vote had been temporarily forced on the South—although couched as a reward for their loyalty and character, not as a right founded in their nature as men, as African American delegates in Virginia and elsewhere had demanded. The Civil Rights Act of 1875 drew, for a moment, accommodations in private theaters, inns, railroad cars, and steamboats into the realm of rights. The right of women to vote, on the other hand, was abruptly set aside. When workers called for the eight-hour day as a basic human right in the late 1860s, their former allies in the Republican Party campaign for free soil and free labor swiftly rejected the idea.[18] On the margins of power, a new array of social rights had been elaborated and thrust against the center, some of them successfully.

## INVENTED RIGHTS

The third era of rights invention, from the 1880s to the mid-1930s, saw the roles of the judiciary and the champions of popular social movements reversed. For the first century of independence, the most expansive talk of rights had been raised outside the courts. For a time, judges in the early republic had played with the principles of natural justice, usually to reaffirm property rights against invasion. But state and federal court judges quickly found their accustomed ground in the written words of common law, statute, and constitution.

The era of business consolidation marked, in this sense, a sharp and unprecedented turn. First in a trickle of dissenting opinions and then in a flood of majority decisions, the courts began to invent natural rights on their own. The first of these, initially pressed in dissent by Justice Stephen J. Field, was a direct offshoot of the Reconstruction debates over rights: the "sacred and imprescriptible" right to choose one's occupation freely. In a different historical setting, Field's "right of free labor," as propounded in the *Slaughter-House Cases*, might have focused on the plight of the ex-slaves, whose labor was being rapidly constrained in tangles of tenantry, debt peonage, and poverty. By the late 1880s and 1890s, however, in an atmosphere acrid with labor disputes and aggressive capital consolidation, the old antislavery slogan was reformulated as the "right of free contract" and thrust into labor law. With it, state and federal courts overturned laws that had banned scrip payment and payment in orders at the company store, laws setting maximum working hours, laws regulating the weighing of miners' coal output, and laws preventing employers from firing union workers—all in the name of lifting "paternal" and "tutelary" burdens from wage earners and setting them free to make whatever employment contracts they had the will and natural "manhood" to make. Freedom of contract adjudication reached its high-water mark in 1923, when the United States Supreme Court invalidated a District of Columbia statute setting a minimum wage for women on the expansive grounds that the "individual freedom of action contemplated by the Constitution" mandated an unrestrained market of prices, the price of labor included.[19]

The sense of urgency in the courts' elaboration of these newly invented rights was manifest in the extraordinary expansion of cases of judicial review. Before the Civil War, the US Supreme Court had, on average, struck down a single state law each year. In the period 1865 to 1898, the figure jumped to five a year; in the 1920s, it leaped to fourteen. State courts followed the same sharp upward slope in declaring state laws unconstitutional. Undergirding the innovations in constitutional practice was a mental reformulation of the courts as not merely institutions of dispute adjudication but also supralegislatures, censoring and policing the work of the popular branches of government. Judicial review, the president of the American Bar Association urged in this vein in 1892, was "the loftiest function and the most sacred duty of the judiciary." It was "the only breakwater against the haste and passions of the people—against the tumultuous ocean of democracy."[20]

Rights invention was only one of the tools of the new judicial activism. The courts mixed constitutional formalism, elastic readings of the Reconstruction amendments, and appeal to the fundamental rights of liberty and the "sacred rights of property" in particular—all with a high degree of eclecticism. Certain though they were that "acquiring, possessing, and protecting property" was a natural right, judges were not interested in thinking backward to property's origins, much less the workers' claims that their labor was property's true foundation. Nor were they interested in all property rights claims. Rights that might have been construed as kinds of property, or essential to property's protection, they let the legislatures annul. The courts' preoccupation was not with the basic ground of rights, or even property rights in general, but the defense of particular sorts of entrepreneurial property claims. Urged on by business lobbies and litigants, theirs was a rights invention project from above, defining, delimiting, and shoring up the ascendant power of their day.

Although the political system was far too complex to move in lockstep, the general drift of the era was clear. During this period of massive immigration, business consolidation, and bitter and continuous labor conflict, the courts threw themselves into politics. Legislatures—sometimes crudely, sometimes with care and sophistication—tried to forestall the worst exploitations of industrial capitalism, citing the principles of public health, safety, and the common good. At times the courts adjusted and complied. But just as often, they wielded a newly expansive rhetoric of rights to resist.

In the face of the courts' aggressive use of natural rights claims, progressives' faith in the efficacy of rights talk was shaken. Echoing the radical rhetoric of an earlier era, the Socialist Labor Party went to the polls in the 1890s with a platform studded with the assertions of inherent rights. Advocates of women's suffrage sustained the language of equal rights until shortly after the turn of the century, when many social feminists traded in arguments rooted in women's special gifts and moral character.[21] Labor organizers insisted on labor's right to strike and organize, independent of what the Bill of Rights or the courts might say. But the more striking phenomenon of the late nineteenth and early twentieth centuries was the abandonment of rights talk by many of the advocates of the social reform movements of the day.

Some of the progressives' desertion of rights talk stemmed from a changed intellectual climate, dominated as never before by a sense of social evolution and history. In this context, the concept of timeless, abstract rights seemed to many progressive thinkers a throwback to eighteenth-century reasoning. This was the ground on which Woodrow Wilson, at Princeton in the 1890s, dismissed Jefferson's natural rights philosophizing as "false," "abstract," and "un-American."[22] Still more powerful was a sense that rights consciousness was shackled to an archaic individualism that was oblivious to the larger good. Better to talk like Theodore Roosevelt and Woodrow Wilson of the people's "will" and "common interest." The Progressive Party in 1912 discarded every reference to rights from its platform and went to the voters with a case for "social and industrial justice" and the "public welfare." Similarly, the Democratic Party platform of 1936 rang with Jeffersonian appeals to "self-evident truths" but not with rights talk, pledging itself instead to secure the people's "safety," "happiness," and "economic security." While the Liberty League railed against the New Deal invasion of property and contract freedoms with a rhetoric of rights, the core language of the New Dealers turned on "the common good," interdependent economic fates, and the "public interest."[23]

Rights consciousness remained a protean and unpredictable force in US political culture. But for almost two generations, progressive activists' consciousness of social bonds and social-evolutionary processes combined with their deepening political contest with the courts to spur them away from rights language. The language of the Revolution had been co-opted by the defenders of narrow entrepreneurial "liberty." To those struggling to bring industrial capitalism under public control, the eighteenth-century heritage had become increasingly problematic: a set of ineffectual and exploded concepts.

### NEW RIGHTS CLAIMS

Then came the Second World War and, with it, a new burst of rights claims. The precipitating event was the rise of fascism—the ascendancy of political systems in which all rights seemed to have been swallowed up by a monstrously swollen state. In the late 1930s, the dominant theme of Franklin Roosevelt's speeches had been "democracy." By 1940, his speechwriters were reaching back to eighteenth-century traditions to talk of "essential human freedoms," whose fate now hung in the balance. The New Dealers' war-accelerated rediscovery of rights culminated in Roosevelt's promulgation of a "second Bill of Rights" in 1944. A translation of the New Deal into language that progressives had spurned less than a decade earlier, it pledged the nation to an "economic bill of rights": the right to a useful job, adequate earnings, a decent home, adequate medical care, and protection from the economic fears of sickness, old age, accident, and unemployment.[24] Four years later, the United States joined the signatories of an equally expansive Universal Declaration of Human Rights. Joined to New Deal liberalism, the language of rights had become protean and unpredictable once more.

The Supreme Court, beaten in its confrontation with the New Deal, took an equally momentous turn in the late 1930s and 1940s. Rejecting the political and economic program of their predecessors, the Court's new appointees shifted their attention from property rights to the issues brought to a head by the specter of fascism: suppression of speech and expression, subversion of fair trial procedures, and the injuries of racial stigmas and inequality. The Court did not arrive at its new program of "preferred rights" without its share of backtracking, particularly during the war and the revived national security scare of the 1950s, but in the shadow of the European dictatorships, its new course was clear.

Dismantling the elaborate edifice built on freedom of contract with the damning observation that the phrase was nowhere in the Constitution, the Supreme Court had reason to keep its distance from assertive rights invention. But the needs of the moment and the war and Cold War–revived talk of political fundamentals all pressed toward appropriation, rather than rejection, of the older lines of rights argument. By the 1940s, the Supreme Court was beginning to pick its way through rights again, establishing some of the sections of the Bill of Rights as so basic and fundamental as to be incorporated into state law through the Fourteenth Amendment. Before the decade was out, the Court had begun again to spin off inventions: rights not directly specified in the Constitution but so fundamental, so fixed a star in our constitutional constellation, that they were morally and logically entailed in the Bill of Rights or the Reconstruction amend-ments themselves.[25] Sometimes through simple assertion, sometimes through ingenious argument, the rights of marriage and procreation, travel, association, the vote, education, and privacy had all been framed as fundamental by the end of the 1960s and laid beside the Bill of Rights as its modern addendum.

The courts were so centrally involved in the postwar rearticulation of rights that the era's burst of rights assertions is often misconstrued as a movement from the top down. But as in the late eighteenth and early nineteenth centuries, the essential fuel came from below. Most important was the African American civil rights movement. Unlike their White counterparts, African American progres-sives had clung to the language of rights through the early twentieth century. In keeping with the mood of the times, the Declaration of Principles from which the NAACP had emerged in the first decade of the century ended with a list of "Negro" Americans' social and civic "duties." But duties were only ancillary to as-sertions of political and "manhood" rights.[26] Rights claims gave immediacy to the talk of freedom that had run so long and eloquently through African American culture. Rights claims challenged core assumptions that a part of humankind was inferior by nature. In the name of a higher and deeper justice, they made defiance of the law into an act of politics. Given urgency by comparisons of racial practice in the United States with Nazi racism, an African American civil and human rights movement mobilized during the war, supplying the courts with arguments and pushing them down the path that would lead to *Brown v. Board of Education* and, in the face of massive resistance to that decision, to the intensified judicial activism of the 1960s.[27]

Equally significant was the contagious effect of the civil rights movement on other outsiders. Through imitation, reaction, or rivalry, the tactics and rights claims of the Black protest movement spread, slowly in the 1950s and then with snowballing effect in the 1960s and early 1970s. The women's rights movement was reborn in a consciousness-intensifying intersection with the African American civil rights protests. Dozens of insurgent movements sprang up, holding deeply entrenched customs to the test of fundamental rights: movements for the rights of gay Americans, Native Americans, Latino Americans, and Asian Americans; movements for the rights of the young, the aged, the poor, the homeless, the institutionalized, and the disabled. Heightened by television and by the historic conjuncture of social movement organization with an activist judiciary willing to give a hearing to the rights claims roiling up from below, rights talk spread with unprecedented speed from out-group to out-group. Rights claims not only mo-bilized out-groups but also, in some cases, created them where group conscious-ness had barely had a public language before—the work of the National Welfare Rights Organization being a striking example.[28]

This eruption of rights claims and rights-claiming organizations generated resistance across a wide and fiercely contested front. Conservatives deplored the unbounded range of the new rights talk and the so-called tyranny of the justices who forced parts of it into the law. From the left, scholars in the critical legal studies movement mounted an even more sweeping critique. The abstractions embedded in rights talk, they objected, were vague and indeterminate, so fully extracted from history and circumstances as to be blind to the core issues of power and justice at stake. A case in point was the American Civil Liberties Union's transformation from a labor defense organization to a defender of rights from whatever social or political position they might come from—the speech rights of rapacious employers equally with the protest rights of their employees, the wielders of hate speech equally with the voices of democracy-enhancing speech. The idea of each person as essentially a rights holder, armored from state and society by a fortress of inviolable rights protections, conservatives cautioned, encouraged withdrawal from social responsibilities into a detached and brittle individualism. From the left, critics warned that legalistic talk distorted claims of justice by narrowing them into the rights categories that courts might accept. Even in a case like *Brown*, whose practical effects were stymied so long by White Southern resistance, these critics argued, rights-grounded strategies were ineffectual compared to the hard work of political mobilization, persuasion, and action.[29]

But this time the dynamics in rights talk overran its critics on both the right and the left. Conservative activists learned how to turn rights claims into weapons for tradition's defense. Repositioning the case for criminal constraints on abortion as defense of the right to life set a powerful model for the battles to come. By the 1980s, social and cultural conservatives were working hard all across the contested social terrain to defend the status quo with counterclaims of rights: parents' rights to keep the traditional family order in place, free speech rights to protect customs of school prayer and Bible reading, taxpayers' rights to hold down public budgets, rights of religious conscience to turn away gay couples seeking to purchase services or refuse to pay taxes that implicated an employer in the provision of contraception. In the early years of its existence, a Moral Majority organizer noted in 1990, "We framed the issues wrong." Framing school prayer as good didn't win the day. "So we learned to frame the issue in terms of 'students' rights.'. . . We are pro-choice for students having the right to pray in public schools."[30] On the political left, the critical legal studies critique of rights came and went, weakened in part by the countercharge that it was itself too distant from real life to understand how, among the truly powerless, rights could alchemize nothingness into visibility and hope.[31]

In the face of these conflicting demands, the Supreme Court tacked back and forth between resistance to the new rights demands and inventions of its own.

After a series of school busing and districting decisions that reached their apogee in *Swann v. Charlotte-Mecklenburg Board of Education* in 1971, the Supreme Court began to back away from efforts to address the social roots of racial segregation and to focus narrowly on the deliberate actions of public authorities. Affirmative measures to correct racial injustices by taking account of race were subject to increasingly tight standards of scrutiny and tailoring. In a decision upholding state sodomy laws in 1986, a conservative Supreme Court majority made clear its determination to get out of the business of instantiating any new "fundamental" rights altogether.[32]

But the pressure toward rights invention was too strong to resist. In 1965, the Court had already announced a "right of privacy older than the Bill of Rights," inherent in the "penumbras" that give the Bill of Rights protections their life and substance.[33] Over the next fifty years, the rights of privacy spread to embrace a woman's right to terminate an early pregnancy without suffering the criminal prosecution of the state, the decriminalization of homosexuality, and the rights of same-sex couples to marry—all fundamentally inherent in people's liberty to express their identity and autonomy of self within the spheres of intimate life. Had they "known the components of liberty in its manifold possibilities" that later generations would realize, Anthony Kennedy wrote for the Court in 2003, the framers of the Fourteenth Amendment would have explicitly enumerated them all.[34]

Just as consequential was the Supreme Court's extension of First Amendment speech rights into economic relations with the same confidence that its late nineteenth-century predecessors had pressed their doctrine of freedom of contract. A series of judgments undermined the effectiveness of campaign finance reform by holding that nonprofit and profit-making corporations had as firm a claim to First Amendment protection when they contributed to election campaigns as did ordinary people. An equally far-reaching set of judgments has extended free speech rights to people and business enterprises seeking new immunities from speech that they deem coercive. Under this heading have come successful challenges to Food and Drug Administration restrictions on the claims that manufacturers of medicines can make for their products; legally mandated payments to public employees' collective bargaining agents whose views might clash with their own; and, in the most striking case, a successful appeals court challenge to the requirement that employers post notices of their employees' National Labor Relations Act rights and grievances procedures, on the grounds that such a posting coerces an employers' speech rights no less severely than the long-abandoned requirement that all citizens, no matter what their religious convictions about oaths might be, recite the Pledge of Allegiance. By one recent count, almost half the free speech cases brought to the Supreme Court now are suits by commercial enterprises.[35]

"Speech is everywhere," Justice Elena Kagan objected. To let the justices pick which speech and which speech holders to protect was to weaponize the First Amendment in the interests of whichever speech holder the courts' majority thought most worthy.[36] By 2018, that was only to state the obvious: that along all these lines of rights reasoning, the courts had inserted themselves deep into politics and policy making once more. Social justice movements, like corporations, organize fleets of lawyers on the wager that court judgment is the surer path to victory than the labor of politics and persuasion. By the second decade of the twenty-first century, these trends in rights assertion have raised the state of rights invention to a volume and cacophony unmatched before. Jurists, commercial enterprises, entrenched and beleaguered defenders of tradition, public interest law firms, libertarian opponents of anything beyond the minimalist state, powerful political lobbies, and aggrieved citizens converge on the language of rights.

But in this intensely crowded field, the older pattern of popular, democratic rights claims persists. The contagious influence of the civil rights movement is, even now, far from spent. In the Black Lives Matter and #MeToo movements, old, deeply entrenched patterns of power are challenged as violations of people's most basic, inherent rights. The rights of immigrants, both legal and undocumented, are a flash point of acute political tension. The human rights of prisoners have returned to the political agenda after decades of aggressive incarceration. The death penalty is under serious debate. The rights of people beyond the United States under the thumb of torture, starvation, genocide, or mass expulsion flare into moments of social activism. The human rights to housing, to wages adequate to care for a family, to medical care, and to maternity and sick leave have awakened, for the moment, a new political left. In its sheer volume of rights invention and cascading rights disputes, the sixty-five years after *Brown* have no historic parallel. But in its harnessing of popular aspirations and grievances to the language of rights, its dynamics are familiar.

## RIGHTS CONSCIOUSNESS

"None of the supposed rights of man," Karl Marx objected in 1843, "go beyond the egoistic man, man as . . . an individual separated from the community, withdrawn into himself, wholly preoccupied with his private interest and acting in accordance with his private caprice."[37] The point cannot be dismissed. Rights claims do not exist outside a situation of real or potential antagonism. Like the Anglo-American legal system itself, rights claims invite sharp distinctions between the rights-holding self and others. It is hardly an accident that a political culture repeatedly flooded by popular claims of rights has no easy time talking directly about common possessions, common interests, or entangled and interdependent destinies. Communities of compromise are not easily made from contentious rights holders. Without a strong language of social relationships larger than the language of rights, political cultures fracture.

But rights consciousness in the United States has never been a simple vehicle for possessive individualism. From the Virginia Bill of Rights through the New Deal's declaration of economic rights and beyond, strong rights claims have gathered individual and collective rights into a common fold. Some rights in the American polity are held by individuals, others by groups, by the "community" (as the Pennsylvania bill of rights of 1776 had it), or the "people" as a whole. That rights claims carry both public and private potential, that social democracy and laissez-faire can both be justified on rights-based foundations, is not due to the capriciousness of language. Rights consciousness contains its own distinctive collective dynamic. Translating pain and injury—a police officer's beating, a "no Jews wanted" sign, or a compulsory religious oath—into claims of rights not only transfers personal wounds into the realm of justice; it translates private experience into a general claim and potentially universalizing language. This is the solidaristic dynamic in rights movements. This is likewise the dynamic of rights contagion, as universally stated rights slip past the tacit restrictions that hedged them in (White, male, Christian, native-born, and the rest) and move out into the hands of unanticipated users.

Above all, what is most striking about the history of rights consciousness in the United States is its democratic character, its invitation to political theorizing from below. To imagine the existence of certain inalienable rights is to think at cross-purposes to history, custom, and massively entrenched convention and to measure each of these against what one can imagine to be the original principles of justice. That has not precluded Americans from trampling massively on rights, not the least in the practice of slavery that bore so hard on the Constitution drafters' minds. But the utopian strain in rights consciousness remains a powerful, unpredictable lever of change.

Since the Revolution, rights consciousness has never been fully consolidated in the existing institutions of law—never separable from inquiry into rights as they ought to be, or must once have been. The result has been a widely diffused, often destabilizing, sometimes convoluted but nonetheless inventive popular debate about the fundamentals of a just society.

The members of the First Congress who served as arbiters of the Bill of Rights' final language had far narrower and more immediate goals than this. As nervous as all centrists about the instability of rights arguments, they pruned the open-ended natural rights abstractions out of the document with the rigor of men determined to close that line of argument from the external democratic clamor. The failure of their effort is one of American history's central events and, even now, the American polity's good fortune.

## NOTES

1. Sally Engle Merry, *Getting Justice and Getting Even: Legal Consciousness among Working-Class Americans* (Chicago: University of Chicago Press, 1990).

2. Oscar Handlin and Mary Handlin, eds., *The Popular Sources of Political Authority: Documents on the Massachusetts Constitution of 1780* (Cambridge, MA: Belknap, 1966), 65.

3. *The Papers of John Adams*, ed. Robert J. Taylor et al., vol. 1 (Cambridge, MA: Harvard University Press, 1977), 137.

4. Bernard Bailyn, *The Ideological Origins of the American Revolution* (Cambridge, MA: Harvard University Press, 1967), 188.

5. Handlin and Handlin, *Popular Sources of Political Authority*, 202–379.

6. Alexander Hamilton, John Jay, and James Madison, *The Federalist Papers* (1787), No. 84.

7. John P. Kaminski et al., eds., *The Documentary History of the Ratification of the Constitution: Digital Edition* (Charlottesville: University of Virginia Press, 2009–19).

8. Gordon Lloyd and Margie Lloyd, eds., *The Essential Bill of Rights: Original Arguments and Fundamental Doctrines* (Lanham, MD: University Press of America, 1998), 320, 325, 341.

9. Helen E. Veit et al., eds., *Creating the Bill of Rights: The Documentary Record from the First Congress* (Baltimore: Johns Hopkins University Press, 1991). See also Library of Congress, "Primary Documents in American History, Bill of Rights," https://www.loc.gov/rr/program/bib/ourdocs/billofrights.html.

10. Veit, *Creating the Bill of Rights*, 300.

11. Lloyd and Lloyd, *Essential Bill of Rights*, 327.

12. Eric Foner, *Tom Paine and Revolutionary America* (New York: Oxford University Press, 1976), 133.

13. John R. Commons et al., eds., *A Documentary History of American Industrial Society*, 10 vols. (Cleveland, 1910–11), 5:86; 6:94.

14. John L. Thomas, *The Liberator: William Lloyd Garrison* (Boston: Little, Brown, 1963), 173.

15. Mary Jo Buhle and Paul Buhle, eds., *The Concise History of Woman Suffrage* (Urbana: University of Illinois Press, 1978), 94–95; Angelina E. Grimké, *Letters to Catherine E. Beecher* (Boston, 1838), 108.

16. Sally G. McMillen, *Seneca Falls and the Origins of the Women's Rights Movement* (New York: Oxford University Press, 2008); Donald B. Johnson, ed., *National Party Platforms*, 2 vols. (Urbana: University of Illinois Press, 1978), 1:175–82, 360–63.

17. Eugene D. Genovese, *The World the Slaveholders Made: Two Essays in Interpretation* (New York: Pantheon, 1968).

18. Steven Hahn, *A Nation under Our Feet: Black Political Struggles in the Rural South from Slavery to the Great Migration* (Cambridge, MA: Harvard University Press, 2003); David Montgomery, *Beyond Equality: Labor and the Radical Republicans, 1862–1872* (New York: Vintage Books, 1967).

19. *Slaughter-House Cases*, 16 Wallace 110 (1873); *Adkins v. Children's Hospital*, 261 U.S. 561 (1923).

20. Quoted in Arnold M. Paul, *Conservative Crisis and the Rule of Law: Attitudes of Bar and Bench, 1887–1895* (Ithaca, NY: Cornell University Press, 1960), 81. See also Robert W. Gordon, "Legal Thought and Legal Practice in the Age of American Enterprise, 1870–1920," in *Professions and Professional Ideologies in America*, ed. Gerald L. Geison (Chapel Hill: University of North Carolina Press, 1983).

21. Johnson, *National Party Platforms*, 1:95, 109; Aileen S. Kraditor, *The Ideas of the Woman Suffrage Movement, 1890–1920* (New York: Norton, 1981).

22. Woodrow Wilson, *Mere Literature and Other Essays* (Boston, 1896), 198–99.

23. "1936 Democratic Party Platform," June 23, 1936, American Presidency Project, ed. Gerhard Peters and John T. Woolley, https://www.presidency.ucsb .edu/node/273216.

24. Franklin D. Roosevelt, State of the Union Message to Congress, January 6, 1941, and State of the Union Message to Congress, January 11, 1944, American Presidency Project.

25. *West Virginia State Board of Education v. Barnette*, 319 U.S. 624 (1943).

26. Francis L. Broderick and August Meier, eds., *Negro Protest Thought in the Twentieth Century* (Indianapolis: Bobbs-Merrill, 1965), 48–52.

27. Patricia Sullivan, *Days of Hope: Race and Democracy in the New Deal Era* (Chapel Hill: University of North Carolina Press).

28. John D. Skrentny, *The Minority Rights Revolution* (Cambridge, MA: Harvard University Press, 2002); Felicia Kornbluh, *The Battle for Welfare Rights: Politics and Poverty in Modern America* (Philadelphia: University of Pennsylvania Press, 2007).

29. Mark Tushnet, "An Essay on Rights," *Texas Law Review* 62 (1984): 1363–403; Robin West, "Critical Legal Studies—The Missing Years," in Robin West, *Normative Jurisprudence: An Introduction* (Cambridge, UK: Cambridge University Press, 2011); Laura M. Weinrib, "Civil Liberties Outside the Courts," *Supreme Court Review* 2014 (2015): 297–362; Gerard N. Rosenberg, *The Hollow Hope: Can Courts Bring about Social Change?* 2nd ed. (Chicago: University of Chicago Press, 2008).

30. Quoted in Steve Bruce, "The Inevitable Failure of the New Christian Right," *Sociology of Religion* 55 (1994): 230.

31. Patricia J. Williams, "Alchemical Notes: Reconstructing Ideals from Deconstructed Rights," *Harvard Civil Rights–Civil Liberties Review* 22 (1987): 401–33.

32. *Bowers v. Hardwick*, 478 U.S. 186 (1986).

33. *Griswold v. Connecticut*, 381 U.S. 479 (1965).

34. *Lawrence v. Texas*, 539 U.S. 558 (2003).

35. Jedediah Purdy, "Neoliberal Constitutionalism: Lochnerism for a New Economy," *Law and Contemporary Problems* 77 (2014): 195–213; "Symposium: A First Amendment for All? Free Expression in an Age of Inequality," *Columbia Law Review* 118 (2018): 1953–2250; John C. Coates IV, "Corporate Speech and the First Amendment: History, Data, and Implications," *Constitutional Commentary* 30 (2015): 223–75.

36. *Janus v. American Federation of State, County, and Municipal Employees*, 585 U.S. ____ (2018).

37. *Karl Marx: Early Writings*, ed. T. B. Bottomore (New York: McGraw-Hill, 1964), 26.

PART II

*Modern Rights in Controversy*

# TWO

—ɯ—

# THE FIRST AMENDMENT AND
# THE FREEDOM TO DIFFER

SUZANNA SHERRY

THE FIRST AMENDMENT PROVIDES THAT "Congress shall make no law . . .
abridging the freedom of speech, or of the press." The incorporation doctrine—by
which the Bill of Rights applies to the states through the Fourteenth Amendment—
makes the amendment effective against state and local governments as well. And
like all constitutional limits, it applies not just to the government itself but to any
state actor—that is, anyone who is acting in an official capacity on behalf of a government entity.

Given that breadth of application, the First Amendment—even more obviously than much of the rest of the Constitution—requires interpretation and line
drawing. In particular, it requires us to think about what the Amendment is for:
Why is it there, and what is its role in a constitutional democracy? This chapter
explores the Supreme Court's answers to those questions as well as considering
scholarly challenges to those answers.

The core of modern First Amendment jurisprudence is what might be called
the anti-censorship principle: The government may not censor speech just
because it disagrees with it or disapproves of it. Even if a majority of citizens
dislikes the speech or the ideas it communicates, the government may not censor it for that reason. Similarly, the government generally cannot favor some
speakers over others, censoring certain viewpoints. Nor may the government
suppress speech because it objects to the consequences the speech is likely to
produce—a right to speak would be illusory if it protected only speech that
had no effect.

Justice Robert Jackson eloquently summarized this principle in 1943: "If there
is any fixed star in our constitutional constellation, it is that no official, high or
petty, can prescribe what shall be orthodox in politics, nationalism, religion,

or other matters of opinion or force citizens to confess by word or act their faith therein."[1]

Somewhat surprisingly, it took the Supreme Court until the middle of the twentieth century to reach agreement on this anti-censorship principle even for written and oral speech on political matters,[2] and somewhat longer to extend it to most types of speech and develop corollary protections for symbolic speech and the right not to speak. The next three sections of this chapter tell the story of how the First Amendment came to embody the anti-censorship principle.

### THE CORE ANTI-CENSORSHIP PRINCIPLE

Governments, including that of the United States, have always tried to suppress dissent and disagreement. The Federalists passed the federal Alien and Sedition Acts of 1798 to silence political dissent and opposition by the Anti-Federalists. During the first half of the nineteenth century, many Southern states enacted laws prohibiting speech that criticized slavery or advocated its abolition. The second half of the nineteenth century saw restrictions on the speech of labor unions and social reformers. And each time the United States has engaged in war, the government has tried to limit speech critical of the war or of the government on the theory that such speech harms the war effort.[3] Until the early twentieth century, all these restrictions met little or no judicial resistance. As late as 1907, the Supreme Court held that the purpose of the First Amendment was "to prevent all *previous restraints* on publications" and not to "prevent the subsequent punishment of such as may be deemed contrary to the public welfare."[4]

The modern history of free speech jurisprudence begins with the momentous events of 1917. In the space of a few months, the United States entered World War I, Congress passed the Espionage Act prohibiting interference with the draft, Lenin established a Bolshevist dictatorship in Russia, and Russia made peace with Germany. American protests against the war, rooted primarily in sympathy toward the Bolsheviks, escalated—and so did American fear of communism, culminating in the postwar Red Scare. The resulting conflict between protest and suppression of dissent generated four influential Supreme Court cases in 1919.

These cases are significant because they contain the seeds of modern First Amendment law, especially as reflected in the developing jurisprudence of Justice Oliver Wendell Holmes. In 1907, Holmes wrote the majority opinion in *Patterson v. Colorado*,[5] which confined free speech protection to the absence of prior restraints. During the course of the four 1919 cases, however, Holmes moved toward a more modern view of free speech. In these cases, then, we can see the roots of a robust protection of expression and the beginnings of the modern view of the First Amendment as a bulwark against government censorship of ideas.

All four cases involved violations of the Espionage Act. Charles Schenck was convicted of violating the act for circulating pamphlets opposing the war, including sending them to men who had been drafted. The pamphlets, distributed in 1917, printed the text of the Thirteenth Amendment—which prohibits slavery—on one side and the heading "Assert Your Rights" on the other. They also contained exhortations to peaceful resistance against the draft and criticism of the war. Schenck argued to the Supreme Court that the First Amendment prohibited punishing him for his written expression. Justice Holmes wrote for a unanimous Court, "The question in every case is whether the words are used in such circumstances and are of such a nature as to create a clear and present danger that they will bring about the substantive evils that Congress has a right to prevent."[6] Finding that Schenck's pamphlet created a clear and present danger of interference with the draft, the Court affirmed the conviction. A week later, the Court used the clear and present danger test to affirm two other convictions under the Espionage Act.[7] In both these later cases—one of which involved Socialist Party leader and presidential candidate Eugene V. Debs—the convictions were based on 1917 speeches or publications decrying capitalism and the war. In both cases, Justice Holmes wrote for a unanimous Court. The clear and present danger test, it seemed, provided no protection for political dissent.

But over the next few months, Holmes had a change of heart. In addition to what he viewed as the excesses of the Red Scare, two influences might have spurred his conversion. One of the country's most influential district court judges, Judge Learned Hand, held (in an opinion later reversed by the Court of Appeals for the Second Circuit) that the government had no authority to suppress dissenting speech unless it contained a "direct incitement" to illegal action—a mere likelihood, or even a clear and present danger, that the words might spark unlawfulness was not sufficient.[8] And Harvard law professor Zechariah Chafee published an article in the *Harvard Law Review* that recast the clear and present danger test in a way that was more protective of political speech.[9]

In November 1919, the Supreme Court again upheld an Espionage Act conviction for speech critical of the war effort, in *Abrams v. United States*.[10] Abrams and his codefendants had circulated leaflets labeling capitalism the only enemy of the workers of the world, urging workers to "Awake!" and informing them that their efforts on behalf of the war were "producing bullets, bayonets, [and] cannon, to murder not only Germans, but also your dearest, best, who are in Russia and are fighting for freedom."[11] Citing *Schenck*, Justice John Clarke's majority opinion rejected the First Amendment defense.

Justice Holmes, joined by Justice Louis Brandeis, dissented, arguing that the convictions ran afoul of the First Amendment. Holmes argued that a "silly leaflet" published by an "unknown man" did not present a real danger to the nation.

In one of the most famous passages in the opinion, he recast the clear and present danger test to reflect his new views:

> The best test of truth is the power of the thought to get itself accepted in the competition of the market.... That at any rate is the theory of our Constitution. It is an experiment, as all life is an experiment.... While that experiment is part of our system I think that we should be eternally vigilant against attempts to check the expression of opinions that we loathe and believe to be fraught with death, unless they so imminently threaten immediate interference with the lawful and pressing purposes of the law that an immediate check is required to save the country.[12]

This passage contains the seeds of the anti-censorship principle.

But Holmes and Brandeis did not prevail, and the official suppression of dissent continued. A wave of state laws outlawing "criminal anarchy" and "criminal syndicalism" were enacted and used to punish socialists, communists, and other unpopular speakers. The Supreme Court continued to uphold these encroachments on free speech. In 1927, Brandeis, joined by Holmes, once again disagreed with the majority's view of the First Amendment, invoking the spirit of "those who won our independence": "They believed that freedom to think as you will and to speak as you think are means indispensable to the discovery and spread of political truth; that without free speech and assembly discussion would be futile; that with them, discussion affords ordinarily adequate protection against the dissemination of noxious doctrine; that the greatest menace to freedom is an inert people; that public discussion is a political duty; and that this should be a fundamental principle of the American government."[13] Application of the clear and present danger test, Brandeis argued, was necessarily tied to these underlying principles: "No danger flowing from speech can be deemed clear and present, unless the incidence of the evil apprehended is so imminent that it may befall before there is opportunity for full discussion. If there be time to expose through discussion the falsehood and fallacies, to avert the evil by processes of education, the remedy to be applied is more speech, not enforced silence."[14]

These two opinions contain the rudiments of two of the three modern justifications for protecting freedom of speech. Holmes espoused the view that unfettered speech helps find truth and that the best ideas will prevail. Brandeis, while agreeing with Holmes, added a new twist: broad public discussion is necessary for democratic self-governance. The third justification, personal autonomy, was developed later, largely in areas outside the First Amendment, and imported into it as the Court began to broaden protections beyond purely political speech. All three rationales support the anti-censorship principle; whether the goal is truth, self-government, or personal autonomy, government censorship undermines it.

The Holmes and Brandeis opinions sketch out a theory of First Amendment protection for political advocacy that was eventually adopted by the Supreme Court, although it did not come to fruition until decades later. In the meantime, the Court—urged on by progressive activists, especially in the labor and civil rights movements—developed a parallel jurisprudence for political speech that did not threaten lawless action. The earliest beneficiaries of the Court's developing First Amendment jurisprudences were labor unions and labor activists. In 1940, the Court held that states could not criminalize union-organizing activities.[15] Next came civil rights activists, when the Court reversed breach-of-the-peace convictions for peaceful protestors against Jim Crow laws in 1963.[16] During the Vietnam era, the Court extended protection to a variety of anti-war protestors, including a man who wore a jacket bearing the words "Fuck the Draft" into a courthouse,[17] schoolchildren who wore black armbands,[18] and the publication of classified government documents relating to the war.[19]

Over the course of a few decades in the middle of the twentieth century, the Court's view of the First Amendment matured; it changed from a means of protecting particular speakers into a recognition of the dangers of allowing government control over speech in general.

The Court gradually implemented its developing vision of the First Amendment as embodying an anti-censorship principle using two key concepts. It first distinguished between content-based and content-neutral restrictions on speech. If the government sought to suppress the speech based on, or because of, its content—that is, based on the ideas that it communicated—that suppression raised the specter of censorship. And to guard against censorship, the Court therefore held that in order to impose content-based restrictions, the government has to show that the restriction is *necessary* to a *compelling* state interest.[20] (Content-neutral restrictions are subject to a more lenient test: they are valid as long as they are "justified without reference to the content of the regulated speech," "narrowly tailored to serve a significant governmental interest," and "leave open ample alternative channels for communication of the information."[21])

The Court eventually officially abandoned the clear and present danger test during the last term of the Warren Court. In *Brandenburg v. Ohio*[22] in 1969, the Court finally held that the First Amendment prohibits the government from outlawing even advocacy of force or illegal action "except where such advocacy is directed to inciting or producing imminent lawless action and is likely to incite or produce such action."[23] Applying the anti-censorship principle and the compelling interest test, the Court has protected a wide variety of speech and speakers, including speech that is clearly political, speech that is only arguably political, and speech that is hard to describe as political but that has been restricted only because the government (or a majority of the citizenry) objects to it or thinks it causes harm. Thus the Court has invalidated, for example, a state law that prohibited candidates in judicial elections from announcing their views on disputed issues,[24] a federal law making it a crime to falsely claim receipt of military honors,[25] a federal statute criminalizing films depicting cruelty to animals,[26] and a section of the federal trademark statute that denied trademark protection to an Asian American rock band using the name The Slants because the name was "disparaging."[27]

Even more controversially, the Court has invalidated campaign finance laws that attempt to limit the role of money in politics. In *Citizens United v. Federal Election Commission*,[28] the Court struck down a federal law limiting independent campaign expenditures (and thus shrinking the amount of speech funded by those expenditures) by corporations and unions. The plaintiff, Citizens United, was a nonprofit corporation that had produced a documentary film critical of one of the Democratic candidates vying for the party's nomination for president. It wished to distribute this film through video-on-demand, for free, shortly before the primary election. Federal law, however, prohibited corporations and unions from using their money to make any "electioneering communication" within thirty days of a primary election (or within sixty days of a general election).

The Supreme Court held that the law violated the First Amendment. Relying on a case decided thirty-five years earlier, the Court held that the speech of corporations (and unions) is within the ambit of the First Amendment and that prohibiting expenditures on speech constitutes a restriction on speech because it reduces the quantity and quality of expression. And attempting to prevent only some persons or entities from speaking is incompatible with the core of the First Amendment: "When the Government seeks to use its full power, including the criminal law, to command where a person may get his or her information or what distrusted source he or she may not hear, it uses censorship to control thought."[29]

Ultimately, then, the Court has adopted the anti-censorship principle and applied it broadly. The government may not suppress speech simply because it is unpopular or offensive or out of step with the majority's views. Nor may it restrict the speech of some in order to enhance the speech of others, as some have suggested as one goal of campaign finance reform. The underlying theory of this interpretation of the First Amendment follows from the early Holmes and Brandeis opinions: "there is no such thing as a false idea,"[30] and the "marketplace of ideas" allows every speaker a chance to persuade other citizens. The ordinary response to harmful speech should therefore be more speech, not less.

The Court has also addressed two concomitant questions. First, what kind of protection does the First Amendment offer to other forms of expression beyond the written or spoken word? Second, is there a right *not* to speak? I turn next to those issues.

## SYMBOLIC SPEECH

It is easy to see how the anti-censorship principle—and thus the First Amendment—is violated when the government punishes people for speaking, writing, or publishing. But expression, especially political protest, can take many forms other than actual speech. Conduct can send a message that is often more powerful than pure speech. The sit-ins for civil rights and protest marches both for civil rights and against various wars are classic examples. An even more powerful message is sent by fire: protesters have burned books, draft cards, bras, flags, and crosses, among other items. The anti-censorship principle suggests that we should not allow the suppression of political expression even when it takes symbolic rather than verbal form. At the same time, these kinds of symbolic expression raise another issue about the appropriate reach of the anti-censorship principle. Sometimes the government wants to restrict conduct for reasons unrelated to censoring ideas: burning things can create a fire hazard, and marches can block traffic.

The Court has solved the puzzle of symbolic speech by focusing not on the speech or conduct itself but on the government's reasons for regulating it. This approach fits naturally with the anti-censorship principle, which is based on the notion that disagreement with the ideas expressed is not a legitimate reason for suppressing speech. Focusing on the government's reasons has the added advantage of generally avoiding the need to define symbolic speech or distinguish it from either pure speech or pure conduct.

The most basic concept is that if the government is regulating the communicative conduct because of its message, the anti-censorship principle is implicated. Along the lines of the *Brandenburg* test, the government may not restrict speech—including symbolic expression—because of its message unless it has a compelling reason, such as preventing imminent violence. *Texas v. Johnson*[31] provides one of the more controversial applications of this principle. To protest the policies of President Ronald Reagan, Gregory Lee Johnson publicly burned a US flag in Dallas while the Republican National Convention was taking place there. While the flag burned, he and his companions chanted, "America, the red, white and blue, we spit on you."[32] Johnson was convicted of flag desecration, but the Supreme Court held the conviction invalid under the First Amendment.

The state argued that restrictions on flag-burning were necessary for two reasons: to prevent breaches of the peace that might occur if onlookers are offended and to "preserv[e] the flag as a symbol of nationhood and national unity."[33] The Court rejected the first proffered justification under *Brandenburg*, because "no disturbance of the peace actually occurred or threatened to occur" because of

Johnson's act.[34] It then turned to the state's second argument, holding that punishing Johnson's expressive conduct in order to preserve the flag as a symbol was in fact suppressing it because of its message—in other words, that the government's purpose was to censor ideas. This, the Court held, Texas could not do: "If there is a bedrock principle underlying the First Amendment, it is that the Government may not prohibit the expression of an idea simply because society finds the idea itself offensive or disagreeable.... We have not recognized an exception to this principle even where our flag has been involved.... [The] enduring lesson [of our prior decisions], that the Government may not prohibit expression simply because it disagrees with its message, is not dependent on the particular mode in which one chooses to express an idea."[35] Confirming that the same anticensorship principle applied to all types of expression, the opinion invoked both Justice Jackson's "fixed star" and Justice Holmes's dismissal of the consequences of a single act by an "unknown man."[36]

The next year, the Court relied on *Johnson* to invalidate a federal flag-desecration law.[37] And in *R.A.V. v. City of St. Paul*,[38] the Court extended protection to other incendiary conduct and struck down an ordinance that prohibited cross-burning if the burning "arouses anger, alarm, or resentment in others on the basis of race, color, creed, religion or gender."[39] Noting that "content-based regulations are presumptively invalid," the Court held that "the First Amendment does not permit St. Paul to impose special prohibitions on those speakers who express views on disfavored subjects."[40] The government may not censor expressive conduct any more than it may censor speech.

But, as with oral or written speech, a more lenient test applies if the government's reasons for restricting symbolic speech have nothing to do with its content. The Court has held, for example, that the government may penalize the burning of draft cards based on its "substantial" interest in the "continued availability" of draft cards.[41] This more lenient test allows the Court to prevent censorship while still permitting the government to ban some harmful conduct, even if the actor means the conduct to be communicative.

## COMPELLED SPEECH

Another issue closely related to the anti-censorship principle is the question of whether the government can force someone to speak or to endorse an idea. Is there a right *not* to speak? The Court has consistently held that there is such a right. As a matter of theory, a right not to speak is a necessary concomitant of the anti-censorship aspect of the right to speak. If the government cannot enforce adherence to its views by suppressing those with which it disagrees, it should not be able to do so by forcing dissenting citizens to act as mouthpieces. Indeed, Justice Jackson's oratory against orthodoxy came in a case that held unconstitutional a law forcing schoolchildren to salute the flag and recite the Pledge of Allegiance. In addition, the Court has often suggested that the First Amendment protects individual autonomy, or "individual freedom of mind."[42]

The Court has therefore held that a state may not punish motorists for covering up the state motto on their license plates, because citizens are free to refrain from speaking.[43] (Ironically, the case involved a motorist who was prosecuted for covering up New Hampshire's motto, "Live Free or Die.") A newspaper cannot be required to publish material that it does not wish to publish,[44] and the state cannot require a business to contribute to advertising it does not support, even if that advertising is favorable to the business.[45] More controversially, the Court has held that a public employee cannot be required to pay dues to a union whose activities she does not support,[46] and an antiabortion center cannot be required to post information about state-subsidized abortions.[47] These cases all illustrate the "basic First Amendment principle that 'freedom of speech prohibits the government from telling people what they must say.'"[48] Doctrines governing compelled speech, then, like doctrines governing symbolic speech, fit comfortably within the anti-censorship principle.

## CRITIQUES

Not everyone agrees with the anti-censorship principle or how the Court has applied it. Some of the cases mentioned so far have generated a great deal of controversy and criticism. This section explores and evaluates those critiques. Critics of the current First Amendment jurisprudence make two arguments: that corporate or commercial speech should be unprotected (or less protected than other speech) and that bigoted speech should be unprotected. Some scholars make both arguments, but some support only one or the other.

Both sets of arguments are part of a larger debate in constitutional law between what one legal historian has called traditional "legal liberals" and self-named "progressives." Traditional legal liberal views were dominant—throughout the legal academy and in the courts—from roughly the New Deal through the 1970s or so.[49] Liberals, who generally favor strong and broad protection under the First Amendment, believe that the greatest threat to liberty and individual rights comes from the government. Courts can and should protect citizens from that threat by vigilantly enforcing constitutional limitations on government power, at least when it comes to personal rights—especially including freedom of speech and ideas—rather than economic ones.[50] Progressives, on the other hand, challenge that traditional view. They believe that the greatest threat comes from the unequal division of private wealth and political power, that it is the duty of government to nullify or rectify that threat, and that courts should therefore be reluctant to extend protection to the wealthy or the politically powerful.[51] Given the gulf between these two views of the courts' role in protecting rights, it is not surprising that they lead to very different interpretations of the First Amendment. The remainder of this section explores those differences and their consequences.

A little history is necessary to understand the progressive arguments about corporate or commercial speech. In the early twentieth century, the Supreme Court invoked the Fourteenth Amendment's due process clause and the rubric of "liberty of contract" to invalidate numerous state and federal laws regulating the economy and economic relationships. Casualties of this so-called Lochnerism—which took its name from the iconic 1905 case of *Lochner v. New York*,[52] invalidating a law imposing maximum hours on bakery employees—included laws establishing minimum wages or maximum hours for employees, laws protecting a right to unionize, and various other social welfare regulations affecting business entities. Essentially the Court used the due process clause as a deregulatory tool, stymying Progressive and New Deal economic and social initiatives. In 1937, however, the Court changed course and announced that it would subject such economic regulations to only "minimal scrutiny," upholding them as long as they were rationally related to a legitimate state interest. It would practice Lochnerism no more, keeping its judicial hands off legislative and executive regulation of the economy.

This brief history is relevant because many contemporary scholars have accused the modern Court of using the First Amendment the way the pre-1937 Court used the due process clause: to implement an economic libertarianism that severely limits government regulation.[53]

Here is how one article described the Court's contemporary First Amendment jurisprudence: "Over the past decade, the Roberts Court has handed down a series of rulings that demonstrate the degree to which the First Amendment can be used to thwart economic and social welfare regulation—generating widespread accusations that the Court has created a 'new Lochner.'"[54] Another scholar noted that "the First Amendment has helped the Supreme Court to do for the consumer capitalism of the information age what freedom of contract did for the industrial age: constitutionally protect certain transactions that lie at the core of the economy [which] makes unequal economic power much harder for democratic lawmaking to reach."[55] Similarly, Justice Elena Kagan, dissenting from the Court's ruling in the union-dues case, wrote that the Court's holding represents a "weaponizing [of] the First Amendment, in a way that unleashes judges, now and in the future, to intervene in economic and regulatory policy."[56]

These scholars (and dissenting justices) criticize a wide range of judicial decisions. One set of decisions affords corporate and commercial entities First Amendment protection from government regulations on advertising,[57] and other cases limit the manner in which federal, state, or local governments can achieve substantive regulatory goals through restrictions on how or what businesses may or must disclose.[58] But the two doctrinal areas that have drawn the most fire are the Court's invalidation of campaign finance reform laws and its reversal of long-standing precedent regarding payment of dues to public-sector unions.

These critiques are varied, complex, and nuanced. But they generally rest on two related arguments. First, these critics describe the First Amendment as instrumental, in the sense that the protection of speech is not independently valuable but rather a means to accomplish other goals. The primary reason to protect speech, they argue, is to enhance democracy by ensuring broad discussion that can inform public opinion. As one scholar puts it, "the Court seems to have lost track of *why* the First Amendment protects speech [and] has begun to apply First Amendment doctrine to all kinds of communication that have nothing to do with the formation of public opinion."[59]

Second, "free speech rights [should] serve an overarching interest in political equality,"[60] and thus the First Amendment should ensure that public discussions "engage the widest possible range of participants and ideas."[61] And to accomplish that equality and diversity, courts should take into account different speakers' ability to contribute to—or undermine—the goals of the First Amendment. Because the Court's recent jurisprudence treats all speakers alike and protects their autonomy regardless of their contribution to democratic discussion, it overvalues some speech and undervalues other speech. Modern free speech jurisprudence is, according to these critics, insufficiently "sensitive to the economic, political, and social inequalities that inhibi[t] or enhance[e] expression."[62] Indeed, these critics believe that First Amendment law should do more than recognize differences among speakers; it should affirmatively "redistribute expressive opportunities among outsider speakers."[63]

Thus the progressives argue that cases protecting corporate speech or undermining the ability of unions to finance their own speech are inconsistent with the values of the First Amendment. To flesh out their arguments in both of these contexts, I begin with campaign finance. Injecting money into politics—and, indeed, including wealthy corporations within the ambit of the First Amendment at all—distorts rather than enhances democracy. It allows business and industry to "dominate the marketplace of ideas."[64] The "corporate takeover" of the First Amendment thus "undermines . . . the robust and inclusive public debate that the First Amendment is supposed to make possible."[65] It follows that the Court erred when it extended First Amendment protection to corporations and compounded the error when it thwarted campaign finance reforms designed to level the playing field by limiting corporate attempts to flood the electoral system with money.

Similarly, denying unions the right to charge public employees dues for services that the union renders to all employees—even nonmembers of the union—is likely to facilitate free riding and diminish (if not ultimately eliminate) funding for public unions.[66] This consequence, according to progressives, undermines "the First Amendment's structural interest in providing protection to the sorts of civic unions that foster informed political participation."[67] The rights of dissenting employees in this context, in other words, ultimately redound to the detriment of democracy and thus are not deserving of protection under the First Amendment as construed by these critics.

Finally let us turn to the arguments against protecting what is often called hate speech: racist, sexist, or other bigoted speech, especially when it is targeted at specific individuals or groups of individuals. The Court has held that the government cannot prohibit or penalize such speech. As mentioned earlier, the Court held that a state cannot punish cross-burning on the basis of the emotions that it engenders in others, nor can the federal government deny a trademark to The Slants, even though it is a derogatory term for Asian Americans. The Court also held, decades before these two cases, that the town of Skokie, Illinois—many of whose inhabitants were survivors of the Holocaust—could not prevent the Nazi party from parading through its streets if it allowed other groups to march.[68] In all these cases, the Court refused to create an exception to the First Amendment for racist or other bigoted speech despite the psychological harm it may inflict on others. Following suit, lower courts have consistently struck down attempts to prohibit racist speech on public college campuses.[69]

Some critics of these cases make arguments similar to the progressives' position on corporate speech. They suggest that hate speech should not be protected because it "'distorts' public discussion by perpetuating imbalances of social and economic power."[70] Analogous to the arguments made in the context of campaign finance reform, these scholars suggest that "those values the first amendment itself is intended to promote are frustrated by an interpretation that is acontextual and idealized, by presupposing a world characterized by equal opportunity and the absence of societally created and culturally ingrained racism."[71]

Others contend that hate speech is not mere speech, but "an action"[72] with harmful consequences: "the harms of denigration, defamation, and exclusion."[73] "In its published, posted, or pasted-up form, hate speech can become a world-defining activity."[74] Finally, some scholars argue that because hate speech undermines equality, another constitutional value, it deserves little or no constitutional protection.

Given the slightly different arguments available to opponents of protection for hate speech, it is possible to endorse the Court's corporate speech cases without endorsing the hate speech cases or vice versa. But many scholars end up conflating the two lines of cases, and with good reason: both lines grow out of the anti-censorship principle, and both refuse to draw distinctions among different speakers when applying that principle. Thus, it is possible to evaluate the progressive critiques together.

What, then, are we to make of these critiques? One can, of course, quibble with some of the factual premises relied on by critics, especially when it comes to *Citizens United* and campaign finance. For example, one study found that individuals—not corporations—were the largest contributors to super PACs during the 2016 election cycle and that unions far outspent corporations.[75] (These data also suggest that unions are less fragile than critics of the union dues case believe.) Of the thirty largest contributors to super PACs in 2016, only one was a corporation.[76]

Progressives also make a broader claim about money in politics. They argue that money undermines "electoral integrity"[77] because "wealth has an increasingly disproportionate influence on our politics."[78] The problem with that claim is that there does not appear to be a direct link between campaign spending and the influence of wealth on politics; the causes of the distorting effect are much more broad and varied.[79] First Amendment jurisprudence is not a major culprit. In other words, as one scholar has put it, "the way to have a more progressive First Amendment is to have a more progressive society, not vice versa."[80]

Moreover, there is a paradox at the heart of the arguments against *Citizens United*. If limits on expenditures are needed, it can only be because excessive spending can skew the results of elections—but at least in theory, giving citizens more information through more communication funded by more contributions should *improve* the results. The only reason it would not do so is if citizens are so gullible that they do not adequately evaluate the information they receive, and whoever advertises more (or better) gets their vote.[81] In other words, the critics of *Citizens United* wish to limit campaign expenditures in the name of democratic decision making, but they don't trust the citizenry to rationally evaluate the campaign ads that those expenditures generate.[82] The same can be said of other limits on corporate speech, including commercial advertising. One defender of strong free speech protections across the board has called the critics' position "highly paternalistic," arguing that "the government ordinarily may not restrict the expression of particular ideas, viewpoints, or items of information because it does not trust its citizens to make wise or desirable decisions if they are exposed to such expression."[83]

These quarrels, however, do not go to the crux of the debate about First Amendment Lochnerism. That debate is really about whether the courts can or should draw lines among different categories of speakers or different types of speech. The problem with advocating that the courts draw such lines is that no principled justification specifies exactly where to draw the lines. And traditional liberals do not trust Congress, or the courts, to draw the lines correctly.

Thus, if Congress can prevent Citizens United from distributing its video, Congress can prohibit the *New York Times* from publishing an editorial endorsing a candidate. Both situations involve corporations wishing to express political views.[84] If a state can punish speech that arouses fear or anger in groups defined by race or gender, there is nothing to stop a prosecutor from applying the law to MAGA caps—and nothing to prevent a legislature from extending the ban to protect other groups, including, for example, Republicans, animal-rights activists, or senior citizens (to name just a few). If California can require antiabortion "crisis pregnancy" clinics to post signs advising visitors of the availability of state funding for abortions, Texas could require Planned Parenthood and other abortion providers to post signs advising patients that a fetal heart begins to beat as early as six weeks.

These potential consequences are not just speculation. A court of appeals relied primarily on several of the corporate speech cases to invalidate a Florida law that prohibited medical professionals from asking their patients about gun ownership.[85] If Supreme Court jurisprudence allowed regulation of corporate speech, it would have been much more difficult to hold the Florida law unconstitutional, because the speech occurs in what is essentially a commercial setting of exchanging money for health care services. And if the antiabortion "crisis pregnancy" case had come out the other way, the Florida law would almost certainly be constitutional as a regulation of the practice of medicine.

What these examples demonstrate is that the strength of the First Amendment lies in its neutrality. Neither the elected branches nor the courts can pick and choose which speech is valuable and which is not. Progressives claim that "instead of providing a shield for the powerless, the First Amendment became a sword used by people at the apex of the American power hierarchy."[86] They miss the possibility that diminishing protection for some speakers opens up arguments in favor of restricting the speech of others. In addition, by castigating First Amendment jurisprudence as a deregulatory tool, the critics risk diminishing its rhetorical power, leading to an increase in restrictions on all kinds of speech.[87] Thus, in seeking to allow restrictions on speech or speakers they disfavor, critics should be careful what they wish for. Their speech could be the next target.

In many ways, the two sides of this argument echo the original debate over *Lochner* itself. The New Deal opponents of *Lochner* and its progeny thought that a regulated economic marketplace was the route to equality and true economic freedom (and proponents took the opposite position). The new progressives think that a regulated speech marketplace is the route to equality and true freedom of speech. Perhaps they are right. But there is much greater risk in entrusting the government with drawing the line when it comes to the communication of ideas than when it comes to regulating economic behavior. Permitting the government to regulate economic behavior risks allowing too much redistribution of wealth. Permitting the government to regulate speech risks allowing it to prescribe orthodoxy.

## CONCLUDING THOUGHTS

The United States affords more protection for freedom of speech than perhaps any other country in the world. Political dissent that would be routinely tolerated in the United States is prohibited and punished elsewhere. But the nation is constantly facing new challenges and new pressure, both from those who would curtail speech in the name of some higher good and those who abuse the freedoms we have. Despite these challenges, as we continue our third century under the Bill of Rights, we must be careful to nurture and cherish what is arguably the most precious of our freedoms, the freedom of ideas: "Freedom to differ is not limited to things that do not matter much. That would be a mere shadow of freedom. The test of its substance is the right to differ as to things that touch the heart of the existing order."[88]

## NOTES

1. *West Virginia State Board of Education v. Barnette*, 319 U.S. 624, 642 (1943).

2. For a suggestion that this delay was *not* surprising (and an account of why the First Amendment jurisprudence emerged when it did), see ROBERT C. POST, CITIZENS DIVIDED: CAMPAIGN FINANCE REFORM AND THE CONSTITUTION 26–43 (2014).

3. For a history of wartime suppression of speech, see GEOFFREY R. STONE, PERILOUS TIMES: FREE SPEECH IN WARTIME FROM THE SEDITION ACT OF 1798 TO THE WAR ON TERRORISM (2004).

4. *Patterson v. Colorado*, 205 U.S. 454, 462 (1907); italics in the original.

5. 205 U.S. 454 (1907).

6. *Schenck v. United States*, 249 U.S. 47, 52 (1919).

7. *Frohwerk v. United States*, 249 U.S. 204 (1919); *Debs v. United States*, 249 U.S. 211 (1919).

8. *Masses Publishing Co. v. Patten*, 244 F. 535, 540 (S.D.N.Y.), rev'd, 246 F.24d (2d Cir. 1917).

9. Zechariah Chafee Jr., *Freedom of Speech in War Time*, 32 HARV. L. REV. 932 (1919).

10. 250 U.S. 616 (1919).

11. *Id*. at 621.

12. *Id*. at 630 (Holmes, J., dissenting).

13. *Whitney v. California*, 274 U.S. 357, 375 (1927) (Brandeis, J., concurring).

14. *Id*. at 377.

15. See *Thornhill v. Alabama*, 310 U.S. 88 (1940). For a history of labor activism's role in the development of the right to free speech, see LAURA WEINRIB, THE TAMING OF FREE SPEECH: AMERICA'S CIVIL LIBERTIES COMPROMISE (2016).

16. See *Edwards v. South Carolina,* 372 U.S. 229 (1963).

17. *Cohen v. California,* 403 U.S. 15 (1971); see also *Hess v. Indiana,* 414 U.S. 105 (1973).

18. *Tinker v. Des Moines Independent School District,* 393 U.S. 503 (1969).

19. *New York Times Co. v. United States,* 403 U.S. 713 (1971) (also known as the Pentagon Papers case).

20. For a history of the development of this test—known as "strict scrutiny"—see, for example, Stephen A. Siegel, *The Origin of the Compelling State Interest Test and Strict Scrutiny,* 48 Am. J. Leg. Hist. 355 (2006).

21. *Clark v. Community for Creative Non-Violence,* 468 U.S. 288, 293 (1984). This test is not without its problems. It requires the Court to decide whether the government was motivated by a desire to censor, but governmental motivation is always difficult to determine. To some extent, requiring a significant government interest and narrow tailoring compensates for the difficulty of distinguishing between regulations motivated by censorship and those prompted by more legitimate motives. The more important the proffered government interest—and the closer to that interest the regulation cuts—the more likely it is that censorship is not the primary motive, or at least that the regulation would have been implemented even in the absence of a desire to suppress dissent. This type of heightened scrutiny of means and ends similarly serves as a substitute for an examination of actual government motive in other constitutional doctrines as well. See John Hart Ely, Democracy and Distrust (1980).

22. 395 U.S. 444 (1969).

23. *Id.* 447. Actually determining whether particular speech meets this definition of punishable incitement is not always easy. Whether President Donald Trump's speech on January 6, 2021, which was followed shortly by his followers rioting and breaking into the Capitol (forcing Congress to stop the process of counting electoral votes and flee to a safe position), did or did not constitute incitement is much debated. For opposing views, see, for example, Alan Dershowitz, *Impeachment Over Protected Speech Would Harm the Constitution,* Newsweek Jan. 12, 2021, https://www.newsweek.com/impeachment-over-protected-speech-would-harm-constitution-opinion-1560512 (not incitement); Beck Reiferson, *Making the Case for Trump's January 6th Speech As Incitement,* Princeton Legal Journal Apr. 19, 2021, https://legaljournal.princeton.edu/making-the-case-for-trumps-january-6th-speech-as-incitement/.

24. *Republican Party of Minnesota v. White,* 536 U.S. 765 (2002).

25. *United States v. Alvarez,* 567 U.S. 709 (2012).

26. *U.S. v. Stevens,* 559 U.S. 460 (2010).

27. *Matal v. Tam,* 137 S. Ct. 1744 (2017).

28. 558 U.S. 310 (2010); see also *Buckley v. Valeo,* 424 U.S. 1 (1976).

29. 558 U.S. at 356.

30. *Gertz v. Robert Welch, Inc.,* 418 U.S. 323, 339 (1974).

31. 491 U.S. 397 (1989).

32. *Id.* at 399.

33. *Id.* at 410.

34. *Id.* at 408.

35. *Id.* at 414–16.

36. *Id.* at 415, 418–19.

37. *United States v. Eichman*, 496 U.S. 310 (1990).

38. 505 U.S. 377 (1992).

39. *Id.* at 380 (quoting ordinance).

40. *Id.* at 382, 391.

41. *United States v. O'Brien*, 391 U.S. 367 (1968).

42. *West Virginia State Board of Education v. Barnette*, 319 U.S. 624, 637 (1943).

43. *Wooley v. Maynard*, 430 U.S. 705 (1977).

44. *Miami Herald Publishing Co. v. Tornillo*, 418 U.S. 241 (1974).

45. *United States v. United Foods*, 533 U.S. 405 (2001). There are complicated exceptions to this rule. See *Glickman v. Wileman Bros.*, 521 U.S. 457 (1997).

46. *Janus v. American Federation of State, County, and Municipal Employees*, 138 S. Ct. 2448 (2018).

47. *National Institute of Family and Life Advocates v. Becerra*, 138 S. Ct. 2361 (2018).

48. *Agency for Int'l Devel. v. Alliance for Open Soc'y Int'l*, 570 U.S. 205, 213 (2013) (invalidating requirement that recipients of federal Leadership Act funds explicitly endorse certain government policies).

49. Laura Kalman, The Strange History of Legal Liberalism (1996).

50. The bifurcation between personal rights and economic rights, and the concomitant difference in how the courts scrutinize laws that affect each type of right, stems from what is often called the "New Deal Compromise" reflected in a famous footnote in a 1938 case. See *United States v. Carolene Products Co.*, 304 U.S. 144, 152n4 (1938). For a fuller defense of the difference between personal rights and economic rights, see Suzanna Sherry, *Selective Judicial Activism: Defending* Carolene Products, 14 Geo. J.L. & Pol'y 559 (2016).

51. See generally Emma Kaufman, *The New Legal Liberalism*, 86 U. Chi. L. Rev. 194, 200–202 (2019); Jeremy K. Kessler and David E. Pozen, *The Search for an Egalitarian First Amendment*, 118 Colum. L. Rev. 1953, 1953 (2018); Louis Michael Seidman, *Can Free Speech Be Progressive?* 118 Colum. L. Rev. 2219 (2018).

52. 198 U.S. 45 (1905).

53. As one scholar has noted, although it is currently progressives accusing conservatives of using the First Amendment in this way, there was a time when the same charges were made against liberals or progressives. Jeremy K. Kessler, *The Early Years of First Amendment Lochnerism*, 116 Colum. L. Rev. 1915 (2016).

54. Kessler and Pozen, *supra* note 51, at 1953. For examples of this scholarly literature, see, for example, Amanda Shanor, *The New* Lochner, 2016 Wisc. L. Rev. 133; Frederick Schauer, *The Politics and Incentives of First Amendment Coverage*, 56 Wm.

& MARY L. REV. 1613 (2015); Louis Michael Seidman, *The Dale Problem: Property and Speech under the Regulatory State*, 75 U. CHI. L. REV. 1541 (2008); Frederick Schauer, *First Amendment Opportunism*, in ETERNALLY VIGILANT: FREE SPEECH IN THE MODERN ERA 174 (Lee C. Bollinger and Geoffrey Stone, eds., 2002) ("ETERNALLY VIGILANT"); Morton Horwitz, *Foreword: The Constitution of Legal Change: Fundamentality Without Fundamentalism*, 107 HARV. L. REV. 30 (1993); Thomas H. Jackson and John C. Jeffries Jr., *Commercial Speech: Economic Due Process and the First Amendment*, 65 VA. L. REV. 1 (1979).

55. Jedidiah Purdy, *Neoliberal Constitutionalism: Lochnerism for a New Economy*, 77 LAW & CONTEMPORARY PROBLEMS 195, 202 (2014).

56. *Janus v. American Federation of State, County, and Municipal Employees*, 138 S. Ct. 2448, 2501 (2018).

57. See, for example, *Lorillard Tobacco Co. v. Reilly*, 533 U.S. 525 (2001) (invalidating a regulation of outdoor cigarette advertisements); *Central Hudson Gas & Elec. v. Public Service Comm'n*, 447 U.S. 557 (1981) (establishing that restrictions on "commercial speech" must be justified by a "substantial" government interest that cannot be served by less speech-restrictive means).

58. See, for example, *National Institute of Family and Life Advocates v. Becerra*, 138 S. Ct. 2361 (2018) (invalidating state law requiring antiabortion "crisis pregnancy clinics" to post information about state-subsidized abortion); *Expressions Hair Design v. Schneiderman*, 137 S. Ct. 1144 (2017) (subjecting to First Amendment scrutiny a state law prohibiting businesses from advertising a credit card surcharge but allowing them to advertise a cash discount); *Sorrell v. IMS Health Inc.*, 564 U.S. 522 (2011) (invalidating limitation on disclosure of information regarding doctors' prescribing practices).

59. Robert C. Post, *The Classic First Amendment Tradition under Stress*, in THE FREE SPEECH CENTURY 106, 109 (Lee C. Bollinger and Geoffrey R. Stone, eds., 2019) ("FREE SPEECH CENTURY"). See also GREGORY P. MAGARIAN, MANAGED SPEECH: THE ROBERTS COURT'S FIRST AMENDMENT 227 (2017) (describing the "normative framework" of ideal First Amendment law as "seek[ing] to advance democratic public discussion"); Vincent Blasi, *Rights Skepticism and Majority Rule*, in FREE SPEECH CENTURY, *supra*, at 13 (criticizing the "noninstrumental" free-speech reasoning of the modern Court).

60. Kathleen Sullivan, *Two Concepts of Freedom of Speech*, 124 HARV. L. REV. 143, 144 (2010) (attributing this view to dissenting justices in *Citizens United*).

61. MAGARIAN, *supra* note 59, at 241. *See also* Kessler and Pozen, *supra* note 51, at 1986 (advocating "impos[ing] speech-redistributive obligations on particularly powerful private entities").

62. Genevieve Lakier, *Imagining an Antisubordinating First Amendment*, 118 COLUM. L. REV. 2117, 2119 (2018).

63. MAGARIAN, *supra* note 59, at 232.

64. WEINRIB, *supra* note 15, at 327.

65. Lakier, *supra* note 62, at 2120.

66. See, for example, *Janus v. American Federation of State, County, and Municipal Employees*, 138 S. Ct. 2448, 2487 (2018) (Kagan, J., dissenting).

67. Tabatha Abu El-Haj, *Public Unions under First Amendment Fire*, 95 WASH. U. L. REV. 129, 1309 (2018). Others argue that compelled payment for services is not the same as compelled speech. See, for example, William Baude and Eugene Volokh, *Compelled Subsidies and the First Amendment*, 132 HARV. L. REV. 171 (2018). This argument is of a different sort than those made by progressives and is beyond the scope of this chapter.

68. *National Socialist Party of Amer. v. Village of Skokie*, 432 U.S. 43 (1977).

69. See, for example, *Dambrot v. Central Michigan University*, 55 F.3d 1177 (6th Cir. 1995); *Bair v. Shippensburg University*, 280 F. Supp. 2d 357 (M.D. Pa. 2003); *UWM Post, Inc. v. Board of Regents of the University of Wisconsin System*, 774 F. Supp. 1163 (E.D. Wisc. 1991); *Doe v. University of Michigan*, 721 F. Supp. 852 (E.D. Mich. 1989). See also *American Booksellers Ass'n, Inc. v. Hudnut*, 771 F.2d 323 (7th Cir. 1985) (invalidating city ordinance that restricted "pornography" because of its alleged harm to women).

70. Robert Post, *Reconciling Theory and Doctrine in First Amendment Jurisprudence*, in ETERNALLY VIGILANT, *supra* note 54, at 168.

71. Charles R. Lawrence III, *If He Hollers Let Him Go: Regulating Racist Speech on Campus*, 1990 DUKE L.J. 431, 437.

72. JEREMY WALDRON, THE HARM IN HATE SPEECH 38 (2012). Catharine MacKinnon has made the same claim about sexualized portrayals of women. CATHARINE A. MACKINNON, ONLY WORDS 30 (1993).

73. WALDRON, *supra* note 72, at 130.

74. *Id.* at 74.

75. Floyd Abrams, Citizens United: *Predictions and Reality*, in FREE SPEECH CENTURY, *supra* note 59, at 81, 85–87. Data for the 2012 election cycle are similar. See *id.* at 88. Not all progressives want to limit corporate speech; some scholars suggest instead a voucher system that provides individual citizens with funds to donate to campaigns in order to level the playing field. See, for example, RICHARD L. HASEN, PLUTOCRATS UNITED: CAMPAIGN MONEY, THE SUPREME COURT, AND THE DISTORTION OF AMERICAN ELECTIONS (2016). The problem is that corporations could outspend any reasonable voucher amount. Most proposals, therefore, also include some kind of cap on corporate spending, condition receipt of voucher funds on a candidate's willingness to forgo other contributions, or increase the amount a candidate can receive depending on whether his or her opponent has forgone other contributions. See HASEN, *supra*; see also *Arizona Free Enterprise Club's Freedom Club PAC v. Bennett*, 564 U.S. 721 (2011).

76. Abrams, *supra* note 75, at 88–89.

77. POST, *supra* note 2, at 60.

78. HASEN, *supra* note 75, at 5 (2016). See also *Citizens United*, 558 U.S. at 396 (Stevens, J., dissenting) (the Court's invalidation of campaign finance laws "threatens to undermine the integrity of elected institutions").

79. See Samuel Issacharoff and Pamela S. Karlan, *The Hydraulics of Campaign Finance Reform*, 77 TEX. L. REV. 1705 (1999); Pamela S. Karlan, *Citizens Deflected: Integrity and Political Reform*, in POST, *supra* note 2, at 141, 143–46.

80. Leslie Kendrick, *Another First Amendment*, 118 COLUM. L. REV. 2095, 2097 (2018).

81. See HASEN, *supra* note 75, at 7 ("advertising . . . could sway enough swing voters—generally the least informed and most easily persuadable voters—to affect the outcome").

82. See Daniel R. Ortiz, *The Democratic Paradox of Campaign Finance Reform*, 50 STAN. L. REV. 893 (1998).

83. Geoffrey R. Stone, *Content Regulation and the First Amendment*, 25 WM. & MARY L. REV. 189, 213 (1983).

84. The federal law invalidated in *Citizens United* actually exempted media corporations from its prohibitions. That, of course, is part of the problem: Congress chose to favor some speakers over others, a core violation of the anti-censorship principle.

85. *Wollschlaeger v. Governor*, 848 F.3d 1293 (11th Cir. 2017) (en banc).

86. Seidman, *supra* note 51, at 2230. See also MAGARIAN, *supra* note 59, at 243 ("the leading First Amendment paladins over the past 45 years have been corporations and commercial interests"); Shanor, *supra* note 54, at 139 ("businesses have increasingly displaced individual litigants as the beneficiaries of First Amendment rights"); John C. Coates IV, *Corporate Speech and the First Amendment: History, Data, and Implications*, 30 CONST. COMMENT. 223 (2015) (empirical support for the idea that corporations are increasingly benefiting).

87. See Frederick Schauer, *Every Possible Use of Language?* in FREE SPEECH CENTURY, *supra* note 59, at 33, 45–46.

88. *West Virginia State Board of Education v. Barnette*, 319 U.S. 624, 642 (1943).

# THREE

## CHURCH AND STATE

### The Religion Clauses

MELVIN I. UROFSKY

THE FIRST AMENDMENT TO THE Constitution contains two clauses concerning religion: "Congress shall make no law respecting an establishment of religion, or prohibiting the free exercise thereof." For most of the first 150 years following the adoption of the Bill of Rights, Congress obeyed this injunction. It was not until 1947 that the Court ruled that the religion clauses applied to the states as well as to the national government. Justice Hugo Black, in his majority ruling in *Everson v. Board of Education*, expounded at length on the historical development of religious freedom in the United States. He concluded:

> The "establishment of religion" clause of the First Amendment means at least this: Neither a state nor the Federal Government can set up a church. Neither can pass laws which aid one religion, aid all religions, or prefer one religion over another. Neither can force nor influence a person to go to or remain away from church against his will or force him to profess a belief or disbelief in any religion. No person can be punished for entertaining or professing religious beliefs or disbeliefs, for church attendance or non-attendance. No tax in any amount, large or small, can be levied to support any religious activities or institutions, whatever they may be called, or whatever form they may adopt to teach or practice religion. Neither a state nor the Federal Government can, openly or secretly, participate in the affairs of any religious organization or groups and vice versa. In the words of [Thomas] Jefferson, the clause against establishment of religion by law was intended to erect "a wall of separation between church and State."[1]

---

Revised and updated for this edition by David J. Bodenhamer.

This paragraph contains the starting point for nearly every religion case decided by the Court in the last seventy years, whether it involves the establishment clause (in which the government promotes a religious function) or the free exercise clause (in which the government restricts an individual from adhering to some practice). For those who believe in a complete and impregnable wall of separation between church and state, Justice Black's statement says all that is necessary. For those, however, who believe that the religion clauses allow accommodation between government and religious groups, provided no one faith is favored or disfavored above others, then the Black reading of history is greatly mistaken.

Yet *Everson* provided an interesting twist. A New Jersey statute authorized school districts to make rules providing transportation for students, "including the transportation of school children to and from school other than a public school, except such school as is operated for profit." One local school board allowed reimbursement to parents of parochial school students for fares paid by their children on public buses when going to and from school, and a taxpayer in the district challenged the payments as a form of establishment.

Justice Black reviewed at length the history of the clauses and language that implied that no form of aid—direct or indirect—could be tolerated under the establishment clause. He concluded that the reimbursement plan did not violate the First Amendment, which only requires that "the state be a neutral in its relations with groups of religious believers and nonbelievers; it does not require the state to be their adversary. . . . [The] legislation, as applied, does no more than provide a general program to help parents get their children, regardless of their religion, safely and expeditiously to and from accredited schools."[2]

The opinion evoked dissents from four members of the Court. Justice Robert H. Jackson noted that Black, after marshaling every argument in favor of a total separation of church from state, weakly allowed that no breach of the wall had occurred. "The case which irresistibly comes to mind as the most fitting precedent is that of Julia who, according to Byron's reports, 'whispering "I will ne'er consent,"—consented.'"[3] Justice Wiley B. Rutledge took the logic of Black's historical argument and reached the inevitable conclusion that if "the test remains undiluted as Jefferson and Madison made it, [then] money taken by taxation from one is not to be used or given to support another's religious training or belief, or indeed one's own. [T]he prohibition is absolute."[4]

Black had written what might be considered the first accommodationist opinion, allowing an indirect form of governmental aid to religious schools, using what would later be termed the "pupil benefit" theory. So long as the aid did not go directly to church-related bodies, and in fact primarily benefited students, the program could pass constitutional muster.

By the time the Court heard its next religion cases, Justice Black had moved to the position Rutledge had suggested, that the prohibition had to be absolute. In a 1948 decision, *McCollum v. Board of Education,* the Court struck down a "released time" program in Illinois, in which classrooms in the public schools were turned over for one hour each week for religious instruction. Local churches and synagogues could send in instructors to teach the tenets of their religion to students whose families approved. To Justice Black, writing for the 8–1 majority, the issue could not have been clearer. "Not only are the state's tax-supported public school buildings used for the dissemination of religious doctrines, the State also affords sectarian groups an invaluable aid in that it helps to provide pupils . . . through use of the state's compulsory public school machinery."[5]

Four years later, the Court issued another accommodationist ruling on the establishment clause. To continue their released time programs, several states had moved the religious instruction off school property, but taxpayers challenged the programs on grounds that they still involved the state in promoting religion. The authority of the school supported participation in the program, they claimed; public school teachers policed attendance, and normal classroom activities came to a halt so students in the program would not miss their secular instruction.

Justice William O. Douglas's opinion for the six-member majority in *Zorach v. Clauson* indicated that the Court had heard the public outcry over the *McCollum* decision, and he went out of his way to assert that the Court was not antagonistic to religion. "We are," he intoned, "a religious people whose institutions presuppose a Supreme Being." Although the First Amendment prohibition against an establishment of religion was "absolute," this did not mean that "in every and all respects there shall be a separation of Church and State." Douglas went on to argue that historically the amendment had been interpreted in a "common sense" manner, because a strict and literal view would lead to unacceptable conclusions; "municipalities would not be permitted to render police or fire protection to religious groups. Policemen who helped parishioners into their places of worship would violate the Constitution." Such a view would make the state hostile to religion, a condition also forbidden by the First Amendment.[6]

The conflicting opinions in *Everson, McCollum,* and *Zorach* left very little clear, other than that the religion clauses now applied to the states as well as to the federal government. In all three cases, the majority as well as the dissenters had seemingly subscribed to the "wall of separation" metaphor and to the absolute nature of the First Amendment prohibitions, but they disagreed on how "absolute" the separation had to be. During the 1960s, it appeared that the separation would be very absolute, as exemplified in the school prayer and Bible cases. Since the early 1970s, however, the pendulum has swung back and forth between strict separation and accommodation, and the issue remains undecided.

The school prayer decision, *Engel v. Vitale* (1962), is a good example of absolutism, and it also indicates the strong feelings that Court decisions touching on religion arouse. In New York, the statewide board of regents had prepared a "nondenominational" prayer for use in the public schools. After one district had directed that the prayer be recited each day, a group of parents challenged the edict as "contrary to the beliefs, religions, or religious practices of both themselves and their children." The New York Court of Appeals, the state's highest tribunal, upheld the school board, providing that it did not force any student to join in the prayer over a parent's objection. The Supreme Court reversed.

In his opinion for the 6–1 majority, Justice Black (who had taught Sunday school for more than twenty years) held the entire idea of a state-mandated prayer, no matter how religiously neutral, as "wholly inconsistent with the Establishment Clause." A prayer, by any definition, constituted a religious activity, and the First Amendment "must at least mean that [it] is no part of the business of government to compose official prayers for any group of the American people to recite as part of a religious program carried on by government." Black saw the nature of prayer itself as essentially religious, and by promoting prayer, the state violated the establishment clause by fostering a religious activity that it determined and sponsored.[7]

The *Engel* decision unleashed a firestorm of conservative criticism against the Court, which, while abating from time to time, has never died out. In the eyes of many, the Court had struck at a traditional practice that served important social purposes, even if it occasionally penalized a few nonconformists or eccentrics. This sense that, as one newspaper screamed, "COURT OUTLAWS GOD" seemed to be reinforced one year later when the Court extended its reasoning in *Abington School District v. Schempp* to invalidate a Pennsylvania law requiring the daily reading of ten verses of the Bible and the recitation of the Lord's Prayer.[8]

Justice Tom Clark, normally considered a conservative, spoke for the 8–1 majority in striking down the required Bible reading. He built on Black's comments in *Engel* that the neutrality commanded by the Constitution stemmed from the bitter lessons of history, which recognized that a fusion of church and state inevitably led to persecution of all but those who adhered to the official orthodoxy. Recognizing that the Court would be confronted with additional establishment clause cases in the future, Clark attempted to set out rules by which lower courts could determine when the constitutional barrier had been breached. The test, he said, may be stated as follows: "What are the purpose and the primary effect of the enactment? If either is the advancement or inhibition of religion then the enactment exceeds the scope of legislative power as circumscribed by the Constitution. That is to say that to withstand the strictures of the Establishment Clause there must be a secular legislative purpose and a primary effect that neither advances nor inhibits religion."[9] In this last sentence, Clark set out the first two prongs of what would later be known as the *Lemon* test, which the Court has used to evaluate all establishment clause challenges. The legislation had to (1) have a secular purpose and (2) neither advance nor inhibit religion.

One can describe the school prayer and Bible cases as instances in which a benign majority unthinkingly imposed its views, unaware that the results restricted the religious freedom of a minority. In the third major establishment clause case of the Warren Court, however, a local majority deliberately attempted to establish its views as official dogma in defiance of what the rest of the country believed.

One of the most famous battlegrounds of the 1920s between the forces of tradition and modernism had been the Scopes "Monkey" trial in Dayton, Tennessee, in which a young teacher named John Scopes had been convicted of violating a state law that banned teaching the theory of evolution. The Tennessee Supreme Court reversed the conviction on a technicality, but the law remained on the statute books, and similar laws could be found in other Bible Belt states. Following the Dayton uproar, however, they remained essentially dead letters, unenforced and in many cases nearly forgotten.

In Arkansas, the statute forbade teachers in state schools from teaching the "theory or doctrine that mankind ascended or descended from a lower order of animals." An Arkansas biology teacher, Susan Epperson, sought a declaratory judgment on the constitutionality of the statute. The Arkansas Supreme Court, aware of anti-evolution sentiment in the state, evaded the constitutional issue entirely. But the US Supreme Court, without a dissenting vote, voided the Arkansas statute as a violation of the establishment clause. Justice Abe Fortas concluded that the Arkansas law "selects from the body of knowledge a particular segment which it proscribes for the sole reason that it is deemed to conflict with a particular religious doctrine, that is, with a particular interpretation of the Book of Genesis by a particular religious group."[10]

Anti-evolutionists in Arkansas and elsewhere sought to bypass the ruling in *Epperson v. Arkansas* a generation later. Instead of removing biology and the evolutionary theory from the schools, they added so-called creation science, which advocated the biblical narrative as supported by allegedly scientific evidence, and required that any school teaching evolution had to give equal time in the classroom to creation science.

The Louisiana Balanced Treatment Act of 1982 reached the Supreme Court in 1987, and Justice Brennan spoke for a 7–2 majority in striking down the statute as a violation of the establishment clause. The Court denounced the stated purpose of the law, to advance academic freedom, as a sham, since the sponsors of the bill had made it quite clear during the legislative debate that they wanted to inject religious teachings into the public schools.[11] It is unlikely that the issue will go away; as with prayer and Bible reading, true believers will keep seeking some way to get their views grafted onto the school curriculum. They believe that the framers of the Constitution and of the Bill of Rights could not possibly have intended to keep religion out of public discourse, and that religion, with the nonsectarian help of the state, had an important role to play in the development of a decent society.

Black's 1947 opinion in *Everson* in which he cited Jefferson's characterization of "a wall of separation between church and State" had opened the door to a flourishing debate over the original intent of the framers. How should justices today interpret not only the First Amendment but the Constitution as a whole? In the courts, in law schools, and among the public, the debate has gone under several names—judicial restraint versus activism and interpretivism versus noninterpretivism—but the core issue is whether judges, in deciding constitutional issues, should confine themselves to norms that are either stated or clearly implicit in the written document (restraint and interpretivism) or whether they can go beyond the four corners of the written Constitution to discover evolving or implied standards (activism and noninterpretivism).

Edwin Meese, who served as attorney general in the second Reagan administration, led the attack for a strict adherence to what he called a "jurisprudence of original intention," in which the courts would determine exactly what the framers had meant and would interpret the Constitution accordingly: "Where the language of the Constitution is specific, it must be obeyed. Where there is a demonstrable consensus among the Framers and ratifiers as to a principle stated or implied by the Constitution, it should be followed. Where there is ambiguity as to the precise meaning or reach of a constitutional provision, it should be interpreted and applied in a manner so as to at least not contradict the text of the Constitution itself."[12]

But what exactly did the framers and ratifiers of the First Amendment religion clauses intend? Did they mean, as Justice Black argued, that the exact meaning of "Congress shall make *no* law" meant just that—that Congress (and, through the Fourteenth Amendment, the states) could not in any way, shape, or form do anything that might breach the wall of separation? Or did they mean that although government could not prefer one sect over another, it might provide aid to all religions on an equal basis? Is the historical record quite as clear as Meese, and proponents of original intent, following the lead of late Justice Antonin Scalia, would have us believe, or is it somewhat murky, so that the original intent of the framers is either not available or irrelevant to contemporary jurisprudence? Many scholars believe that the historic record is, at best, often confused and contradictory.

At the core of the problem is one's view of the Constitution and its role in US government. Advocates of original intent believe that the vision of the framers is as good today as it was two and a half centuries ago, and any deviation from that view is an abandonment of the ideals that have made this country free and great. Judges, they argue, should hew strictly to what the framers intended, and if revisions are to be made, it must be through the amendment process.

Originalists argue the founders never intended a complete prohibition of aid to religion or to establish an impregnable wall. Rather, the originalists believe that the framers meant no single sect would be elevated above the others, and government could aid religious agencies provided it did so on a nondiscriminatory basis. Therefore, state aid to parochial schools, nondenominational prayers, and public involvement in religious activities are not forbidden provided no religion is favored above the others.

Defenders of a "living constitution" agree that courts ought not to amend the Constitution, but believe that for the document to remain true to the framers' intent, it must be interpreted in the light of two lamps: the spirit of the framers and the realities of modern society. They believe that the founding generation never intended to put a straitjacket on succeeding generations; rather, they set out a series of ideals, expressed through powers and limitations, and deliberately left details vague so that those who came after could apply those ideals to the world they lived in.

In this view, conditions have changed dramatically in terms of church and state in the intervening two centuries; in fact, conditions were changing even in the latter part of the eighteenth century. The framers sought language in the First Amendment that would reflect not so much their distaste for a single established church (that model was already passing from the scene) but their fears of church-state entanglement in general. That accounts for the absolute prohibitions expressed in the First Amendment, and courts should, therefore, decide establishment clause cases to preserve an inviolate wall of separation between religion and the state.

The conflict between these two schools of thought can easily be seen in the decisions on state aid to parochial education. Beginning with the Elementary and Secondary Education Act of 1965, both Congress and the states made determined efforts to establish programs that benefited parochial and private schools as well as public systems. Proponents of a strict wall between church and state soon flooded the courts with challenges to the constitutionality of such aid.

The Court heard the first of these cases in 1968, in an attack against a 1965 New York law mandating local school boards to furnish textbooks from a state-approved list to nonprofit private schools within their jurisdictions. Technically, the boards merely "loaned" the books and retained title to them; in fact, the books would remain in the possession of the private schools until the school boards wrote them off for wear and tear. In *Board of Education v. Allen*, the Court upheld the law on what is known as the "pupil benefit theory," which derived directly from Justice Black's opinion in *Everson*. The loan of the texts, according to Justice Byron White, did not aid religion, but benefited the individual student, whether at a public or parochial school, and that, he claimed, had been the primary intent of the legislature. Given these facts, the Court found no violation of the establishment clause.[13]

Under the pupil benefit rule, the Court upheld bus transportation and the loan of textbooks; might not this philosophy be extended to cover the actual costs of instruction in history, mathematics, or science? The launching of Sputnik in 1957 triggered an enormous public clamor for better education, and many parents saw religious schools as an attractive alternative. Why should not tax monies be used to support school systems that provided good education to children? The students, and not religious doctrine, would benefit. This argument commanded the support of several justices, and in some cases, it found a majority.

The Warren Court had handed down two tests in establishment clause cases—legislation had to have a secular purpose, and it could neither advance nor inhibit religion. In *Walz v. Tax Commission* (1970), the Court added a third test, a prohibition against "an excessive government entanglement with religion."[14] One year later the Court heard *Lemon v. Kurtzman*, a case challenging a Rhode Island program in which the state would pay 15 percent of the salaries of parochial school teachers who taught only secular subjects and who had state teaching certificates. In his opinion, Chief Justice Burger articulated the three-pronged test that has governed all subsequent establishment clause cases, the so-called *Lemon* test: "First, the statute must have a secular legislative purpose; second, its principal or primary effect must be one that neither advances nor inhibits religion; finally the statute must not foster an excessive government entanglement with religion."[15]

In articulating the three-pronged test, the chief justice seemed to be sending several messages. First, proponents of the pupil benefit theory should not rely on the limited application of that doctrine in *Everson* and *Allen* to justify further support. Second, he wanted to provide lower courts with a clear and easily applied constitutional rule that could be used in an anticipated flood of litigation resulting from literally hundreds of state and federal programs.

The Court now had its rule, and one that could be used either to prohibit or approve state aid to religious schools. In cases over the next fifteen years, nearly every majority and minority opinion invoked the *Lemon* rule, often with strikingly opposite conclusions. Some of this unpredictability stemmed from shifting alignments among the justices, but by the early 1980s, the jurisprudential differences between the separationists and the accommodationists had become quite pronounced.

Following the *Lemon* decision, state governments tried a variety of measures either to meet the three-part test or to get around it. This drive increased with the resurgence of fundamentalist and evangelical religious groups as part of the conservative coalition that carried Ronald Reagan into the White House in the 1980 election. But despite the presence of an articulate accommodationist bloc, the Court's rulings during Burger's tenure as chief justice (1969–86) largely reinforced rather than repudiated the separationist doctrine of the Warren years. The government could not support religious practices or institutions; government had to be neutral in its dealings with religions; and in those secular programs that benefited pupils in religious schools, the government had to avoid excessive entanglement in the management or activities of those schools.

By the mid-eighties, however, not only had accommodationist belief on the Court increased, but some justices, most notably Sandra Day O'Connor, found the *Lemon* test rigid and inappropriate and sought a more flexible standard by which to interpret the establishment clause. She was also moved in part by the clumsiness with which Chief Justice Burger had attempted to craft an accommodationist doctrine, and the reaction that followed.

Burger, in *Marsh v. Chambers* (1983), spoke for a 6–3 Court in holding that paid legislative chaplains and prayers at the start of each session of the Nebraska legislature did not violate the establishment clause. Just as Justice Black had elaborated a long historical analysis to justify his view of a wall of separation, so now Burger went back to show that the framers of the First Amendment had been aware of such practices and had not objected to them, and that opening prayers had been a staple of national, state, and local government since the founding of the republic.[16] (A case in 2014, *Town of Greece v. Galloway*,[17] extended this logic to prayers that opened town council meetings.) While Burger's argument offended the most ardent separationists, his reasoning made good sense to many people. One had here a tradition going back to the founding era; it did not favor or disfavor any one religious group; it cost the taxpayers practically nothing; and there was little entanglement as a result. Had Burger stopped here, he would have escaped the harsh criticism that followed his ruling the next year in *Lynch v. Donnelly* (1984).

In that case, the Court, by a 5–4 vote, upheld placing a crèche—the Christmas nativity scene—at public expense in front of the city hall in Pawtucket, Rhode Island. For many people, no matter what their faith or view on the First Amendment, there could hardly be a more religious symbol than a crèche. Nor could one imagine any activity more likely to run counter to all the values enunciated by the Court in regard to the establishment clause since 1947, or more likely to flunk all the criteria of Burger's own *Lemon* test. It was not a secular activity, it advanced religious ideas, and it entangled the government in religion. Moreover, even if one took all the arguments used by the accommodationists to justify previous decisions—free speech, secular benefits, historical exceptions—none of them applied to this case. Public monies were being expended to support an openly religious display.[18]

The majority opinion in *Lynch* was the most extreme accommodationist position taken by the Burger Court; it also was one that dismayed legal scholars and laypeople alike. Burger's opinion stood more than three decades of establishment clause jurisprudence on its head when he claimed that the Constitution "affirmatively mandates" accommodation. He referred to his earlier decision in *Marsh v. Chambers* to prove that the framers had intended there to be public support for some activities religious in nature, although he did not make clear the connection between a chaplain opening Congress with a prayer and the display of a crèche.[19]

The crèche decision carried a message that it is doubtful had been intended by the chief justice—namely, that those who did not subscribe to such "national" symbols, such as atheists, Muslims, Hindus, or Jews, did not belong to the community. Justice Brennan in his dissent recognized the deep spiritual significance of the crèche but objected to the majority's debasing of the religious aspects of Christmas. A spokesperson for the National Council of Churches complained that the Court had put Christ "on the same level as Santa Claus and Rudolph the Red-Nosed Reindeer," and soon many cars exhibited bumper stickers to "Keep Christ in Christmas."[20] For scholars, the decision seemed to constitute a major breach in the wall of separation—one that might not be repairable. Reports of the wall's demise, however, proved premature, and the Court soon reaffirmed its commitment to a wall of separation.

The first case involved the highly emotional issue of school prayer. Fundamentalist groups had never accepted the Court's 1962 *Engel* ruling, and the resurgence of the religious Right in the 1970s led to efforts to overturn the decision by constitutional amendment or to bypass it statutorily. In Alabama, the legislature in 1978 required elementary school classes to observe a period of silence "for meditation" at the beginning of the school day. Three years later it amended the law and called on teachers to announce "that a period of silence not to exceed one minute in duration shall be observed for meditation or voluntary prayer." The following year saw another change, this time authorizing any teacher or professor in any of the state's public educational institutions to lead "willing students" in a prescribed prayer that recognized "Almighty God" as the "Creator and Supreme Judge of the World."[21]

Speaking for a 6–3 majority, Justice John Paul Stevens struck down the Alabama statute in *Wallace v. Jaffree* (1985) and reaffirmed, at least in part, the vitality of the *Lemon* test. Perhaps most important, a majority of the Court rejected a basic challenge to post-*Everson* jurisprudence. Judge W. Brevard Hand, in his district court opinion, had held that the Constitution imposed no obstacle to Alabama's establishment of a state religion. Had this view been articulated in 1947, it would have been considered correct; to say it in the 1980s, however, was a mental and judicial aberration. The incorporation of the protections guaranteed in the Bill of Rights and their application to the states had been going on for more than six decades, and with few exceptions, they had been accepted throughout the judicial, academic, and political communities. No one on the Court supported this view, and Stevens provided the strongest opinion in support of the traditional jurisprudence that the Court had issued in many years.[22]

Establishment clause jurisprudence during the William Rehnquist years (1986–2005) included some important accommodationist rulings, some decisions that seemed to reaffirm strict separation, and a few in which Justice O'Connor tried to find a middle ground. The Court ruled in 1993 that if a school allowed its facilities to be used by secular groups, then it had to allow religious societies equal access, no matter how evangelical their messages might be.[23] Two years later, a divided Court held that the University of Virginia could not discriminate in funding student religious groups by denying funds to a student publication because of its religious orientation.[24]

Some of the Court's cases seemed commonsensical to most people. In *Witters v. Washington Department of Services to the Blind* (1986), the Court held that no violation of the First Amendment occurred when a visually handicapped student used state vocational rehabilitation money to pay tuition to a Christian college in order to prepare himself for the ministry.[25] Nearly a decade later, in *Zobrest v. Catalina Foothills School District* (1993), the Court held that providing a publicly funded sign-language interpreter to a deaf student in a parochial school did not violate the establishment clause. The problem that the Court's accommodationist bloc faced is that its members could not agree on a rationale. Justice O'Connor wanted to make the test one of exclusion—that is, if the program tended to exclude any one group and thus make its members feel like outsiders, then the program went too far. Justices Scalia and Clarence Thomas rejected the whole line of reasoning that flowed from *Everson* and would have supported most forms of state aid to religious schools. Others still found the *Lemon* test viable.[26]

In 2004, however, the Court ruled in *Locke v. Davey* that states are free to deny college scholarships to students who plan on becoming ministers by studying theology. The case involved a Washington State program, the Promise Scholarship, which provided college tuition support for needy students. The state rejected Joshua Davey's application when he noted that he intended to pursue a double major in pastoral ministries and business administration at Northwest College.

Washington and thirty-five other states prohibit the spending of public money on religious education.[27] But in 2017 when Missouri refused to allow a church to apply for a state program to resurface playgrounds, citing the state constitution and relying on *Locke*, the Court rejected its argument. Unlike *Locke*, the justices reasoned, state funds did not further a religious purpose; thus, denial of the funds discriminated against an otherwise permissible use.[28] Significantly, the decision rested on the free exercise clause, not the establishment clause, suggesting how closely intertwined these two clauses are.

Three years later, under the same rationale, the Court, 5–4, overruled the Montana Supreme Court, which, following a provision of the state constitution that prohibited any state aid for sectarian purposes, struck down a law that provided tuition assistance to a child attending a parochial school. A state need not support private education, Chief Justice Roberts wrote for the majority, but when it does, "it cannot disqualify some private schools solely because they are religious."[29]

Publicly funded teachers in parochial schools posed another problem. By 1997, most of the justices believed that some of their earlier separationist decisions could not be squared with intervening accommodationist rulings, which allowed greater flexibility in using public funds in parochial settings. The Court now reversed itself, finding that it was not a violation of the First Amendment for state-funded teachers to instruct at religious schools if the material was secular. The justices overruled two 1985 decisions that had invalidated popular publicly funded after-school programs that took place in parochial schools.[30]

Nonetheless, the bloc of Scalia, Thomas, and Rehnquist could not get the centrists, O'Connor, Anthony Kennedy, and David Souter, to join them in overturning the key Warren Court decisions regarding school prayer, Bible reading, and the ban on teaching evolution. In *Lee v. Weisman* (1992) the Court, albeit by a slim majority, reaffirmed the wall of separation, holding that having ministers pray at public school graduations violated the First Amendment.[31] The centrists held together in another highly controversial case from Texas, where students had voluntarily chosen to have a public, student-led prayer before football games. In *Santa Fe Independent School District v. Doe* (2000), a 6–3 majority ruled that the prayer imposed itself on too many people—players, band members, cheerleaders—who could not avoid participation.[32]

Then in what seemed to be a triumph of accommodationist thought, the Court upheld an Ohio school voucher program whose recipients, chosen through a lottery, overwhelmingly used them at parochial schools. Justice Rehnquist for the 5–4 majority explained that the voucher plan met constitutional standards because the program had been enacted for the valid secular purpose of providing educational assistance to poor children in a demonstrably failing public school system. It did not advance or inhibit religion (the second prong of the *Lemon* test), nor did it involve religion and government too closely in administrative details (the third prong of the *Lemon* test).[33] President George W. Bush, long a proponent of vouchers, immediately called on Congress to enact a national program, but Rehnquist's decision was carefully worded to meet the factual situation and was not a blanket endorsement of vouchers.

Toward the end of Rehnquist's tenure, the Supreme Court wrestled with the question of whether display of the Ten Commandments, a basis of Judeo-Christian religious thought, violated the establishment clause of the First Amendment. (Oral argument, ironically, took place beneath a marble frieze in which Moses holds the Ten Commandments in a display of historic lawgivers.) Part of the problem confronting the Court, as many commentators noted, was that its record of establishment clause decisions had failed to mark out a clear-cut jurisprudence. Once the Court wandered away from Black's separatist view, it proved unable to come up with an alternative jurisprudence that had the clear-sightedness of the *Everson* ruling. But the Court also faced the dilemma of how to read the First Amendment with its seemingly absolute bar to any officially endorsed religious statement in light of the fact that religion has always played an important role in American civil life. Ultimately, the justices approved the display of the Ten Commandments in a Texas monument because it was part of a privately donated larger display that had been in place for forty years.[34] But by a similar 5–4 vote, it disallowed the efforts of Kentucky to place copies of the Ten Commandments in each school, since this constituted an effort by the state itself to introduce religious teaching in the schools.[35]

Justice Stephen Breyer was in both majorities, playing the centrist role that in the past had often been occupied by O'Connor, and his concurrence is worth noting. He called the Texas situation a "borderline case" that depended not on any single formula but on context and judgment. The monument's physical setting suggested "little or nothing of the sacred." The fact that forty years had passed without dispute suggested that the public understood the monument not as a religious object but as part of a "broader moral and historical message reflective of a cultural heritage." For the Court to decide otherwise, he said, would lead to the removal of many long-standing depictions of the Ten Commandments in public places, and "it could thereby create the very kind of religiously based divisiveness that the Establishment Clause seeks to avoid." The Court in 2019 followed this logic when it decided that a government-maintained Peace Cross in Maryland was constitutional even though it was modeled on the Latin cross, a Christian symbol, because it had stood since 1925 as a war memorial without causing controversy.[36]

This pragmatic approach continued the Court's practice of avoiding any hard-and-fast jurisprudential rule regarding the establishment clause. Given how complex a subject it is, and how intertwined the religious is with the secular in American life, perhaps that is a good thing.

### FREE EXERCISE OF RELIGION

In some ways, but only some, free exercise cases are easier than establishment problems because they involve the state restricting an individual's religious practices. There is, of course, much overlap between the two clauses, and often a governmental program that tries to help religion in general may in fact restrict the freedoms of individuals. The school prayer and Bible readings offended the Court not just on establishment grounds but also because they limited the free exercise of those who disagreed with the prayer or worshipped from another sacred text.

Free exercise claims also overlap with claims to freedom of expression; several important cases prior to 1953 involved Jehovah's Witnesses, who claimed a right to proselytize, without state regulation, as essential to the free exercise of their beliefs. In these cases, the Court's analysis concentrated almost solely on the criteria used to safeguard speech. In addition, there are some issues unique to free exercise claims.

First is the belief/action dichotomy first enunciated by Chief Justice Morrison Waite in *Reynolds v. United States* (1879), the Mormon bigamy case. While the First Amendment absolutely prohibits government efforts to restrict beliefs, it does not prevent the state from forbidding practices, such as bigamy (or polygamy), that the government believes threaten public order or safety. In the example Waite used, if a sect believed in human sacrifice, the government could do nothing to restrict that belief, but it could, without violating the free expression clause, bar the actual sacrifice.[37] The Court soon recognized, however, that one could not divide belief and action so easily, and in *Cantwell v. Connecticut* (1940) the justices modified Waite's rule. The case involved a Connecticut statute requiring solicitors to obtain a certificate of approval before going door-to-door. Jehovah's Witnesses were arrested for failure to follow the law when proselytizing. Although convicted in Connecticut, the US Supreme Court reversed the decision and incorporated the free exercise clause under the Fourteenth Amendment as a protection against state action. The problem in this case was that the Connecticut law allowed the state to decide whether the solicitation was legitimate. For the unanimous Court, Justice Roberts wrote that "to condition the solicitation of aid for the perpetuation of religious views or systems upon a license, the grant of which rests in the exercise of a determination by state authority as to what is a religious cause, is to lay a forbidden burden upon the exercise of liberty protected by the Constitution."[38]

A second problem involves limits placed by the establishment clause on the free exercise clause. The two clauses overlap in their protection, but there are also instances where they conflict. A state's efforts to accommodate certain groups by exempting or immunizing them from general laws may also provide a preference to one sect. The flag salute cases of the 1940s indicated how closely free exercise and freedom of expression are intertwined; the Sunday laws, so-called blue laws, show the interconnectedness of the two religion clauses.[39]

In the 1930s several states required opening the school day not only with a prayer but with the Pledge of Allegiance to the flag, often accompanied by a salute similar to that used by Nazis to salute Hitler. Jehovah's Witness children were expelled when they refused to participate in the salute because they believed it violated the biblical command against worshipping graven images. In the first case on which the Court heard oral argument, *Minersville School District v. Gobitis* (1940), Justice Felix Frankfurter ignored the free exercise issues and held that the necessity to inculcate patriotism outweighed any minor inconvenience to a particular sect.[40] Only Justice Harlan Fiske Stone dissented, but his view ultimately prevailed. Over the next few years the Court gave the Witnesses one victory after another in their battle against local regulations, and then reversed the *Gobitis* decision in *West Virginia State Board of Education v. Barnette* (1943). The earlier ruling had led to instances of persecution, including some physical assaults, inflicted on Witness children because of their beliefs. Justice Robert H. Jackson, normally a conservative, wrote the decision. For the most part, Jackson employed a free speech analysis, but he also captured the quintessential meaning of the free exercise clause: "The very purpose of the Bill of Rights was to withdraw certain subjects from the vicissitudes of political controversy, to place them beyond the reach of majorities and officials and to establish them as legal principles to be applied by the courts. . . . If there is any fixed star in our constitutional constellation, it is that no official, high or petty, can prescribe what shall be orthodoxy in politics, nationalism, religion or other matters of opinion or force citizens to confess by word or act their faith therein."[41]

Interestingly, the Jehovah's Witnesses, who played such a pioneering role in free exercise jurisprudence in the 1940s, returned to the high court in 2002, and the justices reaffirmed rulings made over sixty years ago for the same group. The small Ohio village of Stratton prohibited canvassers from going door-to-door to sell any product or promote any cause without first getting a permit from the mayor's office. Jehovah's Witnesses objected to having to get a permit to carry their message and sued on First Amendment grounds, claiming that it violated their rights to free speech, free exercise of religion, and freedom of the press. The Supreme Court, by an 8–1 vote in *Watchtower Bible & Tract Society v. Village of Stratton* (2002), upheld the claims of the Witnesses that any effort to limit or regulate their proselytizing infringed on their free exercise rights.[42]

A number of states had, and some still have, laws requiring certain businesses to close on Sunday—for example, liquor stores or car dealerships. In 1961 the Court heard four cases challenging these laws as violations of the First Amendment, and in three of them the Court refused to consider free exercise claims. In *McGowan v. Maryland*, Chief Justice Earl Warren conceded that "the original laws which dealt with Sunday labor were motivated by religious forces." He rejected, however, the argument that this constituted an establishment of religion, because in modern times the laws represented an effort by the state to enforce one day's rest in seven.[43]

In the companion case of *Braunfeld v. Brown*, Orthodox Jewish merchants attacked Pennsylvania's Sunday laws on free exercise grounds. The merchants' religious beliefs required them to close on Saturdays, and having their shops closed two days a week would seriously undermine their ability to earn a livelihood. Chief Justice Warren recited the accepted distinction between belief and action and noted that nothing in the law forced the appellants to modify or deny their beliefs; at worst, they might have to change occupations or incur some economic disadvantages.[44]

There is a striking insensitivity, almost callousness, in Warren's opinion to the problem raised by the Jewish merchants, especially when one considers the great empathy he showed to the plights of other minority groups. In his dissent, Justice William Brennan pointed the way toward future First Amendment jurisprudence. He had no doubt that the Sunday law imposed a great burden on the Jewish merchants, forcing them to choose between their business and their religion, and this, he believed, violated the free exercise clause. To impose such a burden, the state had to prove some compelling state interest to justify this restriction on freedom of religion. "Mere convenience" of having everybody rest on the same day did not, in his eyes, constitute a compelling state interest. The Court, he charged, had "exalted administrative convenience to a constitutional level high enough to justify making one religion economically disadvantageous."

Brennan's opinion showed greater concern for the problems economic hardship would cause religious freedom, and his view triumphed fairly quickly. Two years after the Sunday closing law cases, the Court heard a case in which a Seventh-day Adventist in South Carolina had been discharged from her job because she would not work on Saturday. Her refusal to work on her Sabbath prevented her from finding other employment, and then the state denied her unemployment compensation payments. In what we would now term the "modern" approach to First Amendment issues, Justice Brennan posed the same question in *Sherbert v. Verner* that he had in *Braunfeld*: Did the state have a compelling interest sufficient to warrant an abridgment of a constitutionally protected right? This is, of course, the same question the Court asks about speech restrictions, because the analytical process in speech and free exercise claims are similar. Here the Court found that no compelling reason existed; the state would have to make accommodations for minority faiths.[45]

The *Sherbert* case, as well as a later case excusing Amish children from compulsory schooling beyond a certain age (*Wisconsin v. Yoder* [1972]),[46] raises the question of whether the Constitution can be read as totally religion-neutral or religion-blind. Neutrality in religious matters is more of an ideal than a reality in constitutional adjudication, and for the same reason as in matters relating to race: that it is, if anything, even more impossible for people to be neutral in their religious beliefs. Very few issues that reach the Court can be resolved in simple ways; if the cases had been easy, the Court would not have heard them. Religion, like race, is a tangled skein, and not amenable to simplistic solutions. The Court has recognized this, and from the absolutist decisions of the early Warren era, the Court has moved steadily toward a jurisprudence of balancing various considerations.

The Rehnquist Court took a far less accommodating position on free exercise claims than did its predecessors. In two cases involving claims by Native Americans, the Court dismissed free exercise claims. One case involved a road through sacred grounds, and the other addressed the required use of social security numbers for Indian children.[47] Then in *Employment Division, Oregon Department of Human Resources v. Smith* (1990), the Court upheld the dismissal of a Native American from his state job after he had participated in a peyote ritual. Although many western states and the federal government provided exemptions for peyote used in religious programs, Oregon did not. Justice Scalia, writing for a bare majority of the Court, went all the way back to the belief/action dichotomy of *Reynolds* and, dismissing nearly three decades of accommodation to individual beliefs, held that such belief could never be an excuse for violating "an otherwise valid law regulating conduct that the state is free to regulate."[48]

The implications of this decision for other religious groups led to a broad collation of churches asking Congress, in effect, to overrule the Court. This Congress tried to do in the 1993 Religious Freedom Restoration Act, which held that allegedly neutral laws might in fact burden religion, and that in such cases courts should find means to accommodate religious practices.[49] A poorly drawn statute aimed primarily at pleasing constituents, it also challenged the Court's role as the supreme arbiter of what the Constitution means. The Court did not have to wait long until it had a case exposing all the weaknesses of the act, and in which it could reaffirm its primacy in constitutional interpretation.

The city of Boerne, Texas, had passed an ordinance to preserve its historic main square, which had been built in the Spanish mission style. St. Peter's Catholic Church wanted to expand its building but was denied permission to do so on the grounds that it would ruin the architectural integrity of the square. The church sued, claiming that under the Religious Freedom Restoration Act, the town had to accommodate the church's need to grow. The Court disagreed and, in *City of Boerne v. Flores* (1997), noted that if the town allowed the church to build, it would have to allow all other owners on the square to do so as well, thus jettisoning a legitimate restoration plan. More importantly, though, the Court told Congress that it would decide what rules should be followed when interpreting the Constitution.[50]

However, less than a decade later, the Court, without overruling *Oregon v. Smith* or *Boerne v. Flores*, unanimously upheld the Religious Freedom Restoration Act and ruled that a small religious sect had the right to import for its religious services a hallucinogenic tea that the government wanted to seize as a banned narcotic. Chief Justice John Roberts, who wrote the 8–0 opinion in *Gonzales v. O Centro Espirita Beneficente Uniao do Vegetal* (2006), noted that the federal government had allowed peyote for Native Americans to use in their religious ceremonies for more than three decades. If such use is permitted "for hundreds of thousands of Native Americans practicing their faith," the chief justice wrote, "it is difficult to see how these same findings alone can preclude any consideration of a similar exception for the 130 or so American members of UDV who want to practice theirs."[51]

Moreover, when a locality attempted to restrict the free exercise of a particular sect, the Court had no hesitation in striking down such limitations. In *Church of the Lukumi Babalu Aye v. City of Hialeah* (1993), a unanimous Court invalidated a city ordinance clearly aimed at the practices of the Santeria sect, which still practiced animal sacrifice (after which the animals were cooked and eaten as part of the ritual). Justice Anthony Kennedy called the Hialeah law "religious gerrymandering" and "an impermissible attempt to target petitions and their religious practices."[52]

Although argued under establishment clause grounds, a case from 2005 clearly implicated the free exercise clause as well. In *Cutter v. Wilkinson* (2005), a unanimous Court upheld provisions of the Religious Land Use and Institutionalized Persons Act, holding that a new federal law requiring prison officials to meet inmates' religious needs constituted a permissible accommodation of religion that did not violate separation of church and state. The five Ohio inmates who brought the suit belonged to nonmainstream religions and claimed that they had been denied access to religious literature and ceremonial items and denied time to worship. The state argued that by requiring prison officials to cater to the demands of groups like Satanists or White supremacists, the law would attract new adherents to the group and work to the detriment of prison safety. Justice Ruth Bader Ginsburg, speaking for all the justices, dismissed the state's fears as groundless. If one accepted Ohio's argument, then "all manner of religious accommodations would fail." Justice Ginsburg pointed out that Ohio already provided chaplains for "traditionally recognized" religions. "Our decisions recognize," she noted, "that there is room for play in the joints between the clauses, some space for legislative action neither compelled by the Free Exercise Clause nor prohibited by the Establishment Clause."[53]

During the 2010s, conservative groups increasingly turned to the free exercise clause to claim exemptions on moral grounds from otherwise legitimate governmental mandates, often with success. The justices recognized in *Hosanna-Tabor Evangelical Lutheran Church and School v. Equal Employment Opportunity Commission* (2012) that the free exercise clause protected a religious group's internal decisions even if they conflicted with antidiscrimination laws.[54] In *Burwell v. Hobby Lobby Stores Inc.* (2014), the Court by a 5–4 vote excused a commercial family-owned corporation from complying with the "contraception mandate"—a regulation under the Affordable Care Act that required the corporation's health insurance plan to cover what its owners believed were abortion-inducing drugs.[55] Although the Court has never ruled that corporations could hold religious beliefs—Hobby Lobby is a family-owned company, a distinction the justice deemed to be important—some observers were concerned that it might be moving in this direction,[56] although to date it has not. A decision in 2020 raised these concerns again when the justices upheld in a 7–2 vote a Trump administration regulation exempting employers "with religious and conscientious objections" from meeting the regulatory contraceptive requirements of the Affordable Care Act.[57]

This decision and the Court's subsequent determination that states may not deny gays and lesbians the right to civil marriage—state religious freedom restoration acts, or state RFRAs—have become a flash point in disputes over whether commercial vendors with religious objections may refuse their products and services to same-sex couples when the action otherwise would be a violation of equal protection. In a much-publicized case from Colorado, the Court in a 7–2 majority sided with a baker who refused to sell a cake for a gay couple's wedding in violation of a state antidiscrimination statute. The decision, however, rested on the narrow ground that the Colorado Civil Rights Commission did not employ religious neutrality in its ruling that the baker was liable for damages, not that the baker's free exercise rights exempted him from a legal obligation not to discriminate.[58] Although it appears doubtful that free exercise claims under state RFRAs can withstand a major cultural shift on LGBTQ issues, it is not clear how this tension will be resolved.[59] Nor is it certain whether state or federal regulations that protect individuals who refuse services, such as dispensing birth control pills, because of a religious belief will withstand court challenges.

Other cases reveal a court still wrestling with the meaning of the religion clauses in a highly pluralistic society. Questions related to religious liberty and the death penalty, both arising on emergency orders, symbolize this struggle. In a 2019 case, the Court failed to uphold the claim of a Muslim inmate to have his spiritual leader present during his execution.[60] A few weeks later, the Court came down on the other side, blocking the execution of a Buddhist prisoner unless the state allowed a Buddhist spiritual adviser to be present.[61] Although it was easy for some commentators to read the first decision as bias against Muslims, a couple of years earlier, the justices had ruled strongly in favor of Muslim religious liberty plaintiffs in the case of a prisoner whose Islamic beliefs required him to grow a beard longer than regulations allowed[62] and in a case in which an employee was wrongfully discharged for violating a no-headwear policy although her faith required it.[63] Justice Brett Kavanaugh, concurring in the Buddhist death penalty case, emphasized that "governmental discrimination against religion ... violates the Constitution," which brought no dissent. The problem, however, was that few cases before the Court involved bright-line issues.

As the United States grows more diverse, both religiously and ethnically, as well as more secular, the "play between the joints" of the two religion clauses noted by Justice Ginsburg will no doubt invite further scrutiny by the courts, and in situations undreamed of by the framers. The death and retirement of Supreme Court justices have resulted in the appointments of Justices Neil Gorsuch, Brett Kavanaugh, and Amy Coney Barrett. These appointments cement a conservative majority that may be more receptive to the political prominence of the so-called religious Right in the Republican Party and its demands for the primacy of religion freedom over all other rights. Challenges to government regulations that clash with this view likely will lead to prolonged litigation. It is equally plausible that a pluralistic society will reject exclusionist views. To date, the Court has sought to balance a variety of legitimate interests that at times are in conflict. Its challenge will be how to accomplish this goal in an increasingly diverse, secular, and fractious society.

### NOTES

1. *Everson v. Board of Education*, 330 U.S. 15–16 (1947).
2. *Everson v. Board of Education*, 18.
3. *Everson v. Board of Education*, 19.
4. *Everson v. Board of Education*, 44–45.
5. *McCollum v. Board of Education*, 333 U.S. 203 (1948).
6. *Zorach v. Clauson*, 343 U.S. 306 (1952).
7. *Engel v. Vitale*, 370 U.S. 421 (1962).
8. *Abington School District v. Schempp*, 374 U.S. 203 (1963). In a companion case, *Murray v. Curlett*, the noted atheist Madalyn Murray and her son challenged a local

Baltimore school rule that each day begin with the "reading, without comment, of a chapter in Holy Bible and/or use of the Lord's Prayer." The schools did permit children to be excused at the request of the parents.

9. *Abington School District v. Schempp.*

10. *Epperson v. Arkansas,* 393 U.S. 97 (1968).

11. *Edwards v. Aquillard,* 482 U.S. 578 (1987).

12. Edwin L. Meese Jr., "Construing the Constitution," *UC Davis Law Review* 19 (1985): 22–23.

13. *Board of Education v. Allen,* 392 U.S. 236 (1968).

14. *Walz v. Tax Commission,* 387 U.S. 664 (1970).

15. *Lemon v. Kurtzman,* 403 U.S. 602 (1971).

16. *Marsh v. Chambers,* 463 U.S. 783 (1983).

17. *Town of Greece v. Galloway,* 572 U.S. 565 (2014).

18. Norman Redlich, "The Separation of Church and State: The Burger Court's Tortuous Journey," *Notre Dame Law Review* 60 (1985): 1094, 1122–26.

19. *Lynch v. Donnelly,* 465 U.S. 668 (1984).

20. Leonard W. Levy, *The Establishment Clause and the First Amendment* (New York: Macmillan, 1986), 157.

21. The full prayer read, "Almighty God, You alone are our God. We acknowledge you as the Creator and Supreme judge of the world. May Your justice, Your truth, and Your peace abound this day in the hearts of our countrymen, in the counsels of our government, in the sanctity of our homes and in the classrooms of our schools in the name of our Lord. Amen."

22. *Wallace v. Jaffree,* 472 U.S. 38 (1985).

23. *Lamb's Chapel v. Center Moriches Union Free School District,* 508 U.S. 384 (1993).

24. *Rosenberger v. Rector of the University of Virginia,* 515 U.S. 819 (1995).

25. *Witters v. Washington Department of Services to the Blind,* 474 U.S. 481 (1986).

26. *Zobrest v. Catalina Foothills School District,* 509 U.S. 1 (1993).

27. *Locke v. Davey,* 540 U.S. 712 (2004).

28. *Trinity Lutheran Church of Columbia, Inc. v. Comer,* 582 U.S. ____ (2017).

29. *Espinoza v. Montana Department of Revenue,* 591 U.S. ____ (2020).

30. *Agostini v. Felton,* 521 U.S. 203 (1997).The two earlier cases were *Aguilar v. Felton,* 473 U.S. 402 (1985) and *Grand Rapids School District v. Ball,* 473 U.S. 373 (1985).

31. *Lee v. Weisman,* 505 U.S. 577 (1992).

32. *Santa Fe Independent School District v. Doe,* 530 U.S. 290 (2000).

33. *Zelman v. Simmons Harris,* 536 U.S. 639 (2002).

34. *Van Orden v. Perry,* 545 U.S. 677 (2005).

35. *McCreary County v. American Civil Liberties Union of Kentucky,* 545 U.S. 844 (2005).

36. *The American Legion v. American Humanists Association,* No. 17–1717, 588 U.S. ____ (2019).

37. *Reynolds v. United States,* 98 U.S. 145 (1879).

38. *Cantwell v. Connecticut*, 310 U.S. 296 (1940).

39. For a good overview of the Jehovah's Witnesses in court, see Shawn Francis Peters, *Judging Jehovah's Witnesses: Religious Persecution and the Dawn of the Rights Revolution* (Lawrence: University Press of Kansas, 2000).

40. *Minersville School District v. Gobitis*, 310 U.S. 586 (1940). The justices had previously denied review to similar cases, which confirmed lower and state court opinions upholding flag salute laws.

41. *West Virginia State Board of Education v. Barnette*, 319 U.S. 624, 639–41 (1943).

42. *Watchtower Bible & Tract Society v. Village of Stratton*, 536 U.S. 150 (2002).

43. *McGowen v. Maryland*, 366 U.S. 420 (1961).

44. *Braunfeld v. Brown*, 366 U.S. 599 (1961).

45. *Sherbert v. Verner*, 374 U.S. 398 (1963).

46. *Wisconsin v. Yoder*, 406 U.S. 205 (1972).

47. *Bowen v. Roy*, 476 U.S. 693 (1986) and *Lyng v. Northwest Indian Cemetery Protective Association*, 485 U.S. 439 (1988). Despite the title of the latter case, there were no burial grounds involved; the area was used traditionally for retreats and for rites of passage.

48. *Employment Division, Oregon Department of Human Resources v. Smith*, 494 U.S. 872 (1990).

49. Stat. 1488, 42 U.S.C. Sec. 2000bb et seq.

50. *City of Boerne v. Flores*, 521 U.S. 507 (1997).

51. *Gonzales v. O Centro Espirita Beneficente Uniao do Vegetal*, 126 U.S. 1211 (2006).

52. *Church of the Lukumi Babalu Aye v. City of Hialeah*, 508 U.S. 520 (1993).

53. *Cutter v. Wilkinson*, 544 U.S. 709 (2005), quoted at 719.

54. *Hosanna-Tabor Evangelical Lutheran Church and School v. Equal Employment Opportunity Commission*, 565 U.S. 171 (2012).

55. *Burwell v. Hobby Lobby*, 573 U.S. ___ (2014).

56. The Editorial Board, "Limiting Rights: Imposing Religion on Workers," *New York Times*, June 30, 2014.

57. *Little Sisters of the Poor v. Pennsylvania* and *Trump v. Pennsylvania*. 591 U.S. ___ (2020).

58. *Masterpiece Cakeshop v. Colorado Civil Rights Commission*, 584 U.S. ___ (2018).

59. Christopher C. Lund, "RFRA, State RFRAs, and Religious Minorities," *San Diego Law Review* 53, no. 163 (2016).

60. *Dunn v. Ray*, 139 S. Ct. 661 (2019).

61. *Murphy v. Collier*, 139 S. Ct. 1475 (2019).

62. *Holt v. Hobbs*, 135 S. Ct. 853 (2015).

63. *Equal Emp't Opportunity Comm'n v. Abercrombie & Fitch Stores, Inc.*, 135 S. Ct. 2028 (2015).

FOUR

—ᴍ—

# PUBLIC SAFETY AND
# THE RIGHT TO BEAR ARMS

ROBERT J. COTTROL
RAYMOND T. DIAMOND

A well-regulated Militia, being necessary to the
security of a free State, the right of the people to
keep and bear Arms, shall not be infringed.

Second Amendment, US Constitution

ON THE MORNING OF THURSDAY, June 26, 2008, the United States Supreme
Court did something it had not done in nearly seventy years. The high tribunal
rendered a decision in a case involving the Second Amendment, the constitutional provision protecting the right of the people to keep and bear arms. The
case, *District of Columbia v. Heller*, came after decades of controversy concerning
the meaning of the amendment. Was it meant to protect a private right to have
arms for a range of lawful purposes, including personal self-defense? Or was the
provision simply meant to ensure that the militia would have arms for the common defense? The Supreme Court in the anxiously awaited decision in *Heller*
decided by a narrow 5–4 majority that the Second Amendment was meant to
safeguard the right of individuals to have arms not only for citizen participation
in a militia of the whole but also for personal self-defense, especially self-defense
in the home. In its decision, the high court declared the District of Columbia's
ban on the ownership of handguns to be unconstitutional. The decision in *Heller*
would be followed two years later, on June 28, 2010, by a decision in the case of
*McDonald v. City of Chicago*. That decision invalidated a similar ban in the Windy
City by an equally narrow margin. In this case, the Court in effect declared that
the Second Amendment acted as a limitation not only on the federal government, of which the District of Columbia is a part, but on state governments as
well. The two decisions, handed down more than two hundred years after the

adoption of the Bill of Rights, would usher in a new era of Second Amendment jurisprudence and debate.[1]

That new era of jurisprudence and debate continues to reflect the decades of often fierce controversy over the very meaning of the Second Amendment that had preceded *Heller.* That debate in turn was part of the larger national quarrel over gun control and whether the framers intended to limit the ability of government to prohibit or severely restrict private ownership of firearms. The debate has been fueled, in part, by the fear generated by this nation's high crime rate, including an average of ten thousand homicides committed annually with firearms, including a small but nonetheless unnerving number of mass shootings. The debate has also been fueled by the existence of broad public support for firearms ownership for self-defense and widespread ownership of firearms in early twenty-first-century America. Survey and social science estimates indicate that there are some three hundred million firearms in private hands in the United States and that between one-third and one-half of the nation's homes contain guns.

Two interpretations, broadly speaking, of the Second Amendment had developed in the debate. Some commentators stressed the amendment's militia clause, arguing either that the constitutional provision was only meant to ensure that state militias would be safeguarded against potential federal encroachment or that the individual's right to keep and bear arms was meant to be protected only in the context of a highly regulated, regularly drilling state militia. Adherents of both variants of what might be called the collective rights view argue that the Second Amendment poses little in the way of an impediment to strict, even prohibitory, gun control given the fact that most Americans today are not regularly engaged in the business of militia training. Supporters of the individual rights view have stressed the amendment's second clause, arguing that the framers intended a militia of the whole, or at least a militia consisting of the entire able-bodied White male population. For them this militia of the whole was expected to perform its duties with privately owned weapons. Advocates of this view have also urged that the militia clause should be read as an amplifying rather than a qualifying clause; that is, while maintaining a "well-regulated militia" was a major reason for including the Second Amendment in the Bill of Rights, it should not be viewed as the sole or limiting purpose. The framers also had other reasons for proposing the amendment, including protecting the right of individual self-defense.

The right to keep and bear arms became controversial in the late twentieth century, and yet for much of the nation's history constitutional commentators extolled the right as a fundamental cornerstone of liberty that could not be denied free people. This widespread agreement occurred in part because of the frontier conditions that existed in many parts of the country from the colonial period through much of the nineteenth century. The role of privately owned arms in achieving American independence, particularly in the early years of the Revolution, helped build this consensus. The often violent and lawless nature of American society also contributed to the widespread view that the right to possess arms for self-defense was fundamental.

But the Second Amendment and the right to keep and bear arms cannot be understood solely through an examination of U.S. history. Like other sections of the Bill of Rights, the Second Amendment was an attempt to secure what was believed to be a previously existing right. The framers of the Bill of Rights did not believe they were creating new rights. Instead, they were attempting to prevent the newly formed federal government from encroaching on rights already considered part of the Anglo-American constitutional heritage.[2]

To understand what the framers intended the Second Amendment to accomplish, it is necessary to examine their world and their view of the right to bear arms as one of the traditional "rights of Englishmen." The English settlers who populated North America in the seventeenth century were heirs to a five-centuries-old tradition governing both the right and the duty to be armed. In English law, the idea of an armed citizenry responsible for the security of the community had long coexisted, perhaps somewhat uneasily, with regulation of the ownership of arms, particularly along class lines. The Assize of Arms of 1181 required the arming of all free men. Lacking both professional police forces and a standing army, English law and custom dictated that the citizenry as a whole, privately equipped, assist in both law enforcement and military defense. By law all men ages sixteen through sixty were liable to be summoned into the sheriff's posse comitatus. All persons were expected to participate in the hot pursuit of criminal suspects, the "hue and cry," supplying their own arms for the occasion. There were legal penalties for failure to participate. The maintenance of law and order was a community affair, a duty of all citizens.[3]

All able-bodied men were considered part of the militia and were required, at least theoretically, to be prepared to assist in military defense. The law required citizens to possess arms. Towns and villages were required to provide target ranges to maintain the martial proficiency of the yeomanry. Despite all these requirements, the English discovered that the militia of the whole maintained a rather indifferent proficiency and motivation. By the sixteenth century, the practice was to rely on select groups of men intensively trained for militia duty rather than on the armed population at large.

Although English law recognized a duty and a right to be armed, both were highly circumscribed by English class structure. The law regarded the common people as participants in community defense, but it also regarded them as a dangerous class—useful perhaps in defending shire and realm but also capable of mischief with their weapons and mischief toward each other, their betters, and their betters' game. Restrictions on the type of arms deemed suitable for common people had also long been part of English law and custom. Game laws had been one tool used to limit the arms of the common people. The fourteenth-century Statute of Northampton restricted the ability of people to carry arms in public places. A sixteenth-century statute designed as a crime-control measure prohibited the carrying of handguns and crossbows by those with annual incomes of less than one hundred pounds. After the English Reformation, Catholics were also often subject to being disarmed as potential subversives.

The need for community security had produced a traditional duty to be armed according to English law, but it took the religious and political turmoil of seventeenth-century England to transform that duty into a notion of a political or constitutional right. Attempts by Stuart Kings Charles II and James II to disarm large portions of the population, particularly Protestants and suspected political opponents, met with popular resistance and helped implant into English—and later American—constitutional sensibilities the belief that the right to possess arms was of fundamental political importance. These efforts led to the adoption of the seventh provision of the English Bill of Rights in 1689: "That the subjects which are Protestants may have arms for their defence suitable to their conditions and as allowed by law."[4]

By the eighteenth century, the right to possess arms, both for personal protection and as a counterbalance against state power, had come to be viewed as one of the fundamental rights of Englishmen on both sides of the Atlantic. Sir William Blackstone, whose *Commentaries on the Laws of England* greatly influenced American legal thought both before the Revolution and well into the nineteenth century, listed the right to possess arms as one of the five auxiliary rights of English subjects without which their primary rights could not be maintained: "The fifth and last auxiliary right of the subject, that I shall at present mention, is that of having arms for their defense, suitable to their condition and degree and such as are allowed by law. Which is also declared by the same statute ... and is indeed a public allowance, under due restrictions, of the natural right of resistance and self-preservation, when the sanctions of society and laws are found insufficient to restrain the violence of oppression."[5]

If some five centuries of English experience had transformed the duty to be armed for the common defense into a right to be armed, in part, to resist potential political oppression, a similar evolution in thought occurred in the American colonies between the earliest seventeenth-century settlements and the American Revolution. Early English settlement in North America had a quasi-military character, an obvious response to harsh frontier conditions. Governors of settlements often held the title of militia captain, reflecting both the civil and military nature of their office. To provide for the defense of often isolated colonies, special effort was made to ensure that White men, capable of bearing arms, were brought into the colonies. Far from the security of Britain and often facing hostile European powers at their borders, colonial governments viewed the arming of able-bodied White men and the requirement for militia service as essential to a colony's survival. The right and duty to be armed broadened in colonial America.

If English law qualified the right to own arms by religion and class, those considerations were significantly less important in the often insecure colonies. Whereas the English upper classes sought to restrict the ownership of arms among the lower classes in part to help enforce game laws, significantly fewer restrictions on hunting existed in North America, with its small population and abundant game. And if by the seventeenth century the concept of the militia of the whole had become largely theoretical in England, in America it was the chief instrument of colonial defense. From the beginning, conditions in colonial America created a vastly different attitude toward arms and the people.

Race provided another reason for the renewed emphasis on the right and duty to be armed in America. Britain's American colonies were home to three often antagonistic races—Indigenous, White, and Black. For the settlers of British North America, an armed and universally deputized White population was necessary to ward off not only dangers from the armies of other European powers but also attacks from the Indigenous populations that resisted the encroachment of English settlers on their lands. And an armed White population was essential to maintain social control over Blacks and Indigenous peoples who toiled unwillingly as slaves and servants in English settlements. This helped broaden the right to bear arms for Whites. The need for White men to act not only in the traditional militia and posse capacities but also to keep order over the enslaved population helped lessen class, religious, and ethnic distinctions among Whites in colonial America. That need also helped extend the right to bear arms to classes traditionally viewed with suspicion in England, including indentured servants.

The colonial experience helped strengthen early Americans' appreciation of the merits of an armed citizenry. That appreciation was of course reinforced by the experience of the American Revolution. The Revolution began with acts of rebellion by armed citizens. And if sober historical analysis reveals that it was actually American and French regulars who ultimately defeated the British and established American independence, the image of the privately equipped ragtag militia successfully challenging the British Empire earned a firm place in American thought and influenced US political philosophy. For the generation that authored the Constitution, this experience reinforced the lessons their English ancestors had learned in the seventeenth century. It revitalized Whiggish notions that standing armies were dangerous to liberty. It helped transform the idea that the people should be armed and security provided by a militia of the people from a matter of military necessity into a political notion—one that would find its way into the new Constitution.

This view that an armed population contributed to political liberty as well as community security found its way into the debates over the Constitution and is key to understanding the Second Amendment. Like other provisions of the Constitution, the clause that gave Congress the power to provide for organizing, arming, and disciplining the militia excited fears among those who believed that the proposed Constitution could be used to destroy both state power and individual rights. It is interesting, in light of the current debate over the meaning of the Second Amendment, that both Federalists and Anti-Federalists assumed that the militia would be one that enrolled almost the entire White male population between the ages of sixteen and sixty and that militia members would supply their own arms.

But many feared that the militia clause could be used both to do away with the state's control over the militia and to disarm the population. Some expressed fear that Congress would use its power to establish a select militia. Many viewed a select militia with as much apprehension as they did a standing army. The English experience of the seventeenth century had shown that a select militia could be used to disarm the population at large. Among others, Richard Henry Lee of Virginia expressed the fear that a select militia might serve this end.[6]

In their efforts to answer critics of the Constitution, Alexander Hamilton and James Madison addressed the charges of those critics who argued that the new Constitution could destroy the independence of the militia and deny arms to the population. Hamilton's responses are particularly interesting because he wrote as someone who was openly skeptical of the military value of an armed populace. The former Revolutionary War artillery officer conceded that the militia had fought bravely during the Revolution, but he argued it proved no match when pitted against regular troops. Hamilton urged the creation of a select militia that would be more amenable to military training and discipline than the population as a whole. Despite this view, he conceded that the population as a whole should be armed.

But if Hamilton gave only grudging support to the concept of the militia of the whole, Madison, author of the Second Amendment, was a much more vigorous defender of the concept. In *The Federalist*, Number 46, Madison left little doubt that he saw an armed population as a potential counterweight to tyranny:

> Let a regular army, fully equal to the resources of the country, be formed; and let it be entirely at the devotion of the federal government: still it would not be going too far to say that the State governments with the people on their side would be able to repel the danger. The highest number to which according to the best computation, a standing army can be carried in any country does

not exceed one hundredth part of the whole number of souls; or one twenty-fifth part of the number able to bear arms. This proportion would not yield, in the United States an army of more than twenty-five or thirty thousand men. To these would be opposed a militia amounting to near half a million citizens with arms in their hands, officered by men chosen among themselves, fighting for their common liberties and united and conducted by governments possessing their affections and confidence. It may well be doubted whether a militia thus circumstanced could ever be conquered by such a proportion of regular troops. Those who are best acquainted with the late successful resistance of this country against the British arms will be most inclined to deny the possibility of it. Besides the advantage of being armed, which the Americans possess over the people of almost every other nation, the existence of subordinate governments, to which the people are attached and by which the militia officers are appointed, forms a barrier against the enterprises of ambition, more insurmountable than any which a simple government of any form can admit of notwithstanding the military establishments in the several kingdoms of Europe, which are carried as far as the public resources will bear, the governments are afraid to trust the people with arms.[7]

This desire to maintain a universal militia and an armed population played a critical part in the adoption of the Second Amendment. The amendment, like other provisions of the Bill of Rights, was designed to prevent the newly created federal government from encroaching on rights already enjoyed by the people. It is important to remember that firearms ownership for self-defense and hunting was widespread with few restrictions, at least for the White population. It is also significant that the universally accepted view of the militia at the time was that militiamen would supply their own arms. One year after the ratification of the Bill of Rights, Congress passed legislation reaffirming the notion of a privately equipped militia of the whole. The act, titled "An Act more effectually to provide for the National Defense by establishing a Uniform Militia throughout the United States," called for the enrollment of every free, able-bodied White male citizen between the ages of eighteen and forty-five into the militia. The act required every militia member to provide himself with a musket or firelock, a bayonet, and ammunition.[8]

The decades between the adoption of the Second Amendment and the Civil War brought little opportunity for judicial interpretation of the constitutional provision. Although some jurisdictions had laws prohibiting the carrying of concealed weapons, there were few restrictions concerning the ownership or the open carrying of arms in antebellum America. Most laws restricting the possession of firearms were in the slave states of the antebellum South. These laws generally prohibited the possession of firearms among enslaved people and free Blacks. Outside of the slave states, the right to have arms was generally not impaired, even for free Negroes.* There was no federal legislation restricting firearms ownership, and since *Barron v. Baltimore* (1833) held that the Bill of Rights only limited the power of the federal government, there was no occasion before the Civil War for the federal courts to examine the issue.

Despite the era's absence of federal court decisions on the Second Amendment, there was nonetheless widespread agreement concerning the scope and meaning of the provision among antebellum commentators and in the few state court decisions that examined the issue. Noted jurist and legal commentator St. George Tucker contrasted the Second Amendment's robust guarantee of a right to keep and bear arms with the more restrictive English guarantee, noting that class restrictions and game laws had not limited the American right in the way that the English right had been limited. Supreme Court Justice Joseph Story also regarded the right as fundamental, writing, "The right of the citizens to keep, and bear arms has been justly considered, as the palladium of the liberties of a republic; since it offers a strong moral check against the usurpation and arbitrary power of rulers; and will generally, even if they are successful in the first instance, enable the people to resist, and triumph over them."[9]

If leading antebellum commentators saw the right to keep and bear arms as central to a free people, federal courts were largely silent on the subject. The only discussion in the Supreme Court on the subject before the Civil War came with Justice Roger Taney's opinion in *Dred Scott v. Sandford* (1857). Taney indicated that African Americans, enslaved or free, could be denied the right to possess arms just as they could be denied freedom of speech, assembly, and travel.

Despite the federal courts' silence on the subject, state courts began developing a jurisprudence of the right to keep and bear arms, interpreting relevant provisions of state constitutions. These cases attempted to balance the right to bear arms against competing interests in public safety. Generally state courts upheld prohibitions against carrying concealed weapons. Some state courts limited the right to carry arms to those weapons that were deemed suitable for use in "civilized warfare," in an attempt to prohibit the carrying of weapons that were thought to be used exclusively for criminal purposes. Most of these cases involved restrictions on carrying concealed firearms. In one antebellum case, the Georgia Supreme Court decided that the Second Amendment applied to that state.[10]

It would take the turmoil of the Civil War and Reconstruction to bring the Second Amendment before the Supreme Court. The end of the Civil War brought about a new conflict over the status of former enslaved people and the power of the states. The defeated White South sought to preserve as much of the antebellum

---

* Several generations of Black people, including both of our parents, fought to make *Negro* a term of dignity and respect. We are unwilling to give it up and use it here and elsewhere in honor of this history and their sacrifice.

Southern social order as could survive Northern victory and national law. Southern states were not prepared to accord to the newly emancipated Black population the general liberties enjoyed by White citizens. Indeed, former slaves did not have even the rights that Northern states had long given their free Negro populations.

In 1865 and 1866, Southern states passed a series of statutes known as the Black Codes. These statutes were designed, in part, to ensure that traditional Southern labor arrangements would be preserved. They often required Blacks to sign labor contracts that bound Black agricultural workers to their employers for a year. Black people were forbidden from serving on juries and could not testify or act as parties against Whites. Vagrancy laws were used to force Blacks into labor contracts and to limit freedom of movement. And as further indication that the former enslaved population had not yet joined the ranks of free citizens, Southern states passed legislation prohibiting Black people from carrying firearms without licenses, a requirement to which Whites were not subjected. A Mississippi statute provides a typical example of restrictions of this kind:

> Be it enacted, . . . that no freedman, free Negro or mulatto, not in the military
> service of the United States government, and not licensed so to do by the
> board of police of his or her county, shall keep or carry firearms of any
> kind, or any ammunition, dirk or bowie knife, and on conviction thereof in
> the county court shall be punished by fine, not exceeding ten dollars, and
> pay the cost of such proceedings and all such arms or ammunition shall be
> forfeited to the informer; and it shall be the duty of every civil or military
> officer to arrest any such freedman, free Negro or mulatto found with any
> such arms or ammunition, and shall cause him or her to be committed to
> trial in default of bail.[11]

Such measures deeply concerned Northern Republicans. Many charged that the South was trying to reinstate slavery and deny former slaves those rights long considered essential to a free people. The news that the freedmen were being deprived of the right to keep and bear arms was of particular concern to champions of Negro citizenship. For them, the right of the Black population to possess weapons went beyond symbolic importance. It was important as a means of both maintaining the recently reunited union and ensuring against the virtual re-enslavement of those formerly in bondage. Faced with a hostile South determined to preserve the antebellum social order, Northern Republicans were particularly alarmed at provisions that preserved the right to keep and bear arms for former Confederates while disarming Blacks—the one group in the South with clear unionist sympathies. This helped convince many Northern Republicans to seek national enforcement for the Bill of Rights. This effort would play a major role in the adoption of the Fourteenth Amendment.

The debates over the Fourteenth Amendment and the civil rights legislation of the Reconstruction era indicate the intention of many members of Congress to protect the right to keep and bear arms and other provisions of the Bill of Rights against state infringement. Representative Jonathan Bingham of Ohio, who authored the Fourteenth Amendment's privileges or immunities clause, and other Republican supporters of the Fourteenth Amendment expressed the view that the clause applied the Bill of Rights to the states. The Southern efforts to disarm the freedmen and to deny other basic rights to former slaves played an important role in convincing the Thirty-Ninth Congress that traditional notions of federalism and individual rights needed to change.[12]

If the events of Reconstruction persuaded the Thirty-Ninth Congress of the need for applying the Bill of Rights to the states, the Supreme Court in its earliest decisions on the Fourteenth Amendment moved to uphold the antebellum federal structure. The Supreme Court's first decision on a Second Amendment claim came about after the enactment of the Fourteenth Amendment. The decision examined the extent to which the amendment protected citizens against private actions infringing on the right to bear arms. The decision came in *United States v. Cruikshank*, which was decided on October 1, 1875. The case involved charges brought by federal officials against William Cruikshank and others for violating the constitutional rights of a group of Black men who were attempting to vote. The charges included claims that Cruikshank and his associates violated the right of the Black men to peaceably assemble and to bear arms. The men were carrying weapons to the polls because they feared a mob attack to prevent them from voting. The Court, in a majority opinion authored by Chief Justice Morrison R. Waite, held that the First and Second Amendments were limitations on Congress, not on private individuals. The opinion held that the federal government had no power to protect citizens against private actions that deprived them of their constitutional rights. For protection against private criminal action, the individual was required to look to state governments.[13]

The next case in which the Court examined the Second Amendment, *Presser v. Illinois*, more directly involved the question of whether the Second Amendment in combination with the Fourteenth Amendment sets limits on the ability of states to restrict the right to bear arms. The case involved a challenge to an Illinois statute that prohibited individuals who were not members of the organized militia from parading with arms. Justice William Woods's majority opinion interpreted the statute as not infringing on the right to keep and bear arms. Woods nonetheless used the case to indicate that the Second Amendment did not limit state governments even in light of the Fourteenth Amendment. Woods also indicated that because the citizenry at large constituted a reserve militia that was a resource for the US government, it could not be disarmed by state governments independent of Second Amendment considerations. *Presser* would be cited as precedent that the Fourteenth Amendment did not apply the Second Amendment to the states until the Court's decision in *McDonald* in 2010.[14]

The nineteenth century would come to an end with legal commentators in general agreement that the right to keep and bear arms was an important one for a free people. Michigan jurist Thomas M. Cooley discussed the subject in his treatise on constitutional law. Anticipating some of the modern debate on the subject, Cooley expressed the view that the amendment should not be seen as restricted only to members of the militia. He noted that the purpose of the Second Amendment was to allow the people to provide a check against potential governmental usurpation of power. Cooley went on to note that a restriction of the right to arms to members of the militia, whose membership could be limited by the government, would allow the government to defeat the very purpose of the amendment.[15]

The nineteenth century ended with reasonably broad agreement among those constitutional commentators who considered the right to have arms was an important safeguard for the freedoms of the American people. It should be added that this broad agreement in principle usually did not extend to the messy details of which types of firearms regulation were consistent with the principle. Because firearms regulation was a matter of state and local law, the federal courts, adhering to the view that the Second Amendment did not apply to the states, had little to say on the subject.

State courts did develop a jurisprudence examining state firearms regulation in light of provisions in state constitutions protecting the right to have arms. These cases usually provided state and local governments more leeway in regulating the carrying of arms, particularly concealed weapons, than in restricting the ownership of arms. Thus, the 1871 Tennessee case of *Andrews v. State* held that the right to bear arms was an incident of militia service and subject to reasonably broad state regulation, while the right to own arms was a private right with limitations on state restriction.[16]

The early twentieth century would bring about new efforts at firearms regulation and, with them, new attitudes toward arms and the Second Amendment. Traditional beliefs about the importance of arms were frequently being tempered by the view that whole classes of people were unfit to exercise this prerogative. In the South, state governments, freed from the federal scrutiny of the Reconstruction era, used laws regulating concealed weapons to accomplish what had been attempted with the postwar Black Codes. Discriminatory enforcement of these laws often left Blacks disarmed in public places while Whites remained free to carry firearms. This state of affairs facilitated lynchings and other forms of racial violence during the Jim Crow era.

But the South was not the only region where social prejudice restricted the right of disfavored minorities to possess firearms. If the White South saw armed Black people as a threat, politicians in other regions saw a similar threat arising from large-scale immigration from Southern and Eastern Europe. The new immigrants, like others before them, often met hostile receptions. They were associated with crime and anarchy and stereotyped as lazy and mentally unfit. Many native-born Americans feared the immigrants would bring anarchist-inspired crime from Europe, including political assassinations and politically motivated armed robberies. In 1911 these fears led to the passage of New York's Sullivan Law. This state statute was aimed at New York City, a place where the large foreign-born population was believed to be peculiarly susceptible to crime and vice. The Sullivan Law went far beyond typical gun control measures of the day, prohibiting the unlicensed carrying of weapons and requiring a permit for the ownership or purchase of pistols. Violation of the statute was a felony. The first person convicted under the statute was a member of one of the suspect classes, an Italian immigrant.[17]

It was in this early twentieth-century atmosphere that the collective rights view of the right to bear arms first began to attract serious attention from the judiciary. In one of the earliest cases to adopt this view, *Salina v. Blaksley*, which involved a person convicted of carrying a revolver while intoxicated, the Supreme Court of Kansas interpreted that state's constitutional provision protecting the right to bear arms as a protection that applied only to the militia and not for individual purposes.[18] In 1915 Maine Chief Justice Lucillius A. Emery authored an essay titled "The Constitutional Right to Keep and Bear Arms," which appeared in the *Harvard Law Review*. In the essay, Emery argued that the right to bear or carry arms should be viewed as a right limited to militia service. He also noted that legislatures could not prohibit the keeping or ownership of arms, echoing the distinction made by the Tennessee court in *Andrews*.[19]

These developments affected relatively few Americans at the beginning of the twentieth century. The nation was still largely rural. Firearms ownership for both self-defense and hunting were fairly commonplace, and statutes regulating firearms ownership were relatively rare and unobtrusive. For most citizens, access to firearms was unimpaired, and there was little occasion for either the courts or constitutional commentators to say much about the Second Amendment.

This situation would change after the First World War. Prohibition brought about the rise of organized gangs engaged in the sale of bootlegged alcohol. Territorial rivalries among the gangs led to open warfare on the streets of the nation's major cities. That warfare was made even more terrifying by the introduction of a terrifying new weapon, the Thompson submachine gun. A fully automatic weapon developed too late for use in World War I, the tommy-gun was one of the first submachine guns in widespread use. Used by violent criminals in their wars with one another, the Thompson claimed the lives of a fair number of members of the general public as well.

The end of the twenties and the end of Prohibition did not bring a halt to notorious misuse of automatic weapons. The rise in the 1930s of such desperadoes as John Dillinger, "Pretty Boy" Floyd, "Ma" Barker, George "Machine Gun" Kelly, and Clyde Barrow and Bonnie Parker became a part of American folklore. The exploits of such criminals were made more vivid and terrifying by the then new medium of talking motion pictures. Thus, the horrors of criminal misuse of automatic weapons were powerfully brought home to the public.

These events caused the Roosevelt administration to propose the first federal gun control legislation. The National Firearms Act of 1934 required registration, police permission, and a prohibitive tax for firearms that were deemed gangster weapons, including automatic weapons, sawed-off shotguns, and silencers. It is interesting in light of the current debate that the Roosevelt administration regarded the act as a revenue measure, conceding that an outright ban on such weapons would probably be beyond Congress's powers.

The 1934 act gave rise to the Supreme Court's last decision before *Heller* on the Second Amendment, *United States v. Miller*. It was a curious case. Both sides of the Second Amendment debate have claimed that the decision authored by Justice James C. McReynolds supports their views. Interestingly, the Court only heard arguments by the government. The federal government appealed a decision by a federal district court invalidating the National Firearms Act of 1934 in a case involving the unlicensed transportation of an unregistered sawed-off shotgun. Focusing on the weapon in question, the Court noted, "In the absence of any evidence tending to show that the possession of a [sawed-off shotgun] at this time has some reasonable relationship to the preservation or efficiency of a well-regulated militia, we cannot say that the Second Amendment guarantees the right to keep and bear such an instrument. Certainly it is not within judicial notice that this weapon is any part of the ordinary military equipment or that its use could contribute to the common defense."[20]

Advocates of the collective rights view have pointed to the Court's emphasis in *Miller* on the militia, claiming that it was an indication that the Court saw the Second Amendment as being concerned only with the preservation of state militias. But the Court's discussion of the militia indicates that it saw a clear relationship between the individual right and the maintenance of the militia: "The signification attributed to the term Militia appears from the debates in the Convention, the history and legislation of Colonies and States, and the writings of approved commentators. These show plainly enough that the Militia comprises all males physically capable of acting in concert for the common defense. 'A body of citizens enrolled for military discipline.' And further, that ordinarily when called for service these men were expected to appear bearing arms supplied by themselves and of the kind in common use at the time."[21]

Probably the most accurate way to view what the Court did in *Miller* is to see it as an update of the nineteenth-century civilized warfare doctrine. McReynolds's decision relied on the antebellum Tennessee case *Avmette v. State*, which had allowed the state to restrict the carrying of those types of weapons that were frequently used by criminals and not suitable for the common defense.[22] The Supreme Court in *Miller* remanded the case to the lower courts to determine whether a sawed-off shotgun was a weapon appropriate for militia use. That determination was never made.

Although *Miller* was the Court's most comprehensive exploration of the Second Amendment before *Heller*, it had little effect on either firearms regulation or the general public's view on the right to keep and bear arms. For nearly three decades after *Miller*, little existed in the way of federal firearms regulation. The Federal Firearms Act of 1938 added a prohibition against individuals with felony convictions possessing firearms. But that prohibition affected a relatively small percentage of the population. State and local legislation existed, but with few exceptions—such as the New York Sullivan Law—these were usually traditional regulations governing the manner of carrying weapons, not outright prohibitions. Some states banned the sale but not the possession of pistols. These restrictions were easily circumvented by purchasing handguns from mail-order catalogs. There were few serious attempts to mount constitutional challenges to these restrictions. The Second Amendment was thus bypassed in the postwar Supreme Court's process of applying most of the provisions of the Bill of Rights to the states, although Justice Hugo Black, who had participated in the *Miller* decision, was an advocate of the view that the Fourteenth Amendment made the entire Bill of Rights applicable to the states.[23]

It would take the turmoil of the 1960s and the tragedy of three high-profile assassinations to generate the modern gun control movement and create the ongoing debate over the meaning of the Second Amendment. The assassination of President John F. Kennedy in 1963 brought calls for stricter national controls over the sale of firearms. Urban riots and the assassinations of civil rights leader Martin Luther King Jr. and Senator Robert F. Kennedy led to the passage of the Gun Control Act of 1968, the first federal legislation that seriously affected the purchasing of firearms for large numbers of Americans. This legislation limited the purchase of firearms through the mail and restricted the importation of surplus military rifles. The act also prohibited the purchase of firearms by those with felony convictions, even though the legislation provided no means of checking a purchaser's record. Some of the provisions of the 1968 act would later be modified by legislation passed in 1986.[24]

The 1968 act proved to be something of a watershed. Since then a national debate over gun control and a subsidiary debate over the meaning of the Second Amendment have become perennial features in US politics. The rise of a highly visible national gun control movement has been something new in American political life. Some adherents of this movement have advocated relatively moderate measures, such as screening designed to prevent individuals with suspect backgrounds, criminal records, or histories of mental instability from purchasing firearms. Such measures are essentially extensions of firearms regulations that have long existed in many states as attempts to limit firearms use by undesirable persons—and even in states with state constitutional protection for the right to bear arms and courts willing to enforce such guarantees. These relatively modest measures pose little threat to the general public's right to possess firearms.

But since the 1960s, others have argued for more radical measures. Their view has been that state and local governments and, more importantly, the federal government can and should outlaw the general public's right to possess whole categories of firearms that had previously been owned by large numbers of law-abiding citizens. Many in the gun control movement have argued that ownership of guns for self-defense or as part of a universal citizens' militia is dangerous and atavistic. They have claimed that the only legitimate reason for civilian firearms ownership is for sporting purposes, usually hunting, and even that ownership should be permitted only under stringent licensing. Efforts were made to ban firearms that did not meet this "sporting purposes" definition. In the 1970s and 1980s, gun control advocates urged the banning of handguns, particularly cheap ones popularly known as "Saturday night specials." The prohibitions on handgun ownership in Washington, DC, and Chicago that gave rise to the *Heller* and *McDonald* litigation were two of the rare successes of the handgun prohibition movement. In the 1990s, many gun control supporters advocated bans on "assault weapons," a term employed without great precision to include semiautomatic rifles with military features such as bayonet lugs and pistol grips, or virtually all semiautomatic rifles, depending on the user's definition. The gun control movement scored some success with its campaign against assault weapons. A handful of states enacted bans on some semiautomatic firearms. Congress enacted a ten-year prohibition on the sale of semiautomatic rifles with military-style features in 1994. Congress refused to renew the ban in 2004.

Such advocacy of wholesale restrictions on firearms ownership helped bring about the modern debate over the meaning of the Second Amendment. Much of the effort to reinterpret the Second Amendment as a collective right has been an attempt to justify proposed firearms restrictions that, at earlier periods in US history, would have been regarded as unconstitutional. Since the 1960s, a vigorous polemical debate over whether the amendment should be seen as a broad individual right or as a right limited to a highly controlled militia context has been waged in the nation's editorial pages and broadcast media.

Despite the passion with which the public debate had been waged, the Supreme Court managed to keep a curious silence on the issue during the latter decades of the twentieth century. For decades, the Court basically ducked the issue. In the seventies, eighties, and nineties, the lower federal courts upheld gun control legislation either by citing *Miller* for the proposition that the Second Amendment only protected the right to bear arms in a militia context when addressing federal legislation or by citing *Presser* for the proposition that the amendment did not apply to the states. The Supreme Court declined to grant certiorari in these cases.[25]

If the Court had an institutional reluctance to directly address the issue of the Second Amendment and its applicability to the gun control issue, in dicta, it was, curiously enough, willing to acknowledge the right to bear arms in cases extraneous to the gun control issue. Starting with Justice John Marshall Harlan II's dissent in the 1961 case *Poe v. Ullman*, involving a Connecticut anti-contraception statute, the right to bear arms was often noted in privacy cases: "The full scope of the liberty guaranteed by the Due Process Clause cannot be found in or limited by the precise terms of the specific guarantees elsewhere provided in the Constitution. This 'liberty' is not a series of isolated points priced out in terms of the taking of property; the freedom of speech, press and religion; *the right to keep and bear arms*" (italics added).[26] Statements by other justices—sometimes in dicta, at other times in statements to the press—gave heart to supporters of either the individual or collective rights viewpoints, but the Court would end the twentieth century maintaining its institutional silence on the subject.

If the Supreme Court was reluctant to address the controversy, other important legal actors were making pronouncements on the Second Amendment and the right to arms more generally. Before the Court's decision in *Heller,* forty-four states had provisions in their constitutions for the right to keep and bear arms. If the federal jurisprudence on this right was somewhat thin, state courts had developed a robust jurisprudence on the subject, ranging from a fairly restrictive to fairly expansive views of the right. Congress had also played a role in Second Amendment interpretation. In 1982, the Senate Judiciary Committee's Subcommittee on the Constitution issued a report supporting the individual rights view of the amendment. Four years later, Congress passed the Firearms Owners Protection Act supporting the right of interstate travel with firearms. The statute was prefaced with congressional findings declaring that the Second Amendment was an individual right.[27]

The 1980s would see increased academic debate over the Second Amendment. At first it was a debate that mainly engaged independent scholars not affiliated with universities and usually connected to groups supporting or opposing

stricter gun controls. Because the subject inherently involves a debate over original intentions or understandings, historians tended to enter the debate somewhat sooner than scholars in the legal academy. Something of a milestone in the
history of the debate came in 1989 with the publication of Sanford Levinson's
"The Embarrassing Second Amendment" in the *Yale Law Journal*. For the first
time since gun control had become a national issue in the 1960s, a major constitutional scholar in a leading law journal was arguing that the Second Amendment deserved serious examination and that the individual rights view was likely
the more accurate one. Levinson's article spurred other leading scholars in law,
history, and political science to take up the issue, including Akhil Amar, Saul
Cornell, Leonard Levy, Jack Rakove, Paul Finkelman, Laurence Tribe, William
Van Alstyne, and Gary Wills.[28]

The new scholarship undoubtedly played a part in reawakening the judiciary's
interest in the Second Amendment. Supreme Court Justice Clarence Thomas indicated a favorable disposition toward the individual rights reading of the amendment in the 1997 case *United States v. Printz*.[29] Justice Scalia, who would later write
the majority opinion in *Heller*, expressed support for the individual rights view
in scholarly commentary. A major breakthrough for individual rights advocates
came in 2001 with the Fifth Circuit case *United States v. Emerson*.[30] In *Emerson*,
which involved a Second Amendment challenge to the federal prosecution of an
individual who possessed a firearm in violation of a restraining order, the Fifth
Circuit Court of Appeals held that the Second Amendment was an individual
right but that a restraining order prohibiting possession of firearms on the part
of an individual suspected of domestic violence was reasonable regulation. A
2002 decision by the Ninth Circuit Court of Appeals in *Silveira v. Lockyer* upheld
California's ban on assault weapons, holding that the Second Amendment was a
collective right. The decision seemed written in part to rebut the Fifth Circuit's
opinion in *Emerson*.[31]

National politics would also play a role in issues of Second Amendment interpretation. The close election of George W. Bush in 2000 brought to national
office an administration that had enjoyed the support of the National Rifle
Association—support that may have tipped the electoral balance in a number
of states. One result of Bush's election was a new attitude in the Justice Department more in line with the individual rights view than had been the case in
recent decades. In 2004, the attorney general's office, under Attorney General
John Ashcroft's direction, issued a formal memorandum on the Second Amendment. The memorandum reflected Ashcroft's long-standing support for the
individual rights interpretation. As might be expected, the memorandum was
met with strong criticism by proponents of stricter gun control and received
strong support among opponents of gun control. The Ashcroft memorandum

was marked by a detailed analysis of the history and meaning of the Second Amendment, taking into account much of the new scholarship that had developed since the 1990s.[32]

The debate would continue into the twenty-first century, waged in academic journals and the popular media. As the controversy grew more strident, it would make its way into the 2005 Senate confirmation hearing for future Chief Justice John Roberts. Under questioning from Wisconsin Senator Russell Feingold, Roberts indicated that he believed that the proper interpretation of the Second Amendment was still an open issue, one that the courts had not resolved.[33] If the courts at the time were still reticent concerning the Second Amendment, the political branches of government had traditionally been largely sympathetic to protecting the right to have arms. During the 1990s and continuing into the twenty-first century, an increasing number of states have passed legislation liberalizing the right of citizens to carry guns for self-protection—a reflection of both public fears of crime and the political skill of the National Rifle Association. More than forty states have statutes permitting almost anyone legally eligible to own a pistol to carry a concealed weapon. In 2006, Congress passed legislation prohibiting lawsuits against firearms manufacturers for criminal misuse of firearms. The legislation contained findings that the Second Amendment protected a right of individuals regardless of whether they were members of the militia. That same year, Congress also passed legislation prohibiting public officials from disarming citizens during times of natural disaster. This measure was enacted in part in response to actions taken by New Orleans officials during Hurricane Katrina, when police confiscated guns from citizens in New Orleans, sometimes in dramatic confrontations played out on national television.

The political movement to vindicate the right to keep and bear arms had had considerable political success, limiting national gun control legislation, passing statewide preemption legislation that prevented municipalities from enacting bans on various kinds of firearms, and enacting and reenacting state constitutional provisions for the right to keep and bear arms. But vindication in the form of a Supreme Court ruling proclaiming that the Second Amendment protected the right of individuals for lawful private purposes such as self-defense remained elusive, and for many it seemed as though it might be out of reach. The National Rifle Association and others looked for a possible case. The handgun ban in the District of Columbia seemed the likeliest target. The District of Columbia is federal territory. The incorporation question would not be an issue in the nation's capital. The District of Columbia ban was draconian—no handguns allowed, and rifles and shotguns had to be disassembled so they could not be used for home defense. The District government could not claim that this ban was consistent with a private right to have arms for self-defense.

A suit against the District of Columbia and its handgun ban looked promising, but it was also fraught with peril. The courts had not been friendly to the Second Amendment in recent decades, dicta and out-of-court statements by some justices notwithstanding. A case that lost would be disastrous to supporters of the right to keep and bear arms. The National Rifle Association was reluctant to bring the case, fearing that a lost case would do far more harm than good. The suit against the District's statute was brought by independent attorneys Alan Gura, Robert A. Levy, and Clark M. Neilly III. The attorneys represented Richard Heller, a special police officer in the District of Columbia who was authorized to carry a handgun while guarding a DC courthouse but was prohibited from having an operable handgun at home for self-defense.

The District Court for the District of Columbia dismissed the complaint on the grounds that the Second Amendment applied only to the organized militia. In March 2007, the US Court of Appeals for the DC Circuit, in a 2–1 decision, reversed the district court. The higher court, in an opinion written by Judge Laurence H. Silberman, declared the ban unconstitutional, a violation of the Second Amendment. The full DC Circuit denied the District of Columbia's petition for an en banc hearing or hearing by the full court, thus letting the panel opinion stand. The issue could no longer be avoided. For the first time, a federal court had declared that a specific piece of gun control legislation violated the Second Amendment. The government of the District of Columbia petitioned the Supreme Court for certiorari. It was granted in November 2007.

The Supreme Court would hear the case and render its decision in June 2008. The Court's opinion, written by Justice Scalia, upheld the circuit court's decision: "In sum, we hold that the District's ban on handgun possession in the home violates the Second Amendment, as does its prohibition against rendering any lawful firearm in the home operable for the purpose of immediate self-defense."[34] The opinion commanded a bare 5–4 majority. It was contested by dissents from Justices Breyer and Stevens, joined by Justices Ginsburg and Souter.

But Scalia's opinion did become the law of the case and the law of the land. The majority opinion in *Heller* left many questions unresolved. It stated that the Second Amendment's protections were most important for protection of home and family but only hinted at constitutional protection for a right to carry firearms outside the home for protection. Scalia's opinion indicated that the link envisioned by the framers between the armed citizen and the militia at large was still part of the Second Amendment's purpose, but his opinion also indicated that the government could ban automatic weapons, the weapons most likely to be put to military purposes. The majority opinion also stated that weapons in common use were constitutionally protected, but the opinion did not directly address the assault weapons controversy, even though semiautomatic rifles with military features had been in public hands in large quantities since at least the 1950s. For lawyers and future courts, the decision was frustrating, because the Scalia opinion did not provide a methodology, a level of scrutiny, through which future courts should examine Second Amendment claims. Would allegations that Second Amendment rights were being violated be subject to the rigors of strict scrutiny that had long been the standard in First Amendment claims, or would they be subject to some lesser standard of review? The Scalia opinion was silent on the subject.

Most significantly of all, the opinion in *Heller* did not address whether the Second Amendment applied to the states. Most gun control measures are the products of state and local legislation. A decision that simply recognized the Second Amendment but did not say that the amendment, in combination with the Fourteenth Amendment, provided a limitation on state governments could leave many Americans with a major right unprotected from serious infringement.

Application of the Second Amendment to the states would come two years later, when the Supreme Court decided the case of *McDonald v. City of Chicago*. The named plaintiff in the case was Otis McDonald, a veteran of the Korean War who lived in a dangerous Chicago neighborhood. He brought suit for the right to keep a pistol in his home for protection against gang members. The elderly veteran feared retaliation because he led an antidrug campaign in his community. McDonald was joined by other plaintiffs from Chicago and the nearby suburb of Oak Park, which also had a prohibition on handgun ownership.[35]

*McDonald*, like *Heller*, produced a 5–4 decision. The Court's opinion was written by Justice Samuel Alito. That opinion, joined by Chief Justice Roberts and Justices Kennedy and Scalia, rooted the Second Amendment's application to the states in the Court's previous jurisprudence that held that most provisions of the Bill of Rights applied to the states through the Fourteenth Amendment's due process clause. The fifth vote for application of Second Amendment rights to the states came from Justice Thomas, who wrote a concurring opinion emphasizing the history of the Fourteenth Amendment. Thomas opined that the amendment's history indicated that the framers of that constitutional provision intended that the privileges or immunities clause would be the vehicle for applying the Bill of Rights to the states. Dissenting opinions were written by Justices Breyer and Stevens. Both dissenting opinions were joined by Justices Ginsburg and Sotomayor.[36]

With the decisions in *Heller* and *McDonald*, the Second Amendment would gravitate from being the subject of academic and polemical debate to being a concern of working attorneys and jurists. *Heller* and *McDonald* had affirmed that the right to keep and bear arms protected a right of the individual. But the decisions gave few guidelines as to how far that right extended or how rigorously the courts were supposed to examine restrictions on firearms ownership or use.

Like *Heller*, *McDonald* provided no specific answer about which types of firearms were constitutionally protected or whether the right to bear arms protected a right to bear firearms outside the home. Cases addressing these issues would start appearing in the lower federal courts and in state courts after *McDonald*. For the most part, the courts have tended to take a narrow view of the protection afforded by the Second Amendment, reflecting the hostility that the courts exhibited toward the constitutional provision before the decision in *Heller*. There have been a few exceptions. The Seventh Circuit Court of Appeals and Court of Appeals for the DC Circuit both struck down bans on carrying firearms for protection in Illinois and in the District of Columbia on Second Amendment grounds.[37]

Some federal courts have indicated that while the general ban on individuals with felony convictions owning firearms is, as the Scalia opinion in *Heller* noted, "presumptively lawful," there may be individuals who are barred from owning firearms because of felony convictions who may have valid Second Amendment claims for relief.[38]

In the years between the 2010 decision in *McDonald* and 2019, the Supreme Court seemed to have returned to its pre-*Heller* reluctance to examine Second Amendment claims. In that period, the Court declined to revisit the Second Amendment issue, denying petitions for certiorari in cases where federal circuit courts have issued opinions on assault weapons bans and the right to carry firearms outside the home. The Court did reiterate its decisions in *Heller* and *McDonald* in *Caetano v. Massachusetts*, a 2016 case involving a Massachusetts ban on electric stun guns. The Massachusetts Supreme Judicial Court upheld the ban on the grounds that stun guns employed a technology unknown to the framers of the Second Amendment. The Supreme Court, in a per curiam opinion joined by all the justices, vacated the Massachusetts court's opinion and indicated that the state court ruling was inconsistent with *Heller* and *McDonald*. The decision was as much an affirmation of the notion that lower courts must follow Supreme Court rulings as it was a vindication of the right to bear arms.[39]

With a grant of certiorari on January 22, 2019, the Court signaled its willingness to return to the Second Amendment fray. The case *New York State Rifle and Pistol Association v. City of New York* involved a restrictive pistol control measure in New York City, where residents are required to have a permit to possess pistols in their homes. Those with a residence permit were allowed to transport their handguns in a locked container to a range in New York City, but they were forbidden to transport their pistols to ranges outside the five boroughs or to second homes that they may have had elsewhere. The regulation was upheld by the Second Circuit Court of Appeals. Faced with the likelihood that that provision

would be declared unconstitutional, the New York State legislature passed legislation permitting premises permit holders to travel with their firearms outside of
New York City. Over the dissents of Justices Thomas, Alito, and Gorsuch, a majority of the Court declared the case moot in light of the change in New York law.[40]

On April 26, 2021, the Supreme Court signaled that its reluctance to return
to the Second Amendment issues might have come to an end. On that date the
Court granted certiorari in the case of *New York State Rifle and Pistol Association
v. Corlett*. The case involves issuance of licenses to carry handguns outside the
home. The case has the potential to determine whether the Court sees the right
protected by the Second Amendment as one that includes the right to carry or
"bear" arms outside the home for self-protection. As we write this chapter in
mid-August of 2021, oral arguments in this case have not yet been held before
the Supreme Court.[41]

*Heller* and *McDonald* and the cases that have followed in the wake of the two
decisions should lead us to a new consideration of the Second Amendment's
meaning and how it might be applied in the twenty-first century. The idea that
the right to keep and bear arms was meant to be tied so closely to membership
and participation in a militia that the government has total power to organize or
fail to organize is one that can only be sustained through a highly strained reading of the history. Like nineteenth-century jurist Thomas Cooley, we also believe
that such a reading creates an illusory right that the government can defeat at any
time simply by the way it decides to organize the militia. We would accept no
such reading with any other provision of the Bill of Rights, nor should we with
the Second Amendment.

But to say that the slim majorities were right in *Heller* and *McDonald* and
that the individual rights reading of the Second Amendment is the more plausible and stronger reading should not end the debate. There should be a debate,
as Justice Stevens has intimated, about the appropriateness of a constitutional
amendment to limit the reach of the Second Amendment as pronounced by *Heller*
and *McDonald*, and even whether the amendment should simply be repealed.[42]
Clearly, many advocates of strong gun control measures believe the amendment
to be an anachronism, a relic of an atavistic age of universal militias, posses, slave
patrols, vigilantes, and citizens armed against one another. If so, they should
make that case. It is a hard case to make for modern America, where the right to
self-defense is rightly considered fundamental and where private gun ownership
is widespread. It is also a hard case to make in a nation where forty-four states
have enacted or reenacted right-to-bear-arms provisions in their state constitutions in the twentieth and twenty-first centuries. In the final analysis, radical
constitutional change, such as eliminating a right long considered fundamental,
should be the result of sustained debate, national consensus, and constitutional

amendment and not simply the result of ignoring or creatively reinterpreting key constitutional provisions.

There is, however, an even more interesting debate that might be had with respect to public safety and the right to bear arms. That debate would involve examining how best to recognize and protect the right while also allowing legislatures leeway to develop criminologically sound measures designed to limit, as much as possible, access to weapons among career criminals and those who are mentally unstable. Such a debate would involve recognizing that the right to have arms has been and remains part of the US constitutional tradition, that it is valued by large segments of society, and that it sets real limits on governmental regulation. It also involves recognizing that measures designed to keep weapons out of undesirable hands are not inconsistent with this right. We have, to date, been unable to develop this kind of consensus in part because of the previous effort to render the Second Amendment meaningless, a nonexistent protection for the right of the people to keep and bear arms. It is to be hoped that with *Heller* and *McDonald* and with a maturing jurisprudence that provides strong protection for the right to bear arms we can begin a meaningful dialogue on how to protect both the right to bear arms and enhance public safety.

### NOTES

1. *District of Columbia v. Heller* 554 U.S. 570 (2008); *McDonald v. City of Chicago* 561 U.S. 742 (2010).

2. Bernard Bailyn, *The Ideological Origins of the American Revolution* (Cambridge, MA: Belknap Press, 1967).

3. See generally Joyce Lee Malcolm, *To Keep and Bear Arms: The Origins of an Anglo-American Right* (Cambridge, MA: Harvard University Press, 1994), esp. at 1–15.

4. 1 Wm and Mary, Sess. 2.c2 (1689).

5. William Blackstone, *Commentaries on the Laws of England*, vol. 1, *Of the Rights of Persons* (London, 1765–1769; repr., Chicago: University of Chicago Press, 1979), 139.

6. C. M. Kenyon, ed., *The Anti-Federalists* (New York: Bobbs-Merrill, 1966), 228.

7. James Madison, *Federalist*, No. 46 (1788; rev. ed. New York: New American Library, 1961), 299.

8. 1 Statutes at Large 271 (May 1792).

9. Joseph Story, *Commentaries on the Constitution of the United States*, 2 vols. (Boston: Little, Brown and Co., 1858; Durham, NC: Carolina Academic Press, repr. 1987), 1:708.

10. See *Nunn v. State*, 1 Georgia 243 (1846).

11. See Walter L. Fleming, ed., *Documentary History of Reconstruction: Political, Military, Social, Religious, Educational and Industrial, 1865–1906* (New York, 1909; New York: McGraw-Hill, repr. 1966), 290.

12. The most comprehensive discussion of the incorporation issue is Michael Kent Curtis's *No State Shall Abridge: The Fourteenth Amendment and the Bill of Rights* (Durham, NC: Duke University Press, 1986). For an important discussion of the Thirty-Ninth Congress's views concerning the Second Amendment, its applicability to the states through the Fourteenth Amendment, and the importance of Reconstruction-era civil rights legislation to an understanding of this issue, see Stephen P. Halbrook, *Freedmen, the Fourteenth Amendment and the Right to Bear Arms, 1866–1876* (Westport, CT, 1998).

13. *United States v. Cruikshank*, 92 U.S. 542 (1876).

14. *Presser v. Illinois*, 116 U.S. 252 (1886). As late as 2009, the United States Court of Appeals for the Seventh Circuit ruled against Otis McDonald's claim that Chicago's handgun ban was unconstitutional, citing *Presser* for the proposition that the Second Amendment did not limit the actions of state governments. See *McDonald v. City of Chicago*, 567 F.3d 856 (2009). The Supreme Court reversed the Seventh Circuit the following year.

15. Thomas M. Cooley, *Principles of Constitutional Law* (Boston: Little, Brown, and Co., 1898), 298; Thomas M. Cooley, *A Treatise on the Constitutional Limitations*, 7th ed. (Boston: Little, Brown, and Co., 1903), 498–99.

16. *Andrews v. the State*, 50 Tenn. 154 (1871).

17. Don B. Kates, "Towards a History of Handgun Prohibition in the United States," in *Restricting Handguns: The Liberal Skeptics Speak Out*, ed. Don B. Kates (Croton-on-Hudson, NY: North River Press, 1979), 7–30; Lee Kennett and James La Verne Anderson, *The Gun in America: The Origins of a National Dilemma* (Westport, CT: Greenwood, 1975), 174–80.

18. *Salina v. Blaksley*, 72 Kans. 230 (1905).

19. Lucillius A. Emery, "The Constitutional Right to Keep and Bear Arms," *Harvard Law Review* 28 (1915): 473.

20. *United States v. Miller*, 307 U.S. 178 (1939).

21. *United States v. Miller*.

22. *Aymette v. State*, 21 Tenn. 154 (1840).

23. *Adamson v. People of State of California*, 332 U.S. 46, 59–62 (Black dissenting) (1947).

24. Public Law 90-618, "An Act to Amend Title 18 USC, to Provide for Better Control of the Interstate Traffic in Firearms, Title 1 State Firearms Control Assistance"; Public Law 99-308 (Ninety-Ninth Congress), "An Act To Amend Chapter 44 (Relating to Firearms) of Title 18, US Code and for Other Purposes."

25. See, for example, *Quilici v. Village of Morton Grove*, 695 F.2d 261 (1982).

26. *Poe et al. vs. Ullman*, 367 U.S. 497, 543 (Harlan dissenting) (1961).

27. See Public Law 99-308, op. cit.

28. Sanford Levinson, "The Embarrassing Second Amendment," *Yale Law Journal* 99 (1989): 637. For a brief discussion of Second Amendment scholarship, see the suggestions for further reading at the end of this volume.

29. *United States v. Printz*, 521 U.S. 898 (1997).

30. *United States v. Emerson*, 270 F.3d 2003 (2001).

31. *Silveira v. Lockyer*, 312 F.3d 1052 (2002).

32. "Whether the Second Amendment Secures an Individual Right: Memorandum Opinion for the Attorney General," August 24, 2004, http://www.usdoj.gov/olc/secondamendment2.htm.

33. *Confirmation Hearing on the Nomination of John G. Roberts, Jr. to Be Chief Justice of the United States: Hearing before the Senate Judiciary Committee United States Senate*, 109th Cong., 1st Sess. (September 12–15, 2005), 360–61.

34. *District of Columbia v. Heller*, 554 U.S. 570, 629 (2008).

35. *McDonald v. City of Chicago*, 561 U.S. 742 (2010).

36. *McDonald v. City of Chicago*.

37. *Moore v. Madigan*, 702 F.3d 933 (2012); *Wrenn v. District of Columbia*, 864 F.3d 650 (2017).

38. See, for example, *Binderup v. Atty Gen*, 836 F.3d 336 (3d Cir. 2016).

39. *Caetano v. Massachusetts*, 136 S. Ct. 1027 (2016).

40. *New York State Rifle and Pistol Association v. City of New York*, 140 S. Ct. 1525 (2020).

41. *New York State Rifle et al. v Corlett etc.*, WL 1002643.

42. John Paul Stevens, *The Making of a Justice: Reflections on My First 94 Years* (New York: Little, Brown, 2019), 515.

FIVE

—‿𝔪‿—

# THE ENIGMATIC PLACE OF PROPERTY RIGHTS IN MODERN CONSTITUTIONAL THOUGHT

JAMES W. ELY JR.

THE BELIEF THAT PROPERTY OWNERSHIP is essential for the enjoyment of liberty has long been a fundamental tenet of Anglo-American constitutional thought. "Property rights," Justice Anthony Kennedy proclaimed in 2017, "are necessary to preserve freedom, for property ownership empowers persons to shape and to plan their own destiny in a world where governments are always eager to do so for them."[1] Envisioning property ownership as establishing the basis for individual autonomy from government coercion, the framers of the Constitution placed a high value on the security of property rights. As Chief Justice John Roberts aptly noted in 2021: "The Founders recognized that the protection of private property is indispensable to the promotion of individual freedom."[2] Echoing the philosopher John Locke, John Rutledge of South Carolina advised the Philadelphia convention that "Property was certainly the principal object of Society."[3] Further, the framers believed that respect for property rights was crucial to encourage economic growth and to increase national wealth. The framers relied primarily on a variety of institutional arrangements, such as the separation of powers, to guard the rights of property owners. Still, the Constitution and Bill of Rights contain important provisions designed to restrain legislative incursions on property rights.

Not surprisingly, therefore, throughout most of US history, the Supreme Court as well as state courts functioned as guardians of property and economic rights against legislative encroachments. They stressed that property was more than the physical possession of an object. The concept of ownership encompasses a range of interests, including the right to acquire, use, develop, and dispose of property.

The Progressive movement of the early twentieth century, however, challenged the high constitutional standing of property and called for greater governmental management of the economy.[4] The Supreme Court sustained much of the regulatory legislation promoted by the Progressives and, in the process, began to downplay the constitutional guarantees of the rights of owners. The Court's occasional defense of traditional property rights in the 1930s threatened the New Deal program to combat the Great Depression, eventually causing President Franklin D. Roosevelt to propose his plan to pack the Court. This constitutional crisis was avoided when in 1937 the justices abruptly abandoned scrutiny of economic regulations. Known as the constitutional revolution of 1937, this shift had a profound impact on property rights. Deference to the economic and social judgments of lawmakers became the new orthodoxy. Thus, judicial review of economic legislation since 1937 has been largely perfunctory.[5] Liberal constitutionalism moved in other directions, with scant attention to property rights. Indeed, after the New Deal, it became rather fashionable for scholars to ignore or belittle the significance of constitutionally protected property. Desirous of achieving a more egalitarian distribution of wealth and pursuing a host of regulatory objectives, liberal scholars formulated doctrines to eviscerate private property rights and enlarge governmental power over the economy. This skeptical attitude toward private property has permeated modern legal culture.

The New Deal political hegemony gradually dissolved, and starting in the 1970s new political and intellectual currents were more solicitous of the rights of property owners. There were important intellectual trends sympathetic to the defense of property rights. Classical economic thinking, which stressed the efficiency of free markets, was increasingly employed in the analysis of legal issues. The law and economics movement stressed the deficiencies of governmental regulation of economic activity. Warning that regulations often imposed heavy compliance costs, hampered competition, and restricted economic opportunity, this school of thought argued that the operations of the free market should ordinarily determine the price of goods and services. Another group of legal scholars mounted a sustained challenge to the statist jurisprudence that has dominated thinking about property rights since the New Deal.[6] Urging the federal courts to defend the free market and prevent government transfers of private wealth, they were instrumental in reopening public debate regarding the constitutionality of economic regulations. Among other arguments, these scholars have reasserted the vision of the framers that economic and individual rights were fundamentally inseparable.

Since the 1980s there have been some indications that the Supreme Court under Chief Justices William Rehnquist and John Roberts was in the process of reinvigorating the property clauses of the Constitution. A focus solely on the Supreme Court, however, does not give us the full picture with respect to property rights. Many property issues are presented in state courts. Some of these courts have become more assertive than their federal counterparts in defending property against legislative infringement under state constitutional provisions. In this essay, I briefly review current law dealing with the property clauses of the Constitution, assess the judicial record in this area, and consider the probable course of future developments with respect to property rights.

### DUE PROCESS CLAUSE

The Fifth and Fourteenth Amendments provide that no person shall be "deprived of life, liberty, or property, without due process of law." For many years after the Civil War, the Supreme Court gave a substantive interpretation to the due process clauses, reasoning that these guarantees went beyond procedural protection and encompassed certain fundamental but unenumerated rights. Foremost among these were the right to acquire and use property and the right to make contracts and to pursue common occupations. This doctrine, known as economic due process, reflected a close identification between constitutional values and the free market economy. Congress and the states could control property usage and business activity under the police power to protect the public health, safety, and morals, but the Supreme Court required lawmakers to justify such regulations. The justices did not accept legislative assertions of regulatory purpose at face value and invalidated laws deemed unreasonable or arbitrary as a violation of due process. In effect, the doctrine of economic due process allowed the courts to exercise a degree of supervisory review over economic and social legislation.[7]

Critics associated with the Progressive movement of the early twentieth century charged that courts were substituting their judgment for that of legislators, but in fact most regulatory statutes passed constitutional muster.[8] However, courts did invalidate laws that arbitrarily interfered with the property rights of individuals. In *Buchanan v. Warley* (1917), for example, the Supreme Court struck down a residential segregation ordinance as an infringement of the fundamental right to buy and sell property guaranteed by due process.[9] Economic liberty was the standard against which legislation was measured, and restraint was approved only if found necessary to promote public health, safety, or morals.

As a consequence of the constitutional revolution of 1937, the Supreme Court repudiated economic due process and retreated from judicial review of economic and social legislation. In *United States v. Carolene Products Co.* (1938), the Court placed the rights of property owners in a subordinate category entitled to a lesser degree of due process protection. The justices declared that economic regulations would receive only minimum judicial scrutiny under a permissive "rational basis" test. In a striking reversal of previous decisions, economic legislation was accorded a virtually irrebuttable presumption of validity.[10]

It is difficult to reconcile *Carolene Products* with either the text of the Constitution or the Supreme Court's long defense of property rights. The language of the due process clauses draws no dichotomy between the protection of property and other liberties. Indeed, the framers of the Constitution and Bill of Rights believed that property rights and personal liberty were indissolubly linked. As the distinguished jurist Learned Hand observed, "It would have seemed a strange anomaly to those who penned the words in the Fifth to learn that they constituted severer restrictions as to Liberty than to Property."[11] There are still other problems with the *Carolene Products* ruling. Although couched in terms of deference to lawmakers, the decision actually exemplified judicial activism by ranking rights into categories not expressed in the Constitution. This judicial distinction has produced the curious result that under the due process clauses, there is in fact no meaningful judicial review of legislation affecting the rights of property owners.

Moreover, the asserted justification offered for the Court's double standard for reviewing property rights differently than claims of other individual liberty was questionable. The Court's belief that heightened scrutiny for claims of certain individual rights was necessitated by the failure of the political process, while economic regulations reflected majoritarian preferences in a properly functioning legislative process, has proved to be particularly dubious. Much of the economic legislation upheld under the teachings of *Carolene Products* was classic protectionist legislation enacted not for the public's benefit but at the behest of special interest groups.[12] Because *Carolene Products* based its jurisprudence on a theory of the political process, it is a theory that scholars have increasingly revealed as in clear conflict with reality.

From a historical and jurisprudential perspective, the ruling in *Carolene Products* is highly problematic, but the outcome harmonized with the emergence of statist liberalism after 1937. By weakening the constitutional barriers that secured property ownership, the Court increased legislative control over economic matters and facilitated programs designed to redistribute wealth.

Despite the call by several prominent scholars for revitalization of economic due process, the Supreme Court has shown no sign of reestablishing due process as a safeguard for property owners or of resuming its traditional role as an arbiter of economic legislation. Some state courts, on the other hand, continue to review economic regulations by applying a substantive interpretation of due process to strike down irrational or arbitrary statutes.[13]

### ANTICOMPETITIVE LICENSING AND ENTRY BARRIERS

Recent years have seen the right to pursue ordinary callings in the face of extensive occupational licensing and legislation limiting economic opportunities emerge as subjects of litigation under the due process norm.[14] Sheltered under an expansive reading of the police power, occupational licensing and entry barriers received little judicial oversight for decades. In *Williamson v. Lee Optical* (1955), the

Supreme Court adopted an extremely deferential attitude toward state economic regulation, brushing aside arguments grounded on the due process right to do business. In this climate, occupational licensing and entry barriers proliferated. Critics charged that such regulations had an anticompetitive impact, burdening consumers, raising costs, and stifling economic opportunities for the disadvantaged without demonstrated benefit to the public.

Some courts have begun to look more skeptically at laws restricting occupational choice and imposing barriers to enter certain lines of work. For example, two federal circuit courts have invalidated state regulations that fostered a cartel in the funeral business. They struck down state laws that gave licensed funeral directors the exclusive right to sell caskets. Concluding that the licensing requirement was not rationally related to public health or safety, the courts found that the laws violated the due process right to pursue lawful callings. These decisions represent at least a partial crack in the post–New Deal orthodoxy that economic legislation should receive only cursory due process review. Other federal courts, however, have rejected this reasoning and reiterated the deferential posture concerning licensing laws, even if the effect is to defend monopoly privilege.

Similarly, the application of licensing requirements for cosmetologists to persons engaged in African-style hair braiding or South Asian eyebrow threading has been a source of controversy and has divided federal courts. Some have reasoned that the state-mandated requirements were largely irrelevant to such work, bore no rational relationship to public health and safety, and ran afoul of the due process right to follow ordinary callings. In contrast, a federal circuit court sustained such regulations as applied to hair braiders, emphasizing heavy deference to state economic regulations.

An important decision by the Supreme Court of Texas also warrants attention. In *Patel v. Texas Department of Licensing and Regulation* (2015), the court construed the Texas Constitution to confer greater protection for people seeking to challenge economic regulations than the comparable federal due process norm. It concluded that the requirement to obtain a cosmetology license was onerous and unrelated to eyebrow threading. The court determined that the license provisions as applied were violative of the "due course of law" clause in the state constitution. The record of judicial protection of the right to pursue common occupations has been decidedly mixed, and litigation is likely to persist until the Supreme Court weighs in on the issue.

## CONTRACT CLAUSE

Americans of the founding era assigned a high value to the enforcement of agreements. Not only was there a strong belief in honoring one's commitments, but contracting was central to the emerging market economy. Desirous of assuring the stability of contractual arrangements from state abridgment, the framers inserted language in the Constitution declaring that "No state shall . . . pass any . . . Law impairing the Obligation of Contracts." Chief Justice John Marshall fashioned this provision into an important shield for existing economic arrangements against state legislative interference. In a famous line of cases, he construed the contract clause to cover public contracts to which a state was a party as well as private agreements.[15] Although not part of the Bill of Rights, the clause was at the heart of a great deal of constitutional litigation during the nineteenth century. Indeed, Marshall characterized the various restraints on state legislative power contained in Article I, Section 10, of the Constitution, including the contract clause, as a "bill of rights for the people of each state."[16] In 1878 Justice William Strong, speaking for the Supreme Court, proclaimed: "There is no more important provision in the Federal Constitution than the one which prohibits the states from passing laws impairing the obligation of contracts, and it is one of the highest duties of this Court to take care the prohibition shall neither be evaded nor frittered away."[17]

In the late nineteenth and early twentieth centuries, however, the contract clause gradually declined in importance. To some extent, its functions were superseded by the doctrine of economic due process discussed earlier. Moreover, the Supreme Court recognized that a state legislature could not bargain away its police power to protect public health, safety, and morals.[18] The contract clause was largely left for dead after a sharply divided Supreme Court, in *Home Building and Loan Association v. Blaisdell* (1934), sustained the validity of a state mortgage moratorium statute during the Great Depression. Asserting that the clause's "prohibition is not an absolute one and is not to be read with literal exactness," the Court ruled that an important public purpose could justify state interference with contracts.[19] In effect, the Supreme Court subordinated the contract clause to the authority of the states to adopt regulatory measures. Any vigor remaining in the clause was swept away with the triumph of the New Deal and the constitutional revolution of 1937. It was largely ignored for decades.

In the late 1970s, the Supreme Court applied the contract clause for the first time in nearly forty years. In two decisions the Court struck down both a state impairment of its own financial obligations and legislative interference with private contractual arrangements.[20] Unfortunately, the Court devised an amorphous multifactor test that did more to obfuscate than to clarify contract clause jurisprudence. To compound the confusion, the justices further ruled that a state action that impaired its own obligations should be held to a higher level of judicial scrutiny than abridgment of private contracts. Thereafter, the Court appeared once again to retreat from rigorous application of the contract clause. Subsequent decisions seemingly returned to a more deferential attitude toward state infringement of existing contractual arrangements in order to serve perceived public needs. In *Sveen v. Melin* (2018), the Supreme Court brushed aside a contract clause challenge to a state law providing that, in the event of a divorce, the designation of a now former spouse in a life insurance policy was automatically revoked. The Court majority applied the prevailing multipart test and found that the law did not substantially impair the insurance contract.[21] Dissenting, Justice Neil Gorsuch found a contract clause violation and pointed out that the current test "seems hard to square with the Constitution's original public meaning."[22]

Nonetheless, it may be premature to dismiss the contract clause as a constitutional restraint on legislative power. If nothing else, the Supreme Court has made it clear that the contract clause cannot be treated as a dead letter. In turn, this has emboldened some state and lower federal courts to use the contract clause as a basis to curb legislative power.[23] Consequently, recent decades have witnessed several state and lower federal court decisions invalidating legislation that attempted to alter mortgage foreclosure proceedings, change the terms of existing leasehold arrangements, modify state employee pension plans, or revoke teacher tenure. Likewise, courts have ruled that statutes altering the terms of existing employment or distributorship agreements violate the contract clause. Although it seems unlikely that the contract clause is poised to regain its former eminence in constitutional jurisprudence, the clause will continue to serve a secondary role in protecting property rights and contractual expectations.

## EMINENT DOMAIN

The takings clause of the Fifth Amendment provides: "nor shall private property be taken for public use, without just compensation." Contemporary champions of property rights have centered their hopes on a more vigorous application of the takings clause. Reflecting both common law principles and colonial practice, the clause limited the government's power of eminent domain by mandating that individual owners were entitled to compensation when property was appropriated for "public use."[24] The rationale behind the takings clause is that the financial burden of public policy should not be unfairly concentrated on individual property owners but shared by the public as a whole through taxation. Thus, the desire to achieve a public objective does not justify confiscation of private property without compensation. Consistent with the traditional high standing of property rights, the just compensation norm of the takings clause was the first provision of the Bill of Rights to be applied to the states under the due process clause of the Fourteenth Amendment.[25]

Nonetheless, the law governing the use of eminent domain has not evolved in a manner favorable to property owners. Eminent domain is one of the most intrusive powers of government because it compels owners of property to transfer it to the government for "public use." Yet the Supreme Court has been unwilling to rein in the increasingly aggressive exercise of eminent domain by state and local governments to acquire private property for public projects. In *Hawaii Housing Authority v. Midkiff* (1984), the Court virtually eliminated the public use requirement as a restriction on the exercise of eminent domain power. At issue was a Hawaii land reform statute that authorized tenants under long-term leases to acquire by compulsory purchase the landlord's title to the land. The justices conflated public use with public purpose. They also emphasized that courts must defer to legislative determinations of public use, even if eminent domain is employed to transfer private property from one person to another. Under this rationale, legislators hold almost untrammeled authority to decide whether eminent domain is appropriate in a particular situation.

This evisceration of the public use limitation was underscored by a sharply divided Supreme Court in *Kelo v. City of New London* (2005). The case involved a city development plan under which land acquired from residents by eminent domain would be transferred to private parties for the construction of new residences, stores, and recreational facilities. The rationale for this scheme was the promise of new jobs and enhanced tax revenue. By a 5–4 vote, the Court put its seal of approval on the exercise of eminent domain for purposes of economic development by private parties. The majority stressed deference to legislative judgments regarding the need for eminent domain and asserted that the public interest might be best served by private enterprise. Dissenting, Justice Sandra Day O'Connor charged: "Under the banner of economic development all private property is now vulnerable to being taken and transferred to another private owner." She warned that under the expansive view of eminent domain adopted by the majority, nothing prevented states "from replacing any Motel 6 with a Ritz-Carlton, any home with a shopping mall, or any farm with a factory."[26]

In 2021, the Supreme Court declined to hear an appeal that provided an opportunity to reconsider the *Kelo* case and tighten the expansive reading of the "public use" requirement.[27] It is noteworthy, however, that three justices voted to consider the case. Justice Clarence Thomas argued that the Court should "correct the mistake we made in *Kelo*." He denied that taking land from one party for transfer to another in order to prevent possible future blight satisfied "public use," and warned the open-ended exercise of eminent domain benefited those with disproportionate political influence.[28]

State courts, of course, are free to construe their own constitutions to expand protection for their citizens' property rights to a greater extent than the Supreme Court has done under the US Constitution. Indeed, several state courts have ruled that the exercise of eminent domain for economic development by private parties did not constitute a valid public use under the state constitution. In *County of Wayne v. Hathcock* (2004), for example, the Supreme Court of

Michigan overruled an earlier decision and rejected the general economic benefit rationale as a basis for condemnation of property for transfer to another private party. "After all," the court declared, "if one's ownership of private property is forever subject to the government's determination that another private party would put one's land to better use, then the ownership of real property is perpetually threatened by the expansion plans of any large discount retailer, 'megastore,' or the like."[29] Similarly, in *City of Norwood v. Horney* (2006), the Supreme Court of Ohio characterized the "right of property" as "a fundamental right" and ruled that economic benefit to the community alone does not satisfy the public use requirement of the Ohio Constitution. Specifically rejecting the reasoning in *Kelo*, the Court also criticized "an artificial judicial deference to the state's determination that there was sufficient public interest."[30] In sharp contrast with the US Supreme Court in *Midkiff* and *Kelo*, the Michigan and Ohio courts refused to adopt a highly deferential attitude toward legislative findings and instead made an independent determination of what constitutes public use. It is also noteworthy that the *Kelo* decision aroused widespread criticism and that several state legislatures enacted measures to curb the condemnation of property for economic development purposes.[31]

### PHYSICAL AND REGULATORY TAKINGS OF LAND

One of the most vexing problems in modern takings jurisprudence is whether governmental actions, short of formal condemnation, effectuate a taking for which compensation is required. Virtually all commentators agree that current takings analysis is a muddle. The Supreme Court has contributed to the confusion by applying the clause in an essentially ad hoc manner with seemingly inconsistent results. The justices have found it difficult to formulate meaningful standards to determine whether there has been a taking. Nonetheless, courts appear to be moving toward a broader view of the takings clause and scrutinizing governmental actions affecting property more carefully.

One line of Supreme Court cases addresses the issue of physical intrusion upon private property by the government or by persons with governmental authorization. In *Loretto v. Teleprompter Manhattan CATV Corp.* (1982), the Supreme Court held that a New York law requiring the installation of cable television facilities on a landlord's property effectuated a taking for which compensation was required. Explaining that a physical invasion of property was particularly serious, the Court established a rule that any permanent physical occupation of property, however slight, amounted to a per se taking. More recently, the Supreme Court ruled that a Department of Agriculture marketing order requiring growers of raisins to deliver a portion of their crop to the government free of charge amounted to a physical taking of personal property for which just compensation must be paid.

The ruling made it clear that personal property as well as land was constitutionally protected against direct physical appropriation.[32]

Temporary physical invasion of land can also constitute a taking of property under the Fifth Amendment. The deliberate flooding of land by government has long given rise to takings litigation.[33] In 2012, the Supreme Court declared that "government-induced flooding temporary in duration gains no automatic exemption from Takings Clause inspection."[34] To permit government to temporarily flood property without payment of compensation would undercut the purpose of the takings clause.

In *Cedar Point Nursery v. Hassid* (2021), the Supreme Court ruled that a California regulation granting labor organizations a right to enter an agricultural employer's property for a number of days annually in order to solicit union membership amounted to a per se physical taking of property under the Fifth Amendment.[35] The Court determined that the access requirement appropriated the owners' right to exclude and conferred a right upon union organizers to physically access the owners' land. It stressed that the right to exclude is a fundamental element of the right of ownership and that a government-authorized physical invasion of property constitutes a per se taking requiring payment of just compensation.

A more difficult question is posed by land use regulations that limit the use of property. Under the doctrine of regulatory taking, a regulation might so diminish the value or usefulness of private property as to constitute a taking. In the late nineteenth century, leading commentators and jurists maintained that regulations might so curtail the use of property as to be tantamount to a physical taking.[36] The Supreme Court affirmed this concept in the landmark decision of *Pennsylvania Coal Co. v. Mahon* (1922). Justice Oliver Wendell Holmes declared: "The general rule at least is, that while property may be regulated to a certain extent, if regulation goes too far it will be recognized as a taking." He cautioned that "the natural tendency of human nature" was to extend regulations "until at last private property disappears."[37] Despite the *Pennsylvania Coal* ruling, the Supreme Court has found it difficult to distinguish between appropriate restrictions and unconstitutional takings. Accordingly, the justices have been reluctant to actually apply the doctrine of regulatory taking.

The issue of regulatory takings has been most frequently raised in the context of land use controls. Historically, landowners could use their property for any lawful purpose, restrained only by the common-law prohibition against creating a nuisance and piecemeal land use regulations directed toward specific health and safety concerns. By the early twentieth century, however, urbanization and industrialization had created novel land use problems. With more congested living conditions, the manner in which one person used his or her land directly affected his or her neighbors. When nuisance laws proved inadequate to cope with urban land use problems, states and localities began to control land use more systematically. Yet public restrictions on the use of privately owned land raised difficult constitutional questions. Landowners often complained that the cost of achieving social objectives was unfairly placed on their shoulders rather than imposed on the general public.

During the 1920s, zoning emerged as a land control technique. Zoning was justified as an exercise of the police power to safeguard public health and safety. But such regulations restricted an owner's dominion over the land and often impaired its value. In *Village of Euclid v. Ambler Realty Company* (1926), the Supreme Court upheld the constitutionality of a comprehensive zoning ordinance that divided a locality into residential and commercial districts and restricted the type of building construction in each district. Reasoning that such limitations served the health, safety, and morals of the public, the Court ruled that state police power included the authority to classify land and prevent the erection of commercial buildings in residential areas. To bolster its decision, the Court drew an analogy between zoning and the power to abate a common-law nuisance.

Almost from the outset, regulatory bodies moved beyond the purported health and safety rationale to control land usage. Many zoning restrictions, such as the requirement of large lot sizes for homes, serve to preserve residential amenity features and to inflate the cost of housing. Such regulations often have an exclusionary impact on people with lower incomes and contribute to urban sprawl. Nonetheless, the Supreme Court upheld an ordinance that restricted construction on a five-acre tract to between one and five single family residences.[38]

Likewise, in *Penn Central Transportation v. New York* (1978), the Court sustained the designation of Grand Central Station as a historic landmark despite the fact that such action prevented the owner from modifying the building and significantly reduced its value. In its decision, the Court articulated a confusing multifactor balancing test to ascertain whether a particular governmental action amounts to a regulatory taking of property. The *Penn Central* ad hoc test sets forth a cluster of malleable factors that can be manipulated to justify any outcome. In practice, the *Penn Central* formulation has produced results highly deferential to governmental authority. It affords little real protection for landowners.[39]

Increasingly controversial in recent years has been the practice of many communities to levy impact fees or require donations of land in order to approve new building projects. This practice is based on the notion that a land developer should reimburse a community for the impact of a project on local facilities such as schools, parks, and water services. At first these exactions were closely related to the actual impact of a new development. Faced with growing resistance to higher taxes, however, many local governments have aggressively turned to exactions as an alternative source of general revenue to provide services and infrastructure. The connection between building projects and exactions has become progressively unclear. For instance, localities have required land developers to pay fees to support public transportation, to dedicate land for public parks, to subsidize the construction of low-income housing, and to pay for improvements on land owned by local government. The increased reliance on exactions raises the possibility that local governments may improperly use their power to leverage benefits from landowners without payment of just compensation, in circumvention of the Fifth Amendment. Such exactions, moreover, constitute a kind of special tax levied on developers but ultimately paid by newcomers through higher land prices. Sensitive to the concerns of current residents, local zoning authorities find it politically convenient to place these costs on outsiders such as nonresident land developers.

In addition to zoning, legislation to protect the environment can drastically curtail a landowner's ability to take advantage of property ownership. For instance, landowners must obtain a government permit before the filling of any wetland. The imposition of a permit requirement in order to develop land does not by itself constitute a taking. But the permit process is often expensive and lengthy, and denial of a permit may well prevent any development of the land. Similarly, some states restrict the construction of structures on beachfront property. Such environmental regulations, which sometimes leave the owner with no economically viable use of land, have been challenged as a taking of property. Still other laws seek to mandate public access over privately owned beachfront property, thus diminishing the owner's control of the land.

As this discussion indicates, zoning and environmental regulations have made substantial inroads upon the traditional rights of owners to make use of their land. It appeared that there was no meaningful constitutional limit on the power to regulate land. Perhaps concerned about the increasingly complex web of land use controls, the Supreme Court, starting in the 1980s, took a fresh look at the question of regulatory taking. As a result, the justices somewhat strengthened the position of property owners against governmental authority to reduce the value of their property by regulation. In the notable case of *Nollan v. California Coastal Commission* (1987), the Supreme Court, for the first time since the 1920s, struck down a land use regulation. The case arose when a state agency conditioned a permit to rebuild a beach house on the owner's grant of a public easement across the beachfront. The Court held that the imposition of such a condition constituted a taking because the requirement was unrelated to any problem caused by the development. Further, the Court indicated a willingness to examine more carefully the connection between the purpose and the means of regulations. Writing for the Court, Justice Antonin Scalia added: "We view the Fifth Amendment's property clause to be more than a pleading requirement and compliance with it to be more than an exercise in cleverness and imagination."[40]

The Supreme Court also tightened the test for reviewing the constitutional validity of conditions or exactions imposed on land development projects in *Dolan v. City of Tigard* (1994). The Court ruled that local governments must demonstrate a "rough proportionality" between the regulation placed on the landowner and the particular harm posed by the development. The Court insisted that the burden of showing such a connection was on the government. Conditions unrelated to the proposed development, the Court reasoned, constituted an uncompensated taking of property in violation of the Fifth Amendment. In *Koontz v. St. Johns River Water Management District* (2013), the Supreme Court placed further limitations on the imposition of exactions. It determined that the *Nollan* and *Dolan* requirements applied when a building permit is denied as well as when a permit is granted with conditions, and that monetary exactions are subject to the same level of scrutiny as mandated donations of land.[41]

In *First Evangelical Lutheran Church v. County of Los Angeles* (1987), the justices ruled that a property owner may be entitled to compensation for the temporary loss of land use when controls are later invalidated. This decision raised the prospect of damage awards against excessive regulations.

Some lower federal and state courts have taken a closer look at conditions imposed on landowners. In *Seawall Associates v. City of New York* (1989), for example, the New York Court of Appeals struck down a municipal ordinance that prohibited conversion or demolition of single-room-occupancy housing and that required the owners to lease such rooms for an indefinite period. The declared purpose behind this ordinance was to alleviate the plight of the homeless. The court invalidated the ordinance as both a physical and regulatory taking of property without compensation. Finding that the ordinance abrogated the owners' fundamental right of possession and right to exclude others, the court concluded that the law effected a per se physical taking. Moreover, the court invalidated the ordinance as a regulatory taking. The court ruled that the rental provisions denied the owners economically viable use of their property and that the ordinance did not substantially help the homeless. In the court's view, the tenuous connection between the means adopted by the city and the ends of alleviating homelessness could not justify singling out a few property owners to bear this burden. Rather, this was the type of social obligation that should be placed on the taxpayers as a whole.

Aside from the *Nollan, Dolan,* and *Koontz* decisions governing requirements imposed on landowners who wished to build on their land, the Supreme Court has scrutinized regulations that prevent any meaningful use of a parcel. At issue in *Lucas v. South Carolina Coastal Commission* (1992) was a South Carolina ban on beachfront construction. Designed to prevent beach erosion and preserve a valuable public resource, the law prevented the owner of two residential lots from erecting any permanent structure on his land. The owner contended that this prohibition destroyed the economic value of his property and effectuated a taking for which just compensation was required under the Fifth Amendment.

By a 6–3 vote, the Supreme Court, in an opinion by Justice Scalia, held that regulations that deny a property owner "all economically beneficial or productive use of land" constitute a taking notwithstanding the public interest advanced to justify the restraint. Justice Scalia cogently explained that the total deprivation of economic use is the practical equivalent of physical appropriation of land. And he expressed concern that regulations that prevent economic use "carry with them a heightened risk that private property is being pressed into some form of public service under the guise of mitigating serious public harm."[42] The Court recognized an exception to the rule that eliminating all economic use of land effectuates a taking. No compensation would be required if the owner was barred from putting the land to use by already existing common-law principles of property law or nuisance.

In practice, the *Lucas* decision made only a modest advance in defending the rights of property owners. It addressed an extreme situation, because most land use regulations do not have the effect of denying all productive use of land. The decision has been successfully invoked in only a few cases. But environmental regulations, such as wetlands restrictions that require land to be left in its natural state, might be vulnerable to a *Lucas* challenge.

The Supreme Court has also taken other steps to safeguard the rights of owners from regulatory abuse. In *City of Monterey v. Del Monte Dunes at Monterey, Ltd.* (1999), the Court upheld an award of damages for a regulatory taking. It further ruled that a jury trial was appropriate for ascertaining regulatory takings damages.

In 2010, a plurality of the Court endorsed the doctrine of judicial takings. This doctrine holds that a state court decision that results in the destruction of an existing property right has taken the property no less than if the state had taken the property by legislative fiat. There is certainly no textual reason why courts, as well as legislatures, should not be bound by the Fifth Amendment. As the plurality opinion explained, "The Takings Clause bars the State from taking private property without paying for it, no matter which branch is the instrument of the taking."[43] Whether the judicial takings doctrine will ultimately find acceptance by the Supreme Court remains to be seen, but the door is open for such a possibility.

In *Knick v. Township of Scott* (2019), the Supreme Court, overruling a prior decision, eliminated procedural barriers to a landowner seeking relief in federal courts when his or her property was taken by state or local government. Stressing that the constitutional right to compensation under the Fifth Amendment arises automatically when government takes property without payment, the Court concluded that the owner may proceed directly to federal court without first exhausting state law procedures. It pointed out that other constitutional claims grounded in the Bill of Rights are guaranteed a federal forum. The Court explained that this decision restored "takings claims to the full-fledged constitutional status the Framers envisioned when they included the [Takings] Clause among the other provisions in the Bill of Rights."[44] This decision does not, of course, guarantee that a takings claimant will prevail in federal court, but it eliminates the burdensome exhaustion requirement that such claimants pursue state court remedies first. It simply mandates that takings claims against state and local governments be heard on the same basis as other claims arising under the Bill of Rights.

In 2021, the Supreme Court unanimously extended the *Knick* decision and further strengthened the ability of property owners to file takings cases in federal court against state and local governments.[45] It held that a taking claimant need not first exhaust state administrative procedures once government has reached a conclusive position on the issue. The Court concluded by emphasizing that property owners have the same right of access to federal court as persons asserting other constitutional claims.

Notwithstanding this positive line of decisions, which demonstrates some degree of continuing judicial solicitude for the rights of owners, the Supreme Court has failed to fashion a coherent regulatory takings jurisprudence. The Court's overall pattern of decisions in this area has been hesitant and uncertain.

Substantive rules continue to make it difficult for a regulatory takings claimant to prevail. In *Tahoe-Sierra Preservation Council, Inc. v. Tahoe Regional Planning Agency* (2002), for example, the Supreme Court, by a 6–3 vote, determined that a temporary moratorium on land development, even one depriving the owner of all economic value for a number of years, was not a per se taking of property requiring payment of just compensation. Instead, the Court ruled that the temporary nature of the regulation was one element to be considered under the multifactor *Penn Central* balancing test. The dissenters maintained that the ban on development amounted to a taking of property. This decision had the effect of limiting the protection afforded landowners under the *Lucas* case.

Developments at the state level regarding regulatory takings also warrant mention. A number of state courts have given greater protection to landowners. For example, in 2016, the Supreme Court of North Carolina ruled that state designation of land as part of a highway corridor, thereby heavily restricting the owners' right to develop or subdivide the parcel for an indefinite period, constituted a taking of property requiring just compensation. In reaching this conclusion, the court characterized property as a "fundamental right" under the state constitution.[46] On the other hand, many state courts have resisted enlarged regulatory takings jurisprudence and have narrowly construed Supreme Court takings decisions. State courts in California, an important jurisdiction in fashioning land use regulations, have been especially hostile to regulatory takings claims and have upheld highly intrusive land use controls. A few states, including Florida and Texas, have enacted legislation designed to provide compensation to landowners who experience a regulatory taking as defined by statute.[47]

## TAKINGS OF OTHER PROPERTY INTERESTS

The significance of a reinvigorated takings clause is by no means confined to land use. A wide variety of governmental policies have been challenged as unconstitutional takings of property. At issue in *Eastern Enterprises v. Apfel* (1998) was a congressional statute imposing a retroactive financial liability on a former employer to bolster the solvency of a coal industry retirement and health fund. A plurality of the Supreme Court found that the statute amounted to an unconstitutional taking of property. Justice O'Connor, speaking for the plurality, explained that when a legislative remedy "singles out certain employers to bear a burden that is substantial in amount, based on the employer's conduct far in the past, and unrelated to any commitment that the employers made or to any injury they caused, the governmental action implicates fundamental principles of fairness underlying the Takings Clause."[48] Concurring, Justice Kennedy agreed that the statute was unconstitutional as applied to Eastern Enterprises but concluded that the retroactive effect of the act ran afoul of the due process clause. He reasoned that the regulatory takings doctrine should be confined to situations involving specific property interests, not the imposition of a general obligation to make payments.

Given the fragmented opinion in *Eastern Enterprises*, the significance of the decision is uncertain. Nonetheless, it is noteworthy that the four justices were prepared to invoke the regulatory takings doctrine in the context of a general regulatory statute. Further, the decision suggests that the Court could profitably revisit the question of due process as a guarantee of economic rights.[49]

Local rent control ordinances have long been a source of controversy because they clearly involve a compelled wealth transfer. In an attempt to hold down the cost of rental housing, such measures fix rent payments and thereby prevent property owners from leasing residential property at market prices. It follows that rent control laws effectively require owners to subsidize tenants. Historically, however, courts have rarely taken a hard look at rent regulations. The Supreme Court has upheld the general validity of rent ceilings but insisted that the regulatory schemes must yield landlords a reasonable return on investment. Applying this test, several state and lower federal courts have struck down local rent controls as confiscatory in violation of the takings clause.

## SIGNIFICANCE OF TAKINGS JURISPRUDENCE

The takings clause, of course, does not prevent governmental interference with existing property relationships. Rather, the Fifth Amendment simply requires that owners receive just compensation, defined as an equivalent, for any property taken by government action. In an era of tight budgets and widespread resistance to higher taxes, however, lawmakers are often tempted to achieve public benefits by placing regulatory burdens on a relative handful of property owners instead of on society as a whole through higher taxes. Takings jurisprudence, therefore, has a potentially significant impact on economic regulations and proposed social reforms. As a practical matter, reformist zeal often withers when taxpayers are called on to pay for the results.

Important libertarian considerations undergird the Supreme Court's moves to strengthen the rights of property owners under the takings clause. First, reinvigorated enforcement of the just compensation requirement would enhance democratic accountability. Governmental officials would be compelled to address directly the financial implications of land use controls and social programs and not rely on regulations as a politically attractive substitute for general taxation. Officials could use public revenue, for instance, to provide low-income housing or to acquire beachfront property by eminent domain. This would afford citizens an opportunity to debate the desirability of such policies and to decide how much they are prepared to pay if private property is taken to accomplish them. Second, the takings clause, like the other provisions of the Bill of Rights, was crafted to protect individual liberty by restricting the reach of government power. As Chief Justice Rehnquist tellingly declared in 1994: "We see no reason why the Takings Clause of the Fifth Amendment, as much a part of the Bill of Rights as the First Amendment or the Fourth Amendment, should be relegated to the status of a poor relation."[50] To the founding generation, respect for the rights of property owners reinforced the basic constitutional design of limited government. Experience in the twentieth and twenty-first centuries has amply demonstrated that individual liberties do not flourish in nations where private property is not recognized.[51]

### CONCLUSION

Since the mid-1980s, the Supreme Court has been more solicitous of the rights of property owners than at any time since the pre–New Deal Court of the early 1930s. Certainly the Court has done much to restore property rights to the constitutional agenda after decades of neglect.

Still, the Supreme Court has yet to fulfill the hopes of property rights advocates for muscular takings jurisprudence. Several factors were at work to limit the Court's revival of property rights. Further, despite its conservative reputation in recent years, the Court never had a consistent majority willing to uphold the property rights of individuals in the face of governmental controls. The majority of the Court has been unable to break free of statist thinking about property emanating from the New Deal. Hence, the overall record of the Court on property rights, despite some promising developments, remains mixed.[52]

Accordingly, the place of property rights in modern constitutional thought remains uncertain. The modern welfare state rests on the assumption that redistribution of resources is an appropriate governmental function. The current Supreme Court, perhaps fearful of igniting a political firestorm, has shown no inclination to challenge any major national economic regulations, and courts continue to uphold most land use regulations. Yet it is difficult to reconcile unfettered legislative control of private property with either the language of the Constitution or the course of constitutional history.

Indeed, the Constitution and the Bill of Rights affirmed the central place of property ownership in US history. In defending the rights of property owners, courts have reflected not only the views of the framers but also values deeply embedded in the political culture. Questioning the fashionable dichotomy between personal and economic liberty, Justice Scalia observed: "Few of us, I suspect, would have much difficulty choosing between the right to own property and the right to receive a Miranda warning."[53] In the same vein, the Supreme Court of Ohio cogently observed: "The rights related to property, i.e., to acquire, use, enjoy, and dispose of property, are among the most revered in our law and traditions. Indeed, property rights are integral aspects of our theory of democracy and notions of liberty."[54] Fortunately for Americans, the framers of the Constitution and Bill of Rights understood the vital role of property rights more than two hundred years ago.

## NOTES

1. *Murr v. Wisconsin*, 137 S. Ct. 1933, 1943 (2017).

2. *Cedar Point Nursery v. Hassid*, 141 S. Ct. 2063 2071 (2021).

3. Max Farrand, ed., *The Records of the Federal Constitution of 1787*, rev. ed., 5 vols. (New Haven, CT: Yale University Press, 1937), 1:534.

4. James W. Ely Jr., "The Progressive Assault on Individualism and Property Rights," *Social Philosophy and Policy* 29 (2012): 255–82.

5. James W. Ely Jr., *The Guardian of Every Other Right: A Constitutional History of Property Rights*, 3rd ed. (New York: Oxford University Press, 2007), 139–41, 149–50.

6. See, for example, Richard A. Epstein, *Takings: Private Property and the Power of Eminent Domain* (Cambridge, MA: Harvard University Press, 1985); Bernard H. Siegan, *Economic Liberties and the Constitution*, 2nd ed. (New Brunswick, NJ:

Transaction, 2006). See also Richard Pipes, *Property and Freedom* (New York: Vintage Books, 1999).

7. Ely, *Guardian of Every Other Right*, 87–91.

8. James W. Ely Jr., "The Supreme Court and Property Rights in the Progressive Era," *Journal of Supreme Court History* 44, no. 1 (2019): 14–15; Melvin I. Urofsky, "State Courts and Protective Legislation during the Progressive Era: A Reevaluation," *Journal of American History* 72 (1985): 63.

9. See James W. Ely Jr., "Reflections on *Buchanan v. Warley*, Property Rights, and Race," *Vanderbilt Law Review* 51 (1998): 953.

10. See Geoffrey P. Miller, "The True Story of Carolene Products," *Supreme Court Review* 1987 (1987): 397.

11. Learned Hand, *The Bill of Rights* (Cambridge, MA: Harvard University Press, 1958), 50–51.

12. Randy E. Barnett, "Judicial Engagement through the Lens of Lee Optical," *George Mason Law Review* 19 (2012): 845, 860.

13. See, for example, *State v. Balance*, 229 N.C. 764, 51 S.E.2d 731 (1949) (invaliding requirement that persons practicing photography for compensation must pass an examination and pay a fee).

14. For a review of this litigation, see James W. Ely Jr., "Buchanan and the Right to Acquire Property," *Cumberland Law Review* 48, no. 2 (2018): 423, 427–61.

15. For example, *Fletcher v. Peck*, 10 U.S. 87 (1810) (land grant); *New Jersey v. Wilson*, 11 U.S. 164 (1812) (grant of tax exemption on certain land); *Dartmouth College v. Woodard*, 17 U.S. 518 (1819) (grant of corporate charter).

16. *Fletcher*, 138 U.S. at 138 (1810) (Marshall, C. J.).

17. *Murray v. Charleston*, 96 U.S. 432, 488 (1878).

18. See James W. Ely Jr., *The Contract Clause; A Constitutional History* (Lawrence: University Press of Kansas, 2016), 160–65, 196–98.

19. *Home Building and Loan Association v. Blaisdell*, 290 U.S. 398, 428 (1934).

20. *United States Trust Company v. New Jersey*, 431 U.S. 1 (1977); *Allied Structural Steel Company v. Spannaus*, 438 U.S. 234 (1978).

21. *Sveen v. Melin*, 138 S. Ct. 1815, 1822–24 (2018).

22. *Id.* at 1827.

23. See, for example, *Equipment Manufacturers Institute v. Janklow*, 300 F.3d 842 (8th Cir. 2002); *In re Workers' Compensation Refund*, 46 F.3d 813 (8th Cir. 1995); *Maze v. Board of Directors for Commonwealth Postsecondary Education Prepaid Tuition Trust Fund*, 559 S.W.3d 354 (Ky. 2018); *North Carolina Association of Educators, Inc. v. State*, 368 N.C. 777, 786 S.E.2d 255 (2016) *Federal Land Bank of Wichita v. Story*, 756 P.2d 588 (Okla. 1988).

24. James W. Ely Jr., "'That Due Satisfaction May Be Made': The Fifth Amendment and the Origins of the Compensation Principle," *American Journal of Legal History* 36 (1992): 1.

25. *Chicago, Burlington, and Quincy Railroad Company v. Chicago*, 166 U.S. 226 (1897).

26. *Kelo v. City of New London*, 545 U.S. 469, 494, 503 (2005).

27. *Eychaner v. City of Chicago*, 141 S. Ct. 2422 (2021).

28. Id. at 2423.

29. *County of Wayne v. Hathcock*, 471 Mich. 445, 482, 684 N.W.2d 765, 786 (2004).

30. *City of Norwood v. Horney*, 110 Ohio St.3d 353, 371, 853 N.E.3d 1115, 1136 (2006).

31. For an insightful analysis of the *Kelo* decision and the judicial and legislative response, see Ilya Somin, *The Grasping Hand:* Kelo v. City of New London *and the Limits of Eminent Domain* (Chicago: University of Chicago Press, 2015).

32. *Horne v. Department of Agriculture*, 135 S. Ct. 2419 (2015).

33. *Pumpelly v. Green Bay Co.*, 80 U.S. 166 (1871).

34. *Arkansas Game & Fish Commission v. United States*, 568 U.S. 23, 38 (2012).

35. *Cedar Point Nursery v. Hassid*, 141 S. Ct. 2063 (2021).

36. See, for example, David J. Brewer, "Protection to Private Property from Public Attack," *New Englander and Yale Review* 55 (1891): 97, 102–5; John Lewis, *A Treatise on the Law of Eminent Domain* (Chicago: Callaghan, 1888), 40–46.

37. *Pennsylvania Coal Co. v. Mahon*, 260 U.S. 393, 415 (1922).

38. *Agins v. City of Tiburon*, 447 U.S. 225, 260 (1980).

39. See Stephen J. Eagle, "The Four-Factor Penn Central Regulatory Takings Test," *Penn State Law Review* 118 (2014); Gideon Kanner, "Making Laws and Sausages: A Quarter-Century Retrospective on *Penn Central Transportation Co. v. City of New York*," *William and Mary Bill of Rights Journal* 13 (2005): 679.

40. *Nollan v. California Coastal Commission*, 483 U.S. 825, 841 (1987).

41. *Koontz v. St. Johns River Water Management District*, 133 S. Ct. 2586 (2013).

42. *Lucas v. South Carolina Coastal Council*, 505 U.S. 1003, 1017 (1992).

43. *Stop the Beach Renourishment, Inc v. Florida Department of Environmental Protection*, 580 U.S. 702, 715 (2010).

44. *Knick v. Township of Scott*, 139 S. Ct. 2162, 2170 (2019). For a helpful discussion of this decision, see Ilya Somin, "*Knick v. Township of Scott*: Ending a Catch-22 That Barred Takings Cases from Federal Court," *Cato Supreme Court Review* 2018–19 (2019): 153–87.

45. *Pakdel v. City and County of San Francisco*, 141 S. Ct. 2226 (2021).

46. *State v. North Carolina Department of Transportation*, 368 N.C. 847, 786 S.E.2d 919, 923–925 (2016).

47. Steven J. Eagle, "The Development of Property Rights in America and the Property Rights Movement," *Georgetown Journal of Law and Public Policy* 1 (2002): 77, 121–24.

48. *Eastern Enterprises v. Apfel*, 524 U.S. 498, 537 (1998).

49. See Steven J. Eagle, "Substantive Due Process and Regulatory Takings: A Reappraisal," *Alabama Law Review* 51 (2000): 977.

50. *Dolan v. City of Tigard*, 512 U.S. 374, 392 (1994).

51. Pipes, *Property and Freedom*, 211–25.

52. See Eric A. Claeys, "Takings and Private Property on the Rehnquist Court," *Northwestern University Law Review* 99 (2005): 127.

53. Antonin Scalia, "Economic Affairs as Human Affairs," in *Economic Liberties and the Judiciary*, ed. James A. Dorn and Henry G. Manne (Fairfax, VA.: University Publishing Association, 1987), 31.

54. *City of Norwood*, 110 Ohio St.3d at 361–62, 853 N.E.2d at 1128 (2006).

# SIX

—⚬—

# EQUAL PROTECTION AND
# AFFIRMATIVE ACTION

PAUL MORENO

AFFIRMATIVE ACTION, AND THE QUESTION of its compatibility with equal protection, emerged as part of the "Second Reconstruction" in the post–World War II United States. The second Reconstruction differed from the first fundamentally in the redefinition of equality and rights. In the nineteenth century, Americans established governments to protect the rights of individuals—as in the language of the Declaration of Independence and the 1866 Civil Rights Act. Racial discrimination was defined as disparate treatment of individuals on the basis of race. In the twentieth century, especially after the New Deal, government began to provide substantive rights or "entitlements"—not merely protecting the right to work, for example, but providing jobs.[1] Fifty years of affirmative action have confirmed the conclusion of a prominent scholar of its first twenty-five, Herman Belz, that "the central argument for affirmative action . . . in accordance with the disparate impact theory of discrimination, posits the ideal of a racially balanced society organized on the principles of group rights and equality of result, regulated by government policies aiming at proportional representation."[2] In the context of the entitlement-welfare state, racial equality came to be understood as providing equal outcomes for racial groups. Equal protection in this view was not an individual right to equal treatment but a racial entitlement to equal outcomes. And those entitlements would be provided by the new institutions of the "administrative state."

## I. TO THE SECOND RECONSTRUCTION

The Fourteenth Amendment essentially applied the Fifth Amendment to the states. It forbade them to deprive any person of life, liberty, or property without due process of law, which repeated the wording of the Fifth Amendment and added that states could not deny to any person the equal protection of the laws.[3] This provision was intended to protect primarily (though not exclusively) the millions of recently emancipated enslaved people in the South.

The equal protection clause may have been redundant, as some commentators considered equal protection to be a part of due process. Thomas McIntyre Cooley, the most renowned nineteenth-century analyst of the Constitution, noted that due process included equal protection—and more.[4] Indeed, the whole Fourteenth Amendment (at least Section 1) could be seen as redundant, because the mere abolition of slavery by the Thirteenth Amendment made the freedmen citizens and protected them through the original privileges and immunities clause of Article IV. The Thirty-Ninth Congress enacted the Civil Rights Act of 1866 under the Thirteenth Amendment, before the Fourteenth Amendment was proposed. This act declared the freedmen to be citizens entitled to "the same right . . . to make and enforce contracts," have access to the courts, to property rights, and "to full and equal benefit of all laws and proceedings . . . as is enjoyed by white citizens" and be subject to the same criminal laws.[5] President Andrew Johnson vetoed the civil rights bill. He opposed equal Black citizenship, but also objected that the bill went beyond equal protection and gave special privileges to the freedmen. He saw in the bill's provision to protect the freedmen a "distinction of race and color . . . made to operate in favor of the colored race and against the white race."[6] Congress overrode the veto and passed the Fourteenth Amendment to protect the act from repeal in the future.

Thus, the Reconstruction period presented the first debate over the meaning of equal protection and what would later be called affirmative action—programs designed to benefit disadvantaged minorities. Twentieth-century defenders of affirmative action claimed that Reconstruction-era programs such as the Freedmen's Bureau were the prototypes of contemporary affirmative action.[7] This is a rather fanciful case of lawyer-historians in search of a "usable past."[8] It is fairly clear that the Reconstruction-era Republicans did not favor special treatment for Blacks—indeed, they frequently and roundly denied it. Moreover, they were willing to accept state racial classifications such as segregated public schools, prohibitions on racial intermarriage, and segregation in public accommodations if equal accommodations were provided.[9] Racial egalitarians such as Frederick Douglass called for a "color-blind Constitution."[10] Historian Eric Foner notes, "At their most utopian, blacks in Reconstruction envisioned a society purged of all racial distinctions," and Black nationalists had a difficult time making their case for positive color consciousness.[11] Justice John Marshall Harlan expressed this aspiration in his dissent in *Plessy v. Ferguson* (1896), in which the Court upheld "separate but equal" in public accommodations. "In respect of civil rights, common to all citizens, the Constitution . . . does not, I think, permit any public authority to know the race of those entitled to be protected in the enjoyment of such rights. . . . There is no caste here. Our Constitution is color-blind, and neither knows nor tolerates classes among citizens."[12] Nevertheless, the Court has never insisted on a completely color-blind Constitution.[13] What closed the door to Black aspirations in the nineteenth century opened the door for affirmative action in the twentieth.

By the end of the nineteenth century, even the limited aims of Reconstruction had been overwhelmed by a system of segregation and political disfranchisement that fell far short even of a separate-but-equal standard. The federal judiciary did not help the situation by adopting an overly liberal interpretation of the Constitution and laws, but it was mostly the loss of political will by Republican lawmakers and Northern public opinion that delayed meaningful Reconstruction.[14]

## II. AFFIRMATIVE ACTION EMERGES

The Supreme Court reoriented itself in the New Deal period. Though it had not ignored minority-group rights, the Court was more energetic in defending economic liberty and entrepreneurial property rights, principally by the due process clause of the Fifth and Fourteenth Amendments. In 1937, the Court relaxed its scrutiny of state and federal economic regulation and became more solicitous of the rights of minorities and of noneconomic rights. "The existence of facts supporting the legislative judgment is to be presumed, for regulatory legislation affecting ordinary commercial transactions," the Court declared. But there would be "narrower scope for the operation of the presumption of constitutionality when legislation appears on its face to be within a specific prohibition of the Constitution" or in cases affecting "discrete and insular minorities."[15] It appeared that Black Americans would benefit most from this double standard of constitutional protection.

The Second Reconstruction arose out of the Great Migration of Black Americans from the rural South to Northern and western cities. What had previously been an isolated, sectional issue became a national problem that Northern Whites could no longer ignore. A new Black bourgeoisie arose that was more educated and organized and able to vote, and began to press for the vindication of their civil rights. The most important Black organization was the National Association for the Advancement of Colored People (NAACP), founded in 1909. Black lawyers, principally out of Howard University School of Law, embarked on a litigation campaign to overturn segregation. They won several victories against residential apartheid and segregation in professional education, culminating in the landmark decision of *Brown v. Board of Education* in 1954, in which the Supreme Court held that school segregation violated the equal protection clause.[16] *Brown* held only that states could not segregate public school students on the basis of race, and it did so on the basis of social science arguments about the effects of segregation on Black children's self-esteem. It did not declare that segregation in other areas of public life was unconstitutional (though it gradually would), and it did not declare that the Constitution was color-blind, though it was widely regarded as having done so. The decision was largely ignored by Deep South states for the next decade.

World War II and the US presidency were of even greater importance to the progress of Black civil rights. The war against Hitler's genocidal regime had a profound effect on American racial attitudes, dealing a fatal blow to White supremacy. The war accelerated the Great Migration and brought Blacks into industrial jobs previously closed to them. In 1941, A. Philip Randolph, the president of the all-Black Brotherhood of Sleeping-Car Porters, threatened a "march on Washington" unless President Franklin D. Roosevelt outlawed discrimination in defense industries and desegregated the military. A compromise was arranged in which Roosevelt did the former but not the latter.[17] Executive Order 8802 declared that the nation could not afford to waste any available manpower and so ordered all businesses with contracts with the federal government to cease discrimination on the basis of race, creed, color, or national origin.[18] It established the President's Committee on Fair Employment Practice (usually called the FEPC) to monitor it. This was a significant example of the potential power of the federal government as contractor, and of the presidential power of executive orders.[19] The FEPC is largely regarded as having had little more than symbolic impact, and Congress cut its funding when the war ended. But it was the first important federal civil rights action since Reconstruction, and it provided an example for the future.

After the war, each US president established some kind of nondiscrimination executive order and committee to oversee compliance.[20] As during World War II, the Cold War caused American leaders to exhort the nation to live up to its egalitarian founding ideals.[21] At the same time, many northern and western states outlawed discrimination in private employment, beginning with New York in 1945. These commissions, like the original FEPC, almost always avoided calls for preferential rather than equal treatment and considered individual complaints rather than investigate the racial composition of companies or industries.[22]

As the civil rights movement became more militant in the 1960s, the first steps were taken toward affirmative action. President John F. Kennedy's 1961 executive order required contractors to take "affirmative action" to ensure nondiscrimination.[23] The term had its origin in the National Labor Relations Act of 1935, which prohibited discrimination against union members. An employer that violated the act could be required to reinstate, make back pay, and take any other such affirmative action as the National Labor Relations Board might order. For Presidents Kennedy and Lyndon Johnson, who headed Kennedy's committee and continued his policies, this was mostly a matter of encouraging large businesses to reach out and try to recruit qualified minority workers. This relatively uncontroversial outreach is sometimes called "soft" affirmative action, as opposed to the "hard" affirmative action of preferences and quotas.[24]

President Johnson moved his antidiscrimination committee to the Department of Labor, which pursued an enhanced campaign against exclusive skilled trade unions in several cities, Cleveland and Philadelphia chief among them. Contractors agreed to collect racial data and establish specific numbers of minorities to hire by a particular date (called "manning tables" and "goals and timetables").[25] Unions resisted, and the comptroller general said that the plan violated federal law requiring competitive bidding, so the Labor Department shelved the plan.[26]

President Richard Nixon revived the Philadelphia Plan and was in many ways the father of affirmative action. Nixon had been the head of President Eisenhower's antidiscrimination committee, which had flirted with a similar program toward the end of his administration.[27] Nixon was widely accused of conniving to divide two important interest groups in the Democratic Party—civil rights and organized labor—but it appears more likely that he was genuinely interested in Black economic advancement.[28] His secretary of labor, George Shultz, believed that the power of discriminatory White unions impeded Black economic progress. The Nixon administration ran into the same obstacles that the Johnson administration had encountered, in addition to the claim that the plan violated the Civil Rights Act of 1964. Nixon actively intervened in Congress to prevent it from killing the plan by legislation. Finally, the federal courts upheld the Philadelphia Plan in 1970.[29] Ironically, the discriminatory unions were soon exempted from the Philadelphia Plan and left to devise more malleable "hometown plans," while the plan was extended to *all* federal contractors, covering about half of the entire US workforce.

Affirmative action became part of American economic life and was soon built into corporate organization. Although the Republican Party declared itself opposed to quotas in the 1980 campaign and promised that the president would abolish affirmative action "with the stroke of a pen," once in office, Ronald Reagan opted to maintain affirmative action for government contractors, who had learned to live with it.[30] Employers were willing to hire less efficient minority workers if doing so saved them the greater expense of defending themselves against discrimination suits or losing government contracts.[31] Today most large contractors would maintain affirmative action even if they were not legally required to, because they have come to embrace diversity as a positive good and accept the norm of a racially and sexually proportionate workforce.[32]

### III. THE CIVIL RIGHTS ACT OF 1964

The ethos of affirmative action—of equal group outcomes first on the basis of race and then on the basis of sex and other identities—also became part of the enforcement of the Civil Rights Act of 1964, the landmark statute of the Second

Reconstruction. Whether the Constitution itself was color-blind was an open question, but the text of the Civil Rights Act was clearly so. Nevertheless, bureaucrats and courts were able to refashion it to support race-conscious preferential treatment.

After dramatic civil rights demonstrations provoked violent suppression in the South, President John F. Kennedy sent a civil rights bill to Congress in June 1963. The act was principally aimed at desegregation in "places of public accommodation"—hotels, restaurants, theaters. Notably, the act did not purport to enforce equal protection under the Fourteenth Amendment. Rather, it was enacted under Congress's power to regulate interstate commerce. It also made use of the grant-in-aid or "spending power" by requiring any institution that received federal funds to comply.

Kennedy's bill contained a provision to give a statutory basis to his job antidiscrimination committee, but congressional liberals added a robust fair employment section, which would become Title VII, outlawing discrimination by private sector employers.[33] The bill also added sex to the protected classes of race, color, religion, and national origin. Liberals wanted the act to resemble the National Labor Relations Act, with the Equal Employment Opportunity Commission (EEOC—the new name for the FEPC) issuing cease-and-desist orders to offending employers. They settled for a compromise establishing a commission that would attempt to mediate individual complaints and then provided for lawsuits by dissatisfied individuals and by the attorney general in "pattern or practice" cases. This resort to judicial enforcement, insisted on by conservatives, turned out to be of great advantage in the development of affirmative action.[34]

The crucial question was how the act defined discrimination. The act said only that it was unlawful to "fail or refuse to hire or to discharge any individual . . . because of such individual's race." This language was taken almost verbatim from the original state antidiscrimination statute, the New York Law Against Discrimination (1945). The court-enforcement provision held that guilt involved *intentional* discrimination. Further sections protected merit pay and hiring qualifications so long as they were not "the result of an intention to discriminate" or "designed, intended or used to discriminate." The act also prohibited "preferential treatment to any individual or group" due to statistical "imbalance which may exist" between the minority group and the total population. On the whole, the text of the act evinced the traditional definition of discrimination as intentional unequal treatment of an individual on the basis of race.

Several members of Congress objected to the bill's overly broad definition, which left too much discretion to administrative interpretation. Georgia Senator Richard Russell remarked that the act's lack of definition of discrimination would be "the realization of a bureaucrat's prayers."[35] It resembled the broad delegation of legislative power to agencies that had been going on since the Interstate Commerce Act of 1887. Congress would not make the legislative choice but would defer to bureaucrats, as when it required "just and reasonable" railroad rates or prohibited "unfair methods of competition" in the Federal Trade Commission Act.[36] Southern segregationist opponents warned that the act would lead to racial preferences and quotas. Though liberal congressional managers denied it, this is exactly what happened.

A year after the Civil Rights Act was passed, and as Congress was considering the Voting Rights Act, President Johnson lent his voice to the call for preferential treatment and equal group outcomes in his commencement address at Howard University. The new legislation had secured freedom, he said, "but freedom is not enough." It was now necessary to "wipe away the scars of centuries. . . . You do not take a person who, for years, has been hobbled by chains and liberate him, bring him up to the starting line of a race and then say, 'you are free to compete with all the others,' and still justly believe that you have been completely fair." Providing opportunity was not enough; government must provide the ability to take advantage of opportunity. "We seek . . . not just equality as a right and a theory but equality as a fact and equality as a result."[37] This argument for affirmative action as compensation or reparations for past discrimination did not appear in any civil rights legislation and was not often explicitly presented even by affirmative action advocates. But in reality it provided the basis for racial preferences.[38]

The reparations principle also animated the NAACP and the lawyers who pursued affirmative action. Charles Hamilton Houston, the dean of Howard University School of Law; his student Thurgood Marshall, the NAACP general counsel; and other lawyers of their generation had absorbed the jurisprudential creed of legal realism. They accepted the progressive idea that law was the tool of the dominant class or race in a society. Houston prepared his students to be "social engineers," to use the legal system for political ends.[39] Their goal was not to restore the principles of the Constitution or the Fourteenth Amendment, which in this view were merely the instruments of White supremacy.[40] The goal was not to restore the Constitution to its original principles of justice but to use it to compensate its former victims. As Marshall told his colleagues, "You guys have been discriminating for years. Now it is our turn."[41] Realism of this kind reduced law to politics, and politics as understood in mid-twentieth-century "interest-group liberalism" theory, in which there was no common good above that of particular interest groups competing for power.

As Title VII complaints made their way through the EEOC and the lower federal courts, bureaucrats and judges widened the scope of the act. They shifted its focus from individual rights to group rights by encouraging class action suits and giving other procedural advantages to plaintiffs. One of the commission's first impositions was Form EEO-1, which required employers to provide statistics on the racial composition of their workforces. It began to apply the act retrospectively, taking into account the "present effects of past discrimination." Above all, the commission developed the "disparate impact" theory of discrimination. If an employer used a standard, such as a degree requirement or test score, which had a disparate impact on minorities, the qualification would be presumed to be unlawful unless the employer could prove that it was necessary to carry on the business. This reinterpretation met some resistance in the lower courts, but the Supreme Court accepted the disparate impact theory in the 1971 case of *Griggs v. Duke Power Co.*

The Duke Power Company had hired Black people for only its lowest-level jobs. When the company opened all jobs to Blacks, it instituted the requirement of a high school diploma or an acceptable score on a standardized test. Since Blacks had lower levels of education and scored below Whites on the test, the Court held that these requirements had the effect of perpetuating past discrimination. Employer good faith or intent, Chief Justice Warren Burger wrote for a unanimous Court, did not "redeem employment procedures or testing mechanisms that operate as 'built-in headwinds' for minority groups and are unrelated to measuring job ability."[42]

Rutgers University law professor Alfred W. Blumrosen was the EEOC counsel who was most responsible for promoting the disparate impact standard and getting judges to endorse it. He emphasized what he called the "law transmission system" of broad discretion given by Congress to administrative agencies, whose freedom to interpret statutes would be ratified by the courts.[43] Affirmative action had become a "programmatic right"—an entitlement derived from this interaction of broad congressional delegation and bureaucratic and judicial application.[44] Acts such as the Civil Rights Act were not exactly constitutional amendments, but they were more than ordinary statutes. Some called them fundamental or "superstatutes."[45] Blumrosen and civil rights organizations were amazed at how far the Court had gone in *Griggs*, which they did not think was a very strong case. Blumrosen's commentary on the result was entitled "Strangers in Paradise."[46]

The difficulty of proving business necessity led employers to adopt racial preferences and quotas to avoid lawsuits. Eventually, the EEOC adopted a "bottom-line" policy in which an employer would be left alone if its workforce had 80 percent of the number of minorities in the area labor pool. But this "four-fifths compromise" did not shield employers from lawsuits by Whites who claimed that preferences and quotas violated Title VII. The Supreme Court provided this insulation from reverse discrimination suits in the 1979 *Weber* case. In 1974, the Kaiser Aluminum Company agreed to set aside half of the places in its apprentice training program for Black people. (Though the program was presented as voluntary, the company had been pressured by the Labor Department and EEOC, as was evidenced by its expression in a legally enforceable consent decree.) Brian Weber claimed that the agreement violated his constitutional right to equal protection and won in the lower federal courts. The Supreme Court overturned these decisions, holding that, although Title VII did not *require* preferential treatment, it did not *prohibit* it. Such programs were acceptable so long as they did not "unnecessarily trammel the interests of white workers."[47]

Congress did nothing to restore the original intent of the Civil Rights Act. In 1972, it expanded the reach of Title VII, covering state and local government employment and giving the commission the power to sue on its own. Under President Jimmy Carter there was an enormous expansion in civil rights enforcement agencies—Office of Federal Contract Compliance Programs staff grew from sixty-eight to thirteen hundred, and EEOC staff increased from fewer than three hundred to more than three thousand.[48] In 1977, Congress rather casually, without hearings or debate, included a 10 percent quota for minority-owned companies in the Public Works Employment Act, the first ever racial set-aside enacted by the national legislature.[49] Congress provided no rationale for the set-asides and no proof that previous discrimination was being remedied. In 1980, the Court upheld the program under Congress's commerce and spending powers as well as Congress's power to enforce the equal protection clause of the Fourteenth Amendment.[50] Similarly, the Federal Communications Commission gave tax and other incentives to broadcast license owners to sell to minorities, and the Court upheld this program in the 1990 *Metro Broadcasting* case.[51]

Some thirty-six states and almost two hundred local governments adopted minority set-asides in the 1980s. The Court drew the line on these when the city of Richmond, Virginia, adopted a 30 percent minority quota. The Court now held that such quotas would face "strict scrutiny"—the government must show a compelling interest, and the remedy must be narrowly tailored to address that interest. The city's general claim that "societal discrimination" accounted for racial disparity was not sufficient. (The set-aside included Eskimos and Aleuts; it was implausible to think that the Virginia city had engaged in discrimination against them.) The Court warned that "the dream of a nation of equal citizens in a society where race is irrelevant to personal opportunity and achievement would be lost in a mosaic of shifting preference based on inherently unmeasurable claims of past wrongs."[52] In 1995, the Court extended strict scrutiny to federal contracting set-asides, overruling its *Metro Broadcasting* decision. *Adarand v. Pena* involved advantages given to firms designated as disadvantaged by the Small Business Administration. Simple equation of minority ownership and disadvantage was not sufficient proof under the strict scrutiny standard.[53] Though affirmative action set-asides have continued since *Croson* and *Adarand*, they are supposed to meet the more stringent standards established in those cases. Nevertheless, in 2005, the US Commission on Civil Rights reported that government agencies were quite lax in following the standard.[54]

At the state level, racial preferences were sometimes prohibited by citizen referenda. California's Proposition 209, enacted in 1996, read simply, "The state shall not discriminate against, or grant preferential treatment to, any individual or group on the basis of race, sex, color, ethnicity, or national origin in the operation of public employment, public education, or public contracting." Michigan voters adopted a similar constitutional amendment ten years later, in response to affirmative action cases in higher education. The state of Washington adopted a similar ban in 1998. These state initiatives underscore the point that affirmative action remained controversial because it lacked popular consent, being largely engineered by unelected bureaucrats and judges.

At the same time that the Court was becoming more restrictive about contracting quotas, it began to rein in the disparate impact principle. It had, as early as 1976, stated that disparate impact applied only to the Civil Rights Act of 1964—it was a statutory, not a constitutional, right and could not be claimed under the original Civil Rights Act of 1866.[55] In several cases in 1988–89, the Court, inter alia, shifted the burden of proof in disparate impact cases to help employers defend against statistical disparity suits, eased the definition of business necessity, and made it easier for White people to bring reverse discrimination suits against consent decrees to which they were not parties.[56]

Congress responded to these cases with a civil rights bill in 1990. The civil rights lobby endeavored not just to restore *Griggs* but to go beyond it—strengthening the business necessity standard, for example, and allowing damage awards in disparate treatment cases. President George H. W. Bush vetoed the proposal as a "quota bill," and the veto was sustained by one vote in the Senate. Bush accepted a somewhat milder version that became the Civil Rights Act of 1991, giving legislative consent to the disparate impact standard after a quarter century.[57] The question of disparate impact's compatibility with the equal protection clause remains open.[58]

### IV. AFFIRMATIVE ACTION IN SECONDARY EDUCATION

The equivalent of affirmative action—the quest for equal racial group outcomes or proportional representation—in education came about as the *Brown* decision's prohibition of racial segregation became a requirement of integration. For more than a decade after *Brown*, the Court maintained that it had forbidden only the assignment of students to schools on the basis of race.[59] Initially, the Deep South states engaged in "massive resistance"—most dramatically in the Little Rock crisis of 1957, where President Eisenhower had to use federal troops to desegregate

Central High School. (The border states and the District of Columbia mostly complied peacefully.) The most common tactic was for states to establish "freedom of choice" plans, which allowed students to choose whichever school they wanted. Usually all the White students would choose the traditionally White school, and all but a few intrepid Blacks would remain in the traditionally Black school. The result was token desegregation.

Bureaucrats and judges began to demand more in the late 1960s. Title IV of the Civil Rights Act was enacted for school desegregation but stated, "'Desegregation' means the assignment of students to public schools and within such schools without regard to their race, color, religion, or national origin, but 'desegregation' shall not mean the assignment of students to public schools in order to overcome racial imbalance."[60] Of more significance in the long run was Title VI, which prohibited discrimination in any program that received federal funds. Though colleges and universities received significant federal subsidies, secondary schools did not until the Elementary and Secondary Education Act of 1965. As with affirmative action in government contracting, it would be the spending power that fueled an equal-outcomes policy in education. This was particularly important with the explosion of federal grants-in-aid that came with the Great Society.[61]

The "law transmission system" in education began with the Department of Health, Education and Welfare's reinterpretation of the Civil Rights Act to require active integration.[62] The lower federal courts confirmed the administrative redefinition. The Supreme Court reinforced the shift by holding that freedom of choice no longer satisfied the constitutional standard of equal protection in the 1968 case of *Green v. New Kent County*.[63] The next step was to require busing, or the reallocation of students to achieve racial balance.[64] The Court then began to apply integration and busing outside of the states that had imposed segregation by law. In a 1973 case involving Denver, Colorado, schools, the Court assumed that any public policies that *resulted* in segregation violated the equal protection clause.[65] In other words, de facto segregation was as culpable as de jure segregation. This was the educational equivalent of the disparate impact standard.

Busing to achieve school integration blew up in the justices' faces. Violent reaction by working-class Whites in Boston would become the national symbol of the backlash. Busing accelerated the phenomenon of White flight, as White parents removed their children from integrated public schools or moved to the suburbs. The Court appeared to respond to this in 1974, when it struck down a plan to integrate predominantly Black Detroit schools with the city's predominantly White suburbs. A 5–4 decision held that suburbs that had not engaged even in de facto segregation could not be used to integrate cities that had.[66] Intracity busing would continue, along with city-suburban integration in some border cities, but *Millikin* marked the end of the expansion of affirmative action in secondary education.[67]

Denied the stick of busing, integrationists turned to the carrot of magnet schools—public schools with enhanced programs and facilities to attract White students. States established several thousand magnet schools in the 1970 and 1980s with assistance of federal funds, and these became a less controversial method of school integration. Federal courts imposed them in cases where discrimination had been indicated—as in Kansas City and St. Louis, Missouri—and compelled states to raise taxes to make the improvements. In the 1995 case of *Missouri v. Jenkins*, the Supreme Court said that enhanced schools could not be used as interdistrict lures for intradistrict violations.[68] As in employment cases, the Court did not insist on a color-blind standard but held that for race to be taken into account, the state needed to show a compelling interest, and the racial consideration had to be narrowly tailored to meet that interest—for example, as a remedy to a proven case of discrimination. Thus, in 2007, it struck down a Seattle freedom-of-choice plan that made race a plus-factor in student assignment.[69]

### V. AFFIRMATIVE ACTION IN HIGHER EDUCATION

In higher education, affirmative action involved preferences in admission to selective institutions. The Department of Health, Education and Welfare's Office of Civil Rights could use Title VI of the Civil Rights Act to compel nondiscrimination compliance for any institution that received federal financial assistance. In 1972, the Title IX amendment to the act added sex to Title VI. The Office of Civil Rights demanded an assurance of compliance letter from all colleges and universities, even those that had never discriminated and received no direct federal financial assistance. The Office of Civil Rights maintained that if any of an institution's students received federal financial aid, such assistance bound the entire institution. Grove City College (in Pennsylvania) and several other institutions refused to comply. The Department of Education won a decision by an administrative law judge; the college won an appeal in federal district court; the Department of Education won a reversal in the Third Circuit Court of Appeals.[70]

The Supreme Court essentially split the difference.[71] Indirect financial aid such as federal student loan guarantees did compel the institution to comply with Title IX, but compliance was limited to the specific program or activity involved—in this case, the college's financial aid office. This prompted civil rights organizations to urge Congress to amend Title IX to apply via *any* financial aid to the *entire* institution in the Civil Rights Restoration Act of 1988, enacted over President Reagan's veto.

The Department of Education showed that civil rights laws could be the vehicle for wide-ranging social policy initiatives. The Obama administration required schools to permit transgender students to use the bathroom of the sex with which they currently identified, notwithstanding the fact that the term *gender* appeared nowhere in any civil rights law.[72] Feminists believed that Title IX administration could be used to restore the Violence Against Women Act, which was struck down by the Supreme Court in 2000.[73] Similarly, the Department of Education required colleges to adopt policies on sexual assault that showed scant regard for the rights of male defendants. The Obama administration also targeted secondary school discipline policies that had a disparate impact on minority students. These mandates were simply imposed through letters (addressed to "Dear Colleagues") by the secretary to the institutions, without any formal rulemaking procedures.[74]

Most institutions of higher education eagerly embraced affirmative action. The University of California, Davis established a new medical school in 1966. It then set aside sixteen of one hundred places in its new class for minorities. Alan Bakke, denied admission though he had superior qualifications than admitted minorities, sued.[75] In the Supreme Court, four justices were willing to allow the minority quota; four insisted that it violated the Civil Rights Act. Justice Lewis Powell decided that, though outright quotas were illegal, a college could take race into account to achieve the legitimate goal of a diverse student body.

Diversity rapidly became the talisman of US higher education and spread throughout American culture.[76] It had not been a significant part of UC Davis's defense of its quota system. Indeed, diversity in the US education system up to this point had meant a wide variety of institutions—public and private, religious and secular, male and female, liberal arts and vocational—and had been praised by liberals.[77] Now it allowed institutions to practice affirmative action as long as they were not too blatant about it. In this way, diversity acted as a proxy for race. Pursuing race-based outcomes by racially neutral means was nothing new in US history. Before the Second Reconstruction, majorities pursued policies with a disparate impact that burdened minorities rather than benefited them. Southern states that could not explicitly prevent Blacks from voting imposed literacy tests and poll taxes, which most Black people could not pass or pay. Ivy League colleges used geographical quotas to keep the number of Jews down. After the Second Reconstruction, state authorities contrived to find racial proxies that would help minorities. The University of Maryland established a scholarship program exclusively for Black students. When it was struck down by a federal court, the state made it available to "students of any race who are committed to the advancement of minorities in science."[78]

When the Fifth Circuit Court of Appeals essentially overturned *Bakke* and struck down the affirmative action admissions program at the University of Texas, the state responded with a "ten percent plan," guaranteeing admission to anyone in the top 10 percent of a state high school.[79] This essentially made a virtue of de facto segregation in secondary education, giving top Black students at inferior schools an advantage over average White students at more competitive schools.[80] The issue returned to the Supreme Court in a pair of Michigan cases in 2003. The large University of Michigan adopted a 200-point scale for admission and awarded applicants twenty points for being Black. The smaller University of Michigan Law School did not assign race any specific value but took it into consideration in its "holistic" admissions policy. The Bush administration Justice Department advocated a proxy strategy, arguing that the state should use "race-neutral alternatives that have proven effective in meeting the important and laudable educational goals of educational openness, accessibility, and diversity in other states."[81] An array of educational, business, political, and military leaders emphasized the importance of diversity in American society in sixty-eight amicus briefs. The Court essentially reaffirmed *Bakke*, holding that the undergraduate program was too obviously discriminatory, while the law school program was passable.[82] The decision resembled a political compromise above all. Justice Sandra Day O'Connor emphasized the temporary nature of affirmative action, predicting that "we expect that, twenty-five years from now, the use of racial preferences will no longer be necessary."[83] Justice Ruth Bader Ginsburg candidly averred that overt quotas were "preferable to achieving similar numbers through winks, nods, and disguises."[84]

Affirmative action in higher education remains a volatile issue. The University of Michigan Law School program was undone by the Michigan Civil Rights Initiative, a referendum that prohibited racial preferences in 2006. Several justices in dissent argued that the Fourteenth Amendment prohibited state abolition of affirmative action.[85] Texas, on the other hand, tried to amend its percentage plan to include more Black students from better-integrated schools.[86] The Supreme Court narrowly upheld this "percentage-plus" program in 2016.[87] In 2019, a federal district court upheld a Harvard University admissions system that Asian Americans said discriminated against them, but the decision was appealed and will probably end up before the Supreme Court.[88]

These cases illustrate how multifaceted affirmative action has become over a half century. What was primarily designed as a policy to help African Americans has been extended to an array of other groups. The list of protected classes now includes sex, age, disability, and sexual orientation.[89] Demographic changes, especially those resulting from the Immigration Reform Act of 1965, have transformed the debate. Hispanics as a whole now outnumber African Americans as a racial minority group, and Whites are expected to become a national minority by midcentury. The non-Hispanic White population fell from 80 percent of the total in 1980 to 64 percent in 2010. Of thirty-five million immigrants who arrived between 1965 and 2000, twenty-six million could claim affirmative action prefer-ences.[90] Over a quarter of the Black students at elite universities are immigrants.[91]

## VI. AFFIRMATIVE ACTION IN VOTING RIGHTS

Affirmative action in voting rights came about as the 1965 Voting Rights Act was held to guarantee not just the right to vote for Blacks (and other minorities) but to have a maximum number of minorities elected to office.

Blacks in the South had been mostly (but never completely) disfranchised through literacy tests and poll taxes (which also reduced the number of poor White voters), by the discriminatory application of literacy tests, and by vio-lence and intimidation. As violent resistance to desegregation in Birmingham, Alabama, had prompted Congress to enact the Civil Rights Act of 1964, so brutal suppression of Black voting rights demonstrators at Selma led to the extraordi-nary Voting Rights Act of 1965. Section 2 of the Voting Rights Act gave statutory expression to the Fifteenth Amendment, declaring, "No voting qualification . . . shall be imposed or applied by any State or political subdivision to deny or abridge the right of any citizen of the United States to vote on account of race or color." This section was permanent and applied throughout the country. Section 4 im-posed federal control over elections in states and localities where less than half of the voting-age population was registered, known as the trigger provision or coverage formula.[92] In these areas (mostly in the old Confederacy), no intent or proof of discrimination was needed—here the Voting Rights Act had a disparate impact or effects test *ab initio*. Section 5 suspended voting qualifications in these areas for five years. In what was called the preclearance provision, these states and localities could not alter anything about their voting systems without the ap-proval of the Justice Department or the District of Columbia Court of Appeals.[93] The decision to apply the act was not reviewable in court.[94]

The act was an immediate success; Black voting rates soon equaled or ex-ceeded those of Whites. But the Justice Department and federal courts quickly determined that the act also prohibited the dilution of voting power by protected classes. Thus, it voided a Mississippi racial gerrymander that allowed counties to switch from a district to an at-large system to elect county commissioners.[95] The goal soon became to create the maximum number of majority-minority districts to elect the greatest possible number of minority officials. But in 1976 the Court held that the act did not require absolute maximization. Electoral alterations were acceptable if they did not reduce the current number of minority officeholders who were likely to be elected.[96]

The Voting Rights Act was repeatedly extended and strengthened—for five years in 1970, seven years in 1975, and twenty-five years in 1982 and 2006. These extensions often overturned restrictive Court interpretations of the act.[97] In 1980, for example, the Court held that plaintiffs had to prove intent to discriminate in Section 2 suits, though intent could be inferred from "the totality of the circumstances."[98] The 1982 amendments wrote the disparate impact standard into the entire statute.

The Justice Department continued to press for the maximum number of minority elected officials, using the same racial gerrymandering methods that had once been employed to minimize those numbers. Republicans cunningly supported this project, since packing reliably Democratic Black voters into "safe" Black districts made it easier for Republicans to compete in the rest.[99] After the 1990 census redistricting, the Justice Department and civil rights lobby had nearly reached their goal of proportional racial representation. As of the 1992 election, the House of Representatives had thirty-eight Black members—almost 9 percent of the House.[100] But in 1994 Republicans won control of the House for the first time in a half century. Some analysts attributed this to the "max-Black" gerrymandering.

The Supreme Court attempted to blunt the racial gerrymandering campaign and held that race could not be the predominant factor in districting.[101] But it was exceedingly difficult, given racial polarization, to distinguish a racial gerrymander from an old-fashioned partisan gerrymander. One of the most egregious racial gerrymanders was North Carolina's Twelfth Congressional District, drawn after the state gained a seat by the 1990 census. The goal was to give Blacks (22 percent of the state population) two safe districts of twelve. This required a district that snaked from north to south along Interstate 85, so narrow at points, as one legislator quipped, that "if you drove down I-85 with both car doors open, you'd kill most of the people in the district."[102] The Court voided this plan, with Justice O'Connor commenting on its "uncomfortable resemblance to political apartheid."[103] But the district was sustained in a retrial in federal district court and has remained a political football ever since.[104]

The Voting Rights Act had veered far from its original purpose to guarantee the individual right to vote and had become a racial group entitlement to offices.[105] As one scholar observed, much like affirmative action under the Civil Rights Act, "Voting rights policy was fashioned by government bureaucrats and judges rendering decisions far below the radar screen of most Americans."[106] Its constitutional legitimacy eroded while its Selma symbolism was milked for decades—as demonstrated in the name of the Fannie Lou Hamer, Rosa Parks, and Coretta Scott King Voting Rights Act Reauthorization and Amendments Act of 2006.[107] The Supreme Court released the country from the preclearance provisions of the act in 2013, when it held that the trigger formulas were based on outdated data—1972 registration and voting numbers.[108] In *Shelby County v. Holder*, Chief Justice John Roberts noted that the Voting Rights Act was extraordinary—a federal takeover of traditionally state-controlled functions—and could only be justified by extraordinary circumstances. Those conditions obtained in the 1960s, but Congress had provided no proof that they still existed.[109] This decision was equivalent to *Milliken* in school integration, imposing a historical limit on the effects of discrimination where *Milliken* had imposed a geographic one, and threatened the perpetuity of affirmative action.[110]

Four dissenters in *Shelby County* recognized the import of the decision, claiming that the Court had terminated "the remedy that proved to be best suited to block" voting discrimination. They argued that "it cannot tenably be maintained that the Voting Rights Act . . . is inconsistent with the Fifteenth Amendment," but Justice Thomas's concurring opinion suggested exactly that. The dissenters admitted that "history did not end in 1965" but insisted that "the past is prologue," assuming that discrimination was permanent. *Shelby County*, "striking at the heart of the nation's signal piece of civil rights legislation," was akin to "throwing away your umbrella in a rainstorm because you are not getting wet."

With Republicans in control of at least one house of Congress since 2013, there was no congressional response to the *Shelby County* case. In 2019, the Court held that federal courts could not hear challenges to partisan gerrymanders.[111] It also remains to be seen whether the Court will decide that the 1982 amendment to Section 2 of the Voting Rights Act, applying the disparate impact standard, violates the Fifteenth Amendment or equal protection clause.[112] This parallels the question of whether the Civil Rights Act of 1991 and its disparate impact standard violate the Fourteenth Amendment.

## CONCLUSION

All these areas of public policy—government contracting, employment discrimination, secondary and higher education, and voting—have undergone two fundamental changes. First has been the redefinition of civil rights from an individual right to pursue happiness to a group entitlement to substantively equal outcomes, under the theory that proportional racial equality is the proper understanding of equality. Affirmative action thus fit into the transformation of the old, natural-rights-based Constitution into the entitlement state of modern liberalism. If the first fifty years of affirmative action established the disparate impact theory of discrimination and "the ideal of a racially balanced society organized on the principles of group rights and equality of result, regulated by government policies aiming at proportional representation,"[113] the second quarter century has relied on the new concept of diversity to pursue the same goals.

Second, the equal racial outcomes in employment, education, and voting were to be provided by the rising power of the post–New Deal administrative state. Civil rights historian Hugh Davis Graham concluded that affirmative action developed through "a closed system of bureaucratic policymaking, one largely devoid not only of public testimony but even of public awareness that policy was being made."[114] Affirmative action thus continues to bear a taint of illegitimacy, lacking the essential constitutional element of the consent of the governed. And even when the legislature has affirmed the constructions of bureaucrats and judges, as in the Voting Rights Act of 1982 and the Civil Rights Act of 1991, the question remains of these acts' conformity to the Constitution. After a half century, affirmative action and equal protection continue to pose an American dilemma.

## NOTES

1. Charles Kesler, "The Public Philosophy of the New Freedom and the New Deal," in *The New Deal and Its Legacy: Critique and Reappraisal*, ed. Robert Eden (New York: Praeger, 1989), 162.

2. Herman Belz, *Equality Transformed: A Quarter-Century of Affirmative Action* (New Brunswick, NJ: Transaction, 1991), 234.

3. For an introduction to the extensive debate over how the Fourteenth Amendment incorporated, or applied, the Bill of Rights to the states, see Richard C. Cortner, *The Supreme Court and the Second Bill of Rights: The Fourteenth Amendment and the Nationalization of Civil Liberties* (Madison: University of Wisconsin Press, 1981).

4. Rodney L. Mott, *Due Process of Law* (New York: Da Capo, 1973 [1926]), 277; Thomas M. Cooley, addendum to *Commentaries on the Constitution of the United States*, 2 vols. (Boston: Little, Brown, 1891), 2:688.

5. 14 Stat. 27 (1866).

6. *Congressional Globe*, 39th Cong., 1st Sess. (March 27, 1866), 1679.

7. Eric Schnapper, "Affirmative Action and the Legislative History of the Fourteenth Amendment," *Virginia Law Review* 71 (1985): 73–98; Paul Moreno, "Racial Classifications and Reconstruction Legislation," *Journal of Southern History* 61 (1995): 271–304.

8. Alfred H. Kelly, "Clio and the Court: An Illicit Love Affair," *Supreme Court Review* 1965 (1965): 119–58; John Finnis, "'Shameless Acts' in Colorado: Abuse of Scholarship in Constitutional Cases," *Academic Questions* 7 (1994): 10–41.

9. Stephen J. Riegel, "The Persistent Career of Jim Crow: Lower Federal Court and the 'Separate-but-Equal Doctrine,' 1865–96," *American Journal of Legal History* 28 (1984): 17–40.

10. Ronald R. Sundstrom, *The Browning of America and the Evasion of Social Justice* (Albany: SUNY Press, 2008), 11–12.

11. Eric Foner, *Reconstruction: America's Unfinished Revolution, 1863–77* (New York: Harper & Row, 1988), 288, 372.

12. *Plessy v. Ferguson*, 163 U.S. 537 (1896), 559.

13. Andrew Kull, *The Color-Blind Constitution* (Cambridge, MA: Harvard University Press, 1992).

14. Pamela Brandwein, *Rethinking the Judicial Settlement of Reconstruction* (Cambridge: Cambridge University Press, 2011).

15. *U.S. v. Carolene Products*, 304 U.S. 144 (1938), 152.

16. *Brown* is a good example of the fungibility of the due process and equal protection clauses discussed above. One of the companion cases challenged segregation in the District of Columbia, where Congress acted as a state. The Fourteenth Amendment applies only to the states, and the Fifth Amendment, which limits Congress, does not contain an equal protection clause. The Court decided that the due process clause of the Fifth Amendment would do just as well. *Bolling v. Sharpe*, 347 U.S. 497 (1954).

17. President Harry S. Truman would desegregate the armed forces in 1948.

18. 3 CFR (1938–43), 957.

19. Employers resisting unions were compelled to recognize them or be ineligible for government contracts. Steve Fraser, "The Good War and the Workers," *American Prospect*, September 20, 2009.

20. These were the President's Committee on Government Contract Compliance (Truman), the President's Committee on Government Contracts (Eisenhower), the President's Committee on Equal Employment Opportunity (Kennedy), and the Office of Federal Contract Compliance (Johnson), housed in the Department of Labor. It became today's Office of Contract Compliance Programs in 1975.

21. Mary L. Dudziak, *Cold War Civil Rights: Race and the Image of American Democracy* (Princeton, NJ: Princeton University Press, 2000).

22. Paul Moreno, *From Direct Action to Affirmative Action: Fair Employment Law and Policy in America, 1933–72* (Baton Rouge: Louisiana State University Press, 1997), 107–61.

23. 3 CFR (1959–64), 448.

24. Loan Le and Jack Citrin, "Affirmative Action," in *Public Opinion and Constitutional Controversy*, ed. Nathaniel Persily et al. (Oxford: Oxford University Press, 2008), 163–65.

25. Sex had been added to the nondiscrimination requirement by President Johnson in 1967.

26. A low bid that did not contain an affirmative action provision would not be awarded the contract. Hugh Davis Graham, *The Civil Rights Era: Origins and Development of National Policy, 1960–72* (Oxford: Oxford University Press, 1990), 294.

27. Belz, *Equality Transformed*, 15.

28. Belz, *Equality Transformed*, 39; Dean J. Kotlowski, *Nixon's Civil Rights: Politics, Principle, and Policy* (Cambridge, MA: Harvard University Press, 2001), 8, 24, 30, 37, 98, 106.

29. *Eastern Contractors Association v. Shultz*, 311 F. Supp. 1002 (1970).

30. Roger E. Meiners and Bruce Yandle, "Regulatory Lessons from the Reagan Era: An Introduction," in *Regulation in the Reagan Era: Politics, Bureaucracy and the Public Interest*, ed. Roger E. Meiners and Bruce Yandle (New York: Holmes &

Meier, 1989); Hugh Davis Graham, "The Civil Rights Act and the American Regulatory State," in *Legacies of the 1964 Civil Rights Act*, ed. Bernard Grofman (Charlottesville: University of Virginia Press, 2000), 59; Steven A. Holmes, "Affirmative Action Plans Are Now Part of the Normal Corporate Way of Life," *New York Times*, November 22, 1991, 20.

31. Michael H. Gottesman, "Twelve Options to Consider Before Opting for Racial Quotas," *Georgetown Law Journal* 74 (1991): 1750.

32. Erin Kelly and Frank Dobbin, "How Affirmative Action Became Diversity Management: Employer Response to Antidiscrimination Law, 1961–96," *American Behavioral Scientist* 41 (1998): 960–84.

33. Phased in from large employers to smaller ones, today all employers of fifteen or more.

34. Alfred W. Blumrosen, *Modern Law: The Law Transmission System and Equal Employment Opportunity* (Madison: University of Wisconsin Press, 1993), 49.

35. Graham, "The Civil Rights Act," 46.

36. The Civil Rights Act was out of step with much of the new social regulation of the Great Society Era, in which Congress was more specific and less deferential to bureaucrats. R. Shep Melnick, "The Courts, Congress, and Programmatic Rights," in *Remaking American Politics*, ed. Richard A. Harris and Melnick (Boulder, CO: Westview, 1989), 190.

37. Commencement address at Howard University, June 4, 1965, in *Public Papers of the Presidents of the United States: Lyndon B. Johnson* (Washington, DC: Government Printing Office, 1966), 2:635–40.

38. Randall Kennedy, *For Discrimination: Race, Affirmative Action, and the Law* (New York: Pantheon, 2013), 78.

39. Genna Rae McNeil, *Groundwork: Charles Hamilton Houston and the Struggle for Civil Rights* (Philadelphia: University of Pennsylvania Press, 1983), 133, 214–24.

40. In 1987, Thurgood Marshall praised the Fourteenth Amendment as the *real* Constitution worth celebrating, not the original 1787 Constitution. But this was a Fourteenth Amendment that he and his colleagues had re-created.

41. William O. Douglas, *The Court Years, 1939–75: The Autobiography of William O. Douglas* (New York: Random House, 1980). Although Douglas had a deep personal dislike of Marshall and was an inveterate liar, Marshall never disputed this quote.

42. *Griggs v. Duke Power Co.*, 401 U.S. 424 (1970).

43. Blumrosen, *Modern Law*, 102–7.

44. Melnick, "The Courts, Congress, and Programmatic Rights."

45. Belz, *Equality Transformed*, 171; William N. Eskridge Jr. and John Ferejohn, *A Republic of Statutes: The New American Constitution* (New Haven, CT: Yale University Press, 2010); Reva Siegel, "The Constitutionalization of Disparate Impact—Court-Centered and Popular Pathways: A Comment on Owen Fiss's Brennan Lecture," *California Law Review* 106 (2018): 2005; Gerald Pomper, "Labor and Congress: The Repeal of Taft-Hartley," *Labor History* 3 (1965): 340.

46. Blumrosen, *Modern Law*, 98; "Strangers in Paradise: *Griggs v. Duke Power Co.* and the Concept of Employment Discrimination," *Michigan Law Review* 71 (1972): 59–110. The one area in which the Court did show some concern for the original intent of the Civil Rights Act was its protection of union-negotiated seniority rights under section 703(h).

47. *United Steelworkers v. Weber*, 443 U.S. 193 (1979).

48. Graham, "The Civil Rights Act," 53.

49. Some federal agencies had experimented with racial quotas in the 1930s, but these were never tested in court. Moreno, *From Direct Action to Affirmative Action*, 54–65.

50. *Fullilove v. Klutznick*, 448 U.S. 448 (1980).

51. *Metro Broadcasting v. FCC* 497 U.S. 547 (1990); Mitchell F. Rice, "Government Set-Asides, Minority Business Enterprises, and the Supreme Court," *Public Administration Review* 51 (1991): 119.

52. *Richmond v. Croson*, 488 U.S. 469 (1989).

53. 515 U.S. 200.

54. U.S. Commission on Civil Rights, *Federal Procurement after* Adarand (Washington, DC: U.S. Commission on Civil Rights, 2005); Roger Clegg, "Unfinished Business: The Bush Administration and Racial Preferences," *Harvard Journal of Law and Public Policy* 32 (2009): 971–95.

55. *Washington v. Davis*, 426 U.S. 229 (1976). The Court held that the Civil Rights Act of 1866 applied to acts of private discrimination in 1968 (*Jones v. Mayer*, 392 U.S. 409 [1968]). This was itself a bold example of judicial activism, especially notable because it interpreted the act's right "to make and enforce contracts" as an entitlement—a requirement that employers (or, in this case, landlords) contract without regard to race. The fact that the Fourteenth Amendment did not prohibit discrimination in the private sphere was one reason that Congress enacted the 1964 act (especially Title VII) under the commerce power rather than Section 5 of the Fourteenth Amendment.

56. The lead case was *Wards Cove Packing v. Atonio*, 490 U.S. 642 (1989). Others were *Watson v. Fort Worth Bank*, 487 U.S. 977 (1988) and *Martin v. Wilks*, 498 U.S. 755 (1989).

57. Roger Clegg, "A Brief Legislative History of the Civil Rights Act of 1991," *Louisiana Law Review* 54 (1994).

58. Siegel, "The Constitutionalization of Disparate Impact"; Kenneth L. Marcus, "The War Between Disparate Impact and Equal Protection," *CATO Supreme Court Review* (2008–9): 53–83.

59. This was referred to as "the Briggs dictum," after the decision by Judge John J. Parker in *Briggs v. Elliot*, 132 F. Supp. 776 (1955).

60. Sec. 401(b).

61. Gareth Davies, "Toward Big-Government Conservatism: Conservatism and Federal Aid to Education in the 1970s," *Journal of Contemporary History* 43 (2008): 621–35; Willis Rudy, *America's Schools and Colleges: The Federal Contribution*

(Cranbury, NJ: Cornwall, 2003), 102; Graham, "The Civil Rights Act and the American Regulatory State," 46.

62. 34 CFR sec 100.3(b)(vii)(6). This was undertaken by the Office of Civil Rights in HEW, later in the Department of Education.

63. 391 U.S. 430.

64. *Swann v. Charlotte-Mecklenburg*, 402 U.S. 1 (1971).

65. *Keyes v. Denver*, 413 U.S. 189 (1973).

66. *Millikin v. Bradley*, 418 U.S. 717 (1974).

67. Raymond Wolters, *The Burden of* Brown: *Thirty Years of School Desegregation* (Knoxville: University of Tennessee Press, 1984).

68. 515 U.S. 70 (1995).

69. *Parents Involved in Community Schools v. Seattle*, 551 U.S. 701 (2007).

70. Hugh Davis Graham, "The Storm over Grove City College: Civil Rights Regulation, Higher Education and the Reagan Administration," *History of Education Quarterly* 38 (1998): 407–29; Lee Edwards, *Freedom's College: The History of Grove City College* (Chicago: Regnery, 2000), 195–226; Horace E. Johns, "The Grove City College Case: A Relatively Short-Lived Aberration in American Higher Education," *Higher Education Management* 2 (1990): 147–55.

71. *Grove City College v. Bell*, 465 U.S. 555 (1984).

72. R. Shep Melnick, *The Transformation of Title IX: Regulating Gender Equality in Education* (Washington, DC: Brookings, 2018).

73. Karen M. Tani, "An Administrative Right to Be Free from Sexual Violence? Title IX Enforcement in Historical and Institutional Perspective," *Duke Law Journal* 66 (2017): 1847–1903.

74. Siegel, "The Constitutionalization of Disparate Impact," 2015–16.

75. *Regents of California v. Bakke*, 438 U.S. 265 (1978).

76. Peter Wood, *Diversity: The Invention of a Concept* (San Francisco: Encounter, 2003).

77. Wood, *Diversity*, 108.

78. Victoria Benning and Valerie Strauss, "Area Colleges Open Up Black Scholarships," *Washington Post*, November 6, 1996.

79. *Hopwood v. Texas*, 78 F.3d 932 (1996).

80. Jeffrey Selingo, "What States Aren't Saying About the 'X-Percent Solution,'" *Chronicle of Higher Education*, June 2, 2000.

81. President George W. Bush had signed the Texas 10 percent plan into law as governor in 1997.

82. The cases were *Grutter v. Bollinger*, 539 U.S. 306 (law school) and *Gratz v. Bollinger*, 539 U.S. 244 (college).

83. *Grutter v. Bollinger*, 310; Evan Thomas, "Why Sandra Day O'Connor Saved Affirmative Action," *The Atlantic*, March 19, 2019.

84. *Gratz v. Bollinger*, 305.

85. *Schuette v. Coalition to Defend Affirmative Action*, 572 U.S. 291 (2014).

86. For example, a Black student in the fifteenth percentile of a predominantly White school who was better qualified than a Black student in the fifth percentile of a predominantly Black school.

87. *Fisher v. Texas*, 579 U.S. ___ (2016).

88. Stuart Taylor Jr., "Racial Preferences on Trial as Harvard Goes to Court," *Weekly Standard*, October 12, 2018; Anemona Hartocollis, "Harvard Won a Key Affirmative Action Battle. But the War's Not Over," *New York Times*, October 2, 2019; Robert Barnes, "Supreme Court Puts Off Decision on Reviewing Harvard Race-Conscious Admissions System," *Washington Post*, June 14, 2021.

89. In 2014, President Obama added sexual orientation or gender identity to the list of protected classes in the government contracting program, and the Department of Justice said that it would apply Title VII to cases of gender identity.

90. Hugh Davis Graham, *Collision Course: The Strange Convergence of Affirmative Action and Immigration Policy in America* (New York: Oxford University Press, 2002), 195.

91. Douglas S. Massey et al., "Black Immigrants and Black Natives Attending Selective Colleges and Universities in the United States," *American Journal of Education* 113 (2007): 243.

92. Voting age could vary by state until the Twenty-Sixth Amendment established a national eighteen-year-old right to vote in 1971.

93. Poll taxes had been prohibited by the Twenty-Fourth Amendment in 1964; literacy tests were permanently suspended in the Voting Rights Act extension of 1975.

94. The act also provided for federal monitors and inspectors to supervise elections, but these were little used after the first few years and were not renewed in later extensions of the act.

95. *Allen v. State Board of Electors*, 393 U.S. 544 (1969). The simplest illustration of a racial gerrymander would be a city, 60 percent White and 40 percent Black, divided into five electoral districts, three all-White and two all-Black. Assuming strictly race-based voting, this would produce three White and two Black representatives. A switch to an at-large (no district) system would produce five White representatives. Likewise, altering the district lines so that each of five districts was 60 percent White would produce five White representatives. The Court had already held an obvious racial gerrymander to be a violation of the Fifteenth Amendment in *Gomillion v. Lightfoot*, 364 U.S. 339 (1960). The Court also heard voting rights claims under the equal protection clause of the Fourteenth Amendment. Earl M. Maltz, "The Coming of the Fifteenth Amendment: The Republican Party and the Right to Vote in the Early Reconstruction Era," *Rutgers Law School Research Paper* (2019).

96. William M. Leiter and Samuel Leiter, *Affirmative Action in Antidiscrimination Law and Policy: An Overview and Synthesis*, 2nd ed. (Albany: SUNY Press, 2011), 197.

97. Abigail Thernstrom, "Section 5 of the Voting Rights Act: By Now, a Murky Mess," *Georgetown Journal of Law and Public Policy* 5 (2007): 45.

98. *Mobile v. Bolden*, 446 U.S. 55 (1980); Raymond Wolters, *Right Turn: William Bradford Reynolds, the Reagan Administration, and Black Civil Rights* (New Brunswick, NJ: Transaction, 1996), 48.

99. John J. Miller, "Every Man's Burden," *National Review*, April 10, 2006, 24.

100. Blacks were about 12 percent of the total population. The 2012 elections returned forty-three Blacks to the House.

101. Leiter and Leiter, *Affirmative Action in Antidiscrimination Law*, 212.

102. Joan Biskupic, "North Carolina Case to Pose Test of Racial Districting," *Washington Post*, April 20, 1993.

103. *Shaw v. Reno*, 509 U.S. 630 1993), 647.

104. Vann R. Newkirk, "The Supreme Court Finds North Carolina's Racial Gerrymandering Unconstitutional," *Atlantic*, May 22, 2017.

105. Justice Antonin Scalia was roundly scolded for suggesting this description in oral argument. Gary May, "Scalia's Understanding of the Voting Rights Act Is Shortsighted," *Washington Post*, April 26, 2013.

106. Thernstrom, "Section 5 of the Voting Rights Act," 77.

107. Carol M. Swain, "Reauthorization of the Voting Rights Act: How Politics and Symbolism Failed America," *Georgetown Journal of Law and Public Policy* 5 (2007): 29.

108. Some observers warned that Congress's failure to update the trigger mechanisms would lead to this. Charles S. Bullock III and Ronald Keith Gaddie, "Good Intentions and Bad Social Science Meet in the Renewal of the Voting Rights Act," *Georgetown Journal of Law and Public Policy* 5 (2007): 6.

109. *Shelby County v. Holder*, 570 U.S. 529 (2013). Roberts repeatedly drew on the "extraordinary" phraseology used by the Court when it originally upheld the Act in *South Carolina v. Katzenbach*, 383 U.S. 301 (1966).

110. Desmond S. King and Rogers M. Smith, "'Without Regard to Race': Critical Ideational Development in Modern America," *Journal of Politics* 76 (2014): 966.

111. Adam Liptak, "Supreme Court Bars Challenges to Partisan Gerrymandering," *New York Times*, June 27, 2019.

112. The Court upheld the amended Section 2 without opinion, over two dissents, in 1984. *Mississippi Republican Executive Opinion v. Brooks*, 469 U.S. 1002.

113. Belz, *Equality Transformed*, 234.

114. "The Great Society's Civil Rights Legacy: Continuity 1, Discontinuity 3," in *The Great Society and the High Tide of Liberalism*, ed. Sidney Milkis and Jerome M. Mileur (Amherst: University of Massachusetts Press, 2005), 376.

PART III

*Individual Rights and Public Safety*

SEVEN

—ᏁᏁ—

# REVERSING THE REVOLUTION

Rights of the Accused in a Conservative Age

DAVID J. BODENHAMER

IN 1987 AND 1988, THE little-known Office of Legal Policy in the Department of Justice released eight reports on criminal procedure. Under the series title "Truth in Criminal Justice," the reports challenged "a judicially created system of restrictions of law enforcement that has emerged since the 1960s." It sought a return to "the ideal of criminal investigation and adjudication as a serious search for truth."[1]

The series reflected a view that liberal judges had unduly bridled police officers and prosecutors in combating crime, at grave cost to public safety. The Warren Court in the 1960s had abandoned the discovery of truth, the argument went, in a misguided and unjustified expansion of defendants' rights. These rights enabled criminals to escape punishment—and worse, to continue a life of crime—not through a trial determination of guilt or innocence but rather on some technicality that bore little relationship to what happened. As Attorney General Edwin Meese noted in his preface, "Over the past thirty years . . . a variety of new rules have emerged that impede the discovery of reliable evidence at the investigative stages . . . and that require the concealment of relevant facts at trial." Above all else, he proclaimed, "criminal justice . . . must be devoted to discovering the truth."[2]

The reports called for the reversal of landmark decisions from the 1960s that introduced extraconstitutional, judicially created rules that impeded effective law enforcement. These decisions and others from the Warren Court, the reports claimed, unfairly burdened criminal investigation, allowed an explosive rise in the crime rate, and diminished the importance of the criminal trial, traditionally the testing ground for competing claims of truth. The trial would regain its central role in American jurisprudence when police and prosecutors had the freedom to present evidence of guilt or innocence. Convicting the guilty, after all, was the primary mission of the criminal justice system.[3]

This criticism of the 1960s due process revolution was not new to the politics of the 1980s. Richard Nixon made "law and order" a major theme of his 1968 presidential campaign, proclaiming that the Warren Court let "guilty men walk free from hundreds of courtrooms." His first appointment to the Supreme Court, the new chief justice, Warren Burger, shared Nixon's view. While still on the appellant bench, Burger wrote that the Court's actions made guilt or innocence "irrelevant in the criminal trial as we flounder in a morass of artificial rules poorly conceived and often impossible of application."[4] Election after election saw politicians trot out variations of this theme, often with great success. The criticism remained politically potent during the 1970s and 1980s because it appeared to explain the dramatic increase in violent crimes, especially by Black men.

Yet throughout these decades, the Warren Court reforms remained essentially intact. The Burger Court refused to extend the due process revolution and even trimmed some newfound rights, but it did not repudiate the earlier Court's legacy. Even the Rehnquist Court followed suit initially, despite the new chief justice's view that the Warren Court had erred often by deciding cases without constitutional justification.

In the 1990s, the Court switched direction. Bolstered by the retirement of William Brennan, a liberal holdover from the Warren era and a strong intellectual force on the bench, a new conservative majority abandoned several precedents, some established only a few years earlier. More significant was a different tone to the Court's opinions, a determination to ensure that the rights of the accused did not prevent successful prosecution of guilty suspects. Perhaps more by circumstance than design, the Court's shift paralleled the recommendations of the Department of Justice. After two decades of conservative electoral success, constitutional law finally merged with political opinion.[5]

But what of this change in course? The politics are clear, but what about the interpretation of the past on which it rests? The Warren Court's decisions on criminal procedure were not as revolutionary, as far-reaching, or even as consequential as critics have maintained. This conclusion is less true for the modern Court. An emphasis on convicting the guilty departs significantly from legal traditions that far predate the Warren Court, and a belief that protection of formal trial procedures best ensures justice is at odds with American experience. To understand why the counterrevolution was more radical than the revolution itself, it is first necessary to recall the past.

### PRELUDE TO A REVOLUTION

From the beginning of the nation, the states, not the central government, were primarily responsible for the integrity of criminal due process. State constitutions and state courts defined and protected rights of the accused; the Bill of Rights applied only to federal trials. Even the passage of the Fourteenth Amendment, with its language suggesting national oversight of due process, did not change this division of responsibility. Well into the twentieth century, the Supreme Court adhered to the position first announced in *Hurtado v. California* (1884), that the Fourteenth Amendment did not bind the states to the procedural guarantees of the federal Constitution. Most rights belonging to Americans were attributes of state citizenship and thus were not subject to national regulation or control. Criminal due process referred only to the procedures employed by the state. If criminal prosecutions followed the process required by state law, then the result by definition was just.

Few people found the lack of national supervision troublesome, at least not if they were part of the White majority, because Americans believed they shared a common set of legal values, institutions, and procedures. Chief among them was a commitment to due process of law, which in ideal form pledged procedural fairness in all actions from indictment to trial and punishment. Underlying this notion of fairness was a belief expressed through centuries of Anglo-American experience that the primary purpose of criminal justice was to protect the innocent, not to convict the guilty. The old English maxim remained a guide for nineteenth-century Americans: it was better for twenty guilty persons to escape punishment than for one person to suffer wrongly.[6]

By the mid-nineteenth century, criminal justice was taking new and different shape. The grand jury came under sharp attack in the late antebellum decades, and by the 1880s, almost twenty states, mostly western, allowed the prosecutor to charge a person directly rather than through the traditional indictment. Newly created police departments shifted the focus of law enforcement from reacting to citizen complaints to detecting crime by patrols and investigations. But it was the trial, long the centerpiece of the criminal process, that experienced the most dramatic challenge. Not only did bench trial, or trial by the judge alone, begin to rival jury trial; most defendants avoided trial altogether by pleading guilty in exchange for less severe punishment.[7]

Plea bargaining changed the face of American justice. It made efficient prosecution and conviction of the guilty, not protection of the innocent, the primary goal of the legal system. There were informal, subterranean, and highly particularistic standards for fixing guilt and innocence. Confessions became the desired end, and police interrogations the preferred means for obtaining them. State supreme courts often protested that plea bargaining was a perversion of due process; it represented the sale of justice, and its secrecy mocked the pledge of neutral justice in a public trial. Other critics characterized plea bargaining as an auction, and legal scholars denounced it as a license to violate the law. But the practice continued. Public concerns about order, especially amid rapid urbanization and a flood of immigration from Eastern Europe and Asia, made the control of crime paramount.

These changes led to dissatisfaction during the first decades of the twentieth century with the traditional policy of no federal oversight in matters of criminal justice. Increasingly, events pressured the Supreme Court to extend the protection of the Bill of Rights to criminal defendants under the Fourteenth Amendment, just as it had begun to do for the rights of free speech and free press as well as property rights. The Red Scare following World War I demonstrated the need as states failed to protect even the most basic rights of defendants, especially those belonging to ethnic and racial minorities. During the 1920s and 1930s, studies of criminal justice, including a major national investigation by the Wickersham Commission, revealed the open contempt many police departments held for the rights guaranteed by state and federal constitutions. And the wholesale lynching of Blacks in the South finally became a national disgrace.

By the 1930s, numerous organizations, notably the American Civil Liberties Union and the National Association for the Advancement of Colored People, pressed for nationalization of the Bill of Rights. In 1932, they scored an initial success. *Powell v. Alabama*, the famous Scottsboro case, established that the due process clause of the Fourteenth Amendment guaranteed the assistance of counsel to defendants charged with capital crimes in state courts. Even so, the Supreme Court resisted attempts to incorporate the protections of the Fourth, Fifth, Sixth, and Eighth Amendments into a national standard. The Fourteenth Amendment, the justices held in *Palko v. Connecticut* (1937), imposed on the states only rights essential to a "scheme of ordered liberty."[8] In criminal matters, the assurance of fair trial alone was fundamental to liberty. States could employ widely different procedures without violating due process. Not even trial by jury was essential to fairness, even though the founding fathers had deemed it the bulwark of their liberties.

From the 1930s through the 1950s, the Supreme Court grappled with the meaning of the phrase "due process of law." The fair-trial test meant that the Court would decide case by case which rights of the accused enjoyed constitutional protection. It also suggested that the values and attitudes of individual judges would determine which state procedures created such hardships or so shocked the conscience that they denied fair treatment. Still, the test provided a method for extending the Bill of Rights to the states, and the catalog of nationalized rights—provisions of the Bill of Rights binding on the states—grew extensively by the end of the three decades, especially given the previous absence of such guarantees. Fundamental rights included limited protection against illegal searches and seizures (Fourth Amendment) and coerced confessions (Fifth); public trial, impartial jury, and counsel (Sixth); and protection against cruel and unusual punishments (Eighth). Even so, the interpretation of these rights was not as far-reaching as later Courts would find, and some rights—double jeopardy, protections against self-incrimination, and jury trial, among others—remained totally under state control.

The Court's reliance on the fair-trial test, although maintaining federalism, led to much confusion regarding which criminal procedures were acceptable. Some state practices it permitted, others it rejected; no clear standard guided law enforcement. Continued adherence to the test exposed the Court to charges that defendants' rights depended on judicial caprice. To pursue such an ad hoc approach, Chief Justice Earl Warren cautioned in 1957, "is to build on shifting sands."[9] It was also at odds with the Court's decisions on First Amendment freedoms. These rights applied fully and identically to central and state governments alike under the due process clause of the Fourteenth Amendment. Why should not the same standard govern the rights of the accused? *Palko v. Connecticut*, progenitor of the fair-trial doctrine, Justice Brennan reminded his colleagues, contained no "license to the judiciary to administer a watered-down subjective version of the individual guarantees of the Bill of Rights."[10]

By the late 1950s, four justices—Warren, Black, Douglas, and Brennan—were ready to abandon the fair-trial approach to the Fourteenth Amendment. The 1960s witnessed their triumph. Too much had changed nationally to continue an interpretation that defined rights in terms of state boundaries. State prosecutors and local police alike had grown weary of a distant tribunal deciding long after trial that state practices violated the Constitution. Law schools and bar associations desired more uniform rules. Commentators and legal scholars also questioned why the Fourth, Fifth, Sixth, and Eighth Amendments were not as fundamental as freedom of speech and press.

In a nation where interstate highways collapsed distances and chain stores erased a sense of place, it was only a matter of time before national standards replaced local practice. For criminal law, the shift came in a rush of Supreme Court decisions in the 1960s. In what was termed the "due process revolution," the Bill of Rights became a national code of criminal procedure. Suddenly, rights of criminal defendants became more real, more immediate, and, for many people, more threatening.

## NATIONALIZING THE RIGHTS OF THE ACCUSED

Between 1961 and 1969, the Supreme Court accomplished what previous Courts had stoutly resisted: it applied virtually all the procedural guarantees of the Bill of Rights to the states' administration of criminal justice. Adopting the strategy of selective incorporation, the justices explicitly defined the Fourteenth Amendment phrase "due process of law" to include most of the rights outlined in the

Fourth, Fifth, and Sixth Amendments. The result was a nationalized Bill of Rights that dimmed the local character of justice by applying the same restraints to all criminal proceedings, both state and federal. The majority justices did not seek to diminish states' rights; they desired instead to elevate subminimal state practices to a higher national standard. But in the process, the Court reshaped the nature of federalism itself.

Leading the due process revolution was an unlikely figure: Chief Justice Earl Warren. He was a former California district prosecutor, attorney general, and governor whose pre-Court reputation was of a crusader against corruption and for vigorous law enforcement. Warren's reputation took a sharp turn as chief justice, in large measure because he brought a different style and philosophy to the Court. His long-standing belief in active government challenged the majority justices' embrace of judicial restraint, which included deference for legislative actions, respect for federalism and the diversity of state practice, and reliance on neutral decision making based on narrow case facts rather than broad constitutional interpretation. Warren specifically dismissed as "fantasy" the notion that judges can be impartial. "As defender of the Constitution," he wrote, "the Court cannot be neutral."[11] More important, Court decisions must reach the right result, a condition defined by ethics, not legal procedures.

By the 1960s, the Court was ready to follow the chief justice's lead. Equality joined individualism in the pantheon of modern liberal values. Liberty, long defined as the restraint of power, now required positive governmental action. Individual freedom rested on the protection and extension to all citizens of the fundamental guarantees found in the Bill of Rights and the Fourteenth Amendment. In its emphasis on equality and national standards, the Court was not alone. Liberalism experienced resurgence under the presidencies of Kennedy and Johnson, and the rhetoric of civil rights and social justice framed the agenda of the ascendant Democratic Party. For most of the decade, the justices drew support from a political coalition that preached a similar message.

Popular myth has it that the Court's decisions on criminal justice were highly controversial and came only through the determined efforts of a bare majority of judges. This view distorts what happened. Take, for example, *Gideon v. Wainwright* (1963), which declared that the Sixth Amendment right to counsel applied to the states under the due process clause of the Fourteenth Amendment and that states had to provide a lawyer for felony defendants too poor to hire one. The decision was unanimous, even though it reversed a 1942 precedent (*Betts v. Brady*) allowing a state to refuse such assistance in noncapital cases unless its refusal denied the defendant a fair trial. Twenty-three states filed amicus curiae, or friend of the court, briefs asking the Court to mandate the assistance of counsel in serious criminal cases. The Court's previous deference to the states, the briefs charged, had resulted only in "confusion and contradictions" that failed totally "as a beacon to guide trial judges."[12]

Other decisions affecting the conduct of state trials also met general acceptance, even when the justices divided narrowly. For example, the Court decided in *Malloy v. Hogan* (1964) that the privilege against self-incrimination was part of the due process clause of the Fourteenth Amendment. And the next year, 1965, in *Pointer v. Texas*, the Court ruled that the Sixth Amendment right of an accused to confront a witness against him was a fundamental right that the Fourteenth Amendment required of all states. Neither case occasioned much public comment.

In truth, there was never much objection to the Warren Court's restraints on state trial practices. Pretrial rights were a wholly different matter. The Court discovered early that any challenge to state police practices would be highly controversial. In *Mapp v. Ohio* (1961), the liberal justices narrowly, 5–4, applied the federal exclusionary rule to the states. Even though the case facts revealed a blatant disregard of search-and-seizure guarantees, the Ohio Supreme Court had upheld the state law permitting the use of illegally seized evidence to convict Dollree Mapp of possession of obscene material. The Supreme Court disagreed. One of its earlier decisions, *Wolf v. Colorado* (1948), had extended the Fourth Amendment to the states but without the federal rule of procedure that required the exclusion of any evidence gained in violation of the amendment's guarantees. Now with the amendment's protection went the means to enforce it: the exclusionary rule. "To hold otherwise," Justice Tom Clark reasoned, "is to grant the right but in reality withhold its privilege and enjoyment."[13]

Clark, a former US attorney general, did not believe the decision would impede law enforcement—although, he argued, the Constitution demanded it regardless—but critics of *Mapp* concluded otherwise. They condemned the Court as unrealistic. Police officers engaged in dangerous work that often required quick action, and failure to follow the correct procedures should not nullify the evidence of crime. *Mapp* undermined order, opponents argued, by breaching the federal principle that left criminal matters to state control. The majority justices had overreached their authority and fashioned their decision not on constitutional precedent but on their sense of a right result.

These criticisms surfaced with more force a few years later when the Court extended the right of counsel to the pretrial stages of criminal process, first in *Massiah v. United States* (1964) and then in *Escobedo v. Illinois* (1965) and *Miranda v. Arizona* (1966). The justices concluded that Fifth Amendment guarantees against self-incrimination and coerced confessions and the Sixth Amendment's right to counsel were meaningless unless applied to a police investigation at the point where it focused directly on an individual suspected of crime. Any information gained illegally by denying these protections was not admissible at trial. Significantly, the decisions affirmed and extended the precedents of earlier Courts, stretching back at least to 1945, that automatically overturned convictions achieved through coerced or involuntary confessions, even if the confessions were true and the guilty defendant went free as a result.[14] But for opponents of the decisions, the Court had departed dramatically from past practice, impeding the investigation of crime and jeopardizing public safety.

*Miranda* was by far the most controversial decision, the one still cited as the premier example of a Court gone wrong. Chief Justice Warren's opinion extending the Fifth Amendment protection against self-incrimination to suspects under police interrogation exemplified his ethically based, result-oriented jurisprudence. The opinion first detailed the unfair and forbidding nature of police interrogations. Police manuals and statements by law enforcement officers revealed that beatings, intimidation, psychological pressure, false statements, and denial of food and sleep were standard techniques. For Warren, these tactics suggested that "the interrogation environment [existed] . . . for no other purpose than to subjugate the individual to the will of the examiner."[15] Such police tactics violated the Fifth Amendment protection against self-incrimination.

The longest part of the opinion was a detailed code of police conduct. The new rules quickly became familiar to anyone who watched television crime dramas: suspects must be informed of the right to remain silent; that anything they say can be used against them; that suspects have the right to have counsel present during questioning; and that if they cannot afford an attorney, the court will appoint a lawyer to represent them. These privileges took effect from the first instance of police interrogation while the suspect was "in custody at the station or deprived of his freedom in a significant way." And the rights could be waived only "knowingly and intelligently," a condition presumed not to exist if lengthy questioning preceded the required warnings.[16]

Warren's language vividly portrayed the unequal relationship between interrogator and suspect, an imbalance that the chief justice believed did not belong in a democratic society. "The prosecutor under our system," he commented later, "is not paid to convict people [but to] protect the rights of people . . . and to see that when there is a violation of the law, it is vindicated by trial and prosecution under fair judicial standards."[17] The presence of a lawyer and a protected right of silence created a more equal situation for the accused; thus, these conditions were essential to the constitutional conception of a fair trial.

Police officers, prosecutors, commentators, and politicians were quick to denounce the *Miranda* warnings. They charged that recent Court decisions had "handcuffed" police efforts to fight crime. This claim found a receptive audience in the late 1960s among a general public worried about rising crime rates, urban riots, and racial conflict. The belief that the pretrial reforms threatened public safety even acquired a certain legitimacy from members of the Supreme Court itself. "In some unknown number of cases," Justice Byron White warned in his dissent from the *Miranda* decision, "the Court's rule will return a killer, a rapist or other criminal to the streets . . . to repeat his crime whenever it pleases him."[18]

These alarms were exaggerated. Numerous studies have demonstrated that the decision, like the ones in *Mapp* and *Massiah*, did not restrain the police unduly and, in fact, had little effect on the disposition of most cases. Access to an attorney, usually an overworked and underpaid public defender, may have smoothed negotiations between suspect and prosecutor, but it did not lessen the percentage of cases resolved by plea bargains, nor did it result in lengthy delays, greater bureaucracy, or more dismissals of guilty suspects.

Even as a matter of law, *Miranda* was not as revolutionary as critics claimed. The Supreme Court from the 1930s had held that voluntariness of a confession was essential for its acceptance as evidence, and since 1945 it automatically reversed convictions based on involuntary confessions, regardless of whether the confession was true. Various terms were used to describe the voluntariness test: "free will" and "unconstrained choice" signified a voluntary confession; "breaking the will" and "overbearing the mind," an involuntary one. But, as Justice John Marshall Harlan II noted in his dissent in *Miranda*, the Court's gauge for determining whether a confession was voluntary had been steadily changing, usually in the direction of restricting admissibility.[19] *Miranda* scuttled this case-by-case determination. It established uniform rules of procedure and, equally important, accepted as constitutional any confessions gained under these rules. Although controversial, the reforms in pretrial procedures gradually brought needed improvements in police practices. Police procedures came more fully into public view, resulting in heightened awareness of official misconduct and greater expectations of professionalism. In response, many police departments raised standards for employment, adopted performance guidelines, and improved training and supervision.

The Court, ever aware of public criticism, made concessions to secure more widespread acceptance of its rulings. Most important was the decision not to apply new rulings retroactively. The justices acknowledged that this course denied equal justice to prisoners convicted under abandoned procedures, but they admitted candidly that wholesale release of prisoners was politically unacceptable. Another concession was the adoption of a "harmless-error" test to determine the impact of an unconstitutional act at trial: constitutional errors would not void convictions if "beyond a reasonable doubt that error did not contribute to the verdict obtained."[20] The Court also hesitated to restrict the police unduly. It held in 1966, the same year as *Miranda*, that the government's use of decoys, undercover agents, and paid informants was not necessarily unconstitutional. The justices further approved the admissibility of evidence secured by wiretaps and sustained the right of police "in hot pursuit" to search a house and seize incriminating evidence without a warrant.

These moderating decisions failed to quiet the Court's critics, but mounting pressure did not deter the justices from making further reforms in state criminal procedures. *In re Gault* extended certain due process requirements to juvenile courts. Several important cases incorporated the remaining Sixth Amendment guarantees—specifically, the rights to compulsory process, speedy trial, and trial by jury—into the due process clause of the Fourteenth Amendment as new restraints on state criminal proceedings. The Court continued to insist that poverty should be no impediment to justice by requiring that the state furnish transcripts to indigent defendants. And it strengthened its long-established position that confessions be truly voluntary. Much more controversial were the continuing reforms of pretrial procedures. In 1967, several search-and-seizure decisions especially brought further protest from law-and-order advocates who accused the Court of coddling criminals, a charge that gained momentum during the 1968 election when two presidential candidates—Richard Nixon and George Wallace—made it a major theme in their campaigns.

Such cases, whether controversial or not, departed sharply from the decades-old tradition that defined criminal justice as a local responsibility. Each decision underscored the dramatically changed relationship between the federal Bill of Rights and the state's authority to establish criminal procedures. Earlier Courts had accepted state experimentation with any part of due process unless the justices considered it essential to a scheme of ordered liberty. This standard permitted states to define fairness in a variety of ways, and these definitions may or may not have included the guarantees of the federal amendments. But the Warren Court concluded that rights of the accused were rights of US citizenship.

Throughout the 1960s, the justices repeatedly rejected theory and diversity in favor of history and uniformity—a point emphasized, fittingly, in their reversal of *Palko v. Connecticut*, the landmark case that had justified state experimentation with criminal procedures. Writing for the majority in *Benton v. Maryland* at the end of the decade, Justice Thurgood Marshall noted that recent cases had thoroughly rejected the premise in *Palko* that a denial of fundamental fairness rested on the total circumstances of a criminal proceeding, not simply one element of it. Once the Court decides a guarantee is fundamental to American justice, he continued, then failure to honor that safeguard is a denial of due process. Equally important, these essential protections applied uniformly to all jurisdictions.

Here, then, was the core of the due process revolution: rights of the accused did not vary from state to state; they were truly national rights.

## SLOWING THE REVOLUTION

By 1969, the Court's transformation of criminal procedure was at its end. Neither popular nor political opinion supported further reform. The previous year, stung by rioting in American cities and pressured to curb a recent sharp upturn in crime and violence, Congress had responded by passing the Omnibus Crime Control and Safe Streets Act, the most extensive anti-crime legislation in US history. The measure contained provisions designed to reverse recent Court decisions, especially the *Miranda* rule. And now there was a new chief justice, Warren Burger, who had been appointed by Richard Nixon to redeem his campaign pledge to restore a conservative cast to the Supreme Court. The political thrust was clear: punishment would replace redemption as the goal of criminal justice.[21]

Contrary to expectations, there was no counterrevolution in the law governing defendants' rights, even after three conservative appointees replaced Warren Court justices. The Burger Court did not renounce the due process revolution, but the justices were more tolerant of police behavior and less receptive to further expansion of rights of criminal defendants. Symbolic of the change was the Court's interpretation of the Fourth Amendment's requirement that search warrants be based on probable cause. Previous decisions had challenged the validity of a warrant issued based on rumors or an anonymous informant, yet in *United States v. Harris* (1971), a divided Court held that a suspect's reputation alone was sufficient to support a warrant application. Writing for the majority, Chief Justice Burger denounced "mere hypertechnicality" in warrant affidavits and urged a return to more practical considerations in actions against criminals.[22] In another case, the chief justice bluntly characterized the exclusionary rule as "a mechanically inflexible response." Without a clear demonstration of the rule's effectiveness, he argued, it should be abandoned, because the cost to society—"the release of countless guilty criminals"—was too high.[23]

Subsequent cases confirmed the new direction. Framers of the exclusionary rule, first announced in 1914, believed the principle was part of the Fourth Amendment. Not so, concluded the Court in 1974 in *United States v. Calandra*, which characterized the exclusionary rule as a "judicially created remedy designed to safeguard Fourth Amendment rights generally through its deterrent effect." It was not a "personal constitutional right," and its use presented "a question, not of rights but of remedies"—one that should be answered by weighing the costs of the rule against its benefits.[24]

This new cost-benefit analysis led ultimately to a good-faith exception to the exclusionary rule, announced in *United States v. Leon* (1984): evidence produced by an officer's reasonable or good-faith reliance on the validity of a warrant was admissible in court, even if the warrant later proved defective. The good-faith exception rested explicitly on a balancing of costs and benefits. Using evidence captured innocently under a defective warrant exacted a small price from Fourth Amendment protection when compared to the substantial cost society would bear if an otherwise guilty defendant went free.

In most other areas of criminal procedure, the Court maintained but did little to advance the rights of the accused. Arguing that the law requires only a fair trial, not a perfect one, the Court upheld a conviction even though the police, when giving the required *Miranda* warnings, neglected to tell the defendant of his right to appointed counsel if he could not afford one. In Sixth Amendment cases, the Court guaranteed the right to counsel in all trials that could result in imprisonment, but following the lead of Congress in the Crime Control Act of 1968, it refused to grant the protection to unindicted suspects in a police lineup. Similarly, the justices extended the guarantee of a jury trial to include all petty misdemeanors punishable by imprisonment for six months or longer, yet they allowed states to experiment with the size of juries and accepted 10–2 and 9–3 verdicts in noncapital cases.[25]

## REVERSING THE REVOLUTION

The successes of the Burger Court in slowing the rights revolution of the 1960s did little to dampen the political demand for law and order. Crime rates remained distressingly high, and many Americans accepted the view advanced by President Ronald Reagan, elected in part on a pledge to make crime a major domestic policy issue, that the balance between safety and rights had become dangerously skewed. The exclusionary rule especially was a major target. The Attorney General's Task Force on Violent Crime issued a report in 1982 that labeled its cost as "unacceptably high," and numerous efforts were made throughout the first Reagan administration to restrict or abandon the rule by statute.[26] In this climate, the appointment of William Rehnquist as chief justice in 1986 promised a continued effort to reverse the Warren Court's revolution.

Rehnquist had long signaled his discontent with the Warren Court reforms. In confirmation hearings upon his appointment as associate justice in 1971, he asserted that the personal philosophy of some of justices, not a fair reading of the Constitution, had perversely influenced the Court, causing it to move "too far toward the accused."[27] The proper interpretation of the Constitution rested on principles of strict construction, judicial restraint, and federalism that he found lacking in Warren Court jurisprudence. Nothing in the Constitution, he wrote in 1977, made the Court "a council of revision."[28] He praised the Burger Court for "calling a halt to the sweeping rulings" of the 1960s court, although he viewed the reversal as incomplete.[29]

Initially, the Rehnquist Court followed its predecessor's lead in cases involving rights of the accused, yet the new chief was only partly successful in leading his colleagues to complete the conservative shift, for at least two reasons. Frequent changes in membership slowed efforts to shape a solid majority in favor of a more restrictive stance, but Rehnquist also adopted a leadership style that emphasized persuasion by written opinions rather than the give-and-take of the judicial conference or one-on-one exchanges with colleagues—strategies often used to fashion majorities. Whatever desire the chief justice had to reverse the Warren Court's jurisprudence of rights was never strong enough to overcome his preference for logic over politics as the means of achieving this goal.

In what some scholars have called the "First Rehnquist Court,"[30] roughly from 1986 to 1994, the Court declined to extend defendants' rights and insisted on balancing individual protections with the need for effective law enforcement, but it did not reverse Warren Court decisions despite what appeared to be a conservative majority. Law officers gained greater latitude in applying the *Miranda* rules when, in *Colorado v. Connelly* (1986), the Court adopted a less strict standard to determine the voluntariness of a confession.[31] Strengthening the ability of the police to fight crime was also the result in *United States v. Salerno* (1987), upholding the Bail Reform Act of 1984, which allowed the government to deny bail if release of a defendant would endanger lives or property. Even though an apparent departure from the presumption of innocence, the law itself provided several procedural safeguards, including representation of counsel. These protections, the justices concluded, provided a reasonable balance between the rights of the accused and the need for public safety.

The incremental rebalancing of societal and individual interests gave way to a more comprehensive reassessment of rights of the accused during the 1990 term. For over two decades, politicians' demands for a law-and-order judiciary had reaped electoral windfalls, but not until the appointment of three conservative justices—Kennedy, Scalia, and Souter—did politics and constitutional law join so conclusively.[32] Suddenly the calculus of decision making had changed, and it emboldened the new conservative majority to challenge Warren Court precedents.

The Fourth Amendment was one of the battlegrounds for this new judicial approach. The Rehnquist Court addressed the rule first in two decisions extending the good-faith exception established in *Leon*. In *Illinois v. Krull* (1987),[33] a 5–4 majority extended the exception to situations in which police had relied on a state law later found to be unconstitutional. Eight years later, in *Arizona v. Evans* (1995),[34] the Court applied the same logic to a search conducted upon an arrest based on an error in an official database of outstanding warrants. Significantly, the conservative majority's interest in blunting the expansion of the exclusionary rule outweighed its predisposition to honor federalism. In this instance, the

Arizona Supreme Court had found against the government, arguing that it was "repugnant to the principles of a free society" to take a person into police custody because of official carelessness.

Even though the Rehnquist Court never overturned the exclusionary rule, its rulings marked the success of a strategy, first begun in the 1970s, to limit its use as a guarantor of Fourth Amendment rights. The result was a new body of law about when the rule would apply. The conservative majority defined search narrowly— searches of open fields or of items in plain view were, per se, not searches, which, in turn, meant the rule was not relevant. It upheld numerous exceptions to the warrant requirement that previously had defined a reasonable search, loosened the definition of probable cause, enhanced the stop-and-frisk authority of police, and encouraged police to conduct so-called voluntary searches by holding that suspects need not be warned of their right to refuse consent.[35]

In only two cases did the Court retreat from this stance. In 2000, in *Bond v. United States*, with Rehnquist, surprisingly, writing for a 7–2 majority, the justices upheld a bus passenger's expectation of privacy when faced with an unauthorized, exploratory search of his bags at an immigration checkpoint.[36] The next year, a 5–4 majority of justices halted the "not a search" trend by holding in *Kyllo v. United States* that the use of heat-seeking imaging to probe inside a house was indeed a search and required a warrant.[37]

Other cases also signaled the new direction. The most dramatic departure came in confession law, long a bellwether of constitutional attitudes toward the defendant. Since the 1940s, the Court had reversed convictions based in whole or in part on an involuntary confession, even when there was ample evidence apart from the confession to support the conviction. In *Arizona v. Fulminante* (1991),[38] the 5–4 majority abandoned this precedent. They applied instead the harmless-error test to such evidence, culminating a trend begun in the Burger Court. This new approach classified evidence of a coerced confession not as an automatic violation of due process but simply as a trial error. Like other mistakes at trial, involuntary confessions must now be examined in the context of all the facts presented at trial to determine whether their use was harmless, or inconsequential to the verdict. The harmless-error rule, it appeared, was essential to preserve the central truth-seeking purpose of the criminal trial.[39] The goal was to convict the guilty, not restrain the government.

Judicial restraint and a respect for federalism were other key themes of the new conservative majority. The first principle requires deference to legislative authority; the second, to state practice. The Rehnquist Court retreated from broad constitutional decisions and determined case by case what was acceptable. This approach marked a return to the fair-trial standard that guided the Court before Warren. Fairness is the essential constitutional requirement of due process, and states may achieve this result in a variety of ways. Indeed, the justices appeared to conclude, the federal principle demanded that the Court respect the states' authority to control criminal process.

Tradition and reason were the two criteria used to determine fairness, with the more conservative justices, led by Antonin Scalia, wanting to restrict the standard to history alone: "It is precisely the historical practices that *define* what is 'due' [under due process]," he wrote in *Schad v. Arizona* (1991), a case involving the constitutionality of certain instructions to the jury. "When judges test their individual notions of 'fairness' against an American tradition that is broad and deep and continuing, it is not the tradition that is on trial, but the judges."[40] The conservative majority on the Rehnquist Court rejected the Warren Court's "constant and creative application" of the Bill of Rights to new situations;[41] historical continuity with the Constitution's original meaning, increasingly termed "originalism," was the new guiding principle.

Federalism, too, was a lodestar for the Court. *Coleman v. Thompson* (1991), which with other recent decisions sharply restricted a state prisoner's access to federal courts, is illustrative. The first sentence in Justice Sandra Day O'Connor's opinion for the 6–3 majority—"This is a case about federalism"—established the grounds for the denial of federal habeas review when the prisoner missed the filing deadline for a state court appeal because of his attorney's error. Habeas corpus, while a bulwark against unfair convictions, entailed significant costs, "the most significant of which is the cost in finality in criminal litigation." And in overruling *Fay v. Noia* (1963), the Warren Court decision that expanded federal review of habeas petitions, O'Connor wrote, "We now recognize the important interest in finality served by state procedural rules, and the significant harm to the States that results from the failure of the federal courts to respect them."[42]

Justice Harry Blackmun, joined by Justices Marshall and Stevens, rebuked his colleagues in a stinging dissent, noting that rights are not an issue of federalism; they are constitutional guarantees and as such are superior to state interests. Federal review exists not to diminish state authority but "to ensure that federal rights were not improperly denied a federal forum." The Court, Blackmun charged, "now routinely, and without evident reflection, subordinates fundamental constitutional rights to mere utilitarian interests."[43] The goal of finality alone was not enough to compromise the protection of rights.

Federalism implies a diversity of practice, and the Rehnquist Court repeatedly demonstrated its willingness to accept different criminal procedures for different states, even if it meant reversing precedents it had only recently affirmed. Such was the case in *Payne v. Tennessee* (1991). Various states in the 1980s had enacted laws that permitted sentencing juries in capital cases to consider evidence about the victim when deciding whether to impose the death penalty. These statutes clearly represented a political response to public beliefs that the law favored the criminal and cared little for the victim of crime. In 1987 and 1989, the Court rejected victim impact evidence as a violation of the Eighth Amendment's ban on cruel and unusual punishment. *Payne* abruptly jettisoned these precedents. Writing for the 6–3 majority, Chief Justice Rehnquist rejected the notion that evidence about the victim leads to arbitrary decisions in capital cases, a result forbidden by the Eighth Amendment. States must remain free "in capital cases, as well as others, to devise new procedures and new remedies to meet felt needs." Blind adherence to past mistakes would not accomplish these ends, especially when the precedents "were decided by the narrowest of margins, over spirited dissents."[44] Nowhere in evidence was the Warren Court's concern that due process protected the citizen from the overbearing power of the state. The new jurisprudence increasingly echoed the conservative politics of the past two decades. Now it was the society that had to be protected from the effect of a citizen's claim of constitutional rights.

Federalism became a touchstone for the conservative majority, even though the due process revolution occurred in part because of the failure of states to protect the minimal liberties guaranteed by their own constitutions. It had also come at the request of states, which believed that uniform rules would end the uncertainty and ambiguity that attended law enforcement. Not only did the Court ignore this history in its attempt to revive federalism, it failed to address a question addressed by the Warren Court decisions, namely, whether local standards of due process are appropriate or meaningful in a highly mobile national society, especially when states have repeatedly created artificial distinctions between their citizens.[45]

Only one case during the Rehnquist era suggested that when law became settled, it limited the reach of federalism, or at least this was the conclusion in *Dickerson v. United States* (2000),[46] which upheld the *Miranda* warnings in what surely was among the most surprising decisions reached by the Rehnquist Court on rights of the accused. The case involved a challenge to the admissibility of incriminating statements made in the absence of the required police warning about the suspect's rights. The Fourth Federal Circuit Court reversed a federal district court's suppression of the statements based on Section 3501 of the US Code, which reversed *Arizona v. Miranda* for federal crimes. (The Omnibus Crime Control and Safe Streets Act of 1968 directed trial judges to accept voluntary confessions regardless of whether the accused had received the required warning.) The Supreme Court declined, 7–2, to reverse *Miranda*; the warnings were a constitutional protection that Congress could not override. The issue may have been, in fact, more an institutional claim to supremacy in imposing procedural rules, as some have suggested,[47] than it was a defense of *Miranda*, but, more likely, the justices shied from throwing police practice into chaos. What had once been viewed as "sand in the machinery of justice" was now part of the machine itself.[48]

Whatever the reason, *Dickerson* was an aberration from the Burger-Rehnquist Court tendencies to sharply restrict rights of the accused when those rights conflicted with the state's quest for truth in a criminal proceeding, as a case in 2004 demonstrated. *United States v. Patane* arose when a detective questioned a suspect about the location of a gun without administering the complete *Miranda* warnings. A confession followed, the gun was admitted into evidence, and Patane was convicted, but the Tenth Circuit, relying on Dickerson, unanimously reversed upon appeal. The US Supreme Court disagreed. Even though there was no opinion of the Court, a plurality restated the law as it existed before *Dickerson*, which described the warnings as a subconstitutional rule.[49] By the time of Rehnquist's death in 2005, the law surrounding *Miranda* was murky, but it was clear that a significant number of justices were not willing to give the warning a wide compass if its application interfered with the truth-seeking functions of the criminal process.

The Roberts Court (2005–) did not retreat from the general direction of its predecessor courts in strengthening the state's ability to prosecute crime, but its path was not straightforward. At times its decisions strengthened rights of the accused; a 2015 study, for example, revealed that the Court's most deeply divided decisions more often were favorable to the defendant.[50] But this result reflected less of a liberal-conservative split than the pragmatism of Justice Anthony Kennedy, the swing vote, who rejected a bright-line approach in favor of an assessment of the practical impact of the decision. It is still too soon to know whether Kennedy's retirement in 2018 and Justice Ruth Bader Ginsburg's death in 2020 will significantly reshape the Court's criminal jurisprudence, especially as it relates to rights of the accused.[51] The conservative justices, now in a 6–3 majority, likely will hew more closely to an originalist view advanced by the late Justice Antonin Scalia and will be less interested in an approach that limits the state's ability to seek the truth in criminal proceedings.

The Sixth Amendment right to confront one's accuser and the exculpatory rule were early bellwethers of the Roberts Court's approach. The confrontation clause had arisen out of alarm at the British Crown's use of ex parte interrogations in the seventeenth century to produce evidence against in state trials, thereby depriving the defendant of the right to confront his accusers in court as required in common-law trials. In *Ohio v. Roberts* (1980), the Burger Court allowed admission of out-of-court statements by unavailable declarants where the statements "fall within a firmly rooted hearsay exception" or bear "particularized guarantees of trustworthiness."[52] Originalists on the Roberts Court found this standard both muddled and ahistorical. Under it, the judge, not the jury, determined the reliability of the testimony. Led by Justice Scalia, the Court abandoned this precedent in *Crawford v. Washington* (2004), holding that cross-examination is required to admit prior testimonial statements of witnesses who have since become unavailable.[53] "The only indicium of reliability sufficient to satisfy constitutional demands," Scalia wrote, "is the one the Constitution actually prescribes: confrontation."[54] Four years later, using the same logic, the justices applied the clause to laboratory reports.[55] Ironically, the effort to apply a clear guide itself became muddled as the Court increasingly has grappled with what actions were testimonial, thereby triggering the confrontation clause, and which ones were merely evidentiary.[56]

If decisions regarding the confrontation clause pointed to greater protections for the defendant, cases involving the exculpatory rule strengthened the prosecutorial hand. In two cases, *Van de Camp v. Goldstein* (2009)[57] and *Connick v. Thompson* (2011),[58] the Court strictly limited the degree to which prosecutors could be held liable for failure to release exculpatory evidence, a standard set by the Warren Court in 1963.[59] In 2009, the justices, 5–4, reversed a two-decades-old decision[60] that protected a defendant's Fifth Amendment right to counsel. Once arraigned with counsel assigned, the Sixth Amendment right applied, which could be waived by a defendant's actions rather than explicitly. It was in society's interests, Justice Scalia maintained for the majority, to allow officials to seek voluntary confessions, especially when sufficient safeguards existed through *Miranda* and its offshoots to prevent coerced confessions. "In sum," he wrote, "when the marginal benefits of the *Jackson* rule are weighed against its substantial costs to the truth-seeking process and the criminal justice system, we readily conclude that the rule does not 'pay its way.'"[61]

Capital punishment was one area in which the Court wavered on its commitment to strengthening the state's power to combat crime. In 1972, the justices narrowly struck down a Georgia law that allowed the trial jury to levy the death penalty and reduced all capital convictions to life imprisonment.[62] Four years later, the Court reinstated capital punishment after state legislatures had revised their laws to separate questions of guilt from those of punishment.[63] Only two justices—Brennan and Marshall—confronted the morality of the penalty, which revealed the difficulty of striking down a punishment that most Americans had not yet rejected.

What happened instead was a series of challenges to capital punishment, with the Eighth Amendment serving as a source of procedural rights. Increasingly the justices had to consider case by case whether the punishment met exacting standards of fairness and proportionality, making the cruel and unusual punishment clause a "super due process" standard for capital cases, especially when considered with the more general procedural guarantees derived from other Bill of Rights amendments.[64] The result has been a series of cases that narrowed the reach of the penalty: states could not exact death for the rape of an adult woman[65] or for intellectually disabled individuals who could not understand the reason for their punishment[66] or for juveniles under the age of eighteen at the time the crime was committed[67] or when applied to non-homicidal crimes.[68] But the justices also generally rejected challenges to the death penalty that sought to make the method of execution unconstitutional, even if it resulted in prolonged suffering before death, as happened occasionally with lethal injections.

More than court decisions were in play in the interpretation of the Eighth Amendment, however. A new societal consensus regarding the death penalty, hesitant though it was, accompanied—and at times preceded—the Court's uncertain jurisprudence. From 1976, when the justices affirmed the constitutionality of capital punishment, to 2019, more than seventy-eight hundred defendants had been sent to death row, with more than fifteen hundred executions. Both sentences and executions came from a small number of states in the South and West, with African Americans disproportionately represented among the condemned. With violent crime no longer a major issue, public support began to waver, spurred in part by reform efforts such as The Innocence Project, a nonprofit founded in 1992 that used DNA testing to exonerate wrongfully convicted felons, including capital offenders.[69] By 2019, twenty-one states had abolished the death penalty, although in an additional eleven states' public referenda had reinstated capital punishment after the state supreme court or legislature outlawed it.[70] The nation remained divided but with a trend toward abolition, which explains in part the Court's cautious narrowing of the circumstances in which death is a constitutionally acceptable penalty.

In this emphasis on truth-seeking as the ultimate standard of constitutionality in criminal matters, the Court since the 1980s has hewed to the belief that the goal of criminal justice, indeed its sole standard, is convicting the guilty. This focus makes rights of the accused subject to the judgments of legislative majorities and to the discretion of law enforcement, both of which are dependent on the will of a popular majority. One tragic result, especially when combined with the 1994 Violent Crime Control and Law Enforcement Act crime control statute, with its emphasis on incarcerating repeat offenders (the so-called three strikes provision), was a dramatic increase in the number of individuals convicted of crimes, often minor drug offenses. By 2019, the nation's jails housed over 2.2 million people, with 4.2 million on probation or under court supervision, numbers that were disproportionately weighted toward minorities and the poor. Concerns about fairness and costs led to sentencing reforms, both at state and federal levels, culminating in 2018 with the First Step Act of 2018, which provides for early release of nonviolent offenders.[71]

The truth-seeking functions of trials and punishment of guilty defendants have strong popular appeal, especially in times of societal unrest. Such a stance appeals to democratic tenets, but the framers of the Constitution did not trust rights to the majority. Rights are fundamental. They are essential to the nation's conception of personal liberty. They exist, as James Madison recognized more than two centuries ago, to protect individuals against arbitrary government and oppressive majorities. The Bill of Rights will never prevent all injustices, nor does the original expression of them contain all the rights found necessary to due process. But neither are they subject to diminishment without the loss of liberty. This should be the lesson from our past: we are most faithful to the framers—and to our own freedom—when we strive to advance their legacy of protecting each citizen from the power of overzealous government.

## NOTES

1. Stephen J. Markham, "Foreword: The 'Truth in Criminal Justice' Series," *Journal of Law Reform* 22 (1989): 425.

2. Prefatory statement of Meese, unpublished reports.

3. "If truth cannot be discovered and acted upon, the system can only fail in its basic mission." Markham, "Foreword," 428.

4. Quotations from David J. Bodenhamer, *Fair Trial: Rights of the Accused in American History* (New York: Oxford University Press, 1991), 127, 129.

5. See Michael Willrich, "Criminal Justice in the United States," in *The Cambridge History of Law in America*, vol. 3, *The Twentieth Century and After*, ed. Michael Grossberg and Christopher Tomlins (Cambridge: Cambridge University Press, 2008), 195–231.

6. Chief Justice John Fortescue of the Court of King's Bench in the mid-fifteenth century wrote, "Indeed, one would much rather that twenty guilty persons should escape the punishment of death, than one innocent person should be condemned and suffer capitally." Quoted in Bradley Chapin, *Criminal Justice in Colonial America, 1606–1660* (Athens: University of Georgia Press, 1983), 3.

7. State surveys in the 1920s revealed a heavy dependence on plea bargaining, especially in big-city courts. In Chicago, for example, 85 percent of all felony convictions resulted from a guilty plea. The percentages in other cities were almost as high or higher. See, in general, Albert Alschuler, "Plea Bargaining and Its History," *Columbia Law Review* 79 (January 1979): 1–43.

8. *Palko v. Connecticut*, 302 U.S. 319, 325–26.

9. *Breithaupt v. Abram*, 352 U.S. 432 (1957), 442.

10. *Ohio ex rel. Eaton v. Price*, 364 U.S. 274 (1960).

11. Earl Warren, *The Memoirs of Earl Warren* (New York: Doubleday, 1977), 332.

12. As quoted in Richard C. Cortner, *The Supreme Court and the Second Bill of Rights: The Fourteenth Amendment and the Nationalization of Civil Liberties* (Madison: University of Wisconsin Press, 1981), 196.

13. *Mapp v. Ohio*, 367 U.S. 656 (1961). The history of this case is well told in Carolyn N. Long, *Mapp v. Ohio: Guarding against Unreasonable Searches and Seizures* (Lawrence: University Press of Kansas, 2006).

14. The rule of automatic reversal has governed coerced confession cases since *Malinski v. New York*, 324 U.S. 401 (1945).

15. *Miranda v. Arizona*, 384 U.S. 457 (1966).

16. *Miranda v. Arizona*, 470–75.

17. Anthony Lewis, "A Talk with Warren on Crime, the Court, and the Country," *New York Times Magazine*, October 19, 1969, 126.

18. *Miranda v. Arizona*, 572.

19. *Miranda v. Arizona*, 508.

20. *Chapman v. California*, 386 U.S. 24 (1967).

21. Michael Willech, "Criminal Justice in the United States," in *The Cambridge History of Law in America*, vol. 3, *The Twentieth Century and After*, ed. Michael Grossberg and Christopher Tomlins (Cambridge: Cambridge University Press, 2008), 195–231, esp. 222–31. Willech terms this development as the "severity revolution."

22. *United States v. Harris*, 403 U.S. 582 (1971).

23. *Bivens v. Six Unknown Federal Narcotics Agents*, 403 U.S. 388 (1971), 416.

24. *United States v. Calandra*, 414 U.S. 348, 354 (1974). The Court held that grand jury witnesses could not refuse to answer questions based on illegally acquired evidence.

25. Only in cases involving the death penalty did the Court move beyond the Warren Court's conception of defendants' rights. See Bodenhamer, *Fair Trial*, 132–36.

26. See Long, *Mapp v. Ohio*, 180–81.

27. Senate Judiciary Committee, *Nominations of William H. Rehnquist and Lewis F. Powell, Jr.*, 92nd Cong., 1st Sess. (1971), serial Y4.J89/2: R 26/2, 26–27.

28. *Trible v. Gordon*, 430 U.S. 762 (1977).

29. John A. Jenkins, "The Partisan," *New York Times Magazine*, March 3, 1985, 28. Mark Tushnet has argued that the chief justice had been influenced by Justice Robert Jackson (1941–54), for whom he had clerked. Jackson, an advocate for balancing order and freedom, wrote in a 1949 case, *Watts v. Indiana*, that the Bill of Rights, as interpreted by the Court at that time, imposed the "maximum restrictions upon the power of organized society over the individual that are compatible with the maintenance of organized society itself," a stance that suggested that no further expansion of individual liberties was necessary. Mark Tushnet, *A Court Divided: The Rehnquist Court and the Future of Constitutional Law* (New York: W. W. Norton, 2005), 9–14.

30. See Thomas W. Merrill, "The Making of a Second Rehnquist Court: A Preliminary Analysis," *St. Louis Law Journal* 47 (2003): 569.

31. In *Connelly*, the Court held that police must give the required warnings and stop all questioning if a suspect demanded a lawyer, but they could use

nonthreatening tactics, such as pretending sympathy with the suspect, to secure a valid confession. Four years later, the Court declined 6–2, to weaken *Miranda* further by holding that once the suspect requested counsel, all questioning must stop until a lawyer was present, whether the accused had consulted with an attorney. *Minnick v. Mississippi*, 59 L.W. 4037 (1990).

32. At the time of his appointment, many commentators believed Souter to be more conservative than his record on the Court has demonstrated.

33. U.S. 340 (1987).

34. U.S. 1 (1995).

35. For an excellent discussion of these limits on the exclusionary rule, see Craig M. Bradley, "The Fourth Amendment: Be Reasonable," in *The Rehnquist Legacy*, ed. Craig M. Bradley (New York: Cambridge University Press, 2006), 81–105.

36. U.S. 334 (2000).

37. U.S. 27 (2001).

38. *Arizona v. Fulminante*, 499 U.S. 279 (1991).

39. *Arizona v. Fulminante*, 309. Rehnquist quoted with approval from an earlier case that the harmless-error doctrine is essential to preserve "the principle that the central purpose of a criminal trial is to decide the factual question of the defendant's guilt or innocence."

40. *Schad v. Arizona*, 501 U.S. 651 (1991).

41. Earl Warren, "The Law and the Future," *Fortune*, November 1955, 106.

42. *Coleman v. Thompson*, 501 U.S. 726, 738, 750 (1991).

43. *Coleman v. Thompson*, 758, 765–66.

44. *Payne v. Tennessee*, 501 U.S. 813, 822 (1991).

45. The Roberts Court has continued this emphasis on federalism, especially in habeas corpus and capital punishment cases. See Justin F. Marceau, "Un-Incorporating the Bill of Rights: The Tension between the Fourteenth Amendment and the Federalism Concerns That Underlie Modern Criminal Procedure Reforms," *Journal of Criminal Law and Criminology* 98, no. 4 (2008): 1231.

46. 530 U.S. 428.

47. See, generally, Joshua Dressler, *Understanding Criminal Procedure* (Newark, NJ: LexisNexis, 2002).

48. Richard A. Leo, "Questioning the Relevance of *Miranda* in the Twenty-First Century," *Michigan Law Review* 99 (2001): 1027. Also see William J. Stuntz, The Political Constitution of Criminal Justice, *Harvard Law Review* 119 (2006): 780–851.

49. The justices cited with approval language from a series of cases dating to *Michigan v. Tucker* (1974) that provided exceptions to the required *Miranda* warnings. In *Missouri v. Seibert*, a companion case to *Patane*, the justices found by a 5–4 majority that the police had developed a two-stage process to undermine the *Miranda* requirement. In this case also, the plurality opinion, written by Justice Souter, failed to rely on *Dickerson*, and a concurring opinion by Justice Kennedy

praised an important pre-*Dickerson* case as essentially "correct in its reasoning and its result." 124 S. Ct. 2615. For more on these decisions, see Yale Kamisar, "Dickerson v. United States: The Case That Disappointed Miranda's Critics—and Then Its Supporters," *University of San Diego Public Law and Legal Theory Research Paper Series*, 33 (2005): 119–28, http://digital.sandiego.edu/lwps_public/art33.

50. Christopher E. Smith, Mahdavi M. McCall, and Michael A. McCall, "The Roberts Court and Criminal Justice: An Empirical Assessment," *American Journal of Criminal Justice* 40 (2015): 414.

51. Stephanos Bibas, "Justice Kennedy's Sixth Amendment Pragmatism," *McGeorge Law Review* 44 (2014): 211.

52. *Ohio v. Roberts*, 448 U.S. 56, 66 (1980).

53. *Crawford v. Washington*, 541 U.S. 36 (2004).

54. 541 U.S. at 68–69. Not all scholars agreed with Scalia's historical analysis, noting that the Sixth Amendment also rejected certain common-law practices, such as when it required assistance of counsel. See Randolph N. Jonakait, "The Too-Easy Historical Assumptions of *Crawford v. Washington, Brooklyn Law Review* 71 (2005): 219.

55. *Melendez-Diaz v. Massachusetts*, 557 U.S. 305 (2009).

56. See Jason Widdison, "*Michigan v. Bryant*: The Ghost of Roberts and the Return of Reliability," *Gonzaga Law Review* 47 (2011): 219.

57. 555 U.S. 335.

58. 563 U.S 51.

59. *Brady v. Maryland*, 373 U.S. 83 (1963). See Susan A. Bandes, "The Lone Miscreant, the Self-Training Prosecutor, and Other Fictions: A Comment on Connick v. Thompson," *Fordham Law Review* 80 (2011): 715–36.

60. *Michigan v. Jackson*, 475 U.S. 625 (1986).

61. *Montejo v. Louisiana*, 556 U.S. 778 (2009), at 797.

62. *Furman v. Georgia*, 408 U.S. 238 (1972).

63. *Gregg v. Georgia*, 428 U.S. 153 (1976).

64. Joseph L. Hoffman, "The 'Cruel and Unusual Punishment' Clause: A Limit on the Power to Punish or Constitutional Rhetoric," in *The Bill of Rights in Modern America: Revised and Expanded*, ed. David J. Bodenhamer and James W. Ely Jr. (Bloomington: Indiana University Press, 2008), 172–89.

65. *Coker v. Georgia*, 438 U.S. 534 (1977).

66. *Atkins v. Virginia*, 536 U.S. 304 (2002).

67. *Roper v. Simmons*, 543 U.S. 551 (2005).

68. *Kennedy v. Louisiana*, 553 U.S. 407 (2008).

69. Keith A. Findley and Michael S. Scott, "The Multiple Dimensions of Tunnel Vision in Criminal Cases," *Wisconsin Law Review* 206 (2006): 291. For a best-selling account of wrongfully convicted defendants, see Bryan Stevenson, *Just Mercy: A Story of Justice and Redemption* (New York: Spiegel & Grau, 2014). A more cautionary perspective is offered by Erin Murphy, "The New Forensics: Criminal Justice,

False Certainty, and the Second Generation of Scientific Evidence," *California Law Review* 95 (2007): 721.

70. Statistics from National Conference of State Legislatures, accessed July 30, 2019, http://www.ncsl.org/research/civil-and-criminal-justice/death-penalty.aspx, and Death Penalty Information Center, accessed July 30, 2019, https://deathpenalty info.org/.

71. Nicole Porter, "Top Trends in State Criminal Justice Reform, 2018," Sentencing Project, accessed August 12, 2019, https://www.sentencingproject.org /publications/top-trends-state-criminal-justice-reform-2018/.

# EIGHT

—∽—

# POLICE PRACTICES AND THE BILL OF RIGHTS

LAURENCE A. BENNER
MICHAL R. BELKNAP

IN THE LATE TWENTIETH CENTURY, America's fear of violent crime, fueled by drugs and urban street gangs, spurred the government to get tough on crime. In the law-and-order atmosphere of the day, those Bill of Rights guarantees that secure the right to be free from unreasonable searches and seizures and protect the individual from being subjected to custodial interrogation sometimes seemed to be inconvenient obstacles in the path to winning the war on drugs and street crime. After the tragic events of September 11, 2001, what Americans feared most in the new millennium was terrorism. In the midst of the new war on terror, those same constitutional limitations on governmental authority likewise were seen as impediments to national security. Yet the Fourth and Fifth Amendments are as necessary today as they have ever been.

While limiting what government can do in combating crime and terrorism, these amendments also protect privacy and individual liberty. As the renowned political scientist Edward S. Corwin once pointed out, liberty is "the absence of restraints imposed by other persons upon our own freedom of choice and action."[1] Such restraints can come from two sources. One is other people, such as the mugger who robs us, or the terrorist who blows up the building in which we work. To be sure, the police and the courts safeguard us against the deprivation of our liberty by such individuals when they arrest and confine criminals and terrorists. What we may often forget, however, is that in unleashing these powers to protect our freedom from violent crime and terrorism, we also loosen the restraints on those who wield the levers of government power, enabling them to eavesdrop, search, detain, and coercively interrogate regarding other perceived "emergencies." When that happens, it is not another private citizen but the government itself that deprives us of our liberty and privacy. History has shown that the more unchecked power government has, the greater the likelihood is that it will abuse its power. The Fourth and Fifth Amendments exist to ensure that in the effort to protect us from terrorists and criminals, government does not abuse its powers and become an even greater threat to our freedom than those it is combating.

To understand the important role these provisions play in protecting our freedom, we might consider what society would be like without them. Suppose, for example, police receive an anonymous tip that terrorists are making bombs in a house located somewhere in the French Quarter of New Orleans. Can the police stop and detain anyone who enters or leaves this seventy-eight-square-block area and search their cell phone for suspicious messages? Can they search all the homes in the area or use electronic surveillance to eavesdrop on the conversations occurring in homes? Without the Fourth Amendment, which generally requires individualized justification for such intrusions, there would be no constitutional constraints protecting innocent citizens from such dragnet police practices.

Suppose further that a public demonstration is held to protest US foreign policy. Police arrest several of the demonstrators on charges of disturbing the peace and place them in small, windowless interrogation rooms. One demonstrator is repeatedly shocked with an electric stun gun in an effort to make him reveal the names of the leaders of the demonstration. Another is threatened that unless she cooperates, the authorities will seek to have her mother deported. In a third room, a suspected demonstration leader is questioned around the clock without food, water, or sleep by relay teams of interrogators. His requests to see his lawyer are denied, and his pleas to be left alone are ignored. Such practices, which occur regularly in some countries, are forbidden in the US system of criminal justice because the Fifth Amendment gives each person the right not to be subjected to custodial interrogation.

The framers of the Bill of Rights believed that "in a free society, based on respect for the individual, the determination of guilt or innocence by just procedures, in which the accused made no unwilling contribution to his conviction, was more important than punishing the guilty."[2] They chose to enshrine in the Constitution provisions that would preserve liberty, privacy, and the accusatorial system of criminal procedure that was the legacy of centuries of British common-law privileges and immunities the colonists had fought a war to preserve in America. This founding generation of Americans, who wrote the Bill of Rights into the Constitution in 1791, believed in the existence of natural rights, which no government might invade because they were part of the fundamental law of the land. The principles that the Fourth and Fifth Amendments represented were thus widely accepted, and during the nineteenth century, there was little need to rely on these constitutional rights. Moreover, most crimes were defined and punished by the states, which had their own bill of rights contained within each state constitution.

Although the Supreme Court once held that the amendments to the federal Constitution comprising the Bill of Rights only limited the federal government,[3] the idea that the Bill of Rights did not also protect against state infringement of fundamental protections became untenable after the Civil War and passage of the Fourteenth Amendment. That amendment, ratified in 1868, provides that no state shall "deprive any person of life, liberty, or property, without due process of law." In the 1960s, controversy raged in the Supreme Court over whether this due process guarantee prohibited the states from abridging the same rights that had been secured against federal interference by the Bill of Rights. Over time, under the so-called incorporation doctrine, certain fundamental guarantees in the first eight amendments were incorporated as part of the due process guarantee that the Fourteenth Amendment required states to observe.

Most of the Court's rulings incorporating provisions of the Bill of Rights into the due process clause of the Fourteenth Amendment and applying them to the states came while Earl Warren was chief justice (1953–69). Indeed, between 1961 and 1969, the Warren Court required that the states observe virtually all of the criminal procedure guarantees in the Bill of Rights. The real significance of this "due process revolution," however, lay in the Warren Court's adoption of a judicially created exclusionary rule, which barred the prosecution from using evidence in a state criminal case if it had been obtained in violation of the federal Constitution. Most states had provisions in their state constitutions that mirrored the Fourth and Fifth Amendments. However, the majority of the states in 1960 did not enforce their state constitutional guarantees by making the fruits of their violation inadmissible as evidence in the courtroom. In *Mapp v. Ohio* (1961), the Warren Court made the Fourth Amendment exclusionary rule mandatory in state criminal proceedings, thereby banning evidence obtained as a result of unreasonable searches and seizures. In *Malloy v. Hogan* (1964), it did the same thing with evidence obtained in violation of the Fifth Amendment's prohibition against compulsory self-incrimination.

## THE FOURTH AMENDMENT

The text of the Fourth Amendment provides: "The right of the people to be secure in their persons, houses, papers, and effects, against unreasonable searches and seizures, shall not be violated, and no warrants shall issue, but upon probable cause, supported by oath or affirmation, and particularly describing the place to be searched, and the persons or things to be seized." The historical background giving rise to the Fourth Amendment reveals that this constitutional guarantee originated as a direct result of abusive law enforcement practices suffered by the colonists at the hands of the British. Envisioned by the founders of this nation as an essential bulwark against similar abuses of governmental power in the future, the Fourth Amendment protects two distinct rights: the right to personal liberty and the right to privacy. In the language of the amendment, a governmental restraint on personal liberty by physical force or show of authority is called a seizure. A governmental intrusion upon a person's reasonable expectation of privacy or trespass upon one's home, papers, or effects is called a search. These comprehensive rights to liberty and privacy have been referred to as the "right to be let alone."[4]

The right to be let alone, however, is not absolute. The constitutional guarantee only protects against "unreasonable" governmental searches and seizures. The fundamental question addressed by the Fourth Amendment then is this: Under what circumstances must the individual's right to be let alone yield to the common good? The framers of the Fourth Amendment resolved this question by employing a common-law standard known as probable cause. This traditional standard required individualized justification to believe the person intruded on was engaged in criminal wrongdoing. Today the need to control crime and prevent terrorism has exerted enormous pressure to abandon this strict protective mechanism in order to give greater powers to law enforcement. In response to this pressure, the Supreme Court has created an increasing number of exceptions to the probable cause requirement and limited the scope of the warrant requirement, which requires that probable cause be judicially determined. The result of this judicial reinterpretation of the literal text of the Fourth Amendment has been to diminish greatly the scope of protection that once sprang from this constitutional guarantee.

The late eighteenth-century Americans who adopted the Bill of Rights, however, were not legal positivists who believed that they were creating new manmade rights against government. Rather, they believed the source of such rights lay in a higher, fundamental law, based on principles of natural law and reason. Their intent in drafting the Fourth Amendment was, therefore, to create a mechanism that would prevent the violation of what they viewed as a self-evident and fundamental right to be secure from unjustified governmental invasions of personal liberty and privacy. The procedural mechanism they employed for safeguarding this basic freedom had three essential elements: (1) prior judicial authorization; (2) a requirement of individualized justification (probable cause) for the intrusion; and (3) a requirement that the facts constituting the justification be sworn to under oath.

Probable cause has historically required more than mere suspicion. Using the timeworn, traditional definition, probable cause for a seizure exists when trustworthy information is sufficient to create a reasonable belief that a crime has been committed and that the person to be seized has committed the offense.

Probable cause for a search exists when reliable information produces a reasonable belief that evidence of criminal wrongdoing will be found at the premises to be searched. In applying the probable cause standard, it is therefore elementary that a general justification (such as a laudatory public purpose) will not do. The justification must relate specifically to the individual who is called upon to surrender the liberty or privacy interest in question. This individualized justification standard is not an invention of the founders. Rather, it has roots going back to English common law and even ancient Roman law.

### HISTORICAL ROOTS OF THE FOURTH AMENDMENT

Under Roman criminal procedure at the time of Cicero, criminal prosecutions were normally private lawsuits instituted by the aggrieved party. The accuser had to state his complaint to the court and support it by taking an oath. If the court found that there was probable cause, the accuser could obtain an official writ (the precursor of our warrant) authorizing him to search places for evidence of the crime.[5]

By the seventeenth century, English common law had refined these early protections and developed all the requirements found in the literal text of the Fourth Amendment today. These included: (1) prior judicial approval (2) to search a particularly described place (3) for particularly described items, (4) based on probable cause (5) established by information obtained under oath.[6] The "common law" was, of course, the accumulation of judicial decisions made in cases involving disputes between private citizens. One of the recurring themes throughout the Anglo-Saxon struggle for human rights, however, was the continual (and often unsuccessful) attempt to force the sovereign to recognize these same legal rules of procedure. For example, numerous monarchs from Henry VIII to Charles I used the power of arbitrary search and seizure to stifle dissent. Henry VIII devised a particularly effective method of controlling freedom of expression by licensing his supporters as royal printers. He then issued warrants that officially authorized them to search for and destroy all unlicensed books and papers. During the religious persecutions of the sixteenth century, the notorious Court of Star Chamber also employed the practice of issuing such "general warrants" in its war against nonconformists. Such warrants were not supported by oath, nor were they based on probable cause or any form of individualized justification. Indeed, they specified no person or place. Rather, they broadly authorized the holder of the warrant to search any place for the purpose of discovering heretical books or pamphlets.[7] The use of such general warrants by government officials was finally declared illegal in England shortly before the American Revolution.[8]

Despite the abolition of general warrants in England, a particularly egregious form of general warrant, known as the writ of assistance, was used by British authorities in the American colonies to enforce tariffs designed to implement a mercantilist imperial commercial policy. Armed with a writ of assistance, a customs officer could, at his whim, exercise blanket authority to search any house, business, or warehouse for imports on which the required duties had not been paid. Because the British trade regulations unduly burdened colonial commerce, for many years they went largely unenforced. However, in 1760, while Britain was at war with France, the government ordered strict enforcement of all trade sanctions in the colonies. What had been a semi-legitimate business practice now was prosecuted as smuggling. In the years just prior to the Revolution, well-known patriots either smuggled or defended smugglers in court. For example, Boston merchant John Hancock, later a signer of the Declaration of Independence, was defended in 1769 by a future president, John Adams, on charges stemming from the importation of French wine in violation of the Townshend Acts. Hancock's ship the *Liberty* had been boarded and searched pursuant to a writ of assistance and, under the zero tolerance policy of the day, both the untaxed wine and the ship were subjected to forfeiture, an event that provoked a riot by the citizens of Boston.[9]

Because of the frequent abuse of the arbitrary search powers granted to Crown officers by the writs of assistance, when the writs expired following the death of George II, a group of Boston merchants went to court to attempt to block the issuing of new ones. James Otis, who resigned his position as advocate general of the Admiralty to represent the merchants without fee, gave an impassioned argument. Calling them "remnants of Starchamber tyranny," Otis argued that by stripping away the common-law protections provided by the probable cause standard and the oath requirement, the writs annihilated the sanctity of the home and placed "the liberty of every man in the hands of every petty officer."[10] Although Otis failed to prevent the reissuance of the writs of assistance, John Adams, who attended the argument, later observed that it had been a spark helping to ignite the revolutionary spirit of the colonists. "Every man . . . appeared to me to go away, as I did, ready to take up Arms against Writs of Assistance," he wrote. "Then and there the child Independence was born."[11]

After the Revolution, the founders did not forget the lessons of the past. Indeed, being extremely mistrustful of governmental power, they sought explicit recognition of the fundamental principle that a governmental intrusion on an individual's right to be let alone was reasonable only if there was individualized justification founded on probable cause. This is seen most clearly in the original version of the Fourth Amendment submitted by James Madison: "The rights of the people to be secured . . . from all unreasonable searches and seizures, shall not be violated by warrants issued without probable cause supported by oath or affirmation."[12]

It is readily apparent that this formulation reflects the fear of general warrants and highlights the importance of probable cause as the operative mechanism for curbing unreasonable governmental intrusions. Due to a quirk of history, however, the text of the Fourth Amendment has not come down to us in this form. During debate on the amendment in the First Congress, Representative Egbert Benson of New York objected that Madison's formulation was not strong enough. He moved that the language "by warrants issued without probable cause" be changed to assert affirmatively, "and no warrants shall issue, but upon probable cause." The House rejected this proposed change by a considerable majority. However, Benson was the chair of the Committee of Three appointed to arrange the amendments in final form and the version the House sent to the Senate included his rejected change. No one apparently caught the error and the amendment was subsequently passed by the Senate and ratified by the states in that form.[13]

This seemingly minor change, which Benson intended to strengthen the Fourth Amendment, instead actually weakened it by recasting the amendment in the form of two distinct clauses. What was once a unitary thought—that a search or seizure is reasonable only if it is based on individualized justification in the form of probable cause—became fragmented. The declaration that the right to be free from unreasonable searches and seizures should not be violated was now an independent clause (known today as the reasonableness clause), totally separated from the probable cause requirement.

By destroying the direct link between the probable cause standard and protection from unreasonable searches and seizures, Benson's change created an ambiguity. At the time the Fourth Amendment was adopted, probable cause was universally required for any search or seizure, regardless of the circumstances. The tampered text of the Fourth Amendment, however, seemed expressly to require probable cause only in cases involving warrants. A warrant was at that time, of course, an indispensable prerequisite to the search of a home or business. There was no organized police force in eighteenth-century America. A warrant, therefore, symbolized the authority of the holder to conduct the search. A warrant was not always required, however, for a seizure. For example, a fleeing felon, caught in the act of committing a crime, could be arrested on hue and cry without stopping to get an arrest warrant. This dichotomy laid the basis for an interpretation that would subsequently permit the erosion of the probable cause standard— the very mechanism the framers had employed to protect the liberty and privacy of future generations.

## JUDICIAL INTERPRETATION OF THE FOURTH AMENDMENT

Early interpretation of the Fourth Amendment held true to the founders' original intent. Courts held that for a search or seizure to be reasonable under the Fourth Amendment, the police must, at a minimum, have individualized justification for the intrusion, amounting to probable cause. In recent decades, however, the

Supreme Court, viewing the amendment as an impediment to effective law enforcement, has divorced the warrant clause, which contains the probable cause requirement, from the reasonableness clause, which does not. This has enabled the Court to isolate and make exceptions to the founders' requirement that all searches and seizures be based on particularized probable cause. It achieved this result initially through development of the special needs doctrine. Under this doctrine, if special circumstances made compliance with the warrant or probable cause requirement difficult, the Court employed a balancing test to determine whether the government interest at stake and the needs of law enforcement outweighed the individual's liberty or privacy interest invaded. If so, the search or seizure could still be reasonable under some lesser standard that controlled discretion to prevent arbitrary intrusions.

The first case to apply the balancing test to a street confrontation between police and a citizen was *Terry v. Ohio* (1968).[14] The Warren Court held in this case that even absent probable cause, police could temporarily seize a person and subject him or her to a pat-down search for weapons if there was reasonable suspicion the person was about to engage in violent criminal activity. The Court reasoned that the need to prevent violent crime and the need for investigating officers to protect themselves from the threat of a hidden weapon outweighed the liberty and privacy interests infringed by this minimally intrusive pat-down search and temporary seizure. In an era concerned about crime, this decision certainly seemed reasonable. Once the shield formed by the probable cause standard was pierced, however, it was difficult to prevent further mutilation. Later cases, for example, expanded this exception to permit stops of motorists on the basis of reasonable suspicion of nonviolent criminal behavior. Still, up to this point, the Court had simply lowered the degree of individualized justification from probable cause to reasonable grounds for suspicion. Its next step created an exception that jettisoned the concept of individualized justification altogether.

## SEIZURES: BALANCING AWAY LIBERTY

The seminal case that made such a radical departure from the founders' original understanding involved a limited seizure at a permanent immigration checkpoint set up near San Clemente, California. Employing the balancing test, the Court ruled in *United States v. Martinez-Fuerte* (1976)[15] that the seizure of a motorist and his passengers (simply because of their apparent Mexican ancestry), and their brief detention for questioning, was only minimally intrusive. The need to contain what was perceived as a rising tide of illegal immigration, on the other hand, was deemed great. Hence, such seizures were considered reasonable under the Fourth Amendment, even though they were based solely on racial or ethnic appearance and not otherwise justified by any degree of particularized suspicion of wrongdoing.

As Reverend Martin Niemoller's well-known poem about the Nazi takeover of Germany reminds us, what government is allowed to do to the least powerful, it can one day do to all of us. Today, as a result of the extension of this checkpoint line of cases, the suspicionless seizure of all motorists is permissible in the name of traffic safety. For example, in 1990, the Court upheld the validity of sobriety checkpoints at which motorists are stopped and questioned, even though there is no indication that any driver is intoxicated. Such stops must be brief, and probable cause is still required for an actual arrest. The Court later drew the line at narcotics checkpoints, ruling that the primary purpose of the suspicionless stop could not be solely to search for evidence of ordinary criminal activity. Nevertheless, where police declare that the primary purpose of the checkpoint is not to search for evidence, the Court has upheld even informational checkpoints at which all motorists are stopped for the purpose of asking them if they have knowledge about criminal activity. Thus, for the innocent individual who casts not even a shadow of suspicion, the right to travel freely has been diminished significantly as a result of the Court's use of the balancing test to determine reasonableness.

## SEARCHES: BALANCING AWAY PRIVACY

In light of the greater value placed on privacy and the Fourth Amendment's direct historical connection to abuses suffered under the writs of assistance, the Court initially was reluctant to balance away the probable cause requirement when it came to searches. True, the *Terry* decision had authorized a pat down of outer clothing for weapons based only on reasonable suspicion, and the scope of *Terry* searches had been extended to the passenger compartment of a car, but attempts to expand this exception beyond its officer-safety rationale were unsuccessful. However, with the ascension of William Rehnquist to the position of chief justice and the appointment of three new associate justices by President Ronald Reagan, who had campaigned on a law-and-order agenda, this reluctance soon dissipated.

The Rehnquist Court began by abolishing the warrant and probable cause requirements for administrative searches of both private business premises and personal offices of public employees. In upholding the warrantless search of commercial premises, the Supreme Court ruled that because the activities of the business were subject to regulation, it had diminished privacy interests in its premises. Therefore the warrant and probable cause requirements were not applicable to an administrative search to ensure compliance with such regulations. In another case, the office of a government physician was searched without a warrant or probable cause by a supervisor investigating allegations of malfeasance. The Court found that the "realities of the workplace" made the warrant requirement impractical and that a probable cause requirement would impose "intolerable burdens" on government agencies. Holding the privacy interests of hundreds of thousands of federal, state, and local governmental employees in the balance, the Court found that their right to privacy in their offices was insignificant because they could leave their personal belongings at home.[16]

The most far-reaching search decisions affecting US workers, however, have been the drug-testing cases. At issue in *Skinner v. Railway Labor* (1989)[17] was the validity of federal regulations requiring a private employer (a railroad company) to compel its employees, on pain of suspension for nine months, to submit to blood tests without any individualized suspicion of drug or alcohol abuse. The government maintained that the testing of railroad workers was necessary to determine the cause of train accidents and deter train crews from being intoxicated on the job. Acknowledging that the piercing of the skin and extraction of blood infringed on a worker's right to personal security and that urinalysis could reveal such private medical facts as whether one was pregnant or had epilepsy, the Court nevertheless found these interests insignificant when balanced against the government's special interest in railway safety or a drug-free workforce. Similarly, in *National Treasury Employees Union v. Von Raab* (1989),[18] the Court upheld a urinalysis testing program for a broad category of personnel, including not only customs agents but also clerical workers. The Court has also extended the use of suspicionless drug testing to schools, first upholding the testing of student athletes (because the need to prevent injuries outweighed their diminished expectations of privacy) and later validating drug testing of high school students who engage in any extracurricular activity, including choir and chess club. In these cases, the discretion to conduct suspicionless testing was limited because the testing requirement was triggered either by an event (e.g., a train accident in *Skinner*) or by a voluntary act to engage in a particular activity or apply for a particular job. However, subsequent lower court decisions have permitted suspicionless testing in a wide variety of circumstances.

A fundamental postulate, long thought essential to the survival of individual freedom in America, is that we are guaranteed a government of laws administered according to neutral principles rather than a government of men and women operating according to their personal predilections. The essence of the Fourth Amendment's textually based probable cause standard is objective evidence of individualized suspicion of wrongdoing. The determination that there is probable cause to believe that the person or place to be searched is connected to criminal activity is what makes the search reasonable. The Court, however, has gradually replaced this cornerstone of Fourth Amendment protection by substituting for that objective, neutral principle a subjective balancing test. In weighing the needs of the state against the rights of the individual on the mythical scales of the balancing test, however, the courts necessarily must base their determination of reasonableness on subjective value judgments, which may vary depending on personal beliefs and biases. Thus the Fourth Amendment has increasingly been transformed from a rule of law into a rule of subjective opinion. Amid demands for a more vigorous war on drugs and crime in the latter decades of the twentieth century, it is not surprising that this balancing process resulted in increasing governmental control and diminishing individual liberty and privacy.

The Court's most direct assault on privacy, however, was its redefinition during the 1980s of the Fourth Amendment's operative term *search*. Under traditional analysis, a physical trespass always constituted a search. In the late 1960s, the Warren Court was confronted with the government's use of new electronic surveillance techniques that did not involve a trespass. In *Katz v. United States* (1967),[19] the Warren Court held that a person making a telephone call from a public pay phone booth nevertheless had a "reasonable expectation of privacy" protected by the Fourth Amendment. Under the Rehnquist Court, a "reasonable expectation of privacy" became a divining rod for determining what constituted a search.

The "reasonable expectation of privacy" test, however, is a two-edged sword. Under that test, if the Court is of the opinion that a citizen's expectation of privacy is not "reasonable," then police conduct invading that claimed zone of privacy does not constitute a "search." If no "search" occurs, then the Fourth Amendment does not apply and the protections against arbitrary invasions of privacy afforded by the warrant and probable cause requirements are not available. What constitutes a "reasonable" expectation of privacy can also be influenced by a judge's subjective value judgments. In the 1980s, the Rehnquist Court held that even where police illegally trespassed upon a farmer's land to see what was otherwise secluded from public view, there was no Fourth Amendment violation because, in the Court's judgment, a person had no reasonable expectation of privacy regarding activities that occurred in an open field adjacent to his home. The Court also found privacy expectations were not reasonable if a person had exposed an area, object, or information to a third party. Under this third-party doctrine, the Supreme Court ruled that the police may rummage through our garbage; view fenced-in backyards from the air to see what could not be observed from the street; place radio transmitters on cars to follow our public movements; keep track of whom we correspond with, monitor the number of people we talk to on the telephone; and even look at our checks, deposit slips, and bank statements— all without a warrant, probable cause, or even reasonable suspicion. While such police practices may be regulated by Congress or a state legislature to protect privacy, they remained during this period unchecked by any constitutional restraint, because the Court had determined that any expectation of privacy a person might have in such matters was not "reasonable." Therefore, these police intrusions were not searches to which Fourth Amendment protection applied. Ironically, while the Warren Court originally created the "reasonable expectation of privacy" test to expand the scope of Fourth Amendment protection, in the hands of the Rehnquist Court, this test for defining a search became a vehicle for doing precisely the opposite.

The cramped conception of privacy underlying the third-party doctrine is profoundly misguided. As Professor Laurence Tribe so eloquently explained: "Privacy also encompasses decisions about what to share, whom to share it with and when and how to share it. [Because] creation of our own identities is impossible without a measure of privacy . . . the right to shape our identity [through selective control over personal information] is thus nothing less than the right to control the course of our lives."[20] Justice William J. Brennan repeatedly warned of the dangers of the Rehnquist Court's trend toward diminishing individual privacy. Recognizing that privacy is always an endangered freedom that must be vigilantly protected from the passions of the moment, he explained: "The needs of law enforcement stand in constant tension with the Constitution's protections of the individual. . . . It is precisely the predictability of these pressures that counsels a resolute loyalty to constitutional safeguards."[21]

That police can abuse their powers under the lax constraints afforded by the third-party doctrine is highlighted by a report that police officers took aerial reconnaissance photographs of a television news commentator's home and placed him under continual surveillance for several weeks following his on-air criticism of the local police chief.[22] The danger of such abuses is magnified, moreover, if such relaxed controls extend to the government's use of high-tech surveillance equipment. These innovations run the gamut from miniaturized radio transmitters to parabolic microphones, infrared radiation sensors, and novel use of laser technology—which, by bouncing a laser beam off a closed window, enables police to eavesdrop on a conversation inside a home by means of digital transformation of the windowpane vibrations. The Supreme Court has not had occasion to specifically address this use of laser beam technology, but in *Kyllo v. United States* (2001),[23] it ruled that the use of a thermo-imaging device to measure heat radiating from a home that used artificial light to grow marijuana was a search governed by the warrant and probable cause requirements. Key to the Court's ruling was its finding that people have a reasonable expectation of privacy regarding any detail concerning the interior of their home that could not be otherwise obtained without physical intrusion.[24] While the interior of the home was thus safe from invasive sense-enhancing technology, the threat to privacy created by the third-party doctrine nevertheless remained regarding public movements and anything exposed to public view or third parties. With the enhanced surveillance capability of GPS tracking devices and the advent of the cell phone, which leaves a digital record of a phone user's movements and contains a wealth of personal information, the Court was forced to reconsider the consequences of its earlier privacy decisions.

## PRIVACY REDUX

The Court began restructuring protection for privacy by resurrecting the traditional trespass test for a search and giving it equal status with the reasonable expectation of privacy test. In *United States v. Jones* (2012),[25] the Court held that the attachment by police of a GPS tracking device to the undercarriage of a vehicle and recording public movements linking the owner to a crime was a search because the installation of the GPS constituted a trespass on a protected area. Jones's vehicle was part of his effects protected by the Fourth Amendment's guarantee of an individual's right "to be secure in their persons, houses, papers and effects."[26]

The Court also recalibrated the reasonable expectation of privacy test. In *Carpenter v. U.S.* (2018),[27] the Court held that cell phone users have a "legitimate expectation of privacy" in their service provider's business records that contain tracking data. Known as cell-site location information, this data is generated even when a cell phone is not in use, because a signal is routinely sent out searching to connect with the nearest cell tower so a future call can be received. Chief Justice Roberts, writing for the majority in the 5–4 decision, stressed that these records capture a detailed and comprehensive record of the user's past physical movements that can reveal a wealth of personal information, including a person's social, political, religious, and sexual associations. As Justice Sonia Sotomayor had observed in her concurring opinion in *Jones*, such intrusive government surveillance "chills associational and expressive freedoms . . . and . . . unrestrained . . . is susceptible to abuse [that] may 'alter the relationship between citizen and government in a way that is inimical to democratic society.'"[28] *Carpenter* held that when government accesses third-party records containing location tracking data, even when authorized by statute, it constitutes a search that requires a warrant based on probable cause.

Recognizing the extensive invasion of privacy that would be permitted if police could have unfettered access to information contained inside a cell phone, the Court also ruled in *Riley v. California*[29] that, absent exigent circumstances, a warrant based on probable cause was required to access any electronic data in a cell phone, including phone numbers in the cell phone's call log. This bright-line rule applied, moreover, even though the well-established "search incident to arrest" exception to the warrant requirement otherwise permitted warrantless searches of items, such as a wallet, found on a person who had been arrested and taken into custody.

These decisions have shown the Court has awakened to the consequences of the third-party doctrine and the failure of its precedents to protect individual privacy in this new age of technological advances. However, at the same time, the

Court has continued to use, as the touchstone of Fourth Amendment analysis, a freestanding conception of reasonableness that is determined by the balancing test, and thus does not have to be tethered to any objective requirement of individualized justification, whether in the form of probable cause or reasonable suspicion. An example is seen in *Hein v. North Carolina* (2015),[30] where police stopped a motorist for driving with only one working brake light, even though state law required just a single working tail light. This would seem to be the quintessential unreasonable seizure. However, the Court ruled, with only one dissent, that the Fourth Amendment was not violated by the unjustified stop, because the officer, in the Court's view, made a reasonable mistake in misinterpreting the traffic code. According to the Court, so long as the officer made a reasonable mistake of law, he acted reasonably, and that is all the Fourth Amendment requires. The Court did not explain why the common-law maxim, "ignorance of the law is no excuse," which applies to citizens, does not also apply to government officials— especially police officers whose duty is to know and enforce the law. *Hein*, moreover, sets a dangerous precedent. As a practical matter, it allows a police officer's mistaken interpretation of the scope of an ambiguous law to determine whether the Fourth Amendment was violated. The determination of the scope of constitutional protections should not be left in the hands of mistaken nonjudicial actors, no matter how reasonable their mistake. Rather, as Justice Sotomayor explained in dissent, the law as judicially interpreted should be the backdrop against which the reasonableness inquiry is conducted.

### THE EXCLUSIONARY RULE: THE PRICE OF LIBERTY AND PRIVACY

Supreme Court decisions have eroded not only the scope of Fourth Amendment protection but also the mechanism for enforcing the amendment: the exclusionary rule. When police discover physical evidence of guilt as a result of a search or seizure that violates the defendant's Fourth Amendment rights, the exclusionary rule prohibits the government from using that evidence in court to convict her.

The Supreme Court first ruled that evidence obtained in violation of the Fourth Amendment was inadmissible in a federal court in 1886. In that case, the Court declared that the admission of illegally obtained records into evidence by the trial court had rendered the trial an unconstitutional proceeding that was therefore void.[31] As refined by the Supreme Court in subsequent federal criminal cases, the exclusionary rule initially rested on the duty of the federal courts to give force and effect to the human rights provisions of the Constitution. Reaffirming the Fourth Amendment exclusionary rule in 1913, the justices declared: "If letters and private documents can be seized [illegally] and used in evidence against a citizen accused of an offense, the protection of the Fourth Amendment . . . is of no value, and . . . might as well be stricken from the Constitution. The efforts of the courts and their officials to bring the guilty to punishment, praiseworthy as they are, are not to be aided by the sacrifice of those great principles established by years of endeavor and suffering which have resulted in their embodiment in the fundamental law of the land."[32]

The application of the exclusionary rule to state criminal proceedings, however, was complicated by the fact that the Bill of Rights initially applied only to the federal government. Even after the Supreme Court held that the due process clause prohibited the states from engaging in unreasonable searches and seizures, it at first declined to require the adoption of the exclusionary rule, leaving the states to experiment with other enforcement mechanisms. Such alternatives never materialized. As the chief justice of the California Supreme Court commented in explaining why that court reluctantly changed its position and adopted the exclusionary rule as a matter of state law: "My misgivings . . . grew as I observed . . . a steady course of illegal police procedures that deliberately and flagrantly violated the Constitution. . . . [I]t had become all too obvious that unconstitutional police methods of obtaining evidence were not being deterred."[33] In 1961, after half of the states had adopted the exclusionary rule on their own, the US Supreme Court made it a uniform requirement, as a matter of federal constitutional law, declaring: "[The rule] gives to the individual no more than that which the Constitution guarantees him, to the police officer no less than that to which honest law enforcement is entitled, and, to the court, that judicial integrity so necessary in the true administration of justice."[34]

The exclusionary rule has become the subject of heated controversy, largely because of the popular perception that it unleashes guilty criminals back into society. Exaggerated claims that the exclusionary rule increases the crime rate, however, have not been borne out by statistical studies. Indeed, a comprehensive investigation of the costs of the rule in 1987 revealed that only 1.77 percent of all cases are lost due to its operation. This is because it is infrequently invoked, and even when evidence is excluded, conviction can still be obtained using other evidence that is untainted by constitutional violation. Moreover, examination of the cases lost due to the rule revealed that over 85 percent were not crimes of violence but rather minor drug offenses, such as possession of marijuana, which, while still illegal at that time, were not likely to result in incarceration. Thus, the vast majority of the defendants who go free as a result of the exclusionary rule are not likely to have been imprisoned in any event, even if convicted.[35] Nevertheless, the exclusionary rule has remained a favorite target of politicians. It is especially vulnerable to such attacks because it is a creature of judicial rulemaking, which lacks roots in the express language of the Fourth Amendment.

Today, as a result of judicial modifications, the exclusionary rule has become riddled with exceptions. For example, it does not bar illegally obtained evidence from grand jury proceedings, nor does it apply in deportation cases or other civil proceedings. By far the biggest limitation on the exclusionary rule has been the good-faith exception established in 1984. This retrenchment holds that so long as a police officer reasonably relied on the validity of a search warrant, evidence obtained pursuant to that warrant will not be suppressed, even if the warrant was not based on probable cause. The good-faith exception has also been extended to seizures made in good-faith reliance on a negligently maintained police database that erroneously showed an outstanding arrest warrant for the defendant.

The Roberts Court's assault on the exclusionary rule has been unrelenting. In 2016, the Court refused to exclude evidence obtained as a result of an unlawful stop of a pedestrian without any individualized reasonable suspicion of wrong-doing because of the fortuitous discovery after the stop of an outstanding arrest warrant that otherwise justified the arrest. Because the Court found that the officer was investigating an anonymous tip in good faith, it ruled that the existence of the valid outstanding arrest warrant attenuated the taint of the unlawful stop. Thus, evidence obtained during a search incident to the arrest on that warrant was ruled admissible.

As is readily apparent from these exceptions, the exclusionary rule is no longer based on conceptions of judicial duty and integrity. Indeed, in good-faith exception cases, the judiciary itself has violated a citizen's rights by issuing a warrant without probable cause. Instead of resting on a principled basis, the rule now has a strictly utilitarian rationale: the deterrence of illegal conduct by law enforcement. Under this approach, the Supreme Court engages in a cost-benefit analysis to determine when the exclusionary rule should apply. Thus, in the case creating the good-faith exception, the Court reasoned that the cost of losing relevant evidence outweighed any benefit, because no deterrent purpose would be served by punishing the police for a judge's mistake in issuing a defective warrant. The airtight logic of this position is unassailable if deterrence of police misconduct is the sole objective of the exclusionary rule. However, this rationale does not satisfactorily explain how a judgment of conviction, imposed by the judicial branch, can be constitutionally valid if it rests on evidence obtained as a result of a violation of the Constitution by one of its own members.

A further anomaly posed by the good-faith exception arises from the fact that the right to be secure in one's home unless a search warrant is issued upon probable cause—the core value protected by the Fourth Amendment—would now seem to be a right without a remedy. Do effective alternatives to the exclusionary rule exist? Three have been suggested: civil suits for monetary compensation; disciplinary action against offending officers; and, in egregious cases, criminal prosecution.

A report by the Department of Justice, however, confirms what other studies have repeatedly shown: the failure of these alternatives either to compensate victims adequately or to serve as an effective deterrent. According to the report, while twelve thousand civil actions were filed against federal law enforcement officers from 1971 to 1986, only five plaintiffs actually received an award of damages. Turning to internal discipline for Fourth Amendment violations, the report noted that the Department of Justice itself had conducted only seven investigations of its own agents since 1981 and had imposed no sanctions. Finding a similar dearth of criminal prosecutions, it characterized this alternative as "ill advised."[36] Another possible alternative is independent police review boards, which can be (and have been) established to investigate violations. In practice, however, the police have vigorously opposed any meaningful review by such outsiders, and the political will has been lacking to give such boards adequate investigative powers or to permit them to impose sanctions directly on offending officers.

Despite the demonstrated shortcomings of the various alternatives, the Department of Justice report recommended that the exclusionary rule be abolished and an improved civil remedy established as a deterrent. The major premise underlying its recommendations was that the exclusionary rule, by depriving a court of evidence relevant to a defendant's guilt, interferes with the truth-seeking function of the criminal justice process. Advocates of the exclusionary rule have pointed out, however, that if a fully effective alternative existed, it would cause the same interference that the rule itself does. This is because a fully effective deterrent, by "mak[ing] the police obey the commands of the Fourth Amendment *in advance*," would prevent them from ever obtaining the evidence in the first place.[37]

If the police always obeyed the Fourth Amendment, of course, the cost of the exclusionary rule would not be apparent. The problem with the exclusionary rule is that by removing the visible benefits of a violation of the Constitution, it forces us to come face-to-face with the price society must pay to preserve individual liberty and privacy. There are many who think that price is too high. As Daniel Webster admonished, however, "The first object of a free people is the preservation of their liberty. The spirit of liberty . . . demands checks; it seeks guards . . . it insists on securities. . . . This is the nature of constitutional liberty, and this is our liberty, if we will rightly understand and preserve it."[38]

## POLICE USE OF DEADLY FORCE

Sadly, the United States' shameful history of racial discrimination, lynching, and unpunished domestic terrorism by the Ku Klux Klan has been accompanied by a similar lack of accountability regarding the excessive use of force by law enforcement against people of color.[39] Law enforcement involvement in the murders of civil rights advocates Michael Schwerner, James Chaney, and

Andrew Goodman in 1964 and the televised images of mounted deputies and state police beating peaceful Black civil rights demonstrators at the Edmond Pettis Bridge in Selma, Alabama, in 1965, reflect the persistent vestiges of that lawless era of the early twentieth century. While the civil rights movement inspired by Reverend Martin Luther King Jr. made great progress, the beating of Rodney King by Los Angeles police officers in 1991 signaled that traces from this dark past unfortunately still lingered.[40]

More recently, the racially discriminatory police practices documented by the US Department of Justice in Ferguson, Missouri, and the deaths at the hands of police of Eric Garner in New York City in 2014, Walter Scott in North Charleston, South Carolina, in 2015, Breonna Taylor in Louisville, Kentucky, and George Floyd in Minneapolis, Minnesota, both in 2020, further highlighted the issue of excessive use of deadly force against Black citizens and intensified the Black Lives Matter movement.

The public outcry over the death of Black teenager Michael Brown by a Ferguson police officer prompted an investigation by the US Department of Justice, which found the Ferguson Police Department had engaged in a pattern of unconstitutional stops and arrests, accompanied by a pattern of excessive force that violated the Fourth Amendment. The investigation also concluded that these unconstitutional practices disproportionately impacted African American residents of Ferguson and were motivated in part by racial bias.[41] A separate Justice Department investigation found, however, that the officer did not have the requisite criminal intent required to be charged with a federal crime because he perceived that Brown presented a deadly threat.[42]

Eric Garner died as a result of the use of an illegal choke hold, banned by the New York City Police Department, during his arrest in 2014 for the minor offense of selling untaxed cigarettes. A Staten Island grand jury refused to indict the White officer, and federal prosecutors also declined to bring civil rights charges in 2018. The officer was fired after administrative proceedings in 2019.[43] Following a traffic stop for a defective brake light, Walter Scott fled on foot unarmed and was shot in the back by Officer Slager. After a state prosecution for murder in South Carolina resulted in a hung jury, Slager pled guilty to federal civil rights charges under a deal in which state murder charges were dropped. He was sentenced to twenty years in prison.[44]

In a hail of bullets, Breonna Taylor, an emergency medical technician, was killed just after midnight in her home during the execution of a no-knock search warrant. While three of the officers involved were fired, more than a year later no officer had been held responsible for her death.[45]

Just over two months after Breonna Taylor's wrongful death, the nation's conscience was galvanized by the callous murder of George Floyd on May 25, 2020.

Floyd died after being handcuffed and pinned to the ground, face down, by three Minneapolis police officers. A bystander's video captured officer Derek Chauvin's refusal to heed warnings from onlookers that Floyd had stopped breathing as the veteran officer kept his knee on Floyd's neck for over eight minutes. In a nationally televised trial, Chauvin was convicted of second-degree murder and sentenced to twenty-two and a half years in prison.

These examples of the unjustified use of deadly force against persons of color, from Rodney King to George Floyd, represent just the tip of an iceberg. The inability, for nearly three decades, to eradicate this pattern of unconstitutional police misconduct is systemic and due, to a significant extent, to the failure to hold police accountable for such abuses. One of the contributing factors to that failure of accountability is the legal standard the Supreme Court has employed to determine when an officer is liable for the unconstitutional use of excessive force.

### SUPREME COURT PRECEDENT ON USE OF EXCESSIVE FORCE

Almost two years before the beating of Rodney King, the Supreme Court ruled in *Graham v. Connor* that claims that police had unconstitutionally used excessive force in making an arrest were to be assessed under the Fourth Amendment's reasonableness standard rather than a due process standard.[46] The Court acknowledged that an arrest or seizure, even if justified by probable cause, was not reasonable if the manner in which the seizure was made was unreasonable. Reasonableness, however, is a flexible concept, and the analytical framework established by *Connor* has resulted in significantly restricting judicial enforcement of the right to be free from such unconstitutional seizures.

Conceding that reasonableness is not capable of precise definition, the Court in *Connor* first cautioned that in assessing claims of excessive force, courts must view "the totality of circumstances" from "the perspective of a reasonable officer on the scene, rather than with the 20/20 vision of hindsight." The *Connor* ruling further emphasized that courts must make allowance for the fact that officers often must make split-second judgments about the amount of force necessary in "tense, uncertain and rapidly evolving" circumstances.[47] This special lens for viewing the use of alleged excessive force favors the officer even when deadly force is employed.

While the test is supposed to be one of objective reasonableness determined by a careful balancing that weighs the extent of the intrusion on Fourth Amendment rights against the countervailing governmental interests at stake, a review of the Supreme Court's recent civil rights decisions reveals that, after *Connor*, the scales in fact are tipped in favor of finding that the use of deadly force is reasonable.

For example, prior to *Connor*, the Court had ruled in *Tennessee v. Garner* (1985) that it was not reasonable to use deadly force to prevent the escape of an unarmed fleeing felon.[48] Although the common law had permitted using deadly force, if necessary, to apprehend any fleeing felon, the Court held that the Fourth Amendment did not, because in balancing the interests at stake, it was "not better that all felony suspects die than that they escape."[49] The Court declared that deadly force was reasonable only when a felon was dangerous, either because he threatened the officer with a weapon or "there was probable cause to believe that he had committed a crime involving the infliction or threatened infliction of serious physical harm."[50]

After *Connor*, however, the Court found in *Scott v. Harris* (2007) that it was reasonable for police to deliberately ram the car of a minor traffic violator after a police pursuit at speeds reaching ninety miles per hour. The car overturned and the teenage driver was rendered a quadriplegic. Although the teenager's initial traffic offense was not a felony, the Court concluded that his reckless high-speed escape constituted an "extreme danger" to public safety, which justified the action taken to end the chase.[51] Using the same reasoning in *Plumhoff v. Rickard* (2014), the Court again found that the Fourth Amendment was not violated by police who, after a high-speed chase, fired fifteen shots into a car at close range after it had spun out, come to a stop, and then began pulling away. Both driver and passenger were killed. The driver's only offence before the pursuit had been a minor traffic infraction.[52] Following these decisions, police nationwide, between 2015 and 2017, killed 193 people in moving vehicles, including a fifteen-year-old boy.[53]

Even where a Fourth Amendment violation is found, the Court has made it extremely difficult to obtain redress and deter future violations under 42 U.S.C. § 1983, which provides a federal statutory remedy for the deprivation of constitutional rights. A recent survey, covering nine years of 42 U.S.C. § 1983 civil rights decisions involving any type of Fourth Amendment violation, found that the Supreme Court sided with the defendant/government 80 percent of the time.[54] In addition to restricting standing to bring such actions, the Court has protected police officers from such civil rights litigation by creating the doctrine of qualified immunity. This doctrine requires pretrial dismissal of a civil rights lawsuit unless the constitutional right allegedly violated has been clearly established by prior judicial precedent. The Court has further declared that to be clearly established, there must be a judicial precedent that covers the particularized conduct at issue, so that a reasonable officer would know that his conduct "was unlawful in the situation he or she confronted."[55] Neither the doctrine of qualified immunity nor the clearly established right requirement can be found in the text of 42 U.S.C. § 1983. These restrictions are the result of judicial gloss imposed by the Supreme Court on the remedial statute to reduce its scope.

The Supreme Court has, moreover, used the qualified immunity doctrine to cripple the development of precedent that could clarify the law on the use of deadly force. Reversing prior precedent that required, as a threshold matter, the merits of the claim to be addressed first to determine whether there was a constitutional violation, the Supreme Court subsequently ruled that this was not mandatory. Instead, the Court said in *Pearson v. Callahan* (2009) that lower courts should have the discretion to determine the qualified immunity issue first and grant summary judgment for the defendant officer if the claimed right at issue was not clearly established at the time of the alleged misconduct.[56] This creates a catch-22 situation, especially when the Supreme Court declines to address the merits of a claim that has frequently occurred. By not ruling on the merits and clearly establishing that the use of deadly force was either reasonable or unreasonable in a particular factual context, lower courts are left without clear guidance regarding its use in those circumstances. The issue thus remains unresolved the next time it arises, and the cycle is repeated. This lack of clarity also complicates efforts by police departments to conduct proper training on the use of deadly force.

Justice Samuel Alito, writing for a unanimous Court in *Pearson v. Callahan*, asserted that the development of constitutional law would not be thwarted by declining to address the merits of a 42 U.S.C. § 1983 claim, because constitutional issues can be raised in other contexts where qualified immunity does not apply—for example, criminal cases, civil rights cases against a municipality, and cases seeking to enjoin future unconstitutional conduct. However, significant barriers exist to raising constitutional issues in those contexts. Criminal charges are rarely brought and are even less successful because it must be proven beyond a reasonable doubt that the defendant acted willfully. As the report by the US Department of Justice's investigation into the shooting death of Michael Brown in Ferguson explained: "Even if federal prosecutors determined there were sufficient evidence to convince twelve jurors beyond a reasonable doubt that Wilson used unreasonable force, federal law requires that the government must also prove that the officer acted willfully, that is, with the purpose to violate the law."[57] Civil rights cases against a municipality are also difficult because they require proof that there was either an official policy or a pattern and practice of conduct that was unconstitutional, and lawsuits seeking an injunction generally require a showing of future irreparable harm.

Three recent decisions demonstrate the sweeping grant of immunity the Court has given police under the qualified immunity doctrine. In 2015, the Court ruled in *San Francisco v. Sheehan* (2015) that police officers were immune from Section 1983 liability for shooting an unstable resident of a group home for the mentally disabled. Sheehan had threatened to kill a social worker and refused to open the locked door to her private room when two officers came to take her into custody for transport to a mental facility. Instead of following their training and official police policy that required them to de-escalate the situation and wait for a trained negotiator, the officers broke down the door. After pepper spray failed to subdue

Sheehan, the officers shot her multiple times when she came toward them with a kitchen knife. The Court found the use of deadly force in self-defense was reasonable and ruled that even if the officers' conduct in violently breaking into Sheehan's private room, which provoked the need to use deadly force, was contrary to their training and "imprudent, inappropriate or even reckless," nevertheless no precedent clearly established that the officers had to accommodate Sheehan's mental illness. The Court concluded: "Because the qualified immunity analysis is straightforward, we need not decide whether the Constitution was violated by the officers' failure to accommodate Sheehan's illness."[58]

In *Kinsela v. Hughes* (2018), the Court again failed to clarify how police should deal with someone who appears to be mentally ill. The case involved three officers who responded to a 911 call that an erratic woman was hacking a tree with a knife. The officers arrived to see Hughes standing in her front yard, which was surrounded by a chain-link fence. Hughes was holding a knife at her side, calmly talking with her roommate, who was standing six feet away. The officers were separated from the pair by the chain-link fence. Although the roommate told the officers to "take it easy," they repeatedly ordered Hughes to drop the knife. When she did not respond or seem to even acknowledge their presence, Officer Kinsela, without giving any warning, shot Hughes four times through the fence. Hughes had committed no crime, had not threatened anyone, did not appear angry, and had not raised the knife or approached her roommate at the time she was shot. The Court nevertheless ruled that no clearly established precedent made the shooting unreasonable and granted qualified immunity.[59]

Finally, in *Mullenix v. Luna* (2015), the Court summarily reversed, without full briefing or oral argument, the decisions of both the trial and appellate courts that had denied qualified immunity to a Texas state trooper who, without authorization and after being ordered to stand by, fired his rifle six times from an overpass into an approaching car. The driver, who was a misdemeanor offender being pursued by police, was killed. The officer said he aimed at the engine block to stop the car, although he had no training or experience in such a tactic, which apparently had never been tried. Spike strips that had been previously set up under the overpass appeared to have been sufficient to stop the car, and the trooper's supervisor had in fact told him to wait to see if they worked. Despite the officer's disregard for the chain of command, the Court found no precedent clearly established that this conduct was unconstitutional under the circumstances. Although the driver had no gun, he had apparently called police during the chase and had threatened to shoot the pursuing officers if they stopped him. The Court emphasized that clearly established law cannot be defined "at a high level of generality" using a "broad general proposition." Rather, the Court declared, the dispositive question is whether the particular conduct in light of the specific context of the case has been clearly established as unconstitutional by prior precedent.[60]

The result of these qualified immunity decisions has been to expand the zone of what is considered reasonable use of deadly force. Once deadly force was permissible only when necessary to prevent imminent serious physical harm. Today, however, because of the lack of clarity produced by qualified immunity decisions that simply rest on the fact that there is no clearly established authority, the concepts of necessity and imminence appear to have been distorted out of all sense of proportion. If there is merely a perceived risk of serious physical harm (e.g., the chance of an automobile accident occurring as a result of reckless driving), then the message sent by current Supreme Court decisions is that because no clearly established precedent holds otherwise, police can use force having a high probability of death (e.g., firing fifteen shots into a car at close range) to end the unquantified risk to public safety. The result is tacit approval for using deadly force despite a lack of proportionality between the risk of harm sought to be avoided and the amount of force used by police.

Because police shootings have given rise to a political movement championed by Black Lives Matter, some states have addressed the issue through statutory reforms. California, for example, recently enacted legislation that limits the circumstances in which deadly force can be employed. Assembly Bill 392, enacted in 2019, not only requires that the officer reasonably believe such force is necessary to defend against an imminent threat, but imminence is further defined and limited to circumstances in which a reasonable officer would believe the person against whom deadly force is used "has the present ability, opportunity, and apparent intent to immediately cause death or serious bodily injury to the peace officer or another person."[61] By requiring that it must appear to a reasonable officer that the person intends to cause death or serious bodily injury, this legislation restores a sense of proportionality between the force threatened and the forced used. AB 392 also links the assessment of both necessity and imminence with the immediate need for the action taken, declaring: "An imminent harm is not merely a fear of future harm, no matter how great the fear and no matter how great the likelihood of the harm, but is one that, from appearances, must be instantly confronted and addressed." Under this legislated standard, it is likely that many of the Supreme Court's recent decisions on the use of deadly force, and especially those involving fleeing traffic offenders, would be resolved differently.

In the wake of nationwide protests over the death of George Floyd, the US House of Representatives, on March 3, 2021, passed HR 1280, known as the George Floyd Justice in Policing Act of 2021, which at the time of this writing is pending in the Senate. The House version would, among other things, reform qualified immunity and make it easier to prosecute cases under 18 U.S.C. §242 (which makes the deprivation of civil rights under color of law a federal crime) by lowering the mens rea (intent) requirement from "willfully" to "knowingly or with reckless disregard." HR 1280 further prohibits federal officers from using choke holds and other neck restraint and bans no-knock warrants in drug cases. It also gives incentives to state and local governments to adopt these same policies.

### THE FIFTH AMENDMENT

Hailed as one of the great landmarks in humanity's struggle to make itself civilized, the privilege against self-incrimination reflects, more than any other aspect of criminal procedure, the moral relationship between the state and the individual. Under Talmudic law, which reflected the ancient oral teaching handed down from the time of Moses, confessions were normally not admissible against an accused in a criminal proceeding, even though voluntarily given. The Bible also records that the apostle Paul exercised a status-based privilege under Roman law that protected citizens against compulsory self-incrimination. After arresting him following a riot in Jerusalem, the authorities ordered the apostle whipped until he confessed. Paul, however, asserted his right as a Roman citizen not to be subjected to interrogation by torture and was later released unharmed.[62]

During the Middle Ages, European systems of criminal justice came to rely heavily on confessions for evidence of guilt and regularly used torture to obtain them. While there are examples of torture in English history, this interrogation technique never became an established part of British criminal justice. This is because by the twelfth century, England had developed an accusatorial rather than inquisitorial system of justice. Apparently to protect citizens from unnecessarily having to endure trial by ordeal or trial by battle because of unjustified allegations, the English adopted the principle that proceedings against a person suspected of crime might be commenced only by a formal complaint, made under oath, or by an indictment issued by an accusing jury (the forerunner of our grand jury). After the abolition of trial by ordeal, the use of the oath played a more prominent role in the resolution of guilt or innocence. Once a proper charge had been laid, the defendant was required to answer the charge under oath. Defendants who denied the charge could also be interrogated under oath. Being questioned under an oath to tell the truth before God created a soul-threatening dilemma for the devout Christian. Assuming that a truthful answer would be incriminating, a defendant had the unhappy choice of either telling the truth and suffering immediate temporal punishment or committing perjury, a sin, and suffering eternal damnation. A defendant who refused to plead to the charge under oath could be imprisoned indefinitely.

In its earliest stages, the "privilege" against self-incrimination only shielded the suspect from having to answer an allegation until it was substantiated by a formal charge supported by oath or indictment. When the flames of religious persecution engulfed England in the late sixteenth and early seventeenth centuries, even this limited privilege fell into total eclipse. Both the Court of High

Commission, created by Queen Elizabeth to enforce religious conformity, and the infamous Court of Star Chamber attempted to root out heretics and dissenters by inquisitorial practices. Suspected nonconformists were compelled to take the soul-threatening oath and interrogated at length without benefit of formal charges. In reaction to such abuses of royal power, the privilege against self-incrimination reasserted itself and entered a second stage of development, emerging as the right to be free from compelled self-incrimination. During this stage, the practice of judicially interrogating the accused at trial was abolished and the right to remain silent established as a principle of justice. Englishmen, and, somewhat later, English colonists, viewed the right and accusatorial procedure as essential to protect the individual's right of self-determination. After independence, every one of the eight states that annexed a bill of rights to its new constitution included some form of protection against self-incrimination.

Subsequently, Americans crystallized this principle of justice in the Fifth Amendment's brief and picturesque expression that no person "shall be compelled . . . to be a witness against himself." While these words seem at first glance to prohibit only the use of torture, it was the compulsion created by the use of the oath, not torture, that gave rise to the privilege against self-incrimination in its present form. Early interpretation of the Fifth Amendment by the US Supreme Court followed the English common law in holding that the slightest degree of influence exerted upon an accused to speak gave rise to a presumption of compulsion, rendering the confession inadmissible. Under the pressures of the Prohibition era of the 1920s, however, the Court limited the scope of the amendment's protection by employing a trustworthiness rationale in deciding confession cases. During this period, the privilege yielded to the perceived necessities of law enforcement to such an extent that incriminating statements became admissible unless the methods used to extract them were so harsh that they created a danger that the confession was false. Under this rationale, lengthy, around-the-clock interrogation sessions, featuring relay teams of officers, psychological coercion, and other third-degree tactics (including even minor physical abuse, such as a kick in the shins) became permissible.

Concerned with the abuses that had developed under such a lax standard, the Supreme Court began to tighten restrictions on federal law enforcement in the 1940s by mandating that a confession was inadmissible if it had been obtained during a period of unnecessary delay in bringing the defendant before a magistrate following arrest. Confronted with a 1908 precedent holding that the Fifth Amendment did not apply to the states, the Court initially turned to the due process clause of the Fourteenth Amendment to ensure that state interrogation practices produced only voluntary confessions. In a series of twenty-nine confession cases decided between 1936 and 1964, the Court progressively refined the meaning of due process voluntariness until not only physical force but also certain forms of psychological coercion were forbidden in the backrooms of police stations. The problem with this approach was that it involved an Alice-in-Wonderland journey into the metaphysical realm of the human will. If a confession was the product of free choice, it was voluntary and therefore admissible. If, on the other hand, the suspect's will had been broken by psychological pressure, then due process was violated and the involuntary confession was inadmissible. Because voluntariness varied with the ability of the suspect to withstand pressure, this ad hoc approach to constitutional adjudication failed to provide clear guidance to the police as to which practices were acceptable and made judicial review a morass of subjectivity.

Therefore, in 1964, the Court applied the Fifth Amendment directly to the states and also held, in *Escobedo v. Illinois*,[63] that a suspect had the right to have the assistance of counsel during custodial interrogation. The Court acknowledged that extending the right to counsel from the courtroom to the police interrogation room would diminish significantly the number of confessions obtained but concluded: "If the exercise of constitutional rights will thwart the effectiveness of a system of law enforcement, then there is something very wrong with that system. . . . We have learned the lesson of history, ancient and modern, that a system of criminal law enforcement which comes to depend on the 'confession' will in the long run, be less reliable and more subject to abuses than a system which depends on extrinsic evidence independently secured through skillful investigation."[64]

The *Escobedo* decision provoked an immediate outcry in law enforcement circles. It was feared that if defense lawyers invaded the inner sanctum of the police precinct, the confession would soon become a thing of the past. Confronted by this storm of controversy, the Court retreated from the path it had taken and struck a compromise in the now famous case of *Miranda v. Arizona*.[65] This compromise permitted the police to obtain uncounseled waivers of both the right to have counsel's advice and the right to be free from the compulsion created by custodial interrogation. To provide a mechanism for obtaining valid waivers, the Court created the so-called *Miranda* warnings. This procedural protocol required the police to advise suspects, prior to custodial interrogation, that they have a right to remain silent, that any statement they make can be used in evidence against them, and that they have the right to an attorney's advice before and during questioning, without charge if they are indigent.

*Miranda* held that no statement given by an accused during custodial interrogation is admissible as evidence against the accused if the police failed to give these required warnings. Like *Escobedo*, *Miranda* was also decried by doomsayers who feared that giving warnings would preclude the ability to obtain confessions.

Within six years of this landmark ruling, President Richard Nixon realigned the Court through the appointment of four new justices. One of these appointees was William Hubbs Rehnquist, who, while still an assistant attorney general for the Office of Legal Counsel, had written a memorandum in 1969 to his superior, John Dean (then an associate deputy attorney general), complaining about *Miranda*, the exclusionary rule, and the lack of finality of criminal convictions due to continued litigation permitted by federal habeas corpus.[66] The Nixon appointees, joined by two justices who had dissented in *Miranda*, formed the core of a new majority on the Court that that viewed the *Miranda* warnings not as constitutional rights but as mere judge-made prophylactic rules designed to deter police abuse.

As a result of this reorientation, the Court began making exceptions to the *Miranda* exclusionary rule. Balancing the need to deter perjury by defendants against the need to deter abusive police interrogations, the Court ruled in *Harris v. New York* (1971) that admissions obtained in violation of *Miranda* could be used for the limited purpose of impeachment, to contradict defendants who took the stand at their trials and told a story inconsistent with their prior unwarned statements. Similarly, in *New York v. Quarrels* (1984), the Court created a public safety exception to the *Miranda* rules, reasoning that the need briefly to interrogate an arrested suspect to locate weapons outweighed the value of giving warnings. In *United States v. Patane* (2004), the Court further limited the *Miranda* exclusionary rule to verbal statements, ruling that physical evidence, discovered as the fruit of admissions made in response to custodial interrogation without *Miranda* warnings, was nevertheless admissible.

The Court also limited the scope of the *Miranda* rule by redefining the meaning of custodial interrogation—the event that triggers the *Miranda* warnings. In *Berkemer v. McCarty* (1984), for example, the Court held that *Miranda* did not apply to roadside questioning of a person stopped for suspected drunk driving because the driver was not in custody for the purposes of the *Miranda* rule. In *Illinois v. Perkins* (1990), questioning of a defendant in jail by an undercover officer posing as another inmate was likewise held not to be custodial interrogation.

Not content with just limiting the applicability of *Miranda* and its exclusionary rule, the Court also relaxed the standard for obtaining a waiver of the right not to have to submit to custodial interrogation. *Miranda* held that, to establish such a waiver, the state must meet a heavy burden. The Court's later decisions, however, made this "the lightest heavy burden ... to be found,"[67] allowing a waiver to be inferred without any express statement by the accused. *Miranda* waivers were upheld, moreover, where the police deceived the accused about the charged offence that was the subject of the interrogation and where police withheld information from the suspect concerning their attorney's immediate availability after falsely telling the attorney that the suspect would not be interrogated. In *Colorado v. Connelly* (1986), the Court held that even an insane person suffering from hallucinations could voluntarily waive these so-called *Miranda* "rights."

While the Rehnquist Court crippled *Miranda*'s waiver requirement, the Roberts Court delivered what was perhaps the final coup de grâce, holding in *Berghuis v. Thompkins* (2010)[68] that where a suspect had been read and understood his "rights in full," the police were not required to obtain a waiver of the right to remain silent *before* interrogating him. This decision stands *Miranda* on its head. The whole point of *Miranda* was to create a checkpoint at which police were required to obtain a waiver before subjecting a suspect to custodial interrogation. Thompkins, moreover, had been subjected to almost three hours of calculated interrogation during which he was falsely told a witness had fingered him as the shooter in a murder. The Court nevertheless ruled that there was an implied waiver because Thompkins had "engaged in a course of conduct indicating waiver" when he responded to the question "Do you believe in God?" and then, crying, responded affirmatively when asked "Do you pray to God to forgive you for shooting that boy down?" Finding no evidence of actual coercion such as threats or physical abuse, the Court found the affirmative statement voluntary and admissible.

The Supreme Court also dealt a severe blow to *Miranda*'s enforceability by holding in *Chavez v. Martinez* (2003) that police could not be sued under 42 U.S.C. § 1983 for violating the *Miranda* rules unless the improperly obtained statements were actually introduced in court. Martinez, a farmworker, was riding a bicycle along a path through a vacant lot when he encountered police officers investigating suspected drug activity. When Martinez resisted arrest, he was shot five times, leaving him permanently blind and paralyzed from the waist down. Although in severe pain, Martinez was repeatedly questioned without warnings while doctors attempted to treat him at the hospital. Martinez was never prosecuted for any offense and later sued Chavez, the interrogating detective, for allegedly violating his rights under the Fifth Amendment. A five-justice majority agreed, however, that "the failure to give a *Miranda* warning does not, without more, establish a completed violation [of the Fifth Amendment] when the unwarned interrogation ensues."[69]

The restraints *Miranda* imposes on the police are thus today much more limited than the Warren Court envisioned. While *Miranda* requires police to give the required warnings prior to any custodial interrogation and stop questioning if the accused at any time states they do not want to talk or wish to consult with counsel, in practice the reality is quite different. The police can interrogate in complete disregard of the *Miranda* warnings requirement if they are only seeking information rather than statements admissible in a courtroom. They also know that any physical evidence located as a result of such an interrogation will still be admissible in court.

These numerous exceptions and limitations help explain in part why the final nail in *Miranda*'s coffin was not driven in when the Court agreed to hear *Dickerson v. United States* (2000), a case in which a lower federal appellate court had upheld the admission of a confession taken by the FBI without *Miranda* warnings. The lower court had applied a long disregarded statutory provision enacted by Congress soon after *Miranda* was decided, which declared simply that a confession was admissible in a federal prosecution if it was voluntarily given. Congress had passed this provision in an attempt to nullify *Miranda*'s warning requirements and reimpose the old voluntariness test, which *Miranda* had expressly found inadequate and unworkable. While many speculated that *Dickerson* would provide the vehicle to finally overrule *Miranda*, in an ironic twist, Chief Justice Rehnquist authored the Court's opinion declining the invitation. Instead, he protected the Court's own sphere of power by declaring that Congress may not legislatively supersede a Supreme Court decision interpreting the Constitution. The chief justice acknowledged that the "Constitution does not require police to administer the particular *Miranda* warnings." Observing that the *Miranda* warnings had become part of the national culture, however, he nevertheless concluded that the Constitution does require "procedures that will warn a suspect in custody of his right to remain silent and which will assure the suspect that the exercise of that right will be honored."[70] Because the federal statute failed to require that a suspect in custody be given this information before interrogation, the statute was therefore unconstitutional. *Miranda* thus survived, but like an old coat, tattered and torn, it no longer retains its original shape.

As constitutional scholar Yale Kamisar has observed, this support for *Miranda* by a Supreme Court that made every effort to weaken it reflects how successful that effort has been.[71] Putting aside the fears he once held that *Miranda* would handcuff the police, the chief justice observed in *Dickerson* that "our subsequent cases have reduced the impact of the *Miranda* rule on legitimate law enforcement." Empirical studies, including an American Bar Association survey of judges, prosecutors, and police officers, confirm that *Miranda* creates no significant problem for law enforcement.[72] Indeed, defense attorneys continue to be astonished that their clients confess despite being given *Miranda* warnings. This should not be at all surprising. Central to the *Miranda* decision was the Court's conclusion that the police-dominated atmosphere surrounding custodial interrogation constitutes compulsion, rendering any statement made in such a setting the result of compulsion in violation of the Fifth Amendment. Yet precisely these same pressures operate on suspects who are asked to waive their rights. Indeed, it seems illogical that a sane person would voluntarily subject themselves to the pressures of a custodial interrogation at the hands of a trained interrogator without an attorney at their side if he or she had a truly free and unconstrained choice in the matter.

Because of the erosion of protection caused by the many exceptions to its protocol, *Miranda* today remains as a mere symbol of society's respect for individual self-determination and human dignity. While its ritualized warnings may fail to dissipate the compulsion inherent in the custodial setting, they nevertheless serve to restrain impulses that in other eras have led to unchecked abuses by requiring an officer of the state to acknowledge that even the lowly criminal suspect has certain rights the government must respect so long as he or she affirmatively asserts them.

## A NEW APPROACH TO PREVENTING UNCONSTITUTIONAL POLICE PRACTICES

The weak deterrent effect of the Fourth and Fifth Amendments' exception-riddled exclusionary rules, and particularly the failure of the Supreme Court to adequately address the use of deadly force by police, has called into question the ability of courts to remedy and deter unconstitutional police misconduct. One alternative has been to establish some form of citizen review board. These entities, however, have generally lacked the power to conduct their own independent investigation. Another alternative, employed in other countries and increasingly being utilized in the United States, is an independent investigative agency known as an ombudsman. Such agencies provide a forum for citizen complaints and have subpoena power, staff investigators, and the power to make recommendations and promote their implementation though public reports, which inform public opinion. If given true independence, appropriate powers, and adequate funding for a professional staff, the ombudsman concept may offer a new approach to protecting the freedoms guaranteed by the Bill of Rights.[73]

## CONCLUSION

The history of the Fourth and Fifth Amendments can perhaps best be understood as a struggle between two opposing conceptions of an ideal criminal justice system. One view—the crime control model—sees the primary function of the criminal justice system as the apprehension and punishment of the guilty. Proponents of this view tend to value the efficiency and effectiveness of law enforcement over the protection of human rights and thus permit the restriction of liberty and privacy when it impedes the wars on crime and terrorism. Proponents of the opposing view—the due process model—believe that the rights to liberty, privacy, and self-determination are essential to the continued existence of a free and democratic society. Because the coercive power of government is exercised most forcefully through the criminal law, they insist that the primary function of the criminal justice system must be to safeguard those freedoms from erosion.[74]

The crime control model reflects a short-term view. It seeks to respond to what is perceived as an immediate crisis. The due process model reflects a long-term view. It seeks to prevent the abuses of power that history has shown repeatedly occur when power is left unchecked. One view trusts those exercising government power and sees the greatest threat to social order as crime and terrorism. The other distrusts those who wield governmental power and foresees the disintegration of the type of society we value if fear is permitted to let discrimination and arbitrary abuse gain a foothold. Neither view holds a monopoly on the truth. The challenge for a society that seeks to ensure both freedom from the street mugger and terrorist, on the one hand, and freedom from oppressive government, on the other, is how to strike the proper balance between these two models.

A majority of the Warren Court, molded by the experience of the Second World War and the horrors of Nazi Germany and Stalinist Russia, championed the due process model. The Warren Court's extension of the federal Constitution's human rights guarantees to the states in the 1960s was motivated by a belief that the states were failing to protect racial minorities from abusive law enforcement practices. This discrimination, moreover, was occurring at a time when those groups were attempting to exercise their political rights and participate in the democratic process of mainstream America. The television images of police beating peaceful civil rights demonstrators and the documentation of abuses such as dragnet searches and coerced confessions in backrooms of police stations created public support for extending federal protection for such basic human rights.

In the 1970s and 1980s, however, the public came to feel increasingly vulnerable to street crime, and the pendulum swung the other way. Many Americans began to regard these basic human rights as mere technicalities, which allowed guilty criminals to escape just punishment. The replacement of members of the Warren Court with new justices, appointed by presidents who made crime control a political slogan, led to judicial reinterpretations of the Fourth and Fifth Amendments that significantly diminished liberty and privacy in order to promote efficient law enforcement.

In the aftermath of 9/11, increased police powers to fight the war on terror came to be seen as an even more compelling necessity. Yet as Justice Louis Brandeis warned long ago, "Experience should teach us to be most on our guard to protect liberty when the Government's purposes are beneficent. . . . The greatest dangers to liberty lurk in insidious encroachment by men of zeal, well-meaning but without understanding."[75] Unfortunately, in the past our nation's leaders have not been immune to the pressure created by threats to national security. During World War II, US citizens of Japanese ancestry, totally innocent of any wrongdoing, were confined en masse in detention camps, while the public re-mained largely silent. Those who ignore such lessons from history might find themselves repeating once again the mistakes of the past.

In an age of anxiety, the fear of terrorism makes plausible any police practice that may appear helpful to the protection of national security. In such times, the Bill of Rights might seem like an inconvenient and outdated impediment. The danger, however, is not so much that the Supreme Court will further erode these protections but that the government will exploit to the maximum the many ex-ceptions and loopholes already created by the Court's jurisprudence.

For example, because the Court has ruled that the failure to give *Miranda* warnings does not constitute a completed violation of the Fifth Amendment until the unwarned statement is introduced into court in a criminal case, *Miranda* provides little protection for targets of terrorism-related investigations, where the objective is often to obtain information rather than a confession for use in a criminal prosecution.[76] The fact *Miranda* can be disregarded in such terrorist investigations is all the more troublesome because the line between an investi-gation into terrorism and an investigation of ordinary criminal activity can often be blurred or extinguished altogether where dual purposes can be perceived.

Once an exception has been made to a well-established norm, it can also be difficult to contain the exception. An example of this crossover effect can be seen in the Fourth Amendment context with respect to police use of Stingray surveil-lance technology. This tool allows the user to track the location of a cell phone. Developed for military and national security surveillance, the Stingray device is now in the hands of state and/or local police in more than half of the states, yet its use and operation remain shrouded in secrecy.[77]

Because the Court has previously ruled that citizens have no reasonable ex-pectation of privacy in their banking and other records held by third parties, it has been unclear whether the Fourth Amendment prevents the government from creating databases of personal information now electronically kept by others concerning an individual's transactions and communications. The original ver-sion of Section 215 of the USA Patriot Act, passed in 2001 immediately after 9/11, in fact enabled any agent in charge of an FBI office to obtain records held by a third party by simply issuing a secret subpoena, based merely upon a declaration that the information sought was relevant to an investigation to protect against terrorism. This procedure bypassed not only the Fourth Amendment's normal warrant requirement but also ignored the special court established by the For-eign Intelligence Surveillance Act of 1978, which was empowered to authorize and oversee surveillance of any person reasonably believed to be an agent of a foreign power or foreign group engaged in international terrorism. Section 215 was a temporary provision that was scheduled to sunset in 2005. However, it was repeatedly renewed, with some protections added, and remained in effect for almost twenty years.

It would appear, however, that public opinion did help to preserve the guarantees of the Bill of Rights for US citizens in one instance during this period. This was reflected in the decision of President George W. Bush not to reauthorize a secret program known as the Terrorist Surveillance Program. Under this program, the National Security Agency repeatedly engaged in warrantless monitoring of international telephone and internet communications involving US citizens. Discovery of the secret program, which was reported by the *New York Times*, sparked a public outcry. The president claimed his commander-in-chief powers gave him the authority to authorize the secret warrantless surveillance, but this argument was rejected in *ACLU v. NSA* (2006) by a federal district court judge, who ruled that the program violated the Fourth Amendment. The administration appealed that ruling, which was later overturned on the technical ground that the ACLU and other plaintiffs had no standing to bring the action. However, in the interim, Bush's party lost control of Congress following the midterm elections of 2006. When it became clear that the NSA program would be unlikely to survive closer congressional scrutiny of executive power, the program was apparently not reauthorized.[78]

Legislation was thereafter passed which continued the surveillance authority granted by the Patriot Act but provided safeguards protecting US citizens and anyone inside the United States. The ACLU repeatedly complained to Congress, however, that the NSA was violating the provisions of this reformed surveillance program. The authority to amass such electronic databases under the Patriot Act finally was allowed to expire on March 15, 2020.[79]

The Supreme Court has also recently revisited the issue of electronic privacy, holding in *Riley v. California* (2014) that absent exigent circumstances necessitating an immediate search, a warrant is necessary to access digital data in a cell phone found on a person arrested for a crime. The Court also held in *Carpenter v. United States* (2018) that a warrant is required before the government can access business records of a wireless carrier that reveal the public movements of a cell phone owner. The narrow 5 to 4 ruling, which expressly exempted national security surveillance techniques and real-time tracking from consideration, may thus bring only a limited ray of hope. Moreover, the Supreme Court's refusal to give organizations who advocate for civil rights and journalists standing to contest such surveillance practices unless they can demonstrate a concrete injury,[80] as a practical matter, will likely result in only criminal defendants being able to bring a legal challenge, assuming they know their communications have been monitored. Considering that the overwhelming majority of criminal defendants charged with serious crime are represented by public defenders, who in many jurisdictions work in offices that are understaffed and underfunded, the outlook for vigilant judicial oversight therefore does not seem promising.[81]

In the end analysis, if the Bill of Rights is to flourish in the future, it is necessary that an informed electorate demand accountability from those who exercise government powers to deny liberty and invade privacy. As Alexander Hamilton observed in *The Federalist*, Number 84: "Whatever fine declarations may be inserted in any constitution respecting [liberty], [it] must altogether depend on public opinion, and on the general spirit of the people and of the government. [H]ere, after all, . . . must we seek for the only solid basis of all our rights."

## NOTES

1. Edward S. Corwin, *Liberty against Government: The Rise, Flowering and Decline of a Famous Judicial Concept* (Baton Rouge: Louisiana State University Press, 1948), 7.

2. Leonard W. Levy, *Origins of the Fifth Amendment: The Right against Self-Incrimination* (New York: Oxford University Press, 1968), 432.

3. *Barron v. Baltimore*, 32 U.S. 243 (1833) held that the takings clause of the Fifth Amendment (which prohibited taking of private property for public use without just compensation) did not apply to state governments.

4. Justice Brandeis, dissenting in *Olmstead v. United States*, 277 U.S. 438 (1928).

5. Nelson Lasson, *The History and Development of the Fourth Amendment to the United States Constitution* (Baltimore: Johns Hopkins University Press, 1937), 13–20.

6. Lasson, *History and Development*, 35–36; Matthew Hale, *History of the Pleas of the Crown*, 3 vols. (Philadelphia, 1847), vols. 1 and 2.

7. Lasson, *History and Development*, 20–39.

8. *Entick v. Carrington*, 19 Howell's State Trials 1029 (1765).

9. Lasson, *History and Development*, 51–72.

10. John Adams's abstract of James Otis's argument, in L. Kevin Wroth and Hiller B. Zobel, eds., *The Legal Papers of John Adams*, 3 vols. (Cambridge, MA: Harvard University Press, 1965), 1:142, 144.

11. Wroth and Zobel, *Legal Papers*, 107 (spelling modernized).

12. *Annals of Congress*, 1st Cong., 1st Session, 452.

13. See Osmand K. Frankel, "Concerning Searches and Seizures," *Harvard Law Review* 34 (1921): 361n30.

14. *Terry v. Ohio*, 392 U.S. 1 (1968).

15. *United States v. Martinez-Fuerte*, 428 U.S. 543 (1976).

16. *O'Connor v. Ortega*, 480 U.S. 709 (1987). Note, however, that because of heightened privacy concerns, the Court held in *Riley v. California*, 134 S. Ct. 2473 (2014) that a warrant is required to search a person's cell phone. See discussion *infra*.

17. *Skinner v. Railway Labor Executives' Association*, 489 U.S. 602 (1989).

18. *National Treasury Employees Union v. Von Raab*, 489 U.S. 656 (1989).

19. *Katz v. United States*, 389 U.S. 347 (1967).

20. Laurence Tribe and Joshua Matz, *Uncertain Justice: The Roberts Court and the Constitution* (New York: Henry Holt, 2014), 223–24.

21. *Michigan Dept. of State Police v. Sitz*, 110 S.O. 2481, 2490 (1990) (quoting *Alameida-Sanchez v. United States*, 413 U.S. 266, 273 [1973]).

22. "Newsman Says He Was Target of Probe," *San Diego Union*, December 21, 1990.

23. *Kyllo v. United States*, 533 U.S. 37 (2001).

24. The Court limited its holding, however, to sense-enhancing technology that was not in "general public use." The thermo-imaging device used in *Kyllo* had been obtained from the military. But what if laser technology becomes generally available at one's local Best Buy? Should a police officer standing on a public sidewalk across the street from your home be able to use this technology to eavesdrop on your private family conversations inside the home unless you have protected your windows with soundproofing countermeasures?

25. 132 S. Ct. 945 (2012).

26. In later cases, the Court ruled that attachment of a GPS device to the ankle of a sex offender, following completion of the offender's sentence, was a trespass on the person, and that a police drug detector dog's entry onto a front porch to sniff a home for drugs was also a trespass and thus a search, even though the porch was visible to the public. The Court distinguished its prior decision allowing officers to trespass on an open field, ruling that the porch was within the "curtilage"—a common-law concept that traditionally treated certain areas immediately outside the home as part of the home itself.

27. *Carpenter v. U.S.*, 138 S. Ct. 2206 (2018).

28. Sotomayor, J. concurring opinion, *U.S. v. Jones*, 565 U.S. 400, 416 (2012).

29. *Riley v. California*, 573 U.S. 373 (2014).

30. *Hein v. North Carolina*, 135 S. Ct. 530 (2015).

31. *Boyd v. United States*, 116 U.S. 616 (1886).

32. *Weeks v. United States*, 232 U.S. 393–94 (1913).

33. Roger B. Traynor, "*Mapp v. Ohio* at Large in the Fifty States," *Duke Law Journal* (1962): 321–22.

34. *Mapp v. Ohio*, 367 U.S. 660 (1961).

35. Peter F. Nardulli, "The Societal Cost of the Exclusionary Rule: An Empirical Assessment," *American Bar Foundation Research Journal* (1983): 585; Nardulli, "The Societal Costs of the Exclusionary Rule Revisited," *University of Illinois Law Review* (1987): 223–39.

36. Office of Legal Policy, United States Department of Justice, *Report to the Attorney General on the Search and Seizure Exclusionary Rule: Report No. 2 in the Truth in Criminal Justice Series* (1986), reprinted in *University of Michigan Journal of Law Reform* 22 (1989): 573–659.

37. Yale Kamisar, "Remembering the 'Old World' of Criminal Procedure," *University of Michigan Journal of Law Reform* 23 (1990): 568; italics in the original.

38. Daniel Webster, *The Writing and Speeches of Daniel Webster*, 10 vols. (Boston, 1903), 7:122.

39. See Michal Belknap, *Federal Law and Southern Order* (Athens: University of Georgia Press, 1995).

40. See C. Ogletree et al., *Beyond the Rodney King Story: An Investigation of Police Conduct in Minority Communities* (Boston: Northeastern University Press, 1995).

41. See Investigation of the Ferguson Police Department, US Department of Justice, Civil Rights Division, March 4, 2015, at 15–42, 62–78.

42. According to the report, "the only possible basis for prosecuting [Officer] Wilson under section 18 U.S.C. 242 would therefore be if the government could prove that his account is not true—i.e., that Brown never assaulted Wilson at the SUV, never attempted to gain control of Wilson's gun, and thereafter clearly surrendered in a way that no reasonable officer could have failed to perceive. Given that Wilson's account is corroborated by physical evidence and that his perception of a threat posed by Brown is corroborated by other eyewitnesses, . . . there is no credible evidence that Wilson willfully shot Brown as he was attempting to surrender or was otherwise not posing a threat. Even if Wilson was mistaken in his interpretation of Brown's conduct, the fact that others interpreted that conduct the same way as Wilson precludes a determination that he acted with a bad purpose to disobey the law. The same is true even if Wilson could be said to have acted with poor judgment in the manner in which he first interacted with Brown, or in pursuing Brown after the incident at the SUV. These are matters of policy and procedure that do not rise to the level of a Constitutional violation and thus cannot support a criminal prosecution." Department of Justice Report Regarding the Criminal Investigation into the Shooting Death of Michael Brown by Ferguson, Missouri Police Officer Darren Wilson, March 4, 2015, 86.

43. See Associated Press, "Eric Garner Death: NYPD Judge Recommends Firing Officer over Chokehold Death," *Los Angeles Times*, August 2, 2019, https://www.latimes.com/world-nation/story/2019-08-02/eric-garner-chokehold-death-fired.

44. See A. Blinder, "White Officer Who Shot Black Man in Back Is Sentenced to 20 Years," *New York Times*, December 7, 2017, 15.

45. See Brakkton Booker and Rachel Tiesman, "A Year after Breonna Taylor's Killing, Family Says There's 'No Accountability,'" NPR Daily Newsletter, March 13, 2021, https://www.npr.org/2021/03/13/973983947/a-year-after-breonna-taylors-killing-family-says-theres-no-accountability.

46. *Graham v. Connor*, 490 U.S. 386 (1989).

47. *Id.* at 396–97.

48. *Tennessee v. Garner*, 471 U.S. 1 (1985).

49. *Id.* at 11.

50. *Id.* at 11–12.

51. *Scott v. Harris*, 550 U.S. 372, 383 (2007).

52. *Plumhoff v. Rickard*, 572 U.S. 765 (2014).

53. Wesley Lowery et al., "Police Have Killed Nearly 200 People Who Were in Moving Vehicles since 2015," *Washington Post*, May 3, 2017.

54. American Bar Association, preface to *The Fourth Amendment Handbook*, 4th ed., ed. L. Benner (Chicago: American Bar Association, 2019). The period covered decisions from January 2010 to January 2019.

55. *Saucier v. Katz*, 533 U.S. 194, 202 (2001). The Supreme Court recently appeared to soften the rigidity of this approach in a per curiam decision in *Lombardo v. City of St. Louis*, 594 U.S. ____ (2021), remanding the case (which involved a prone restraint) back to the lower court because it was unclear whether that court had treated a prior precedent as a per se rule, while failing to give "careful attention to the facts and circumstances of [the] particular case."

56. *Pearson v. Callahan*, 555 U.S. 223 at 242–43 (2009).

57. Department of Justice Report Regarding the Criminal Investigation into the Shooting Death of Michael Brown by Ferguson, Missouri Police Officer Darren Wilson, March 4, 2015, 85, citing *Screws v. United States*, 325 U.S. 91, 101–7 (1945) (discussing willfulness element of 18 U.S.C. § 242).

58. *San Francisco v. Sheehan*, 135 S. Ct. 1765, 1778 (2015).

59. *Kinsela v. Hughes*, 138 S. Ct. 1148 (2018).

60. *Mullenix v. Luna*, 136 S. Ct. 305, 311 (2015).

61. California Assembly Bill 392, August 19, 2019, amending section 835a of the California Penal Code at subsection (e)(2), https://leginfo.legislature.ca.gov/faces/billNavClient.xhtml?bill_id=201920200AB392#content_anchor.

62. Acts 22: 24–30.

63. *Escobedo v. Illinois*, 378 U.S. 478 (1964). The Sixth Amendment basis for the right to counsel has subsequently been disavowed by the Court in *Moran v. Burbine*, 475 U.S. 412 (1986).

64. *Escobedo v. Illinois*, 488–89.

65. *Miranda v. Arizona*, 384 U.S. 436 (1966).

66. Rehnquist proposed consideration of a constitutional amendment to restore the balance that had been tipped, in his view, too far toward individual rights during the Warren Court's due process revolution. Such an amendment, of course, never materialized, but in lone dissents in his early years on the Court and later as chief justice, he championed this agenda.

67. Yale Kamisar, prepared remarks at the US Law Week's Constitutional Law Conference, September 17, 1987, Washington, DC, on file in the law libraries of California Western School of Law and the University of Michigan.

68. *Berghuis v. Thompkins*, 560 U.S. 370 (2010).

69. *Chavez v. Martinez*, 538 U.S. 760, at 789 (Kennedy, J., concurring). The justices forming the majority differed in their reasons for this result. A plurality of four justices, in an opinion by Justice Thomas, believed that even if actual coercion

was used to obtain a confession, no Fifth Amendment violation occurred until the confession was admitted into evidence. This resulted from the plurality's extremely narrow reading of the Fifth Amendment, which confined the scope of the amendment's protection to the literal words of the text. The Fifth Amendment states, "No person . . . shall be compelled in any criminal case to be a witness against himself." Taken literally, this means that there can be no completed violation of the Fifth Amendment until a person's compelled statements are actually used in court against him or her in a criminal case, because it is only at that point that the person is "a witness against himself." Thus, even torture would not constitute a violation of the Fifth Amendment under the plurality's view if the torture-induced statement was never admitted against the defendant in court.

Justice Kennedy, however, who cast the fifth vote necessary to make a majority in *Chavez*, disagreed with this reasoning. In Kennedy's view, the Fifth Amendment does protect against torture without regard to the subsequent use of the statements obtained. On the other hand, the mere failure to give *Miranda* warnings does not in Kennedy's view constitute compulsion violating the Fifth Amendment. Therefore, he agreed with the result reached by the plurality that Martinez's Fifth Amendment rights were not violated by the mere failure to give *Miranda* warnings.

70. *United States v. Dickerson*, 120 S. Ct. 2326, 2335 (2000).

71. Yale Kamisar, "Miranda's Reprieve: How Rehnquist Spared the Landmark Confession Case, but Weakened Its Impact," *American Bar Association Journal* 92 (June 2006): 48–51.

72. Stephen J. Schulhofer, "Reconsidering *Miranda*," *University of Chicago Law Review* 54 (1987): 435–61; "Special Commission on Criminal Justice in a Free Society," *Criminal Justice in Crisis* (Chicago: American Bar Association, 1988), 28–29; Richard A. Leo, "Questioning the Relevance of *Miranda* in the Twenty-first Century," *Michigan Law Review* 99 (2001): 1000.

73. See Laurence A. Benner, "Protecting Constitutional Rights in an Age of Anxiety: A New Approach," *Human Rights* (American Bar Association) 29 (Spring 2002), https://www.americanbar.org/groups/crsj/publications /human_rights_magazine_home/human_rights_vol29_2002/spring2002 /hr_spring02_benner/?q=&wt=json&start=0.

Without adequate powers and staffing, however, this approach, too, will be unsuccessful. See ACLU Letter to the European Commission, June 17, 2017, Re: The European Commission's Annual Review of the EU–US Privacy Shield, highlighting the inability of the Privacy Ombudsman (established in the executive branch following negotiations between the European Union and the United States) to adequately address privacy concerns regarding data coming into the United States from EU countries because the ombudsman lacked adequate investigatory powers. Attached as Exhibit A to ACLU Letter to European Commission re: Privacy Shield Annual Review, July 25, 2019, https://www.aclu.org/issues /national-security/privacy-and-surveillance/nsa-surveillance.

74. See Herbert L. Packer, "Two Models of the Criminal Process," *University of Pennsylvania Law Review* 113 (1964): 1–23.

75. *Olmstead v. United States,* 277 U.S. 479 (1928) (dissenting opinion).

76. See *Chavez v. Martinez,* 538 U.S. 760 (1994). It can be argued that torture would violate the due process clauses of the Fifth and Fourteenth Amendments. However, the "shocks the conscience" test used for determining when executive action violates due process, rather than the Fifth Amendment's test of compulsion, creates greater uncertainty about what practices would be unconstitutional under a due process analysis.

77. See Adam Bates, "Stingray: A New Frontier in Police Surveillance," Policy Analysis No. 809, Cato Institute, January 25, 2017.

78. See Richard B. Schmitt and Greg Miller, "U.S. Ceases Warrantless Spy Program," *Los Angeles Times,* January 18, 2007, 1.

79. See India McKinney, "Section 215 Expired: Year in Review 2020," Electronic Frontier Foundation, December 29, 2020, https://www.eff.org/deeplinks/2020/12/section-215-expired-year-review-2020.

80. See *Clapper v. Amnesty Int'l USA,* 568 U.S. 398 (2013) holding that future economic or professional injury due to the inability to communicate confidentially was not sufficiently certain to demonstrate actual injury in fact.

81. See Laurence A. Benner, "The Presumption of Guilt: Systemic Factors that Contribute to Ineffective Assistance of Counsel in California," 45 *California Western Law Review* 263 (2009).

PART IV

*Emerging Rights*

# NINE

—ⅶ—

# PRIVACY RIGHTS IN MODERN AMERICA

ADAM D. MOORE

IN THE US LIBERAL TRADITION, the public–private distinction has been used to mark the boundary of when individuals should be left alone. Building on such thinkers as John Locke and John Stuart Mill, the writers of the US Constitution, federal and state legislation, and subsequent case law placed individual liberty and freedom at the heart of American political thought.

For Locke (1632–1704), the public–private distinction fell out of his conception of a pre-political state of nature, the legitimate function of government, and property rights. The sole reason for uniting into a commonwealth, according to Locke, was to remedy the inconveniencies of the state of nature. The primary function of government was to secure the rights of life, liberty, and property.[1] On estates and behind fences, walls, and doors, individuals secured a domain of private action, free from public pressures or interference.

John Stuart Mill (1806–73) also sought to limit societal or public incursions into private domains. He argued, "The only purpose for which power can be rightfully exercised over any member of a civilized community, against his will, is to prevent harm to others."[2] When an action violates the rights of another, moral harm has occurred and appropriate action or interference is warranted by citizens or government agents. Short of this sort of violation, compulsion or interference is unjustified. A central and guiding principle of Western liberal democracies is that individuals, within certain limits, may set and pursue their own life goals and projects. Rights to privacy erect a boundary that allows individuals the moral space to order their lives as they see fit.

The individualism of Locke and Mill and the liberal, political, and economic experiments that followed the Enlightenment stand in stark contrast to what came before. In prior centuries, individuals were born into various hierarchical

211

social orders that largely determined the arc of their lives. For example, slaves, serfs, peasants, clergy, feudal lords, and monarchs each had various attached duties and obligations. Loyalty to a tribe, obedience to the queen, and submission to religious authorities, along with the surveillance necessary to determine compliance, was the norm. The ascendency of individual rights, as opposed to communal or societal obligations, became the backdrop for the liberal democracies in Western Europe and the United States.

At their core, disputes about the strength and scope of privacy center on the question of what we owe each other as citizens, colleagues, or friends. Imagine that we simply don't owe each other much—that aside from respecting the basic rights of life, liberty, property, and contract, we are each free to order our lives as we see fit and pursue our own values. In the absence of more robust obligations to citizens, colleagues, or friends, privacy may flourish. Imagine a different extreme. Consider that we are "our brother's keeper" and owe a great deal to others in our society. Aside from the basic rights of life, liberty, and property, we add rights to health care, jobs, food, education, income, retirement, respect, security, social justice, and so on. In this society, the moral and legal landscape would be thick with obligations and duties. In the face of these duties and the accompanying demands of moral and legal accountability, the domain of privacy would shrink.

Complicating the tensions between privacy, obligations to others, and accountability is that privacy is difficult to define. Privacy has been used to denote a wide variety of interests or rights, including personal information control, reproductive autonomy, access to places and bodies, secrecy, and personal development. Privacy interests also appear to be culturally relative—for example, opening a door without knocking might be considered a serious privacy violation in one culture and yet permitted in another.

Privacy has always been a commodity secured, more or less, on the basis of wealth, power, and privilege. While recent advances in information technology have highlighted privacy interests and concerns, privacy norms have been found in every culture systematically studied. Alan Westin, former professor of public law and government, argued that aspects of privacy are found in every society.[3] This view is supported by anthropology professors John Roberts and Thomas Gregor, who write, "Societies stemming from quite different cultural traditions such as the Mehinacu and the Zuni do not lack rules and barriers restricting the flow of information within the community, but the management and the functions of privacy may be quite different."[4] For example, in Mehinacu society, where gossip and the lack of physical barriers encourage openness and transparency, many individuals engage in obfuscation by spreading false or misleading rumors, thus attempting to conceal and control private information.

In the United States, legal protections for privacy have been found to exist in the penumbras of certain amendments to the Constitution and as part of common law. Local, state, and federal statutes also protect various dimensions of privacy. From these sources, privacy law has grown to protect the sanctity of the home and bedroom, a woman's right to obtain an abortion, the right to secure publications with anonymity, and rights against intrusions by government officials or other citizens.

In this article I review each of these areas, including (1) philosophical definitions of privacy along with specific critiques; (2) legal conceptions of privacy, including the history of privacy protections granted in constitutional and tort law and various federal and state statutes; and (3) general critiques of privacy protections both moral and legal. My hope is to provide a general overview of the issues and debates that frame this lively area of scholarly inquiry.

## PHILOSOPHICAL DIMENSIONS OF PRIVACY

Different conceptions of privacy typically fall into one of six categories or combinations of the six.[5] In 1890, legal theorists Samuel Warren and Louis Brandeis argued that "recent inventions and business methods call attention . . . for the protection of the person, and for securing to the individual . . . the right to be let alone."[6] While credited with starting the modern debate, the conception of privacy proposed by Warren and Brandeis has been widely criticized as both too broad and too narrow. For example, on this definition any offensive or hurtful conduct would violate a "right to be let alone," yet we may not want to conclude that such conduct is a violation of privacy. Moreover, unobtrusive National Security Agency surveillance may leave someone alone but still violate privacy.[7]

Privacy defined as "limited access to the self" has been defended by numerous authors.[8] Philosopher Sissela Bok writes, "Privacy is the condition of being protected from unwanted access by others—either physical access, personal information, or attention."[9] Ruth Gavison argues that privacy consists of "secrecy, anonymity, and solitude."[10] These conceptions of privacy also seem too broad and too narrow. For example, while I may not want others to notice the color of my eyes as I walk through a public park or when I have friends over for dinner, it would seem overbroad to claim that privacy has been violated if others take note of my eye color in these contexts. Additionally, the undiscovered Peeping Tom may not know who you are or impact your solitude and yet this seems to be a paradigm case of a privacy violation.

Judge Richard Posner has defined privacy as a kind of secrecy. Privacy is the right to conceal discreditable facts about oneself.[11] Judith Wagner DeCew and others have criticized this conception of privacy, noting that "secret information is often not private (for example, secret military plans) and private matters are not always secret (for example, one's debts)."[12] Moreover, it seems that privacy defined as informational secrecy cannot accommodate the areas of locational privacy and decisional privacy. For example, I might wander into your house and not take any information with me, or we might consider the right between consenting adults to use contraceptive devices.

Control over information has also been offered as a definition of privacy. Alan Westin writes, "Privacy is the claim of individuals, groups, or institutions to determine for themselves when, how, and to what extent information about them is communicated to others."[13] Charles Fried claims, "Privacy is not simply an absence of information about us in the minds of others; rather it is the control we have over information about ourselves."[14] Aside from omitting bodily or locational privacy and decisional privacy, this conception is also too broad. Imagine that you share intimate information with a lover. While you may no longer control this information, it may yet still be private, and sharing this information to a wider group may be a privacy violation. We might also wonder about the normative status of this control. For example, a new technology might be invented that limits my abilities to control personal information. Critics of nonnormative accounts of privacy note that we do not actually care whether a condition or state of privacy obtains; what we care about is the normative status—*Should* the condition obtain? For example, your purchase of an X-ray device may cause me to lose control over private information. But the question is not whether you can look; the question is whether you are morally justified in looking.

According to personality-based conceptions, privacy protects personhood and autonomous action.[15] Philosopher Stanley Benn writes, "Respect for someone as a person, as a chooser, implies respect for him as one engaged on a kind of self-creative enterprise, which could be disrupted, distorted, or frustrated even by so limited an intrusion as watching."[16] Zones of privacy protect us from the unwanted gaze of governments, corporations, and neighbors. In private areas, self-examination and critical reflection can occur free from the judgment of others. But rather than offering a definition, critics note that personality-based conceptions explain why privacy is valuable and why we should care about protecting privacy. Additionally, bodily or locational privacy, personal information, and private decisions are clearly connected to personhood, reputation, and self-creation, but so are a host of other values, such as liberty and property.[17]

Privacy has also been viewed as a form of intimacy.[18] Law professor Jeffrey Rosen argues that "in order to flourish, the intimate relationships on which true knowledge of another person depends need space as well as time: sanctuaries from the gaze of the crowd in which slow mutual self-disclosure is possible."[19] Julie Inness notes that privacy is "the state of the agent having control over decisions concerning matters that draw their meaning and value from the agent's love, caring, or liking. These decisions cover choices on the agent's part about access to herself, the dissemination of information about herself, and her actions."[20] Critics counter, arguing that financial information may be private but not intimate, whereas it is also possible to have private relationships without intimacy and to perform private acts that are not intimate.[21] Moreover, data mining and predictive analytics may pose a threat to individual privacy without affecting intimate relationships.

The final area may be viewed as a catchall or hybrid area that joins together different aspects of the privacy definitions already discussed. Philosophers Judith Wagner DeCew and Adam Moore offer normative definitions of privacy. DeCew has proposed the "realm of the private to be whatever types of information and activities are not, according to a reasonable person in normal circumstances, the legitimate concern of others."[22] Moore argues that "privacy is a right to control access to, and uses of, places, bodies, and personal information."[23] Helen Nissenbaum has advanced the view that privacy is a matter of contextual integrity. Nissenbaum writes: "Contextual integrity ties adequate protection for privacy to norms of specific contexts, demanding that information gathering and dissemination be appropriate to that context and obey the governing norms of distribution within it."[24] Each of these hybrid accounts of privacy has strengths and weaknesses, and this brief summary indicates the variety and breadth of definitions of privacy.

## LEGAL CONCEPTIONS OF PRIVACY

Legal privacy protections in the United States can be divided into three categories. Common-law torts protect privacy by allowing individuals to sue others in civil court. Constitutional privacy, including decisional privacy, First Amendment privacy, and Fourth Amendment privacy, protects US citizens from unjustified governmental intrusions into private domains. Finally, various statutory regulations at local, state, and federal levels protect privacy. We will take them up in turn.

### Privacy Torts

While privacy protections were implicated in the common-law doctrines of nuisance, trespass, and restrictions on eavesdropping, one of the first discussions of privacy occurred in Judge Thomas Cooley's treatise on torts in 1880.[25] In *De May v. Roberts* (1881),[26] the Michigan Supreme Court echoed Cooley's view acknowledging an individual's right to be let alone. "The plaintiff had a legal right to the privacy of her apartment . . . and the law secures to her this right by requiring others to observe it, and to abstain from its violation."[27] In 1890, Samuel D. Warren and Louis D. Brandeis issued a call to arms in their article titled "The Right to Privacy."[28] Hinting at times to come, Warren and Brandeis noted: "Recent inventions and business methods call attention to the next step which must be taken for the protection of the person, and for securing to the individual what Judge Cooley calls the right 'to be let alone.' Instantaneous photographs and newspaper enterprise have invaded the sacred precincts of private and domestic life; and numerous mechanical devices threaten to make good the prediction that 'what is whispered in the closet shall be proclaimed from the house-tops.'"[29]

The remedy for such invasions was to create a new tort. Torts are, in general, a negligent or intentional civil wrong that injures someone and for which the injured person may sue for damages. In 1960, in an effort to clarify matters, legal scholar Dean William Prosser separated privacy cases into four distinct but related torts: *intrusion*—intruding (physically or otherwise) on the solitude of another in a highly offensive manner; *appropriation*—using another's name or likeness for some advantage without the other's consent; *private facts*—publicizing highly offensive private information about someone that is not of legitimate concern to the public; and *false light*—publicizing a highly offensive and false impression of another.[30]

Following Warren and Brandeis, Prosser offered a common-law foundation for these privacy torts. The first Restatement of Torts in 1939 recognized this common-law right,[31] and Prosser's four torts were incorporated into the second Restatement of Torts in 1977.[32] Thus, by the mid-1970s, common-law protections of privacy were widespread in the US legal landscape.

Nevertheless, each of Prosser's torts has been limited by other social values such as free speech. *Melvin v. Reid* (1931) set the stage for undermining privacy rights in publicly available information.[33] The *Melvin* case involved Gabrielle Darley, a former prostitute who was tried and acquitted of murder as depicted in the movie *The Red Kimono*. Darley brought suit and lost, although the court also held that the use of the plaintiff's name was actionable. The view that in entering the public domain individuals voluntarily relinquish privacy claims was further solidified as a principle of law in *Gill v. Hearst Publishing Co.* (1953).[34] In *Gill*, a photograph of the plaintiffs embracing was used to illustrate an article titled "And So the World Goes Round." While in public, the plaintiffs argued that the embrace was a private moment not meant to be broadcast to the world as part of an article. Ruling against the plaintiffs and citing *Melvin*, Judge J. Spence reaffirmed the view that privacy rights generally lapse in public places.

Along with *Melvin* and other cases, the death knell for private fact torts came in *Florida Star v. B.J.F.* (1989).[35] In this case, a news agency published the name of a sexual assault victim after obtaining the name from a police report. The Supreme Court decided in favor of the defendant, stating: "The imposition of civil damages on the newspaper . . . violated the First Amendment, because (1) the news article contained lawfully obtained, truthful information about a matter of public significance, and (2) imposing liability under the circumstances was not a narrowly tailored means of furthering state interests in maintaining the privacy and safety of sexual assault victims."[36] Dissenting in *Florida Star*, Justice Byron White argued that "at issue in this case is whether there is any information about people, which—though true—may not be published in the press. By holding that only 'a state interest of the highest order' permits the State to penalize the publication of truthful information, and by holding that protecting a rape victim's right to privacy is not among those state interests of the highest order, the Court accepts appellant's invitation . . . to obliterate one of the most noteworthy legal inventions of the 20th century: the tort of the publication of private facts."[37]

The common-law tort of false light has seemingly transformed into defamation and has little to do with privacy and more to do with a property claim in one's reputation. As with defamation, truth is seen as a defense against a false light charge.[38] The tort of appropriation, which prohibits the commercial use of someone's name or likeness without consent, has also broken free from protecting privacy interests. Typically, it is used by celebrities and public figures to protect commercial value in intangible property such as names, likenesses, and vocal qualities.[39] The scope and power of the intrusion tort has also been severely limited. Some jurisdictions require physical trespass, and virtually no violation can occur in public places. The invasion must be intentional, it must physically intrude, the plaintiff must have a reasonable expectation of privacy, and it must be highly offensive to a reasonable person.[40] Here again, the cases pile up against privacy. *Melvin*, *Gill*, and *Florida Star* each rule out the possibility of an intrusion tort, because the private information disclosed in these cases was, in some sense, publicly available.[41]

## Constitutional Privacy Protections

Constitutional-based protections of privacy can be broken into three areas: decisional privacy, First Amendment privacy, and Fourth Amendment privacy. Privacy related to the Third and Fifth Amendments will not be considered.[42] Due to issues related to constitutional interpretation, this area of privacy is fairly complex and controversial. Many scholars deny that the constitution protects privacy except in a very narrow range of cases—for example, the Fourth Amendment's prohibition against "unreasonable searches and seizures" of "houses, papers, and effects."[43] In any case, the goal in this section is to describe the current state of privacy protections in US constitutional law.

### Decisional Privacy

In *Griswold v. Connecticut*,[44] a statute prohibiting the dissemination of contraceptive devices and information, even to married couples, was struck down because it would, in part, allow the police to violate "the sacred precincts of marital bedrooms."[45] Justice William Douglas, writing the majority opinion in *Griswold*, claimed that a legal right to privacy could be found in the shadows or penumbras of the First, Third, Fourth, and Fifth Amendments to the Constitution.

Douglas argued that by protecting the rights of parents to send their children to private schools and for associations to assemble and restrict access to membership lists, the First Amendment hints at a legal protection for privacy. Combined with the Third and Fourth Amendments, which protect against invasions into one's home, and the Fifth Amendment, which affords individuals the right not to disclose information about themselves, Douglas thought the sum was a legal right to privacy. Also in *Griswold*, Justice Arthur Goldberg invoked the Ninth and Fourteenth Amendments in support of privacy. Goldberg claimed that privacy was one of the rights retained by the people and that the due process clause of the Fourteenth Amendment protects privacy as a value "implicit in the concept of ordered liberty."[46]

Several judicial decisions solidified the Douglas and Goldberg line of argumentation. In *Loving v. Virginia*,[47] *Stanley v. Georgia*,[48] *Eisenstadt v. Baird*,[49] and *Carey v. Population Services*,[50] the Court struck down laws that prohibited interracial marriage, possession of pornographic materials in one's own home, and distribution of contraceptives to unmarried persons. One of the most important and controversial applications of this line of reasoning came in 1973 with *Roe v. Wade*.[51] Justice Harry Blackmun argued, "The right to privacy, whether it be founded in the Fourteenth Amendment's concept of personal liberty and restrictions upon the state action, as we feel it is, or, as the District Court determined, in the Ninth Amendment's reservation of rights to the people, is broad enough to encompass a woman's decision whether or not to terminate her pregnancy."[52] Thus, in general terms, the court recognized that individuals have privacy rights to be free from governmental interference related to certain sorts of decisions.

### First Amendment Privacy

Privacy is also safeguarded by protecting the right to speak anonymously and the confidentiality of one's associations.[53] Sometimes the ability to speak freely relies heavily on anonymity. For example, the Supreme Court of New Jersey has held that an anonymous online speaker has a First Amendment right to remain unidentified.[54] "Anonymous pamphlets, leaflets, brochures and even books have played an important role in the progress of mankind. Great works of literature have frequently been produced by authors writing under assumed names . . . the interest in having anonymous works enter the marketplace of ideas unquestionably outweighs any public interest in requiring disclosure as a condition of entry. Accordingly, an author's decision to remain anonymous . . . is an aspect of the freedom of speech protected by the First Amendment."[55]

Many individuals would not speak their minds, engage in whistleblowing, challenge popular views, or denounce those in power without the ability to remain anonymous. Much of the discourse in online environments would not occur without anonymity and encryption. Just as an example, consider the many anonymous philosophical works or works published under a pseudonym that have challenged religious orthodoxy. Saying something unpopular or anti-religious could, and did, get people killed; anonymity thus played a key role in preserving human life while allowing new ideas to emerge.

As noted by Douglas in *Griswold*, the First Amendment also protects the privacy of associations and groups to peaceably assemble. In *NAACP v. Alabama* (1958), the state of Alabama required the National Association for the Advancement of Colored People to submit the names and address of all members in the state.[56] The US Supreme Court held that compelled disclosure of the NAACP membership lists would have the effect of undermining the association, noting that the "petitioner has made an uncontroverted showing that on past occasions revelation of the identity of its rank-and-file members has exposed these members to economic reprisal, loss of employment, threat of physical coercion, and other manifestations of public hostility."[57]

Privacy has a role in protecting information access as well. Imagine someone visiting a library to learn about alternative lifestyles not accepted by the majority. Remaining anonymous or hiding one's curiosity about, for example, a gay lifestyle may be important in certain contexts. This is true of all sorts of personal information, such as religious preference or political party affiliation. Not having authorities looking over one's shoulder might also be important for conducting research. In *Urofsky v. Gilmore* (2000), six professors employed by several public universities in Virginia challenged "the constitutionality of a Virginia law restricting state employees from accessing sexually explicit material on computers that are owned or leased by the state."[58] Denial of access and requiring permission, they argued, would have the effect of suppressing research and constituted an assault on academic freedom. Ultimately, the Virginia law was upheld and the US Supreme Court refused to hear the case.

## Fourth Amendment Privacy

In a long series of cases and judicial decisions, known as "Fourth Amendment Privacy," the court has protected citizens from unreasonable searches and seizures. The Fourth Amendment states: "The right of the people to be secure in their persons, houses, papers, and effects, against unreasonable searches and seizures, shall not be violated, and no Warrants shall issue, but upon probable cause, supported by Oath or affirmation, and particularly describing the place to be searched, and the persons or things to be seized."[59] This amendment grew out of opposition to writs of assistance, which were general warrants utilized by the English Crown authorizing government agents to enter any house or other establishment and seize contraband. Writs of this sort, often used against political or business rivals, were generally detested by American colonists as "fishing expeditions." In 1760 James Otis attacked such writs, citing the long English tradition that "a man's house is his castle."[60] Addressing the English Parliament in 1763, William Pitt wrote, "The poorest man may in his cottage bid defiance to all the force of the crown. It may be frail—its roof may shake—the wind may blow through it—the storm may enter, the rain may enter—but the King of England cannot enter—all his force dares not cross the threshold of the ruined tenement."[61]

Although many cases and developments in Fourth Amendment jurisprudence took place during the 1800s and early 1900s, our modern view began to take shape with *Olmstead v. United States* (1928).[62] In *Olmstead*, the court ruled that the Fourth Amendment protection against unreasonable searches and seizures applied to physical things such as houses, notebooks, and receipts but not to electronic communications. To violate the prohibition against unwarranted searches and seizures, an officer would have to physically trespass on the property of the defendant. Since electronic eavesdropping did not constitute trespass, such surveillance did not violate the Fourth Amendment. Thirty-nine years later, the Supreme Court, in *Katz v. United States*,[63] overturned the *Olmstead* decision, affirming that privacy interests may be found in personal communications as well as "persons, houses, papers, and effects." In *Katz*, the physical trespass doctrine of *Olmstead* was seemingly repudiated, and it was generally acknowledged that a search could include both physical and electronic or technological invasion.[64]

In place of the physical trespass doctrine of earlier times, the *Katz* court offered a "reasonable expectation of privacy" test. If an individual has a reasonable expectation of privacy, then a warrant must be obtained. Justice John Harlan, in his concurring opinion, offered two requirements for determining whether a search has occurred. "These requirements were, first, that a person have exhibited an actual (subjective) expectation of privacy and, second, that the expectation be one that society is prepared to recognize as 'reasonable'"[65] Also in 1967, the Supreme Court struck down specific sections of a New York eavesdropping statute in *Berger v. New York*, noting that the probable cause requirement of the Fourth Amendment applied to electronic surveillance.[66] Thus, in *Berger* and *Katz*, the Supreme Court sought to extend Fourth Amendment protections to electronic communications. Physical trespass was not necessary, probable cause applied, and the "particularization" requirement—detailing the communications to be seized and the allowable duration of the surveillance—applied as well. These changes in Fourth Amendment jurisprudence affected several statutes, including the Omnibus Crime Control and Safe Street Act of 1968.[67]

The plain view doctrine established in *Coolidge v. New Hampshire*[68] permitted police observations conducted during a warranted intrusion. Thus, a police officer who has a warrant to search for documents and who inadvertently notices, for example, a marijuana plant growing in a planter, would be allowed to use this evidence even though the warrant did not specify a drug search. The open view doctrine, on the other hand, allowed for observations made when no search was being conducted. If a police officer, while walking down the street, noticed a marijuana plant growing in a backyard, the officer could use this information without a warrant because no search was conducted.[69] Unaided observations from a nonintrusive altitude do not run afoul of Fourth Amendment protection. What is observed is also important in that the courts have drawn a distinction between open fields and private dwellings, attaching more protection to the latter than to the former.[70]

In "One Hundred Years of Privacy,"[71] law professor Ken Gormley notes, "A reasonable expectation of privacy has been found, sufficient to ward off governmental intrusion, with respect to the use of . . . bugging devices;[72] administrative searches of homes and businesses;[73] searches of closed luggage and footlockers;[74] sealed packages;[75] . . . random spot checks for automobiles to inspect drivers' licenses and vehicle registrations."[76] On the negative side, "The court had found no reasonable expectation of privacy in an individual's bank records;[77] in voice or writing exemplars;[78] in phone numbers recorded by pen registers;[79] in conversations recorded by wired informants;[80] and a growing list of cases involving automobiles, trunks, glove compartments and closed containers therein."[81]

More recently, and especially after the terrorist attacks of September 11, 2001, Fourth Amendment privacy has been limited further by the Uniting and Strengthening America by Providing Appropriate Tools Required to Intercept and Obstruct Terrorism (USA PATRIOT) Act.[82] The Patriot Act expands the government's ability to conduct covert "sneak and peak" searches; expands the breadth of "trap-and-trace" and "pen register" surveillance by allowing content to be monitored; allows the inclusion of DNA information into databases of individuals convicted of "any crime of violence"; increases government surveillance abilities of suspected computer trespassers (any target suspected of violating the Computer Fraud and Abuse Act may be monitored without a court order); authorizes the attorney general to circumvent probable cause restrictions through the use of national security letters or administrative subpoenas; and increases the government's ability to access records held by third parties.[83]

This last limit on Fourth Amendment privacy protections is now called the third-party doctrine, holding that when citizens voluntarily give personal information to others, they forfeit reasonable expectations of privacy related to government surveillance.[84] The third-party doctrine is the US government's primary defense for the National Security Agency's and FBI's bulk data collection programs (PRISM, IREACH, Stellar Wind, etc.), and it is also why applications for warrants have decreased in favor of using administrative subpoenas.[85] Recently,

however, several legal challenges have sought to limit the scope of these surveillance programs.[86]

## Statutory Privacy

Statutory privacy protections exist at the local, state, and federal levels. While a
comprehensive overview of each level is beyond the scope of this chapter, I will
mention several of the most important federal statutes and a few of the more
interesting state statutes.[87]

- The Omnibus Crime Control and Safe Street Act of 1968 regulated
  electronic surveillance and wiretaps.[88]
- The Fair Credit Reporting Act of 1970 regulated the accuracy and
  use of personal information held by credit agencies.[89]
- The Family Educational Rights and Privacy Act of 1974 regulated
  access to educational records.[90]
- The Privacy Act of 1974 was enacted to promote fair information
  practices between citizens and the government.[91]
- The Right to Financial Privacy Act of 1978 regulated access to personal financial records in reaction to the Supreme Court's ruling
  in *United States v. Miller.*[92]
- The Electronic Communications Privacy Act of 1986 expanded
  the scope of federal wiretap laws to cover electronic communications and stored electronic communications.[93]
- The Computer Matching and Privacy Protection Act of 1988
  amended the Privacy Protection Act related to computer matching and information sharing across different federal agencies.[94]
- Title V of the Gramm-Leach-Bliley Financial Modernization Act
  of 2000 regulated the sharing of personal information by giving
  data subjects the ability to opt out of certain sharing practices
  used by financial institutions.[95]
- The Health Insurance Portability and Accountability Act of 1996
  protects the security, confidentiality, and accessibility of health
  information.[96]
- The Video Voyeurism Prevention Act of 2004 protects individuals
  from intrusions via the use of miniature cameras, camera phones,
  and video recorders in public places.[97]

States have also passed legislation designed to protect privacy.[98] For example,
Washington State's voyeurism statute prohibits the photographing of a person
without that person's knowledge and consent in a "place where he or she would
have a reasonable expectation of privacy."[99] The California Consumer Privacy
Act (CCPA) of 2018, which echoes the European Union's General Data Protection

Regulation, gives California residents the right to access their personal information, to know if their personal information is sold or disclosed and to whom, and to reject the further sale of their personal information to others.[100] Those who fail to comply with the CCPA are subject to fines and penalties. Space does not permit a full accounting of the many statutory privacy protections found at the state and local level in the United States.

## GENERAL CRITIQUES OF PRIVACY

Many scholars and legal theorists view privacy with concern or suspicion. This section describes a few of the more forceful criticisms that dominate the literature.

Judith Jarvis Thomson has argued that privacy is reducible to the more basic rights of property and what she calls "rights over the person."[101] Privacy is not unique, and we may well do better considering these other rights rather than attending to an ambiguous concept. Defenders of privacy have countered, noting that Thomson has not shown which set of rights is more basic. Perhaps property and rights over the person are reducible to privacy and not the other way around. Additionally, many contested concepts such as liberty and autonomy are difficult to define, but this does not mean that they should be jettisoned from meaningful discourse.[102]

Feminists have also been suspicious of privacy. Catharine MacKinnon writes, "For women the measure of the intimacy has been the measure of the oppression.... This is why feminism has seen the personal as the political. The private is public for those for whom the personal is political. In this sense, for women there is no private, either normatively or empirically. Feminism confronts the fact that women have no privacy to lose or to guarantee."[103] Other feminists note that rejecting privacy, especially decisional privacy, would have profound negative effects on the power, standing, and life prospects for women.[104]

In the area of legal privacy, many scholars have complained that the word *privacy* does not appear in the Constitution or the Bill of Rights and thus view the creation of this area of law as a form of judicial activism.[105] Focusing on decisional privacy, Louis Henkin writes, "To date, at least, the right has brought little new protection for what most of us think of as 'privacy'—freedom from official intrusion. What the Supreme Court has given us, rather, is something essentially different and farther-reaching additional zone of autonomy."[106] Defenders of decisional privacy note that privacy rights are a subset of liberty claims centering on consenting adults in private places. Thus, like any right, there is nothing odd about the connection between privacy and autonomy. DeCew expresses this point as follows: "A subset of autonomy cases ... can plausibly be said to involve privacy interests. ... They should be viewed as liberty cases in virtue of their concern over decision-making power, whereas privacy is at stake because of the nature of the decision."[107] More generally, when looking at the First, Third, Fourth, Fifth, Ninth, and Fourteenth Amendments, it would seem that privacy is implicated along with *liberty*—another word that does not appear in the Constitution or Bill of Rights.

### FINAL REMARKS

In *FTC v Wyndham Corp.*,[108] the court held that keeping personal information about patrons on an insecure system and not correcting the security flaws after the first intrusion was deemed to be actionable behavior. Due to defective security practices, Wyndham was hacked on three separate occasions with the result of over $10 million in losses due to identity theft. Section 5 of the Federal Trade Commission Act defines an unfair and actionable behavior as one that "causes or is likely to cause substantial injury to consumers; cannot be reasonably avoided by consumers; and is not outweighed by countervailing benefits to consumers or to competition."[109] This line of thought could be used in a more robust way. Imagine that companies or states that warehouse sensitive personal information about individuals—information not central to the enterprise or business concern—could be held partially liable if this information were stolen, misplaced, or accessed by outsiders. If so, at a minimum, corporations and states would be incentivized to maintain secure systems that hold private information, and at best, this non-essential data would simply be deleted.

Cases such as *FTC v. Wyndham Inc.* and, more importantly, legislation such as the California Consumer Privacy Act and the European Union's General Data Protection Regulation may have a profound impact on how sensitive personal data are controlled, stored, and transmitted. If individuals are given rights of notice, consent, control, and deletion over their own personal information, and if violation of these rights is coupled with fines for misuse, then perhaps we will begin to move past the non sequitur that access equals abandonment—that, if someone has access to your private information, then you must have abandoned all claims to it. Note that the poet does not lose her copyright when she allows you to read her poem. Similarly, it could be argued that granting the government, corporations, or neighbors access to some private fact about yourself is not also to waive all downstream rights over this information. Needless to say, as technology expands the ways personal information may be shared, captured, warehoused, and processed, the philosophical, legal, and technical issues related to control, consent, and deletion will need to be reexamined.

### NOTES

Parts of this article are drawn from previously published material. See Adam D. Moore, *Privacy Rights: Moral and Legal Foundations* (University Park: Pennsylvania

State University Press, 2010), 99–132, and "Privacy," in "Library Hi Tech: Special Issue on Information Ethics," *Library Hi Tech* 25 (2007): 58–78.

1. John Locke, *The Second Treatise of Government* (1690), ed. C. B. Macpherson (Indianapolis, IN: Hackett, 1980), 5–30.

2. John Stuart Mill, *On Liberty* (1859), ed. E. Rapaport (Indianapolis, IN: Hackett, 1978), 9.

3. Alan Westin, *Privacy and Freedom* (New York: Atheneum, 1967).

4. John Roberts and Thomas Gregor, "Privacy: A Cultural View," in *Privacy: Nomos XIII*, ed. J. Roland Pennock and John W. Chapman (New York: Atherton, 1971), 225.

5. See Daniel J. Solove, "Conceptualizing Privacy," *California Law Review* 90 (2002): 1088–155, 1094. For a more recent topology of privacy, see Bert-Jaap Koops, Bryce Newell, Timan Tjerk, et al., "A Typology of Privacy," *University of Pennsylvania Journal of International Law* 38 (2017): 483–575.

6. Samuel D. Warren and Louis D. Brandeis, "The Right to Privacy," *Harvard Law Review* 4 (1890): 194.

7. For example, see Ruth Gavison, "Privacy and the Limits of Law," *Yale Law Journal* 89 (1980): 421–71; Judith Wagner DeCew, *In Pursuit of Privacy: Law, Ethics, and the Rise of Technology* (Ithaca, NY: Cornell University Press, 1997), 53.

8. See Sissela Bok, *Secrets: On the Ethics of Concealment and Revelation* (New York: Pantheon, 1983); Gavison, "Privacy and the Limits of Law."

9. Bok, *Secrets*, 10.

10. Gavison, "Privacy and the Limits of Law," 433.

11. Richard Posner, "The Economics of Privacy," *American Economic Review Papers and Proceedings* 71 (1981): 405–9.

12. DeCew, *In Pursuit of Privacy*, 48.

13. Westin, *Privacy and Freedom*, 7.

14. Charles Fried, "Privacy: A Moral Analysis," in *Philosophical Dimensions of Privacy*, ed. Ferdinand D. Schoeman (Cambridge: Cambridge University Press, 1984), 203–21, 209.

15. See Roscoe Pound, "Interests in Personality," *Harvard Law Review* 28 (1915): 343; Paul A. Freund, "Privacy: One Concept or Many?" in *Privacy: Nomos XIII*, ed. J. Roland Pennock and John W. Chapman (New York: Atherton, 1971), 182; Jeffrey Reiman, "Privacy, Intimacy, and Personhood," *Philosophy and Public Affairs* 6 (1976): 26–44.

16. Stanley I. Benn, 1971, "Privacy, Freedom, and Respect for Persons," in *Privacy: Nomos XIII*, ed. J. Roland Pennock and John W. Chapman (New York: Atherton, 1971), 26.

17. See Gavison, "Privacy and the Limits of Law"; Jed Rubenfeld, "The Right of Privacy," *Harvard Law Review* 102 (1989): 737–807; Solove, "Conceptualizing Privacy."

18. See James Rachels, "Why Privacy Is Important," *Philosophy and Public Affairs* 4 (1975): 323–33; Julie Inness, *Privacy, Intimacy, and Isolation* (Oxford:

Oxford University Press, 1992); Jeffrey Rosen, *The Unwanted Gaze: The Destruction of Privacy in America* (New York: Random House, 2000).

19. Rosen, *The Unwanted Gaze*, 8.

20. Inness, *Privacy, Intimacy, and Isolation*, 91.

21. See Solove, "Conceptualizing Privacy"; DeCew, *In Pursuit of Privacy*.

22. DeCew, *In Pursuit of Privacy*, 58.

23. Adam Moore, *Privacy Rights: Moral and Legal Foundations* (University Park: Pennsylvania State University Press, 2010), 27.

24. Helen Nissenbaum, "Privacy as Contextual Integrity," *Washington Law Review* 79 (2004): 119–57.

25. Thomas Cooley, *A Treatise on the Law of Torts* (Chicago: Callaghan, 1880). See also Warren and Brandeis, "The Right to Privacy."

26. *De May v. Roberts*, 9 N.W. 146 (Mich. 1881).

27. *De May v. Roberts*, 149, cited in R. Turkington and A. Allen, *Privacy Law: Cases and Materials*, 2nd ed. (St. Paul, MN: West, 2002), 23.

28. Warren and Brandeis, "The Right to Privacy."

29. Warren and Brandeis, "Right to Privacy," 194.

30. Dean William Prosser, "Privacy," *California Law Review* 48 (1960): 383, 384. Drawn from E. Alderman and C. Kennedy's *The Right to Privacy* (New York: Knopf, 1995), 155–56.

31. Prosser, "Privacy," 386.

32. Restatement (Second) of Torts 652B-652E (1977).

33. *Melvin v. Reid* (1931) 112 Cal. App. 285.

34. *Gill v. Hearst Publishing Co.* (1953) 40 Cal. 2d 224.

35. *Florida Star v. B.J.F.* (1989), 491 U.S. 524.

36. *Florida Star v. B.J.F.* (1989), 491 U.S. 551.

37. *Florida Star v. B.J.F.*

38. *Machleder v. Diaz* (1986) 801 F.2d 46; U.S. App.

39. *Matthews v. Wozencraft* (1994) 15 F.3d 432, 438, 5th Cir.

40. Restatement of Torts 652B, 1977.

41. See also *Bartnicki v. Vopper*, 121 S. Ct. 1753 (2001). *Cape Publications, Inc. v. Bridges*, 423 So. 2d 426 (Fla. Dist. Ct. App. 1982); *DeGregorio v. CBS, Inc.*, 473 N.Y.S.2d 922 (N.Y. S. Ct. 1984); *Sipple v. Chronicle Publishing Co.*, 154 Cal. App. 3d 1040, 201 Cal. Rptr. 665 (1984).

42. The Third Amendment prohibiting the quartering of soldiers in private homes without consent and the Fifth Amendment prohibiting self-incrimination that is testimonial in nature both protect privacy interests. See, for example, *Engblom v. Carey*, 677 F.2d 957 (2d Cir. 1982), *Boyd v. United States*, 116 U.S. 616 (1886), and *Schmerber v. California*, 384 U.S. 757, 765 (1966).

43. See, for example, Robert Bork, *The Tempting of America: The Political Seduction of the Law* (New York: Simon & Schuster, 1990).

44. *Griswold v. Connecticut*, 381 U.S. 479 (1965).

45. Douglas, *Griswold v. Connecticut*, 381 U.S. 479 (1965).

46. *Griswold v. Connecticut*, 381 U.S. 479 (1965).

47. *Loving v. Virginia*, 388 U.S. 1 (1967).

48. *Stanley v. Georgia*, 394 U.S. 577 (1969).

49. *Eisenstadt v. Baird*, 405 U.S. 438 (1972).

50. *Carey v. Population Services*, 431 U.S. 678 (1977).

51. *Roe v. Wade*, 410 U.S. 153 (1973).

52. *Roe v. Wade*, 164–65.

53. See, for example, Nadine Strossen, "Protecting Privacy and Free Speech in Cyberspace," *Georgetown Law Journal* 89 (2001): 2107; Susan Brenner, "The Privacy Privilege: Law Enforcement, Technology, and the Constitution," *Journal of Technology Law and Policy* 7 (December 2002): 123–94.

54. *Dendrite Int'l v. Doe No. 3*, 342 N.J. Super. 134 (App. Div. 2001). See also *Buckley v. American Constitutional Law Foundation*, 525 U.S. 182, 197–90 (1999); *ACLU v. Miller*, 977 F. Supp. 1228 (N.D. Ga. 1997), *Bates v. City of Little Rock*, 361 U.S. 516 (1960); *NAACP v. Alabama ex rel. Patterson*, 357 U.S. 449 (1958); *McIntyre v. Ohio Elections Comm'n*, 514 U.S. 334 (1995).

55. *Dendrite Int'l v. Doe No. 3*, 342 N.J. Super. 134 (App. Div. 2001) at 149. See also *Talley v. California*, 362 U.S. 60 (1960); *Bates v. Little Rock*, 361 U.S. 516 (1960).

56. *NAACP v. Alabama*, 357 U.S. 449 (1958).

57. *NAACP v. Alabama* 357 U.S. 449 (1958) at 463. See also Edward Bloustein, "Group Privacy: The Right to Huddle," *Rutgers-Camden Law Journal* 8 (1977): 278, quoted in Jonathan Kahn, "Privacy as a Legal Principle of Identity Maintenance," *Seton Hall Law Review* 33 (2003): 401.

58. *Urofsky v. Gilmore*, 216 F.3d 401 (4th Cir. 2000).

59. U.S. Constitution, amend 4.

60. James Otis, "In Opposition to Writs of Assistance," Delivered before the Superior Court, Boston (February 1761). See *Entick v. Carrington*, 19 Howell's State Trials 1029, 95 Eng. 807 (1705).

61. William Pitt the elder, Earl of Chatham, speech in the House of Lords, 1763, in Henry Peter Brougham, *Historical Sketches of Statesmen Who Flourished in the Time of George III*, vol. 1 (London: R. Griffin, 1839), 52.

62. *Olmstead v. United States*, 227 U.S. 438 (1928). For earlier cases, see *Boyd v. United States*, 116 U.S. 616 (1886); *Gouled v. United States*, 255 U.S. 298 (1921); *Weeks v. United States*, 232 U.S. 383, 392 (1914); *Carroll v. United States*, 267 U.S. 132, 158 (1925); *Agnello v. United States*, 269 U.S. 20, 30 (1925).

63. *Katz v. United States*, 389 U.S. 347 (1967).

64. But see *United States v. Jones*, 565 U.S. 400 (2012). Justice Sonia Sotomayor wrote, "As the majority's opinion makes clear, *Katz's* reasonable-expectation-of-privacy test augmented, but did not displace or diminish, the common-law trespassory test that preceded it." *United States v. Jones*, 565 U.S. 400 (2012) at 3.

65. Turkington and Allen, *Privacy Law*, 95. See also *Rakas v. Illinois*, 439 U.S. 128 (1978); *United States v. White*, 401 U.S. 745, 786 (1971); *Smith v. Maryland*, 442 U.S. 735, 740 (1979); *Alderman v. United States*, 394 U.S. 165 (1969); *Mincey v. Arizona*,

437 U.S. 385 (1978); *Payton v. New York*, 445 U.S. 573 (1980); *Rawlings v. Kentucky*, 448 U.S. 98 (1980); *Terry v. Ohio*, 392 U.S. 1, 19 (1968).

66. *Berger v. New York*, 388 U.S. 41 (1967).

67. Omnibus Crime Control and Safe Street Act of 1968, U.S.C. §§ 2510–2520 (1994 and Supp. V 2000). See below.

68. *Coolidge v. New Hampshire*, 403 U.S. 443 (1971).

69. See Tom Bush, "Comment: A Privacy-Based Analysis for Warrantless Aerial Surveillance Cases," *California Law Review* 75 (1987): 1776.

70. See *Oliver v. United States*, 466 U.S. 170, 177 (1984); *Kyllo v. United States*, 533 U.S. 27 (2001).

71. Ken Gormley, "One Hundred Years of Privacy," *Wisconsin Law Review* (1992): 1369.

72. See *Berger v. New York*, 388 U.S. 41 (1967); *United States v. United States Dist. Court*, 407 U.S. 297 (1972). Cited in Gormley, "One Hundred Years of Privacy," n171.

73. See *Camara v. Municipal Court*, 387 U.S. 523 (1967); *G.M. Leasing Corp. v. United States*, 429 U.S. 338 (1977). Cited in Gormley, "One Hundred Years of Privacy," n172.

74. See *United States v. Chadwick*, 433 U.S. 1 (1977); *Arkansas v. Sanders*, 442 U.S. 753 (1979). But see *United States v. Ross*, 456 U.S. 798 (1982). Cited in Gormley, "One Hundred Years of Privacy," n173.

75. See *Walter v. United States*, 447 U.S. 649 (1980). Cited in Gormley, "One Hundred Years of Privacy," n174.

76. See *Delaware v. Prouse*, 440 U.S. 648 (1979). Cited in Gormley, "One Hundred Years of Privacy," n178.

77. *See United States v. Miller*, 425 U.S. 435 (1976). Cited in Gormley, "One Hundred Years of Privacy," n179.

78. See *United States v. Dionisio*, 410 U.S. 1 (1973). Cited in Gormley, "One Hundred Years of Privacy," n180.

79. See *Smith v. Maryland*, 442 U.S. 735 (1979). Cited in Gormley, "One Hundred Years of Privacy," n181.

80. See *United States v. White*, 401 U.S. 745 (1971). Cited in Gormley, "One Hundred Years of Privacy," n182.

81. See *Chambers v. Maroney*, 399 U.S. 42 (1970); *South Dakota v. Opperman*, 428 U.S. 364 (1976); *Rakas v. Illinois*, 439 U.S. 128 (1978); *California v. Carney*, 471 U.S. 386 (1985); *United States v. Ross*, 456 U.S. 798 (1982); *New York v. Belton*, 453 U.S. 454 (1981). Cited in Gormley, "One Hundred Years of Privacy," n183.

82. USA Patriot Act (U.S. H.R. 3162, Public Law 107–56), Title II.

83. USA Patriot Act, Sec. 214–17, 503, 505.

84. See *Smith v. Maryland*, 442 U.S. 735 (1979).

85. See Christopher Slobogin, "Subpoenas and Privacy," *DePaul Law Review* 54 (2005): 805–46.

86. See *Riley v. California*, 134 S. Ct. 2473, 2489 (2014); *Jewel v. National Security Agency*, accessed February 6, 2019, https://www.eff.org/files/filenode/jewel/jewel .complaint.pdf.

87. See also Cable Communications Policy Act 1984, 47 U.S.C. 521; Video Privacy Protection Act of 1988, 18 U.S.C. 2710; Telephone Consumer Protection Act of 1991, 47 U.S.C. 227; Communications Assistance for Law Enforcement Act of 1994; Telecommunications Act of 1996, 47 U.S.C. § 222; Children's On Line Privacy Protection Act of 1999, §§ 6501–6.

88. Omnibus Crime Control and Safe Street Act of 1968, U.S.C. §§ 2510–20 (1994 and Supp. V 2000).

89. Fair Credit Reporting Act of 1970, 15 U.S.C § 1681–81t (1996, 2003).

90. Family Educational Rights and Privacy Act of 1974, 20 U.S.C. §§ 1232g(a)–1232g(g).

91. Privacy Act of 1974, 5 U.S.C. § 552a(a)–552a(v).

92. Right to Financial Privacy Act of 1978, 12 U.S.C. § 3401. *United States v. Miller*, 425 U.S. 435 (1976). In *Miller*, the court rejected the view that bank customers had legal privacy rights to financial information held by financial institutions.

93. Electronic Communications Privacy Act of 1986, 18 U.S.C. §§ 2510–22. See *Smith v. Maryland*, 442 U.S. 735 (1979).

94. Computer Matching and Privacy Protection Act of 1988, 5 U.S.C.A. § 552a.

95. Title V of the Gramm-Leach-Bliley Financial Modernization Act of 2000, Pub. L. No. 106–2, 113 Stat. 1338.

96. Health Insurance Portability and Accountability Act of 1996, Pub. L. No. 104–91, 110 Stat. 1936.

97. Video Voyeurism Prevention Act of 2004, 18 U.S.C. 1801 (2005); Pub. L. No. 108–495.

98. For an overview of state privacy protections, see Electronic Privacy Information Center, accessed February 9, 2019, http://www.epic.org/privacy/consumer/states.html.

99. Washington State, RCW 9A.44.115. See also California's anti-voyeurism statute California Penal Code § 647(k)(1) and Federal Video Voyeurism Prevention Act of 2004, 18 U.S.C. 1801 (2005); Pub. L. No. 108–495.

100. California Consumer Privacy Act, accessed February 6, 2019, https://leginfo.legislature.ca.gov/faces/billTextClient.xhtml?bill_id=201720180AB375. See also UN General Assembly, Universal Declaration of Human Rights, accessed February 7, 2019, http://www.un.org/en/universal-declaration-human-rights/; European Union, accessed February 7, 2019, https://eur-lex.europa.eu/legal-content/EN/TXT/HTML/?uri=CELEX:32016R0679&from=EN. The General Data Protection Regulation allows fines up to 4 percent of a company's worldwide yearly revenues or twenty million euros, whichever is higher.

101. Judith Jarvis Thomson, "The Right to Privacy," *Philosophy and Public Affairs* 4 (1975): 295–314. See also William Parent, "Privacy, Morality, and the Law," *Philosophy and Public Affairs* 12 (1983): 269–88.

102. See Thomas Scanlon, "Thomson on Privacy," *Philosophy and Public Affairs* 4 (1975): 315–22; DeCew, *In Pursuit of Privacy*; Moore, *Privacy Rights*.

103. Catharine MacKinnon, *Toward a Feminist Theory of the State* (Cambridge, MA: Harvard University Press, 2002), 191. See also Carol Gilligan, *In a Different*

*Voice: Psychological Theory and Women's Development* (Cambridge, MA: Harvard University Press, 1982).

104. See Anita L. Allen, *Uneasy Access: Privacy for Women in a Free Society* (Lanham, MD: Rowman & Littlefield, 1988); DeCew, *In Pursuit of Privacy.*

105. See, for example, Bork, *The Tempting of America*; John Hart Ely, "The Wages of Crying Wolf: A Comment on Roe v. Wade," *Yale Law Journal* 82 (1973): 920–49; Louis Henkin, "Privacy and Autonomy," *Columbia Law Review* 74 (1974): 1410–33.

106. Henkin, 1410–11.

107. Judith Wagner DeCew, "The Scope of Privacy in Law and Ethics," *Law and Philosophy* 5 (1986): 165.

108. *FTC v. Wyndham Corp.*, 799 F.3d 236 (3d Cir. 2015).

109. Federal Trade Commission Act, Section 5: Unfair or Deceptive Acts or Practices (15 USC §45), accessed February 6, 2019, https://www.federalreserve.gov/boarddocs/supmanual/cch/ftca.pdf.

# TEN

—ᴧᴧᴧ—

# THE RIGHTS OF NONCITIZENS

## KUNAL M. PARKER

### INTRODUCTION

Most Americans approach the US Constitution from the perspective of those on the inside, where *inside* refers to those inside both the country's territory and its political community. This is a US Constitution by and for Americans: it speaks to the structure of government, limitations on its powers, and individual rights. The overall impression, particularly when one familiarizes oneself with individual rights jurisprudence, is one of individuals empowered vis-à-vis government.

Matters look dramatically different, however, when one approaches the US Constitution from the outside. *Outside* in this sense has multiple meanings. It might refer to those physically located outside US territory but nevertheless subject to US governmental power. It might refer to those located within territories over which the United States claims sovereignty but which are not states. It could refer to groups in the United States possessed of limited sovereignty. It could also refer to the millions of individuals physically within the United States or at its borders who are not US citizens. From these multiple outsides, the US Constitution appears not so much as an instrument that limits governmental power but as one that, in many crucial contexts, simply does not afford recourse against it. Most Americans likely spend very little time thinking about it.

This essay is devoted to an exploration of the constitutional law of immigration and citizenship with a view to showing how the lines between inside and outside have been drawn and redrawn over the long span of American history. Who has counted as a citizen (and therefore who has been designated a noncitizen or "alien") has shifted over time. The various rights associated with the status of citizen (and therefore the lack of rights unique to the status of noncitizen) have changed as well. The historical narrative offered here tracks a mammoth shift from (a) a world in which the citizen/noncitizen distinction coexisted with (but was arguably less important than) a number of legal statuses into which individuals were slotted to (b) a world in which, as many legal statuses crumbled, the citizen/noncitizen distinction became a dominant way of categorizing individuals and rights.[1] This shift is the result of countless (and not always successful) struggles waged by women, racial minorities, the indigent, and immigrants to gain equality under the law. It reveals a complex relationship between status and rights and, hence, how citizen and noncitizen—and the rights associated with each—blend and shift. In this brief essay, I read the historical record to make such themes concrete. I seek to show how *inside* and *outside* have been constructed for purposes of US constitutional law.[2]

## CITIZENSHIP, IMMIGRATION, AND
## RIGHTS BEFORE THE CIVIL WAR

The basic logic of American citizenship—the jus soli rule—derives from England's feudal past. According to the jus soli rule, birth within the realm of the monarch made one an English subject. Subjecthood entailed reciprocal obligations: the subject owed the monarch perpetual allegiance, while the monarch owed the subject protection. Albeit reciprocal, these obligations were unequal. The subject could never forego his or her allegiance, even if the monarch was no longer able to extend protection (for example, if the monarch lost the territory in which the subject was located).[3]

In the early modern period, to be an English subject did not entail many of the crucial rights that Americans of today claim to have guaranteed to them under the US Constitution. First, and perhaps most important, English subjects did not possess rights to movement and presence throughout the kingdom. The earliest colonial charters evidence the subject's need to obtain the monarch's permission to depart the realm. Subjects were also not assured the right to remain within the realm. Those convicted of criminal offenses could be shipped out to distant colonies, virtually ensuring that they would never return, with the result that, during the eighteenth century, the convict trade became the second largest source of involuntary migration to North America after the African slave trade. However, perhaps the most important source of restriction on the subject's rights to presence and mobility grew out of the English poor laws. Beginning in the sixteenth century, a network of laws assigned legal residency, labeled "settlement" or "inhabitancy," to all subjects for the purposes of administering poor relief. Indigent individuals could be refused entrance to places where they were not legally settled and, if they sought public assistance by reason of ill health, injury, or lack of work, could be returned to places where they were settled.

Second, with the exception of propertied adult males, English subjects did not possess rights to participate in government even after the power of the monarchy waned in the aftermath of the Glorious Revolution. Instead, despite being subjects, the majority of English found themselves slotted into a variety of statuses that vested control over them in various legal superiors who represented them in the polity, controlled their labor, and set the terms of their presence and movement. Thus, women were subordinated to their husbands under the system of coverture, children to fathers, servants to masters, the indigent to local poor relief authorities, and so on.

Given this lack of rights, freedoms, and privileges, the substantive distinction between subject and alien in early modern England was perhaps not great. Both subject and alien shared important legal disabilities when it came to rights of movement, presence, and political participation. One important difference, however, was real property rights. English law provided that aliens could neither hold nor transmit real property. Upon the death of an alien, his property would escheat to the state. As England's commercial empire grew, aliens also came to be barred from participating in the lucrative colonial trade. Aliens who wanted access to these valuable economic privileges were compelled to seek naturalization or denization. Naturalization, a cumbersome process regulated by Parliament, ensured that an alien would be treated like a natural-born subject and possess all the rights thereof. Denization, a process controlled by the monarchy, provided a lesser status but proved popular nonetheless because it was easier to navigate.

English colonists carried over to North America many of the ideas, institutions, and practices associated with subjecthood. The imperatives of peopling the country led, however, to a relaxation of some of the restrictions that governed life in Great Britain. Although property holding as a prerequisite for voting remained in place, political participation among adult white men was more widespread in colonial North America than it was in Great Britain. Induction into the community of allegiance also proved easier. The need to attract white Protestant settlers led to an easing of naturalization procedures, on the one hand, and a relaxation of bars to alien rights to hold real property, on the other.

However, restrictions on mobility remained widespread in colonial North America, applicable to subject and alien alike. As the English transplanted the poor laws to North America, towns, counties, and colonies sought to limit their responsibility for the indigent by "warning out" undesirables who lacked legal settlements. Warning out did not necessarily involve immediate physical expulsion. However, it did place the newcomer on legal notice and made it impossible for him to acquire a legal settlement in a particular town or county. Once warning out was accomplished, the newcomer could be permitted to live, work, and pay taxes in the town or county but could be removed to the town, county, or colony to which he legally "belonged" should he need assistance by reason of old age, illness, or injury. The crucial point here is that it was legal settlement—and not subjecthood—that determined rights to presence and mobility. Both subjects and aliens suffered similar legal disabilities.

Indeed, during this period, immigration laws were an extension of the poor laws. Seaports required ship captains to provide bonds for travelers, but such laws did not rigorously distinguish between travelers who were within the community of allegiance (subjects) and those who were not (aliens). Based on the logic of settlement, those excluded could come from overseas, a neighboring colony, or a neighboring town. Studies of removal practices show that it was far more common for towns in New England to remove strangers to neighboring towns and colonies rather than to places "beyond sea."

English colonists also carried with them to North America the plethora of legal statuses that had determined political participation, control over labor, and geographic mobility. However, the demography of colonial North America differed from that of Great Britain in two crucial respects, with serious implications for subjecthood and rights. First, colonists felt compelled to establish a legal relationship to the indigenous populations of the lands they were settling. While legal characterizations of Native Americans varied, it was common practice to represent Native Americans, especially if they lived beyond the frontier of English settlement, as "aliens." It made sense to the English to speak of "naturalizing" Native Americans—something often done to lift alien property disabilities and to facilitate sales of land by Native Americans to Whites. But in what sense were Native Americans aliens? They had come from literally nowhere. They were aliens only because English communities had emerged in their midst and had drawn lines placing them on the outside. The legal construction of Native Americans as aliens illustrates the emergence of the idea of the native-born foreigner. The willingness to deem Native Americans aliens bled into a willingness to deny them rights. Even where Native Americans were not actively represented as aliens, they were subjected to a range of legal disabilities, including political disenfranchisement, stricter controls on mobility, and harsher applications of the poor laws than were applicable to Whites.

Second, the colonists had to work through how people of African descent fitted into the new legal order. The enslavement of Africans and their descendants resulted in slotting a substantial population—even the majority in some places—into an involuntary, perpetual, and oppressive status. Slave owners were vested with control over the labor, mobility, and other rights of the enslaved to an extent that increasingly marked enslaved people off from other working people. Were enslaved people British subjects? What of the small but growing number of free Blacks? During the colonial period, there is evidence that free Blacks were considered British subjects. Nevertheless, like Native Americans, they experienced legal disabilities well in excess of those visited on Whites, including political disenfranchisement and severe constraints on their presence and mobility. Indeed, both Native Americans and free Blacks were likely legally disabled to a greater extent than White aliens.

The American Revolution both altered and retained crucial features of the colonial legal landscape. By legally separating itself from Great Britain, the revolutionary generation engaged in a massive act of self-expatriation, thereby repudiating the idea that allegiance to the monarch was perpetual. As they abandoned allegiance to the British monarch, Americans replaced the category of subject with that of citizen. But who counted as a citizen? How did one become a citizen? What exactly did citizenship entail? How sharply was the citizen distinguished from the alien?

The US Constitution of 1787 mentions the phrase "citizen of the United States" very few times. Perhaps best known is its requirement that the president be a "natural born citizen, or a citizen of the United States" at the time of the adoption of the Constitution.[4] The paucity of references to citizenship of the United States suggests that citizenship at the state level was likely more important than national citizenship at the time of the Constitution's adoption.

Interestingly, the US Constitution of 1787 nowhere specified what made someone a citizen of the United States. This lack of definition points to the fact that most Americans simply assumed that the English jus soli rule would apply. Birth within US territory would mean that one was a natural-born citizen. But did this rule extend to all those born within US territory? The jus soli rule applied most unambiguously to native-born Whites. Its application to Native Americans and free Blacks was a subject of controversy that would carry important implications for the future development of the law of citizenship and immigration. Prominent legal thinkers in the early Republic would argue that Native Americans born within tribes, while not exactly aliens, could not be "considered as subjects born under allegiance."[5] Most concurred that enslaved people were not citizens. But the status of free Blacks was vigorously debated. As the postrevolutionary Northern emancipation and the liberalization of manumission in the Upper South swelled the community of free Blacks, their status in the polity became a flash point. Free Blacks might be deemed citizens of some states (and in some states even possessed the right to vote), but were they citizens of the United States?

According to the Constitution, Congress was given the authority to promulgate a "uniform rule of naturalization," which it did by making citizenship available to free white people who had resided in the United States for at least five years.[6] Thus, non-Whites were statutorily barred from becoming citizens. The relatively low barriers to naturalization for white male aliens, considered highly desirable for the settlement of the country, placed them in a legal status above many of the native-born population, including Native Americans, enslaved people, free Blacks, and others.

However, it should be pointed out that even those native-born Whites who counted as citizens of the United States in terms of the citizen/alien distinction lacked many of the rights we might now associate with citizenship. For the majority of the resident adult white population, a proliferation of legal statuses distinct from citizenship—married woman, servant, pauper, convict, and so on—governed labor, presence, mobility, and participation in government.

The fact that legal statuses other than citizenship governed rights of presence and mobility meant that there was no legal right to travel throughout the United States as an incident of national citizenship. Citizens would face a regime of borders just as aliens would. Article IV of the Articles of Confederation had specified that "the people of each state shall have free ingress and regress to and from any other state." But the preceding sentence had specifically excepted "paupers, vagabonds, and fugitives from Justice" from a state's obligation to extend to the "free inhabitants" of another state the "privileges and immunities of free citizens in the several states."[7] The US Constitution's comity clause omitted the exception for paupers and vagabonds when it provided: "The citizens of each state shall be entitled to all privileges and immunities of citizens in the several states."[8] But this language did not alter the fact that restrictions on the presence and mobility of the poor remained not only legal but entirely uncontroversial. Poor Americans were unable to move into towns, counties, and states as they wished and risked being removed by local officials and returned to where they were from. Married women found their domicile derivative of, and linked to, that of their husbands.

The most severe constraints on mobility and residence were, of course, those on Native Americans and free Blacks. Deemed aliens or noncitizens in many regards, Native Americans could be expelled from their ancestral lands and removed to places beyond the frontier of White settlement. The removal of the Cherokees from the southeastern United States was only the most celebrated of a series of relocations. The situation for free Blacks, who were citizens of some (but not all) states and whose citizenship at the federal level remained in question, was equally dire. In 1816, the American Colonization Society was founded to assist in the repatriation of free Blacks to Africa, where they allegedly "belonged." Throughout the antebellum period, free Blacks were barred from entering states or required to post bond upon entry; could be expelled from states; and, especially in slave states, were prevented from moving around the state and from leaving the states for extended periods of time on pain of not being allowed to reenter. In *Moore v. Illinois* (1852), the Supreme Court recognized a state's authority to exclude free Blacks and paupers as part of a state's general power to regulate: "Some of the states, coterminous with those who tolerate slavery, have found it necessary to protect themselves against the influx either of liberated or fugitive slaves, and to repel from their soil a population likely to become burdensome and injurious either as paupers or criminals."⁹

All of these restrictions on mobility and residence—for native-born Whites, Native Americans, and free Blacks—bore concrete implications for what immigration law in this period looked like. In the antebellum United States, immigration laws were promulgated at the state and local level. Borders were wielded against aliens, citizens, and those in between if they were poor or black. In other words, formal citizenship (or the lack thereof) was not the operative basis of distinction.

The fact that so many native-born people, even those considered citizens for purposes of the citizen/alien distinction, lacked rights to political participation also made the distinction between citizen and alien blurry. At the time of the Civil War, women lacked the vote, while free Blacks possessed the right only in New England. Meanwhile, some states in the West, hoping to attract white settlers, relaxed alien property disabilities and allowed white male aliens to vote after filing a declaration of intent to naturalize. Thus, at a time when not all native-born Americans were deemed citizens, and when even those deemed citizens were not granted the full panoply of rights associated with citizenship, certain white male aliens were granted greater rights than a majority of native-born Americans.

Some developments in the antebellum decades indicating a growing distinction between citizen and alien are worth noting. Owing no doubt to the increasing knitting together of territories and peoples, there was legal recognition here and there that all citizens of the United States should possess some core of common rights. In *Corfield v. Coryell* (1823), Justice Bushrod Washington was called on to give meaning to the Constitution's comity clause, which asked states to extend to citizens of other states the privileges and immunities of citizens in the several states. He expressed the idea as follows:

> We feel no hesitation in confining these expressions to those privileges
> and immunities which are, in their nature, fundamental. . . . [These were]:
> protection by the government; the enjoyment of life and liberty, with the
> right to acquire and possess property of every kind, and to pursue and obtain
> happiness and safety; subject nevertheless to such restraints as the government
> must justly prescribe for the general good of the whole. The right of a citizen of
> one State to pass through, or to reside in any other State, for purposes of trade,
> agriculture, professional pursuits, or otherwise; to claim the benefit of the writ
> of habeas corpus; to institute and maintain actions of any kind in the courts of
> the State; to take, hold and dispose of property, either real or personal; and an

exemption from higher taxes or impositions than are paid by the other citizens of the State; may be mentioned as some of the particular privileges and immunities of citizens, which are clearly embraced by the general description of privileges deemed to be fundamental; to which may be added, the elective franchise, as regulated and established by the laws or constitution of the State in which it is to be exercised.[10]

A few decades later, in the *Passenger Cases* (1849), Chief Justice Roger Taney would state, "We are all citizens of the United States, and as members of the same community, must have the right to pass and repass through every part of it without interruption, as freely as in our own states."[11]

But, as already suggested, the "we" Taney invoked did not include millions of native-born people. The most controversial exclusion from the "we" involved free Blacks. Over the course of the antebellum period, questions surrounding whether free Blacks were citizens of the United States grew ever more pressing. Free Blacks and their allies fought mightily against discrimination at the state level and scored some significant victories in the North. However, in 1857, the Supreme Court ruled that Blacks could not be citizens of the United States by reason of birth or naturalization. This did not mean that Blacks could not be citizens of states that chose to grant them citizenship.[12]

The question of free Blacks' citizenship had direct consequences for the constitutional law of immigration. Even as mass immigration picked up in the 1820s, reaching crisis proportions during the Irish famine migration of the late 1840s and early 1850s, the federal government did not get involved in regulating immigration. The reason was clear. Pro-slavery forces felt that federal involvement in immigration would pave the way for federal involvement in issues regarding the mobility of free Blacks (which the slave states were insistent on controlling). As long as free Blacks remained noncitizens who could be barred from entering states, in other words, states would insist on the right to control the entrance and residence of all outsiders in their territories, including immigrants. The Supreme Court oscillated between recognizing the rights of the slave states to regulate the influx of free Blacks and disapproving the efforts of immigrant-receiving states on the Atlantic seaboard from interfering with Congress's constitutional authority to regulate the commerce with foreign nations that immigration was said to involve. These conflicting signals of the Court alternately upheld and struck down aspects of states' immigration regimes, which kept the laws relatively weak and ineffectual.[13]

Because the US Constitution did not speak unequivocally on the issue, there were also no clear constitutional standards regarding states' laws regarding the treatment of immigrants (beyond some sense that certain restrictions could infringe on Congress's constitutional authority to regulate foreign commerce).

In states such as New York and Massachusetts, the removal of immigrants in the antebellum period appears to have occurred with inadequate procedural protections. Furthermore, although states on the Atlantic seaboard tended to focus their enforcement efforts increasingly on indigent immigrants, they continued to exclude indigent citizens from other states.

## THE EMERGENCE OF A CONSTITUTIONAL LAW OF IMMIGRATION

The Civil War revolutionized the law of citizenship. Ratified in 1868, the Fourteenth Amendment to the US Constitution constitutionalized the English jus soli rule by providing: "All persons born or naturalized in the United States, and subject to the jurisdiction thereof, are citizens of the United States and of the state wherein they reside."[14] The citizenship clause of the Fourteenth Amendment thus ended forever the controversy surrounding the citizenship of native-born Blacks. It also removed the power of the states to deprive their Black residents of the status of citizen. However, the Fourteenth Amendment reached beyond the issue of Black citizenship. After its ratification, all native-born individuals, including the native-born children of immigrants, would be citizens notwithstanding race or national origin.[15]

The matter of native-born aliens did not entirely disappear after passage of the Fourteenth Amendment because the citizenship clause was deemed not to extend to Native Americans born within tribes. In *Elk v. Wilkins* (1884), the US Supreme Court ruled that Native Americans born in tribes were no more citizens of the United States by birth than were Frenchmen born in France: "Indians born within the territorial limits of the United States, members of and owing immediate allegiance to one of the Indian tribes (an alien though dependent power), although in a geographical sense born in the United States, are no more 'born in the United States and subject to the jurisdiction thereof,' within the meaning of the first section of the Fourteenth Amendment, than the children of subjects of any foreign government born within the domain of that government, or the children born within the United States of ambassadors or other public ministers of foreign nations."[16] Thus, it was permissible for Nebraska to deny a Native American who had left his tribe the right to vote. Native Americans would be recognized as citizens of the United States not under the Constitution but by virtue of the Indian Citizenship Act of 1924.[17]

It goes without saying that the ratification of the Fourteenth Amendment did not mean that women, Blacks, Native Americans, and other racial minorities became full members of the polity. In other words, formal recognition of citizenship did not bring with it substantive rights or equality. In the aftermath of the Civil War, an era of second-class citizenship—and hence a reinscription of old statuses—opened for Blacks, Native Americans, and others. With the "separate but equal" reasoning of *Plessy v. Ferguson* (1896) furnishing the overarching logic, the result was a new form of "border control" for racial minorities.[18] Although states could not legally bar Blacks from their territories, a mix of public and private measures were deployed to keep Black people and other minorities from enjoying equal access to towns, neighborhoods, modes of transportation, and a plethora of public and private institutions ranging from schools to hospitals, restaurants to shops, recreational spaces to cemeteries. Discrimination in employment was pervasive. By the early twentieth century, as the result of a battery of restrictive laws, Blacks in the South had effectively been disenfranchised. Native Americans and Latinos experienced similar restrictions on voting in the West and Southwest. In the post–Civil War period, White women hoping to benefit from a new flowering of individual rights would find themselves still subject to legal coverture, barred from various professions, and denied the vote.[19] The continuation of unequal statuses for women and minorities would spark a new wave of struggle that would extend into the twentieth century.

Notwithstanding its unrealized promise for women and racial minorities, the post–Civil War transformation of the law of citizenship bore crucial consequences for the regulation of immigration. During the antebellum period, as noted, the constitutionality of immigration restriction was adjudicated in terms of whether state-level immigration restriction violated Congress's exclusive powers under the US Constitution to regulate commerce with foreign nations. The insistence of the slave states on regulating the mobility of free Blacks kept immigration regulation at the state level.

However, with formal citizenship now extended among more or less the entire native-born population, the inability of states to close their borders to Blacks, and even new judicial intimations in the post–Civil War period of a right to travel, the major obstacle to the emergence of a federal immigration regime was removed.[20] Thus, in the decades following the Civil War, the Supreme Court began to chip away at state-level immigration regimes.[21] By the early 1880s, a federal immigration state, its gaze turned exclusively outward to noncitizens, had come into being. With it came a widening gulf between citizen and alien.

Federal immigration law, and the federal constitutional law of immigration, was developed largely in the context of immigration to the United States from China, the federal government's efforts to exclude and remove Chinese immigrants, and Chinese immigrants' efforts to fight back using the courts. Chinese people had been immigrating to the United States since the late 1840s, drawn to California, as so many were, by the Gold Rush. In 1868, the United States and China concluded the Burlingame Treaty, which would ensure the free influx of nationals of one country into the other.[22] Anti-Chinese sentiment, however, surged in the West, with attacks on Chinese communities and expulsions of Chinese people from towns and communities. White laborers, fearful of competition from Chinese laborers, led the push for legislation to end Chinese immigration.

In 1882, Congress passed the first of a succession of Chinese exclusion laws, which sought to bar the entrance of Chinese immigrants on the ground of their race. The 1888 exclusion law was challenged by a returning Chinese immigrant who found himself in a difficult position. He had obtained the paperwork he needed to reenter the country only to have Congress invalidate the paperwork while he was on his way back. But his challenge failed. The Supreme Court used the occasion to announce a new theory underpinning the federal exclusion power. While the immigration power before the Civil War had been discussed in terms of Congress's foreign commerce power, it now came to be grounded in something as vague and important and potentially limitless as sovereignty. The exclusion power was "plenary," and the Court would not interfere with it. The Court put it thus: "The power of exclusion of foreigners being an incident of sovereignty belonging to the government of the United States as a part of those sovereign powers delegated by the Constitution, the right to its exercise at any time when, in the judgment of the government, the interests of the country require it, cannot be granted away or restrained on behalf of any one."[23]

After giving the federal government plenary power over exclusion, the Supreme Court moved to shelter Congress's deportation power. In 1892, Congress passed the Geary Act, which required Chinese immigrants to produce a certificate from a white witness as evidence of their legal presence in the country; failure to do so would subject a Chinese alien to deportation. Chinese immigrant groups who challenged the deportation law were met with defeat. In *Fong Yue Ting v. United States* (1893), the Court stated: "The right of a nation to expel or deport foreigners who have not been naturalized, or taken any steps towards becoming citizens of the country, rests on the same grounds, and is as absolute and unqualified as the right to prohibit and prevent their entrance into the country."[24] Furthermore, because deportation was deemed a civil sanction and not a criminal one, many of the Constitution's safeguards when it came to the rights of criminal defendants were deemed unavailable to immigrants facing deportation. Thanks to the litigation of Chinese and Japanese immigrants, courts did place some limits on federal plenary power in the context of deportation, but such limits were procedural rather than substantive.[25]

Thus, both crucial aspects of immigration law—the law of exclusion and the law of deportation—were viewed as part of Congress's plenary power with respect to noncitizens and came to be immunized from constitutional review. At a time when laws that were racial on their face risked judicial invalidation ("separate but equal" not being considered an impermissible writing of racial inequality into law), immigration law could freely operate with racial categories. By the early twentieth century, building on the experience with Chinese immigrants and in response to the racialist xenophobia of the period, the federal government had vastly expanded the scope of immigration and deportation law. Federal immigration law barred the entrance of immigrants on grounds of poverty, health, previous criminal background, political opinion, and, increasingly, race and national origin. By the 1920s, immigration from Asia was banned in its entirety, while national origins quotas had severely reduced immigration from Southern and Eastern Europe. Meanwhile, deportation law had increasingly begun to focus not on removing those who should have been excluded but on using deportation as a punishment for post-entry acts, including seeking public assistance, committing crimes, and engaging in political activity frowned on by the state. Despite the severity of deportation as a penalty, because deportation was considered a civil penalty, immigrants facing deportation got none of the protections the Constitution afforded to criminal defendants.

Around roughly this time, the law of naturalization also came to be shielded from constitutional review. Following the passage of the Fourteenth Amendment, Congress altered the naturalization law, which had hitherto restricted naturalization to immigrants who were White. When radical Republicans pushed to remove racial classifications from the law, however, senators from the western states balked. Naturalization law was therefore modified to permit naturalization only by Whites and individuals of African descent. This racial bar to naturalization would last until 1952. Immigrants from the Middle East, South Asia, and East Asia would tie up the federal courts for years in litigation involving whether or not they were White for purposes of the naturalization law. They generally lost. Thus, a legally resident alien who could not be classified as White or Black would be condemned to being a perpetual foreigner, no matter how long he or she had lived and worked in the United States.[26]

The noncitizen's foreignness was also given greater substantive meaning at the state level to the extent that the Supreme Court permitted states to discriminate against noncitizens. There were, to be sure, some limits on what states could do. In *Yick Wo v. Hopkins* (1886), one of the earliest cases to apply the Fourteenth Amendment, the Supreme Court ruled that resident immigrants would be covered by the equal protection clause's prohibition on discrimination on the basis of race.[27] However, in keeping with the older English tradition of alien legal disabilities, the Court also repeatedly declared that states were free to discriminate against immigrants on the ground of noncitizenship—also called alienage—so long as such discrimination did not amount to an interference with Congress's now exclusive plenary power over immigration.[28] In many cases, state laws discriminating against immigrants on grounds of citizenship were allowed to stand even if it was clear to all that alienage functioned as a proxy for race—as in the case of the alien land laws that barred noncitizens from owning land only if they were ineligible to become citizens (a prohibition that targeted only Asians, because White immigrants were eligible to naturalize).[29] With the Supreme Court's blessing, then, states in the early twentieth century passed a torrent of laws that barred immigrants from holding property, engaging in many professions and trades, possessing licenses, and so on. By the early twentieth century, states had also largely repealed laws that had allowed white immigrants to vote in the nineteenth century.

The legal subordination of immigrants was greatly exacerbated in the twentieth century by the emergence of a new phenomenon: undocumented immigration. As historian Mae Ngai has pointed out, the institution of immigration quotas in the 1920s led to numbers of immigrants whose presence was illegal not because they violated a substantive exclusion standard (poverty, prior criminal background, etc.) but simply because they were present in violation of law.[30] The "illegality" of immigrants increased their vulnerability to exploitation in the workplace, community, and home. Fear of law enforcement would drive undocumented immigrants into the shadows, making them uniquely disabled subjects on the American legal landscape.

Thus, the rise of the federal immigration regime, its grounding in plenary power, the permissibility of legal discrimination against noncitizens, and the rise of the figure of the illegal alien collectively placed noncitizens in many important respects outside the purview of the US Constitution. At the same time, a set of complex, contradictory, halting developments fueled by the struggles of Blacks, Native Americans, women, the indigent, and others, swept more and more native-born individuals into the constitutional inside. Although it is beyond the scope of this essay to explore the emergence of this constitutional inside in detail, it is worth noting two interrelated developments.

First, the well-known rights revolution of the twentieth century, which transformed the lives of women, racial minorities, and the poor in different ways, diminished (but never eradicated) legal statuses of race, gender, and class; brought individuals into nonmediated relationships with the state; and allowed them greater rights than before when it came to participation in government. After centuries of occlusion by the legal personalities of their husbands, married women began to represent themselves in the world outside the home. Women won the right to vote, the right to run for office, rights against discrimination in the workplace, and relative equality vis-à-vis men in the context of family law. The status of African Americans and other racial minorities was also transformed relative to their status in the late nineteenth century. The civil rights movement ended the era of formal segregation, while the major civil rights statutes of the 1960s were aimed at safeguarding African Americans' rights in the context of voting, employment, housing, and public accommodations. By the 1970s, laws barring the indigent from voting were also disappearing.

Second, in the twentieth century, indigent Americans finally won more robust rights to presence and movement throughout the country. Despite various judicial expressions of solicitude for a right to travel in the nineteenth century, the poor laws had remained in effect, even experiencing a strengthening as the Great Depression set many people on the march in search of work. In *Edwards v. California* (1941), however, the Supreme Court struck down a California law criminalizing the importation of indigent people into the state.[31] In *Shapiro v. Thomson* (1969), the Court invalidated state laws imposing residence requirements on out-of-state migrants applying for welfare benefits. It stated: "This Court long ago recognized that the nature of our Federal Union and our constitutional concepts of personal liberty unite to require that all citizens be free to travel throughout the length and breadth of our land uninhibited by statutes, rules, or regulations which unreasonably burden or restrict this movement."[32] The centuries-old territorial controls that impeded indigent Americans' rights to presence and movement throughout the country thus came to an end. Meanwhile, the end of legal segregation resulted in a dismantling of some of the barriers that restricted African Americans' presence and mobility.

As a result of such parallel developments—one subjecting immigrants to plenary power and the other bringing more of the native-born population within the purview of the Constitution—the gap between citizen and noncitizen, inside and outside, grew wider than at any previous point in US history. To be sure, the distinction between the two, never having been clean, would remain messy.

To begin with, the rights revolution that brought more and more native-born individuals into the constitutional inside also had a major impact on immigration and nationality law. In 1952, Congress lifted racial bars to naturalization. In 1965, swept up in the civil rights mood of the country, Congress eliminated the national origins quotas of the 1920s, placing all countries under an equal quota system. Notwithstanding such liberalizing tendencies, the Supreme Court did not significantly alter the plenary power doctrine in the context of substantive exclusion and deportation law. Political opinion could be a basis of exclusion or deportation in ways that likely would be found to violate the First Amendment in the domestic context.[33] Similarly, gender could be used in immigration law in ways that would be impermissible under the equal protection clause if used in domestic law.[34] Apart from the Court's attempt to temper the harshness of the plenary doctrine by according immigrants procedural protections,[35] the only requirement it placed on the political branches' substantive power to exclude was that they offer a "facially legitimate and *bona fide* reason" for the decision to exclude—a standard that is very easy for the government to meet.[36] Much of the Court's attempt to curb the federal government's power in recent years

has occurred in the context of detention of aliens pending removal; such efforts have often involved reading statutes aggressively to avoid constitutional
pronouncements.[37]

The Supreme Court has been more aggressive in striking down state laws
regarding immigrants. The rationales here have been a combination of equal
protection and federalism concerns.[38] Perhaps the most celebrated of its efforts
in this context is the landmark case of *Plyler v. Doe* (1982), in which the Court
struck down as a violation of the equal protection clause a Texas law that withheld school funding for undocumented alien minors and authorized schools to
deny such minors enrollment. The Court stated: "This situation raises the specter
of a permanent caste of undocumented resident aliens, encouraged by some to
remain here as a source of cheap labor, but nevertheless denied the benefits that
our society makes available to citizens and lawful residents. The existence of such
an underclass presents most difficult problems for a Nation that prides itself on
adherence to principles of equality under law."[39]

Even as the gulf between citizen and alien, inside and outside, grew throughout the twentieth century, it must be emphasized that the state also repeatedly
sought to transform citizens into noncitizens, thereby seeking (yet again) to blur
the lines between insider and outsider. First, and perhaps most significant, in the
early twentieth century, the federal government began to expatriate Americans
against their will—that is, to literally transform citizens into noncitizens. A variety of acts could trigger involuntary expatriation, such as voting in a foreign
election, working for a foreign government, or, in the case of naturalized citizens,
prolonged residence in a foreign country. Perhaps most outrageous, American
women could lose their citizenship if they married noncitizens, a law the US
Supreme Court upheld in 1915.[40] By the mid-twentieth century, however, the US
Supreme Court shifted course, making it very hard for the government to expatriate citizens against their will.[41]

Second, the US government deliberately blurred lines between immigrants
and citizens, treating citizens like noncitizens in times of war or economic crisis.
Perhaps the most egregious example of this was the internment during World
War II of approximately 110,000 individuals of Japanese descent, more than two-
thirds of whom were US citizens. The same blurring took place in immigration
raids, when US citizens of Mexican descent were shipped to Mexico along with
Mexican nationals.

Finally, particularly in the late twentieth century, the US government began
aggressively to use deportation as a tool to eject insiders. While technically not
citizens, many of those deported had been in the country for most of their lives,
often having come to the United States as children. While deportation had been
on the upswing since the early twentieth century, it spiked sharply following

the 1996 reforms of immigration law. Legal scholar Daniel Kanstroom observes that, including voluntary returns, just under twelve million noncitizens were removed from the United States in the first decade of the twenty-first century, most following convictions for drug-related crimes.[42] This removal of noncitizens reveals striking similarities to the mass incarceration of African American men that began in the closing decades of the twentieth century. Thus, even as the gap between citizen and noncitizen widened over the course of the twentieth century, the lines separating them occasionally blurred.

## CONCLUSION

In the early twenty-first century, the plenary power doctrine is alive and well, placing noncitizens outside the purview of the Constitution in important regards. The Supreme Court's most recent articulation of it came in *Trump v. Hawaii* (2018), in which plaintiffs challenged a September 24, 2017, proclamation by President Donald Trump restricting entry by the nationals of eight countries (six of which were predominantly Muslim) on the ground that such countries' information sharing systems about travelers were inadequate. The proclamation purported to be the result of a bureaucratic review process. To its opponents, however, it was clearly attributable to the xenophobia and Islamophobia that Trump had expressed repeatedly as a presidential candidate. For the majority of the Court, however, plenary power would render the president's proclamation, allegations of religious bias notwithstanding, impossible to dislodge. Chief Justice John Roberts put it as follows: "The upshot of our cases in this context is clear: 'Any rule of constitutional law that would inhibit the flexibility' of the President 'to respond to changing world conditions should be adopted only with the greatest caution,' and our inquiry into matters of entry and national security is highly constrained. . . . A conventional application of [*Kleindienst v. Mandel*], asking only whether the policy is facially legitimate and bona fide, would put an end to our review."[43] Exclusion laws thus cannot be tested against the general constitutional standard prohibiting religious discrimination. The Constitution does not speak on the issue, casting those inside the country and their families whom they cannot bring over essentially outside its purview.

But if the plenary power doctrine has been newly reaffirmed, it is important to keep in mind that immigrants and other noncitizens—following in the steps of Native Americans, Blacks, women, and the indigent—are constantly working to redefine statuses and claims and to make better futures for themselves. The latest and most noteworthy example is the Dreamers, individuals who were brought to the United States as minors, allowed to attend public schools under the rule of *Plyler v. Doe*, and who, now, cast on the outside, are busily making claims for themselves in the halls of legislatures, in the courtroom, and in the public sphere. They are doing what many Americans once deemed noncitizens or lacking crucial rights of citizenship have done in seeking to relocate themselves from the constitutional outside to the constitutional inside. And thus the lines between citizen and noncitizen, drawn and redrawn so many times over the long span of US history, are being redrawn again.

## NOTES

1. This argument has been made for the nineteenth century by William J. Novak, "The Legal Transformation of Citizenship in Nineteenth-Century America," in *The Democratic Experiment: New Directions in American Political History*, ed. Meg Jacobs, William J. Novak, and Julian Zelizer (Princeton, NJ: Princeton University Press, 2003), 85–119. My essay builds on and extends Novak's argument.

2. In writing this essay, I have drawn heavily from Kunal M. Parker, *Making Foreigners: Immigration and Citizenship Law in America, 1600–2000* (New York: Cambridge University Press, 2015). For reasons of length, I have omitted specific references to *Making Foreigners*. Readers who want more detail may consult that book and the sources I have relied on in it, including the bibliographic essay appended to it.

3. *Calvin's Case*, 7 Coke Report 1a, 77 ER 377 (1608) is the most celebrated articulation of the theory of English subjecthood. For a thorough exploration of the idea of perpetual allegiance emerging from *Calvin's Case*, see James H. Kettner, *The Development of American Citizenship, 1608–1870* (Chapel Hill: University of North Carolina Press, 1978), chaps. 1–3.

4. US Constitution Article II, Section 1. Some other references to citizenship are Article I, Section 2 (requiring a member of the House of Representatives to have been "seven years a citizen of the United States") and Article I, Section 3 (requiring a member of the Senate to have been "nine years a citizen of the United States").

5. *Jackson v. Wood*, 7 Johns. Rep. 290, 295 (NY 1810) (opinion of James Kent).

6. US Constitution, Article I, Section 8.

7. Articles of Confederation, Article IV.

8. US Constitution, Article IV, Section 2.

9. *Moore v. Illinois*, 55 U.S. 13, 18 (1852).

10. *Corfield v. Coryell*, 6. F.Cas. 546, 551–52 (E.D.Pa. 1823).

11. *Smith v. Turner* (*Passenger Cases*), 48 U.S. 283, 492 (1849) (Opinion of Taney, CJ).

12. *Scott.v. Sandford*, 60 U.S. 393 (1857).

13. *New York v. Miln*, 36 U.S. 102 (1837) (upholding New York's immigration laws); *Smith v. Turner* (*Passenger Cases*), 48 U.S. 283 (1849) (striking down New York and Massachusetts head taxes on immigrants).

14. US Constitution, Fourteenth Amendment, Section 1.

15. *United States v. Wong Kim Ark*, 169 U.S. 649 (1898).

16. 112 U.S. 94, 102 (1884).

17. 43 Stat. 253 (June 2, 1924).

18. 163 U.S. 537 (1896).

19. See, for example, *Bradwell v. Illinois*, 83 U.S. 130 (1872), upholding an Illinois law barring women from the practice of law.

20. *Crandall v. Nevada*, 73 U.S. 35 (1867) struck down a tax on transporting passengers into and out of Nevada on the ground that the tax was a burden on the citizen's right to travel.

21. *People v. Compagnie Generale Transatlantique*, 107 U.S. 59 (1883).

22. 16 Stat. 739 (July 28, 1868).

23. *Chae Chan Ping v. United States*, 130 U.S. 581, 609 (1889).

24. *Fong Yue Ting v. United States*, 149 U.S. 698, 707 (1893).

25. *The Japanese Immigrant Case (Yamataya v. Fisher)*, 189 U.S. 86 (1903).

26. *Ozawa v. United States*, 260 U.S. 178 (1922); *United States v. Thind*, 261 U.S. 204 (1923).

27. *Yick Wo v. Hopkins*, 118 U.S. 356 (1886).

28. *Truax v. Raich*, 239 U.S. 33 (1915).

29. *Terrace v. Thompson*, 263 U.S. 197 (1923).

30. Mae M. Ngai, *Impossible Subjects: Illegal Aliens and the Making of Modern America*, rev. ed. (Princeton, NJ: Princeton University Press, 2014).

31. 314 U.S. 160 (1941).

32. *Shapiro v. Thompson*, 394 U.S. 618, 629 (1969). The right to travel was reaffirmed in *Saenz v. Roe*, 526 U.S. 489 (1999).

33. *Harisiades v. Shaughnessy*, 342 U.S. 580 (1952); *Kleindienst v. Mandel*, 408 U.S. 753 (1972).

34. *Fiallo v. Bell*, 430 U.S. 787 (1977); *Nguyen v. INS*, 533 U.S. 53 (2001).

35. See, for example, *Landon v. Plasencia*, 459 U.S. 21 (1982) (due process due to a returning alien in exclusion proceedings). Procedural due process protections for aliens in deportation proceedings have been established for much longer.

36. *Kleindienst v. Mandel*, 408 U.S. at 770.

37. *Zadvydas v. Davis*, 533 U.S. 678 (2001); *Clark v. Martinez*, 543 U.S. 371 (2005). But see *Demore v. Kim*, 538 U.S. 510 (2003); *Jennings v. Rodriguez*, 138 S. Ct. 830 (2018).

38. See, for example, *Graham v. Richardson*, 403 U.S. 365 (1971).

39. 457 U.S. 202, 218–19 (1982).

40. *Mackenzie v. Hare*, 239 U.S. 299 (1915).

41. *Afroyim v. Rusk*, 387 U.S. 253 (1967).

42. Daniel Kanstroom, *Aftermath: Deportation Law and the New American Diaspora* (New York: Oxford University Press, 2012), 12.

43. *Trump v. Hawaii*, 585 U.S. ____ (2018).

## ELEVEN

—ᴍ—

# THE COMING OUT OF AMERICAN LAW

MARIE-AMÉLIE GEORGE

OVER THE COURSE OF ONE generation, the constitutional status of LGBTQ-identified individuals has transformed radically.[1] From outlaws to outcasts to community members, the legal evolution has been striking, albeit far from complete. As many questions remain as have been resolved, rendering LGBTQ rights one of the most contested, controversial, and changing areas of contemporary civil rights law.

When the Supreme Court upheld laws criminalizing private, consensual sodomy in 1986, its opinion wavered between blithe indifference and open hostility to same-sex sexuality.[2] Less than thirty years later, the Court invalidated restrictions on same-sex marriage because they served to "disrespect and subordinate" the same population.[3] That decision marked the end of a constitutional metamorphosis, by which gays and lesbians have shifted from deviants whose sexual conduct and gender identity was their defining characteristic, to community members whose immutable same-sex sexuality and gender expression was incidental to their status as citizens.

Although these cases function as constitutional bookends for a jurisprudential transformation, the Supreme Court's decisions have not addressed the LGBTQ community as a whole. The Court decided a transgender rights case for the first time in 2020, but it has yet to hear a dispute involving gender nonconforming gays and lesbians or nonbinary individuals. The LGBTQ movement is a coalition of multiple identity groups, and a relatively new one at that: national gay and lesbian rights groups only expanded to become LGBT rights organizations in the late 1990s and early 2000s, and their legal agendas and strategies reflect that history.[4] As a result, this essay often uses the acronym LGBTQ anachronistically, but does so because the legal issues of the coalition's subgroups often intersect and influence one another.

The Supreme Court has recently become an important arbiter of LGBTQ rights, but LGBTQ rights have advanced in significant part outside the courts. As with other minority rights struggles, legislatures and administrative agencies have been essential forums for rights debates. LGBTQ rights diverge in that LGBTQ individuals have had their rights put to popular vote more than any other minority group, which adds an atypical locus of legal decision making for civil rights contests.[5] Additionally, the majority of these legal struggles have taken place at the state and municipal levels rather than at the federal level. Shifts in social and legal perspectives have been geographically uneven—an important factor since the LGBTQ rights movement has attempted to build from the local to the national, not the other way around.

To illustrate the extent to which the American legal paradigm has changed over the course of half a century, this essay begins by describing the web of laws that disciplined LGBTQ life and rendered both same-sex sexuality and gender nonconformity a legal liability. With this context in place, it then traces the evolution of the Supreme Court's main cases on LGBTQ rights, which mirror the striking shift in US society's treatment of LGBTQ individuals. The essay ends by analyzing three contested doctrinal areas: (1) the conflict between marriage equality and those who object to same-sex marriage because of their religious beliefs, (2) whether federal prohibitions on discrimination based on sex includes sexual orientation and gender identity, and (3) nonbinary rights. These debates demonstrate both the law's transformation and the limits of what constitutional jurisprudence has established for LGBTQ rights.

## GETTING TO TODAY

Social opprobrium against same-sex sexuality and gender variance has long roots, with all thirteen colonies criminalizing sodomy as a "crime against nature."[6] Same-sex assignations nevertheless transpired and relationships flourished within the confines of the queer world. This community also included individuals that today's society might identify as transgender. For example, in 1895, San Francisco police arrested Ferdinand Haisch, a forty-seven-year-old carpenter, who appeared in public in women's clothing at the end of each workday.[7] After the judge conditioned Haisch's release from prison on her ceasing to wear dresses in public, Haisch complied, but continued to don women's clothing at home.[8]

Despite the existence of individuals who transgressed gender norms and engaged in same-sex sexual activity, LGBTQ-identified individuals only became a visible minority group in the second half of the twentieth century. It was not until the 1930s that same-sex sexual conduct became a marker of identity, creating a dividing line between what were then known as homosexuals and heterosexuals.[9] After World War II, gay and lesbian bars proliferated around the country, thereby increasing the subpopulation's visibility.[10] In the 1950s, the national press began reporting on sex reassignment surgeries, which had been available in Europe since the early 1930s, thereby introducing transsexuality to Americans as well as communicating the possibility of surgical intervention to gender-variant individuals.[11]

Federal law developed in tandem with these social changes to codify the LGBTQ community's outsider status. The US military disqualified homosexuals from service in World War II, then later denied GI Bill benefits to gay men who had nevertheless enlisted but then been discharged as "undesirable" because of their sexual orientation.[12] In 1952, Congress barred homosexuals from entering the country under its new immigration code.[13] Throughout the 1950s, as part of the Red Scare's anticommunist investigations into security risks and disloyalty, the executive branch attempted to purge its civil service ranks of all gay and lesbian employees, claiming that "even one homosexual can pollute a Government office."[14] NASA budget analyst Clifford Norton learned how dangerous even the most minor of liaisons could be. After fifteen years of exemplary government service, the agency fired him for his "immoral, indecent and disgraceful conduct" in 1957, when it discovered he had invited a man home for a drink.[15] Government employees who lost their jobs and their security clearances because of their sexuality were often unable to find other work in their field; shame and poverty led some to commit suicide.[16]

At the state and local levels, officials typically deployed existing laws to curtail the rights of gays, lesbians, and gender-variant individuals. Police arrested LGBTQ individuals for disorderly conduct, loitering, vagrancy, lewd and lascivious behavior, and solicitation—all of which were statutory crimes that applied to the population at large.[17] Law enforcement likewise relied on masquerade laws, which were enacted throughout the nineteenth and twentieth centuries to prevent fraud and aid in the detection of criminals, to arrest individuals who were wearing fewer than two or three articles of clothing appropriate to their gender assigned at birth.[18] One lesbian woman recounted being stopped for wearing a man's shirt and pants in the 1950s, but avoiding arrest because she was wearing women's shoes.[19] Law enforcement additionally used obscenity laws to curtail the LGBTQ press and preclude subcultures from developing through national publications.[20] Municipal and state liquor authorities also revoked the licenses of gay and lesbian bars, arguing they had become disorderly by permitting "homosexuals, degenerates, and undesirables" to congregate on the premises.[21]

States additionally created new statutes that they then disproportionately applied to LGBTQ individuals. Beginning in the late 1930s, thirty states and the District of Columbia enacted sexual psychopath laws, under which courts sentenced defendants—including homosexual men convicted of consensual sodomy—to psychiatric institutions until cured.[22] Bert Chapman was thirty-five years old when police arrested him in his home in September 1940 for engaging in a "homosexual act" with another consenting adult. After being adjudicated under Michigan's sexual psychopath statute, he spent the next thirty-one years in state mental hospitals, ultimately securing his release in 1971 by convincing a jury he was not dangerous.[23]

In the decades that followed, the social and legal landscape began shifting in favor of LGBTQ rights. In 1961, Illinois became the first state to decriminalize consensual sodomy, and by 1978, twenty-one other states had followed suit.[24] In 1972, East Lansing, Michigan, passed the first sexual orientation–inclusive antidiscrimination ordinance; three years later, in 1975, Minneapolis, Minnesota, enacted the first comprehensive antidiscrimination law that included both sexual orientation and gender-identity protections.[25] Also in 1975, the federal Civil Service Commission eliminated "immoral conduct" as a disqualification from service.[26] The American Psychiatric Association's 1973 decision to declassify homosexuality as a mental illness promoted these changes, as lawmakers often pointed to homosexuality's pathological status to justify discriminatory laws and policies.[27]

As LGBTQ rights progressed, the religious Right organized in opposition, sponsoring hundreds of anti-LGBTQ ballot measures around the country.[28] In addition to repealing newly instituted antidiscrimination statutes, the measures sought to affirmatively prohibit the state from providing such protections for LGBTQ individuals, prevent gay and lesbian teachers from serving in the classroom, and institute constitutional bans on same-sex marriage.[29] These efforts, which were part of a larger conservative backlash, were overwhelmingly effective at curtailing LGBTQ rights throughout the 1980s and 1990s.

The AIDS crisis of the 1980s compounded the effects of the religious Right's increasing influence. HIV/AIDS was devastating to the LGBTQ community, with the epidemic raging for more than a decade before scientists developed an effective treatment.[30] During that time, more than 380,000 people died, leaving the survivors who had cared for their friends and partners with tremendous senses of loss, depression, fear, anxiety, shame, and anger.[31] Multiplying the devastation was that then president Ronald Reagan did not speak the word "AIDS" in public until 1986 and repeatedly declined to fund research, services, and educational efforts.[32] Many members of the LGBTQ community criticized the leader for his indifference and blamed his inaction for prolonging the crisis. They then channeled their feelings into activism that focused on access to health care, antidiscrimination ordinances, and family recognition.[33] Domestic partnership rights became increasingly pressing after longtime partners found themselves unable to make medical decisions for their loved ones or evicted from their rent-controlled homes because the state did not recognize their relationships.[34]

### DEVELOPING THE DOCTRINE

It was during the height of the AIDS crisis that the Supreme Court agreed to hear its first LGBTQ rights case in decades.[35] Michael Hardwick, who had been arrested in his bedroom for engaging in consensual sodomy with another adult man, took his case to the nation's highest court in 1986. Until 1960, every state outlawed private, consensual sodomy, and at the time the Court heard *Bowers v. Hardwick*, twenty-four states and the District of Columbia continued to do so, with punishments that ranged from fines to life imprisonment.[36] States did not often enforce these laws, but their existence had pernicious effects, promoting discrimination, violence, and stigma, as well as curtailing gays' and lesbians' social interactions and political activism.[37] In bringing the challenge, LGBTQ rights advocates hoped to eliminate a symbol of subordination, which they identified as the "bedrock of legal discrimination against gay men and lesbians."[38] Given that half the states had decriminalized consensual sodomy and the Supreme Court's prior cases seemed to recognize a right to sexual privacy in the home, advocates were hopeful the Court would decide the case in their favor.[39]

However, the Court ruled against Hardwick, disappointing advocates and the LGBTQ community, which felt the blow of the decision all the more acutely because of the AIDS crisis. In its decision, the Court did not just uphold the laws, but also reduced Hardwick's claim to dignity, privacy in his personal relationships, and equality before the law to a mere demand for a "constitutional right of homosexuals to engage in acts of sodomy."[40] In doing so, the Court appeared to denigrate gays and lesbians as lesser citizens. The European Court of Human Rights had struck down consensual sodomy laws in Europe in a decision five years earlier, putting the case at odds with legal trends in other Western countries.[41]

The decision turned on the vote of Justice Lewis Powell, who initially joined four others to strike down the laws as unconstitutional, but later changed his mind and the outcome.[42] The privacy argument that Hardwick made simply did not resonate with Powell's understanding of homosexuality, which he saw as incompatible with family life. Hardwick had emphasized that sodomy laws allowed the police to intrude into both the physical sanctuary of the home and the emotional intimacy of human relationships[43]—a claim Powell described as "repellent" since "home is one of the most beautiful words in the English language" and one that "usually connotes family, husband and wife, and children."[44] At the time, although LGBTQ individuals were increasingly raising children—some born during opposite-sex marriages, others adopted or conceived with same-sex partners through alternative reproductive technologies—long-standing stereo-types of gay men as hedonistic and same-sex sexuality as pedophilic led many to view homosexuality as anathema to parenthood.[45]

The Court did not revisit the issue for seventeen years. During that interval, the Court struck down a citizen-enacted constitutional amendment that pro-hibited Colorado from protecting gays, lesbians, or bisexuals from discrimination due to their sexual orientation.[46] Although *Romer v. Evans*, decided in 1996, was a significant victory of LGBTQ rights, the fact that the constitutional amend-ment targeted gays and lesbians was not central to the majority opinion. Justice Anthony Kennedy emphasized the sweeping breadth of the laws, which made a category of citizens a "stranger to its laws."[47] If sodomy laws had permissibly attacked homosexual conduct in *Bowers*, then Colorado's law was unconstitu-tional because it discriminated against an identity group that happened to be homosexual.

When consensual sodomy laws came before the Court again in 2003, the jus-tices understood both same-sex sexuality and the harm of the laws much differ-ently. The opinion mirrored a broader social shift, one where many Americans accepted same-sex sexuality and refused to countenance discrimination against LGBTQ individuals. In *Lawrence v. Texas*, Justice Kennedy wrote that the Court had previously "misapprehended the claim of liberty" presented in the legal chal-lenge, as the real issue was that the state demeaned and controlled the lives of gays and lesbians through the criminal laws.[48] Consensual homosexual sodomy was no longer a question of conduct, but rather an expressive act integrally related to personhood.[49] Furthermore, the penal code served as "an invitation to subject ho-mosexual persons to discrimination both in the public and in the private spheres," rendering gays and lesbians legal outcasts.[50] The consensual sodomy laws made it both possible and permissible to discriminate against gays and lesbians. To em-phasize the significance of its decision, the Court took the unusual step of stating that "*Bowers* was not correct when it was decided, and it is not correct today."[51] Instead of simply overruling *Bowers* and claiming the nation was shifting course from that point forward, the Court eradicated the opinion, identifying it as a blot in jurisprudential history.

For the dissenting justices, one of the important implications of *Lawrence* was whether the majority's reframing of gay and lesbian identity rendered same-sex relationships equivalent to their opposite-sex counterparts. At oral argu-ment, Chief Justice William Rehnquist asked whether striking down sodomy laws meant that the state could no longer "prefer heterosexuals to homosexuals to teach kindergarten" to prevent children from being "induced . . . to follow the path of homosexuality."[52] Antonin Scalia voiced similar concerns in his dissent, criticizing the majority for failing to recognize that "many Americans do not want persons who openly engage in homosexual conduct as partners in their business, as scoutmasters for their children, as teachers in their children's schools, or as boarders in their home."[53] These objections were slightly different than the ones Justice Powell had raised in 1987, but they were rooted in similar concerns and stereotypes.[54] Lambda Legal, a national LGBTQ rights group that represented the petitioner, tried to preempt these issues by soliciting numerous amicus briefs to support its arguments that gays and lesbians formed lasting relationships and raised children within those families.[55] The organization even went so far as to stress that John Lawrence and Tyron Garner were arrested for engaging in a physical act like any other loving couple, despite the fact that the men were mere acquaintances.[56]

Although *Lawrence* was a marker of jurisprudential change, it took the marriage cases, *United States v. Windsor* and *Obergefell v. Hodges*, decided more than a decade later, to recast gays and lesbians as ordinary citizens. Justice Kennedy's opinion in *Windsor* framed the injustice of marriage laws as one that had always existed but only recently been recognized, identifying same-sex couples as individuals who should always have been seen as integral members of American society.[57] Two years later, in *Obergefell*, the movement for LGBTQ rights had become analogous to the struggle for racial justice, with the Supreme Court noting that same-sex attractions were an immutable characteristic.[58] There, the Court commented that "outlaw to outcast may be a step forward, but it does not achieve the full promise of liberty."[59] The marriage equality decision aimed at moving toward that goal.

In these cases, the Supreme Court's portrayal of the LGBTQ community shifted dramatically, from individuals seeking constitutional protections for torrid assignations to loving family members. In 1986, Justice Powell's perception of same-sex sexuality as incongruous with family led to the Court upholding consensual sodomy laws; by 2015, the ubiquity of gay- and lesbian-headed families supported a constitutional right to same-sex marriage. Indeed, much of the LGBTQ movement's broader success has come from emphasizing families, which has countered long-standing stereotypes of gays and lesbians as harmful to children and reinforced the notion that LGBTQ individuals are like all other Americans.

## CURRENT BOUNDARIES OF LGBTQ RIGHTS

The marriage equality movement created profound legal change and propelled discourse in favor of LGBTQ rights, but the larger implications of the Court's opinions continue to be contested. The cases did not entirely resolve debates over marriage equality because the Court's landmark decisions left open the question of how to resolve competing rights claims between same-sex couples and individuals who have religious objections to marriage equality. At the same time, the way in which the LGBTQ movement secured its victories may have a limited strategic effect. Litigators stressed how same-sex couples were like their opposite-sex counterparts in all but the gender of their sexual partners, but for many in the LGBTQ community, the law should respect their differences rather than require their conformity to social norms.[60] For these individuals, LGBTQ social movement advocacy should focus as much, if not more, on transforming society by challenging hierarchies as securing formal equality. Current debates over LGBTQ rights therefore include protecting marriage rights, expanding the law's reach to protect other members of the LGBTQ community, and using law to reshape the social order.

### Religious Objections to Same-Sex Marriage

For lower courts adjudicating LGBTQ rights in the wake of *Obergefell*, one particularly thorny question has been demarcating the boundary where marriage equality ends and First Amendment religious liberties begin. This issue has come up most often in the context of same-sex weddings, with religious objectors arguing that their provision of goods and services for these events renders them complicit in conduct they consider morally objectionable.[61] Conservative leaders issued calls to resist same-sex marriage as a violation of conscience even before the Court handed down its decision in *Obergefell*, setting up the standoff that came to a head after the ruling. Although state and county officials delayed implementing the Court's decision or defied it altogether, resistance quickly became limited to private providers of wedding-related goods or services, such as photographers and venue owners.[62]

One of the objectors' main claims is that they are a religious minority whose rights deserve protection—a secular argument that provides an opportunity to present the faith-based reasons for their opposition and continue the debate over same-sex marriage.[63] Unlike previous claims against marital rights for same-sex couples, these arguments are presumptively not about whether there is a legal right to same-sex marriage, but rather concern the circumstances under which same-sex couples may obtain the services they need to solemnize and celebrate their marriages. However, since their underlying premise is that the couples' union is morally wrong, these contests propagate the culture wars that underpin the legal challenges around LGBTQ rights.

Supporting religious objectors' constitutional claims are federal and state-level religious freedom restoration acts, or RFRAs (pronounced "rifra"), which enumerate protections for religious practice and belief. States began enacting RFRAs in the early 1990s in response to a shift in Supreme Court jurisprudence that provided less protection to religious liberties.[64] For many decades, the Court interpreted the First Amendment's free exercise clause to protect religious observers whose practices conflicted with laws of general application. For example, in 1963, the Court protected a Seventh-day Adventist's right to receive unemployment benefits after she refused an offered job because it required her to work on the Sabbath.[65] In 1990, the Court changed its approach, only applying heightened judicial scrutiny to laws that directly target religious practices.[66] In that decision, the Court ruled that Native Americans could not use peyote for sacramental purposes in contravention of the state's criminal controlled substance laws.

Religious objectors successfully invoked an RFRA to defend against a claim of sexual orientation discrimination for the first time in 2018.[67] In that case, *Masterpiece Cakeshop Ltd. v. Colorado Civil Rights Commission*, the Supreme Court ruled in favor of a devout Christian baker named Jack Phillips who refused to provide wedding cakes to same-sex couples.[68] However, the decision was a narrow one that provided little guidance on the larger issues. The Court recognized that religious objections generally do not permit business owners to deny protected classes equal access to goods or services, and that any decision in their favor would have to be constrained lest it result in actions that "impose a serious stigma on gay persons."[69] At the same time, adjudicators hearing those cases needed to approach religion neutrally rather than with the hostility to Phillips's sincerely held religious beliefs that the Colorado commission had expressed.[70] The decision was therefore largely limited to how commission members had adjudicated the case, not their ultimate conclusion.

Courts will need to resolve these competing claims to equality and religious liberty in other contexts, particularly since responses to transgender rights will likely follow this same path. Many religious denominations welcome transgender individuals, but a significant number also press transgender members to affirm their sex assigned at birth and identify physical transition as inconsistent with biblical mandates.[71] Religious objectors to transgender rights may press their claims under RFRAs or seek greater statutory protections, similar to what the Mississippi legislature enacted in 2016. Unlike most RFRAs, Mississippi's law protects specific religious views, in that it provides the state will not discriminate against those acting in accordance with their religious beliefs that "marriage is or should be recognized as the union of one man and one woman," "sexual relations are properly reserved to such a marriage," and "male (man) or female (woman) refer[s] to an individual's immutable biological sex as objectively determined by anatomy and genetics at time of birth."[72] An immediate challenge to the law failed on procedural grounds.[73] Thus, although the current legal debate over religious objectors' rights is framed in terms of marriage, it will likely shift in form, raising new contests over LGBTQ rights.

### Employment Discrimination Protections

The marriage equality debate is not entirely resolved, despite the Supreme Court's rulings, yet that ongoing legal battle is only one of the major issues on the LGBTQ rights agenda. The Court recently addressed a different legal question that had been percolating for decades: the applicability of federal antidiscrimination laws to LGBTQ rights. In 2020, it ruled in *Bostock v. Clayton County* that Title VII of the Civil Rights Act, which protects against discrimination on the basis of sex in the workplace, encompasses prohibitions on discrimination due to sexual orientation and gender identity.[74] That landmark decision provided antidiscrimination protections to millions of Americans, though how the Court reached its conclusion may limit advocates' ability to use it to promote the rights of nonbinary and other gender-nonconforming LGBTQ individuals.

The Court came to its conclusion using a textualist methodology, a formalist approach in which courts interpret the law based on the ordinary meaning of the legal text. Title VII prohibits employers from basing an employment decision on the employee's sex. Since sexual orientation–based discrimination requires treating a woman who dates a man differently from a man who dates a man, and gender identity discrimination means an employer is differentiating between a woman who identifies as male and a man who identifies as male, "it is impossible to discriminate against a person for being homosexual or transgender without discriminating against that individual based on sex."[75] In other words, when employers discriminate on the basis of sexual orientation or gender identity, they necessarily treat an employee differently based at least in part on that person's sex.[76]

Advocates began pressing courts to recognize Title VII's protections for LGBTQ individuals in the late 1970s, but rather than a formalist claim, they argued that the law extended to sexual orientation and gender identity discrimination because it proscribed sex stereotyping, or discrimination against people who do not conform to traditional expectations of how men and women act.[77] Judges recognized that stereotypes based on gender and sexual orientation could overlap, which made it difficult to distinguish between sex stereotyping discrimination and sexual orientation discrimination.[78] They nevertheless insisted the two needed to be distinct since "every case of sexual orientation discrimination cannot translate into a triable case of gender stereotyping discrimination, which would contradict Congress's decision not to make sexual orientation discrimination cognizable" under the Civil Rights Act.[79] Despite these concerns, some courts upheld claims where they could isolate the elements of gender-based discrimination.[80] For example, in *Prowel v. Wise Business Forms*, the Third Circuit determined that a gay machine operator's dress, grooming, manner of walking, effeminate demeanor, and high-pitched voice supported a claim of sex discrimination because it was based not on sexual orientation but on the employer's vision of "how a man should look, speak, and act."[81]

As courts increasingly tried to distinguish between sex stereotyping and sexual orientation discrimination, the legal contortions that the boundary drawing required led some judges to determine the line did not exist.[82] The Second and Seventh Circuits consequently held that discrimination on the basis of sexual orientation constitutes sex discrimination as a matter of law under Title VII.[83] The Equal Employment Opportunity Commission, which enforces Title VII, also made the same determination.[84] The division among the circuits is what led the Supreme Court to take up the question in *Bostock*.[85]

The judicial process progressed similarly for transgender employment discrimination, as courts initially rejected arguments that Title VII protected against gender identity discrimination but then changed their position because of sex stereotyping arguments. Early decisions reasoned that "Congress had a narrow view of sex in mind when it passed the Civil Rights Act" and consequently ruled against transgender plaintiffs.[86] After the Supreme Court interpreted Title VII to include sex stereotyping, transgender individuals reframed their claims as failing to conform to expectations of how men and women appeared and behaved.[87] In the 2004 case of *Smith v. City of Salem*, the Sixth Circuit became the first federal appellate court to hold that transgender individuals could bring sex stereotyping claims under Title VII.[88] Central to its decision was that, before the plaintiff transitioned to living as a woman full-time, her coworkers complained that her mannerisms were insufficiently masculine.[89]

The Sixth Circuit later extended *Smith* by determining that gender identity discrimination and sex discrimination are one and the same, a conclusion other judges soon adopted.[90] Like the courts that held they could not distinguish between sex stereotyping and sexual orientation discrimination, the Sixth Circuit explained that "an employer cannot discriminate on the basis of transgender status without imposing its stereotypical notions of how sexual organs and gender identity ought to align. There is no way to disaggregate discrimination on the basis of transgender status from discrimination on the basis of gender nonconformity, and we see no reason to try."[91] Importantly, even federal circuits that rejected claims that Title VII protects against sexual orientation discrimination recognized that the statute encompasses gender identity protections.[92]

These lower court arguments about Title VII emphasized the extent to which LGBTQ individuals defied sex stereotypes and gender norms. In that sense, they were diametrically opposed to arguments of the marriage equality movement, which highlighted how gays and lesbians formed families like their heterosexual counterparts. These Title VII decisions therefore supported LGBTQ individuals' claims for protection based on their differences rather than their sameness. The Supreme Court's reasoning, however, was rooted in the text of the statute, instead of sex stereotyping theory—a perspective that might indicate its unwillingness to extend protections when LGBTQ individuals diverge from the norm. Whether and how Supreme Court precedent that emphasizes gays' and lesbians' similarity serves as groundwork for the rights claims of nonbinary and gender-fluid members of the LGBTQ community therefore remains to be seen.

## Nonbinary Rights

The Supreme Court's reasoning in *Bostock* is particularly important given that advocates are increasingly focused on transgender and nonbinary rights, which both highlight the needs of gender nonconformists. The contemporary transgender rights movement traces back to the 1970s, when advocates prompted many states to change their laws so transgender individuals could modify the gender on their identification documents, including birth certificates and driver's licenses, after undergoing gender confirmation surgery.[93] Since that period, advocates have been lobbying legislatures and administrative agencies to eliminate the surgical requirement because surgery is often unappealing, prohibitively expensive, or both.[94] These efforts have been successful in some states and municipalities, which increasingly accept hormonal treatments or a treating physician's attestation as evidence of gender identity.[95] Most recently, cities and states have begun offering a gender-neutral "X" designation on documents for nonbinary individuals, and a federal court has ordered the State Department to offer a nonbinary gender option on US passports.[96]

An individual's sex designation on identity documents is extremely consequential in that it often determines access to sex-segregated spaces, such as restrooms, store changing facilities, and fitness club locker rooms.[97] Transgender youth have even more encounters with the legal sex imperative, as schools themselves may be limited by gender, and coeducational facilities divide residence halls, sports teams, and other extracurricular activities by sex. The state enforces the gendered division of these spaces by enacting statutes and zoning ordinances that require the segregation, as well as by enforcing these laws when participants and patrons challenge a transgender person's presence. The ability to secure representative identity documents is therefore bound in a larger legal structure that regulates the sexual binary in public life.

However, not all sex-based classifications depend on identity documents, with administrators typically making housing assignments in prisons, jails, and immigration detention facilities according to whether a transgender individual has had genital surgery.[98] These administrative classifications can have extremely harmful consequences, as transgender individuals disproportionately suffer sexual abuse while incarcerated.[99] In 2012, the Department of Justice promulgated regulations under the Prison Rape Elimination Act that required promoting transgender inmates' health and safety by considering factors other than genital status in housing, although few states have complied with these supposedly mandatory standards.[100] States also differ as to whether they provide transgender inmates with hormone treatments and access to gender confirmation surgery, and federal circuit courts are divided on whether the correctional institutions' failure to do so constitutes cruel and unusual punishment under the Eighth Amendment.[101]

Although much of the advocacy around transgender rights has focused on individuals' ability to have their gender identity and legal sex align, an increasingly pressing question is how the law should address those whose gender is fluid or nonbinary. Protecting the right of transgender individuals who identify as male and female is categorically different from recognizing gender neutrality or a third, alternative gender. Indeed, what nonbinary rights should look like is a subject of debate, as the elimination of sex classifications and the acceptance of all forms of self-identification are two distinct approaches, even though both aim to address the needs of the same population.[102] Thus, one of the primary questions that advocates will need to resolve is what legal goal they should pursue.

## CONCLUSION

As much as LGBTQ rights have recently transformed, debates about how to conceptualize sex, gender, and sexual orientation are ongoing, producing legislative enactments and administration regulations that in turn raise constitutional questions for courts to resolve. How the Supreme Court will interpret the state's obligation to LGBTQ individuals is uncertain, particularly since Justice Kennedy, who authored all but the most recent opinions affirming LGBTQ rights, retired in July 2018. The Court's composition will influence the viability of specific claims as well as which objectives and strategies lawyers will press.

The LGBTQ movement's Supreme Court successes have been rooted in claims about sameness, but many of the current legal issues implicate questions of difference. The next stage of LGBTQ rights therefore appears to be unlike the one that has come before, in that it will focus on the accommodation of difference. At the same time, LGBTQ rights advocacy in the 1980s began as outsiders demanding legal rights, which gave rise to a transformational legal movement. LGBTQ rights groups may simply be back in a similar starting place, but they are further down the road.

## NOTES

1. This essay uses LGBTQ to refer to lesbian, gay, bisexual, transgender, and queer, with queer referring to those whose sexual and gender identity is nonnormative. This essay excludes asexual and intersex because of the contested place of these identity categories within the LGBTQ legal coalition and the different rights issues they raise. For a discussion of these issues, see Marie-Amélie George, "Expanding LGBT," *Florida Law Review* 243 (2021): 243–319.

2. *Bowers v. Hardwick*, 478 U.S. 186 (1986).

3. *Obergefell v. Hodges*, 135 S. Ct. 2584, 2604 (2015).

4. Marie-Amélie George, "The LGBT Disconnect," *Wisconsin Law Review* 2018, no. 3 (2018): 503–91.

5. Brad Sears, Christy Mallory, and Nan D. Hunter, "Voters' Initiatives to Repeal or Prevent Laws Prohibiting Employment Discrimination against LGBT People, 1974–Present," Williams Institute, UCLA, 2009, https://escholarship.org /uc/item/58j4w7k3.

6. William N. Eskridge Jr., *Dishonorable Passions: Sodomy Laws in America, 1861–2003* (New York: Viking, 2008), 16.

7. Clare Sears, *Arresting Dress: Cross-Dressing, Law, and Fascination in Nineteenth-Century San Francisco* (Durham, NC: Duke University Press, 2015), 64.

8. Sears, *Arresting Dress*, 73.

9. George Chauncey, *Gay New York: Gender, Urban Culture, and the Making of the Gay Male World, 1890–1940* (New York: Basic Books, 1994), 12–14. For contemporary terminology and terms to avoid, see GLAAD, *GLAAD Media Reference Guide*, 10th ed. 2016, https://www.glaad.org/reference.

10. John D'Emilio, *Sexual Politics, Sexual Communities: The Making of a Homosexual Minority in the United States, 1940–1970*, 2nd ed. (Chicago: University of Chicago Press, 1998), 32.

11. Joanne Meyerowitz, *How Sex Changed: A History of Transsexuality in the United States* (Cambridge, MA: Harvard University Press, 2002), 19–21, 62–69. Like homosexuality, transsexuality is a dated term but one that people used at the time to self-identify.

12. Allan Bérubé, *Coming Out Under Fire: The History of Gay Men and Women in World War II*, 20th anniv. ed. (Chapel Hill: University of North Carolina Press, 2010), 9–12, 164–69, 201–3, 230.

13. Margot Canaday, *The Straight State: Sexuality and Citizenship in Twentieth-Century America* (Princeton, NJ: Princeton University Press, 2009), 216, 220.

14. D'Emilio, *Sexual Politics*, 41–42.

15. David K. Johnson, *The Lavender Scare: The Cold War Persecution of Gays and Lesbians in the Federal Government* (Chicago: University of Chicago Press, 2004), 191.

16. Johnson, *Lavender Scare*, 158, 167–68, 192.

17. Elizabeth Lapovsky Kennedy and Madeline D. Davis, *Boots of Leather, Slippers of Gold: The History of a Lesbian Community* (New York: Penguin Books, 1993), 180; Steven A. Rosen, "Police Harassment of Homosexual Women and Men in New York City 1960–1980," *Columbia Human Rights Law Review* 12 (1980–81): 164.

18. Kennedy and Davis, 180; Martin B. Duberman, *Stonewall* (New York: Dutton, 1993), 299n39.

19. Kennedy and Davis, 180.

20. William N. Eskridge Jr., *Gaylaw: Challenging the Apartheid of the Closet* (Cambridge, MA: Harvard University Press, 1999), 116–23.

21. Rosen, "Police Harassment," 170.

22. Estelle B. Freedman, "'Uncontrolled Desires': The Response to the Sexual Psychopath, 1920–1960," *Journal of American History* 74, no. 1 (1987): 89, 94, 103–5.

23. Marie-Amélie George, "Deviant Justice: The Transformation of Gay and Lesbian Rights in America" (PhD diss., Yale University, 2018), introduction.

24. Melinda D. Kane, "Timing Matters: Shifts in the Causal Determinants of Sodomy Law Decriminalization, 1961–1998," *Social Problems* 54, no. 2 (2007): 214.

25. Amy L. Stone, *Gay Rights at the Ballot* Box (Minneapolis: University of Minnesota Press, 2012), 12; Jami K. Taylor et al., "Content and Complexity in Policy Reinvention and Diffusion: Gay and Transgender-Inclusive Laws against Discrimination," *State Politics and Policy Quarterly* 12, no. 1 (2012): 93n6.

26. Johnson, *The Lavender Scare*, 210.

27. Marie-Amélie George, "Bureaucratic Agency: Administering the Transformation of LGBT Rights," *Yale Law and Policy Review* 36, no. 1 (2017): 111–16.

28. Stone, *Gay Rights at the Ballot Box*, 6, 12–13; George, "The LGBT Disconnect," 514–15.

29. Stone, *Gay Rights at the Ballot Box*, 1, 6–7.

30. Steven Epstein, *Impure Science: AIDS, Activism, and the Politics of Knowledge* (Berkeley: University of California Press, 1996), 45, 323–24.

31. Centers for Disease Control, "HIV and AIDS—United States, 1981–2000," *Morbidity and Mortality Weekly Report*, June 1, 2001.

32. Jennifer Brier, *Infectious Ideas: U.S. Political Responses to the AIDS Crisis* (Chapel Hill: University of North Carolina Press, 2009), 80.

33. Marc Stein, *Rethinking the Gay and Lesbian Movement* (New York: Routledge, 2012), 159, 161–63, 176–77.

34. George Chauncey, *Why Marriage? The History Shaping Today's Debate over Gay Equality* (New York: Basic Books, 2004), 96–104.

35. The Court had previously decided cases in favor of gay and lesbian publications, ruling they did not constitute obscenity, as well as addressed immigration restrictions on gays and lesbians. Joyce Murdoch and Deb Price, *Courting Justice: Gay Men and Lesbians v. the Supreme Court* (New York: Basic Books, 2002), 82–83, 97, 114–16.

36. *Bowers v. Hardwick*, 478 U.S. 186, 193–94 (1986).

37. Eskridge, *Dishonorable Passions*, 189, 296.

38. Eskridge, *Dishonorable Passions*, 235.

39. Eskridge, *Dishonorable Passions*, 235.

40. *Bowers v. Hardwick*, 478 U.S. 186, 191 (1986).

41. *Dudgeon v. United Kingdom*, 45 Eur. Ct. H.R. (1981).

42. Vote Tallies, n.d., File 85–140, Bowers v. Hardwick, Lewis F. Powell, Jr. Archives, Supreme Court Case Files Collection, Sydney Lewis Hall, Washington and Lee School of Law (hereafter cited as Powell Archives); Lewis F. Powell, Conference Notes, n.d., File 85–140, Bowers v. Hardwick, Powell Archives; Lewis F. Powell, memorandum to the Conference, April 8, 1986, File 85–140, Bowers v. Hardwick, Powell Archives.

43. Brief for Respondent at *17, Bowers v. Hardwick, No. 85–140, 1986 WL 720422 (January 31, 1996).

44. Lewis J. Powell, memorandum to Michael Mosman, March 31, 1986, File 85–140, Bowers v. Hardwick, Powell Archives.

45. Marie-Amélie George, "Agency Nullification: Defying Bans on Gay and Lesbian Foster and Adoptive Parents," *Harvard Civil Rights–Civil Liberties Law Review* 51, no. 2 (2016): 371–74.

46. *Romer v. Evans*, 517 U.S. 620 (1996).

47. *Romer v. Evans*, 635.

48. 539 US 558, 567, 578 (2003).

49. 539 US 558, 567.

50. 539 US 558, 575.

51. 539 US 558, 577.

52. Transcript of Oral Argument, Lawrence v. Texas, No. 02–102, 2003 WL 1702543, at *20–21 (March 26, 2003).

53. *Lawrence*, 539 U.S. at 602.

54. John Gallagher and Chris Bull, *Perfect Enemies: The Religious Right, the Gay Movement, and the Politics of the 1990s* (New York: Crown, 1996), 217.

55. Eskridge, *Dishonorable Passions*, 319.

56. Dale Carpenter, *Flagrant Conduct: The Story of* Lawrence v. Texas (New York: W. W. Norton, 2012), 45.

57. *United States v. Windsor*, 133 S. Ct. at 2689.

58. *Obergefell*, 135 S. Ct. at 2594.

59. *Obergefell*, 2600.

60. Cynthia Godsoe, "Perfect Plaintiffs," *Yale Law Journal Forum* 125 (2015): 153–54; Jane S. Schacter, "The Other Same-Sex Marriage Debate," *Chicago-Kent Law Review* 84, no. 2 (2009): 382.

61. Douglas NeJaime and Reva B. Siegel, "Conscience Wars: Complicity-Based Conscience Claims in Religion and Politics," *Yale Law Journal* 124, no. 7 (2015): 2518.

62. George, "Deviant Justice," epilogue.

63. NeJaime and Siegel, "Conscience Wars," 2553.

64. Douglas NeJaime and Reva B. Siegel, "Religious Accommodation, and Its Limits in a Pluralist Society," in *Religious Freedom, LGBT Rights, and Prospects for Common Ground*, ed. William N. Eskridge Jr. and Robin Fretwell Wilson (New York: Cambridge University Press, 2018), 74.

65. *Sherbert v. Verner*, 374 U.S. 398 (1963).

66. *Employment Div. v. Smith*, 494 U.S. 872, 883–85 (1990).

67. J. Stuart Adams, "Cultivating Common Ground," in Eskridge and Fretwell, *Religious Freedom*, 445.

68. 138 S. Ct. 1719 (2018).

69. 138 S. Ct. 1719, 1728–29.

70. 138 S. Ct. 1729. The Court noted the importance of balancing the baker's First Amendment rights against those of gay and lesbian citizens; decisions would need to avoid a situation where "all purveyors of goods and services who object to gay marriages for moral and religious reasons in effect be allowed to put up signs saying

'no goods or services will be sold if they will be used for gay marriages,' something that would impose a serious stigma on gay persons." 138 S. Ct., 1728–29.

71. Aleskandra Sandstrom, "Religious Groups' Policies on Transgender Members Vary Widely," Pew Research Center, December 2, 2015, http://www .pewresearch.org/fact-tank/2015/12/02/religious-groups-policies-on-transgender -members-vary-widely/. Churches that do not accept transgender identity include the Assemblies of God, Church of Jesus-Christ of Latter-day Saints (the Mormon Church), Lutheran Church-Missouri Synod, Southern Baptist Convention, and Roman Catholic Church. Sandstrom, "Religious Groups."

72. H.B. 1523, 2016 Reg. Sess. (Miss. 2016).

73. *Barber v. Bryant*, 860 F.3d 345 (5th Cir. 2017), *cert. denied* 128 S. Ct. 652 (2018).

74. *Bostock v. Clayton Cty.*, 140 S. Ct. 1731 (2020); Mary Anne Case, "Legal Protections for the 'Personal Best' of Each Employee: Title VII's Prohibition on Sex Discrimination, the Legacy of *Price Waterhouse v. Hopkins*, and the Prospect of ENDA," *Stanford Law Review* 66, no. 6 (2014): 1345–54.

75. *Bostock*, at 1741.

76. *Bostock*, at 1743.

77. Kimberly A. Yuracko, "Soul of a Woman: The Sex Stereotyping Prohibition at Work," *University of Pennsylvania Law Review* 161, no. 3 (2013): 757–805.

78. See, for example, *Hamm v. Weyauwega Milk Products, Inc.*, 332 F.3d 1058, 1065n5 (7th Cir. 2003); *Williamson v. A.G. Edwards & Sons, Inc.*, 876 F.2d 69 (8th Cir. 1989); *Wrightson v. Pizza Hut of America, Inc.*, 99 F.3d 138, 143 (4th Cir. 1996); *Fredette v. BVP Management Assoc.*, 112 F.3d 1503, 1510 (11th Cir. 1997); *Higgins v. New Balance Athletic Shoe, Inc.*, 194 F.3d 252 (1st Cir. 1999).

79. *Prowel v. Wise Business Forms, Inc.*, 579 F.3d 285, 292 (3d Cir. 2009).

80. *EEOC v. Boh Bros. Const. Co.*, 731 F.3d 444, 457 (5th Cir. 2013); *Prowel*, 579 F.3d at 292.

81. *Prowel*, 579 F.3d at 291–92.

82. *Videckis v. Pepperdine Univ.*, 150 F. Supp. 3d 1151, 1159 (C.D. Cal. 2015); *Centola v. Potter*, 183 F. Supp. 2d 403, 408 (D. Mass. 2002).

83. *Zarda v. Altitude Express, Inc.*, 883 F.3d 100, 112 (2d Cir. 2018); *Hively v. Ivy Tech Cmty. C. of Indiana*, 853 F.3d 339 (7th Cir. 2017).

84. *Baldwin v. Foxx*, EEOC Doc. 0120133080, 2015 WL 4397641 (EEOC July 15, 2015).

85. *Evans v. Ga. Regional Hospital*, 850 F.3d 1248 (11th Cir. 2017); *Sanches v. Carrollton-Famers Branch Independent Sch. Dist.*, 647 F.3d 156 (5th Cir. 2011); see also *Tumminello v. Father Ryan High School, Inc.*, 678 Fed. Appx. 281 (6th Cir. 2017).

86. *Ulane v. Eastern Airlines, Inc.*, 742 F.2d 1081, 1086 (7th Cir. 1984); *Holloway v. Arthur Anderson & Co.*, 566 F.2d 659, 661–63 (9th Cir. 1977); *Sommers v. Budget Mktg., Inc.*, 667 F.2d 748, 750 (8th Cir. 1982).

87. Transgender plaintiffs were increasingly successful, but not all courts have held that they could bring lawsuits under Title VII. See, for example, *Etsitty v. Utah Transit Auth.*, 502 F.3d 1215 (10th Cir. 2007).

88. *Smith v. City of Salem, Ohio*, 378 F.3d 566, 572 (6th Cir. 2004).

89. *Smith v. City of Salem*, 575.

90. *EEOC v. R.G. & G.R. Harris Funeral Homes, Inc.*, 884 F.3d 560, 576–77 (6th Cir. 2018).

91. *EEOC v. R.G. & G.R. Harris Funeral Homes, Inc.*

92. *Evans v. Ga. Regional Hospital*, 850 F.3d 1248, 1254–55 (11th Cir. 2017).

93. Meyerowitz, *How Sex Changed*, 242–53.

94. Dean Spade, "Documenting Gender," *Hastings Law Journal* 59 (2008): 754–55.

95. Jessica A. Clarke, "Identity and Form," *California Law Review* 103, no. 4 (2015): 794–98.

96. Jessica A. Clarke, "They, Them, Theirs," *Harvard Law Review* 132, no. 1 (2019): 896–97; *Zzyym v. Kerry*, No. 15-cv-02362-RBJ, 2018 WL 4491434 (D. Colo. Sept. 19, 2018).

97. Clarke, "Identity and Form," 797–99.

98. Janei Au, Comment, "A Remedy for Male-to-Female Transgender Inmates: Applying Disparate Impact to Prison Placement," *American University Journal of Gender, Social Policy, and Law* 24, no. 3 (2016): 375–76.

99. Julia C. Oparah, "Feminism and the (Trans)Gender Entrapment of Gender Nonconforming Prisoners," *UCLA Women's Law Journal* 18, no. 2 (2012): 263–65.

100. United States Department of Justice, Prison Rape Elimination Act Prisons and Jails Standards, 28 C.F.R. § 115.41–42 (2012); Elliot Oberholtzer, "The Dismal State of Transgender Incarceration Policies," *Prison Policy Initiative*, November 8, 2017.

101. Circuits ruling in favor of transgender litigants: *Rosati v. Igbinoso*, 791 F.3d 1037 (9th Cir. 2015); *Kothman v. Rosario*, 558 Fed. Appx. 9–7 (11th Cir. 2014); *Fields v. Smith*, 653 F.3d 550 (7th Cir. 2011); *Brown v. Zavaras*, 63 F.3d 967 (10th Cir. 1995). Circuits ruling against: *Gibson v. Collier*, ____ F.3d ____, 2019 WL 141721 (5th Cir. 2019); *Kosilek v. Spencer*, 774 F.3d 63 (1st Cir. 2014); *De'Lonta v. Johnson*, 708 F.3d 520 (4th Cir. 2013); *Smith v. Hayman*, 489 Fed. Appx. 544 (3d Cir. 2012); *Praylor v. Texas Dep't of Crim. Justice*, 430 F.3d 1208 (5th Cir. 2005).

102. Clarke, "They, Them, and Theirs," 937–45.

PART V

*State Constitutional Rights*

# TWELVE

—∞—

# SECOND WIND FOR STATE BILLS OF RIGHTS

RANDALL T. SHEPARD

AMERICANS GROWING UP IN THE twenty-first century regularly observe citizens who believe their constitutional rights have been violated seeking vindication in state or federal courts. What may not be apparent to them is that the active engagement of courts in both systems represents a distinct third phase in how the nation has approached vindication of individual rights over its history.

From the nation's founding until roughly the opening of the twentieth century, state constitutions and their accompanying bills of rights were the leading sources of law in the defense of citizens' rights. Thereafter began a process by which federal jurisprudence and federal court authority came to overshadow state constitutional rights—slowly at first and then accelerating until the 1970s. More recently, state courts have emerged once again as a focus for controversies over how far individual rights extend.

It was a curious phenomenon in light of the postcolonial debate over whether there should even be a federal list of rights in the Constitution of the United States. Early Americans saw little threat to their liberties emanating from state capitals, but they feared unchecked power exercised by a new and distant sovereign. The Anti-Federalists had attacked the constitution proposed in 1787 on the grounds that it would afford the new national government too much control over the lives of individual citizens. It was only late in the campaign for ratification that the Federalists pledged to support a federal bill of rights, thus helping bring the last two key states, Virginia and New York, into the new union. Fear of national power and loyalty to state governments were so strong that even the prospect of amendments spelling out individual freedoms was barely enough to carry the day. Ratification forces prevailed in New York by just three votes.

As people like James Madison, Thomas Jefferson, and Roger Sherman began to ponder the shape such federal guarantees should take, there were plenty of models from which they could borrow. One reason Americans worried little about state governments was that most state constitutions written in the revolutionary period contained guarantees of enumerated rights. The earliest of these was the Virginia Declaration of Rights in 1776, adopted three weeks before the Declaration of Independence. Many provisions in the Virginia declaration and other such charters became part of the federal amendments eventually proposed to the states.

Notwithstanding the prompt adoption of ten amendments to the federal Constitution, the bills of rights in the state constitutions remained the principal force in American civil liberties for a century and a half. Madison had argued that the federal restraints should bind both national and state governments, but he did not prevail. The First Congress, taking up these questions in 1791, specifically rejected efforts to insert in the Bill of Rights provisions limiting state authority.[1] If there had ever been any doubt that the federal Bill of Rights was not a limitation on state activities, that doubt vanished when the US Supreme Court heard a case in which one John Barron argued that the city of Baltimore had violated his rights under the Fifth Amendment by taking property without compensation. Chief Justice John Marshall was not impressed: "The question thus presented is, we think, of great importance, but not much difficulty."[2] Marshall made quick work of Barron's claim: "Had the framers of these amendments intended them to be limitations on the powers of the State governments they would have imitated the framers of the original Constitution, and would have expressed that intention."[3]

Even after the adoption of the Thirteenth, Fourteenth, and Fifteenth Amendments following the Civil War, federal due process and equal protection were deemed to require only that state procedures provide for fundamental fairness, not that they embody specific guarantees in the same manner in which they were written in the Bill of Rights. In the familiar *Slaughter-House Cases* of 1873, the Supreme Court held that the Fourteenth Amendment did not add to any rights, privileges, or immunities of the citizens of the several states.[4] Twelve years later, in *Hurtado v. California*, the Court declared that "due process of law" referred to "that law of the land in which each State, which derives its authority from the inherent and reserved powers of the State."[5]

Americans who thought their rights had been violated regularly went to state court and frequently found vindication. The Indiana Supreme Court, for example, spent forty years asserting its authority in the fight against slavery. The very first volume of that court's decisions records its ruling in *State v. Lasselle*, which set aside a writ of habeas corpus and directed that an enslaved woman named Polly Strong be freed. The Indiana court observed that "the framers of our constitution intended a total and entire prohibition of slavery in this State;

and we can conceive of no form of words in which that intention could have been more clearly expressed."[6] The court likewise later barred contracts of indenture and also invalidated the state's runaway slave law.[7]

The spirit of individual liberty motivated muscular action by state courts in other fields. When the Wisconsin Supreme Court held in 1859 that indigent criminal defendants were entitled to counsel at public expense, it acknowledged that it could not find any provision in the state constitution or statutes expressly providing such assistance.[8] Still, it pointed to the right to appear with counsel and stated that "it would be a reproach upon the administration of justice, if a person, thus upon trial could not have the assistance of legal counsel because he was too poor to obtain it." Similar sentiments had prompted declaration about the right to counsel at public expense in Indiana in 1854 and in Iowa in 1850.[9]

## THE FEDERAL RIGHTS REVOLUTION UNLEASHED

By the middle of the twentieth century, however, the national Bill of Rights was more commonly deployed against states than against the federal government, and state constitutions in general were swept nearly into obscurity. The cause of this transformation can be best explained in one word: race.

Race was at the heart of the Civil War amendments. The sponsors of the Fourteenth Amendment were largely motivated by a desire to protect the Civil Rights Act of 1866.[10] They sought to "embody" the act in the Constitution so as to remove any doubt about its constitutionality and place the act beyond the power of a later Congress to repeal. Whatever shift in authority they intended between the national government and state governments was largely designed to make the power of the national government available to ensure that the Southern states recognized and protected the basic rights of former slaves.

Clearly, the Fourteenth Amendment was not intended to expand the general authority of Congress. The leading architect of what became Section 1 of the Fourteenth Amendment was Representative John A. Bingham, an Ohio Republican, whose original proposal would have indeed expanded the authority of Congress. It read: "The Congress shall have the power to make all laws which shall be necessary and proper to secure to the citizens of each State privileges and immunities of citizens in the several States, and to all persons in the several States equal protection in the rights of life, liberty and property."[11]

Opponents of the Fourteenth Amendment criticized Bingham's proposal precisely because it gave too much power to Congress, arguing that this sweeping grant of power to the national legislature was a serious invasion of state sovereignty and an alteration of the basic fabric of the federal system. They also criticized the draft amendment on the grounds that it gave Congress the right to define the liberties of the citizens according to Congress's will. These complaints led to a compromise on Section 1 of the amendment, the adopted version of which makes a general declaration of constitutional principle ("No State shall make or enforce any law which . . .") and adds to congressional authority the power "to enforce, by appropriate legislation, the provisions of this article."

The democratic accommodation reflected in this restrained language remained intact during the first several decades after the Fourteenth Amendment was adopted. The nation's courts honored the compromise by deploying the Fourteenth Amendment largely to protect the basic freedoms contemplated by the Civil Rights Act. In *Ex Parte Virginia*, for example, the US Supreme Court held that the Fourteenth Amendment was a sufficient constitutional basis for a federal indictment of a state judge who excluded Blacks from jury lists.[12] In *Yick Wo v. Hopkins*, the Court granted relief to a defendant who violated a facially neutral California statute that in actual practice discriminated against Chinese laundries, saying: "Whatever may have been the intent of the ordinances as adopted, they are applied . . . with a mind so unequal and oppressive as to amount to a practical denial by the State of that equal protection of the laws which is secured by the petitioners . . . by the broad and benign provisions of the Fourteenth Amendment to the Constitution of the United States."[13] Generally, though, the Court declined to use the amendment for more sweeping purposes. For most of the first fifty to seventy-five years after its adoption, courts did not regard the Fourteenth Amendment as a basis for expanded federal judicial authority.

Around the turn of the twentieth century, however, federal judges began to assert that the Fourteenth Amendment gave them the power to enter orders against state and local governments for violations of the federal Bill of Rights. Most observers regard the 1897 decision in *Chicago, Burlington & Quincy R.R. Co. v. Chicago* as the beginning of what eventually became the incorporation doctrine, by which various federal Bill of Rights guarantees were held to be implicit in Fourteenth Amendment due process or equal protection.[14] The city of Chicago had adopted an ordinance setting one dollar as the amount of damages a railroad should receive when a new public street crossed its tracks. The Court struck down the ordinance, asserting that the railroad was entitled to "just compensation"—a Fifth Amendment concept—because just compensation was an essential element of due process under the Fourteenth Amendment.

Along similar lines, in 1925, the Supreme Court ruled in *Gitlow v. New York* that the Fourteenth Amendment limited a state's regulation of free speech and free press, incorporating elements of the First Amendment.[15] A little at a time, the Court held that various provisions of the Bill of Rights were incorporated into the Fourteenth Amendment and thus enforceable against the states. This approach grew so ubiquitous that by the twenty-first century, one could hear a justice suggesting from the bench that all provisions of all ten amendments were likely incorporated.

It was not railroad crossing condemnations or even free speech protection that led federal judges in the mid-twentieth century to use the Fourteenth Amendment in new and expansive ways. The reason for this expanded use was the same reason the amendment was enacted in the first place: race. The civil rights movement of the 1950s and 1960s presented case after case to the Supreme Court in which African Americans sought redress for grievances suffered at the hands of segregation-minded Whites. Many of these grievances arose in criminal cases where the prosecutor, the victim, the judge, and the jury were all White, and the defendant was Black. Even the highest state courts in the South were not all willing to take cognizance of the potential for injustice in such situations.

The Supreme Court was rightly suspicious of the treatment Black people received in the courts of the Deep South. Some of those courts played a particularly prominent role in civil rights litigation, and a few of them represented a fierce resistance to African American rights and the federal authority. Indeed, one might argue that the Fifth and Sixth Amendments became incorporated because of the old Supreme Court of Alabama. That tribunal alone offered up a series of cases we now remember partly because they have "Alabama" in the caption: *Boykin v. Alabama, Powell v. Alabama,* and *NAACP v. Alabama,*[16] to name just three.

Faced with local unwillingness to protect the rights of Black people, the Supreme Court expanded the incorporation doctrine at a breakneck pace during a period more or less marked by the arrival of Justice Abe Fortas in 1965 and the appointment of Chief Justice Warren Burger in 1969. Whether it was school desegregation, criminal defense rights, or prison reform, the Supreme Court cut down its own precedents and state constitutional law like so much wheat, and state constitutions and lesser rules of law were rendered nearly irrelevant by a galloping nationalization of a wide variety of matters.[17]

## A RENAISSANCE IN STATE CONSTITUTIONAL LAW

This race to compel every state to afford civil liberties in accord with some minimum defined by the federal judiciary eventually abated for two reasons. First, the Supreme Court's membership shifted throughout the 1970s and 1980s, a period in which Republican presidents made multiple appointments. These appointments produced a court much less likely to expand federal judicial supervision of state governments and state courts. Second, a series of state judges emerged who were dedicated to a renaissance in state constitution jurisprudence.[18] This renaissance produced hundreds of appellate opinions, scores of journal articles, and dozens of books.

A good many law scholars credit Justice William Brennan with launching the renewal of state constitutional law. Brennan's 1977 article in the *Harvard Law*

*Review*[19] has been called the "starting point of the modern re-emphasis on state constitutions."[20] Another scholar called Brennan's piece "a clarion call to state judges to wield their own bills of rights."[21]

Of course, Justice Brennan had spent much of his time on the US Supreme Court brushing aside various state constitutional provisions. It might therefore be more accurate to credit Brennan and Oregon's Justice Hans Linde.[22] Linde had been a professor of law at the University of Oregon before his appointment to that state's high court. He argued in a 1979 lecture at the University of Baltimore that state court judges confronting a constitutional question should always examine it under their own state's constitution before analyzing it under the federal Constitution. A probable third member of this pantheon is Justice Robert Utter of the Washington Supreme Court. Utter helpfully pointed out that state constitutions were relatively lengthy and commonly newer than the federal documents and thus were capable of application to particular modern political issues.[23]

Justice Brennan's own renewed interest in state constitutions actually predated his 1977 article, and the genesis of it is easy to identify. The change in the Supreme Court's composition meant that Brennan and Chief Justice Earl Warren no longer regularly marched to victory. By the mid-1970s, Brennan began to find himself on the losing end of cases. He concluded that the rights revolution was over as far as the Supreme Court was concerned and quite candidly announced that liberals and civil libertarians should take the war to a different front. He made his announcement in the 1975 case of *Michigan v. Mosely*.[24] Dissenting in a search-and-seizure case was a relatively novel experience for Brennan, and he used his dissent to remind state judges that they had the power "to impose higher standards governing police practices under state law than is required by the Federal Constitution."[25] The timing of this plea was hardly a coincidence. During the 1975 term, Justice Brennan wrote twenty-six dissenting opinions, his second-highest number for that decade. In cases disposed of during that term by written opinion, he also cast fifty-six dissenting votes, which tied his record for the decade. Of course, this represented both rights cases and others.[26]

Justice Brennan's 1975 conversion ultimately became the stuff of folklore because of his own considerable standing and because he identified a method by which certain litigants and advocacy interest groups might achieve their objectives despite their increasing inability to succeed through the vehicle of the Supreme Court. He is undoubtedly an important part of the new state constitutionalism story.

On the other hand, both scholars and judges had been working this idea long before Justice Brennan realized he would no longer be able to engineer congenial outcomes at the Supreme Court. New legal scholarship on state constitutions began to appear as early as the 1960s, much of it providing the intellectual foundation for the renaissance ahead.[27]

More important to real-world litigants, state courts exercised their constitutional authority in a variety of settings well before Justice Brennan's exhortation. Where no parallel federal provision existed, for example, the state constitution regularly provided the sole basis for a constitutional challenge.[28] The state constitution was also pertinent where a parallel federal provision had not yet been incorporated into the Fourteenth Amendment, such as the Fifth Amendment right to indictment only through a grand jury or the Second Amendment right to bear arms.[29] Of course, the Supreme Court's declarations that a given part of the federal Bill of Rights is incorporated under the Fourteenth Amendment and thus applicable as a limit on state actors has continued apace. In 2010, the court held in *McDonald v. City of Chicago* that the Second Amendment was incorporated and thus could render unconstitutional parts of a Chicago ordinance banning possession of handguns and imposing other limits on rifles and shotguns.[30] Most recently, the Court announced that the excessive fines clause of the Eighth Amendment applied to forfeiture proceedings conducted in state courts as to property used in committing a crime.[31]

The state constitution was also deployed where a parallel federal provision had been construed in such a way that it clearly did not apply to the facts of a given case.[32] In still other instances, state courts heard cases involving claims under parallel federal and state constitutional provisions and gave the state constitutional claim independent consideration.[33]

The level of scholarship reflected in such opinions varied enormously. Some high-quality work provided an early foundation for further jurisprudential refinement of state constitutions, while others were woefully inadequate. A commendable example of the former was the Georgia Supreme Court's decision in 1962 on the subject of free expression, *K. Gordon Murray Productions, Inc. v. Floyd.*[34]

The Georgia Supreme Court invalidated a provision of Atlanta's municipal code that required exhibitors of motion pictures to obtain prior approval for each film they showed from a Board of Motion Pictures Censors. Designed to prevent exhibition of obscene films, the ordinance nevertheless subjected all films to the screening process. The court first concluded that the ordinance did not violate the First Amendment. The Georgia court then proceeded to a detailed consideration of the state's free expression provision, which had been crafted in its own special way: "No law shall ever be passed to curtail or restrain the liberty of speech, or of the press; any person may speak, write and publish his sentiments, on all subjects, being responsible for the abuse of that liberty. Protection to person and property is the paramount duty of government, and shall be impartial and complete."[35] After analyzing this discreet text and reflecting on the history of free speech case law under the Georgia Constitution, the court invalidated the ordinance because it subjected all motion pictures to prior approval, not just obscene ones.

## EVERY MOVEMENT HAS ITS DETRACTORS

While the Georgia court and others provided demonstrable evidence that state constitutional doctrine could rest capably on text, legal history, and jurisprudence long in the making, not everyone was convinced. Even as the renaissance gathered steam in the 1990s, a few law scholars challenged both its legitimacy and its efficacy.

Professor James Gardner's article, "Failed Discourse of State Constitutionalism," in the *Michigan Law Review*,[36] argued that the foundation of the new state constitutionalism movement was a specific vision of state sovereignty. As Gardner put it, "State constitutionalism . . . holds that a state constitution is the creation of the sovereign people of the state and reflects the fundamental values, and indirectly the character, of that people. An important corollary of this proposition is that the fundamental values and character of the various states actually differ, both from state to state and as between the state and national polities."[37] Having done some empirical research on this point, Gardner asserted that his studies demonstrated that state constitutionalism is, and will remain, "impoverished" and "pedestrian" despite the scholarly attention lavished on it.

While Professor Richard Boldt and Judge Dan Friedman see value in state court attention to their own organic documents, they see danger when those courts act solely on their own state provisions. They opine that when a state supreme court departs from the US Supreme Court's position on a constitutional guarantee, especially on open-ended provisions such as due process and equal protection, the state judges are rightly suspected of effectuating "their personal preferences instead of implementing neutral principles in reaching their decision." They also complain that even courts claiming to adhere to a primacy approach for state constitutional law do not always follow it in every case. The approach they outline is called "pragmatic prudentialism."[38]

One might say that in some respects the federal judiciary initially thought of the state constitutional renaissance as a matter of little consequence. In *United States v. Singer*, sheriff's deputies in Wisconsin had seized evidence, plausibly in violation of the Wisconsin Constitution, and subsequently passed it along to the United States attorney for use in prosecution. Singer sought to suppress this evidence on grounds that the state's seizure had contravened Wisconsin's bill of rights. It was a plausible request, since the Supreme Court had held in 1960 that state courts could not admit evidence ruled inadmissible in federal court but subsequently transferred to state prosecutors on a "silver platter."[39] The US Court of Appeals for the Seventh Circuit brushed away this argument, stating simply that Wisconsin law was "irrelevant" and directing that the evidence be admitted.[40] The Seventh Circuit had excellent company. Considering whether a federal district court could order a tax increase in Kansas City to finance the judge's crafted effort to entice White parents to move back into urban schools, Justice Byron White saw little value in the pertinent taxation provisions of the Missouri Constitution. He simply said they "hinder the process" of shaping the district court's plan for integrating the city's school.[41]

Around the turn of the twenty-first century, the Rehnquist Court gave further impetus to state law and state constitutions. Oddly, this effect flowed both from cases in which the Court exercised its constitutional power and from cases in which it did not. Two very different cases reflect these events.

In 1942, the Court had held that a farmer in Montgomery County, Ohio, who grew crops on his own land and consumed them on the same farm was part of interstate commerce and subject to congressional regulation under the commerce clause.[42] For most of the ensuing half century, the Court gave Congress every reason to imagine that the commerce clause empowered it to legislate on anything that moved and most of what did not. Chief Justice William H. Rehnquist believed that such breadth of authority was not consistent with the notion of a government of enumerated powers. In 1995, the Court sustained the Rehnquist view in *United States v. Lopez*,[43] in which a student had been convicted under the federal Gun-Free School Zones Act after bringing a handgun to school for another student who intended to use it in a gang war. The Rehnquist Court vacated the conviction, declaring that Lopez's possession of the gun had little to do with the purpose of granting power to Congress through the commerce clause. The act did not purport to regulate commerce across state lines, Rehnquist argued in authoring the Court's opinion. If mere possession of a gun could be deemed somehow connected to other activities in commerce across state lines, he said, the commerce power would be imbued with more or less infinite reach, covering virtually any activity by individual citizens.

The *Lopez* decision was highly unpopular in a Congress that believed in the breadth of its own authority and many of whose members desired to be seen as willing to combat school violence. The collective effect of *Lopez* and other decisions restraining the authority of Congress, however, was to foster the impression generated during the Reagan presidency that the action was being "returned to the states." If anything, this impression bolstered the interest in state legislation and state constitutions.

The Court's 2005 decision in *Kelo v. City of New London*[44] also propelled resort to state constitutions. Municipal authorities in Connecticut had decided to condemn land in preparation for a multiple-use economic development project. Suzanne Kelo resisted the acquisition of her home and contended that it violated the Fifth Amendment requirement that property might not be taken for a public use except upon payment of just compensation. Most condemnees are largely concerned with just how much money "just compensation" turns out to be. Instead, Kelo argued that taking her home for economic development was not seizure for a public use.

The Court declined to impose a uniform federal definition of public use on state governments and let stand Connecticut's condemnation of the Kelo home. On this occasion the Court's decision to defer to state decision makers drew broad criticism from advocates of private property rights. Opponents of easy condemnation sought relief through state legislation and state constitutions. The high courts of Ohio and Oklahoma responded by placing judicial limits on the taking of private land, in direct reaction to the Kelo announcement that the Fifth Amendment did not contain a substantive definition of public use that was binding on states.[45] In a somewhat different vein, the courts of Pennsylvania and Missouri invalidated condemnations by affirming statutes that sought to restrain the sort of condemnation in Kelo. Both courts saw these statutes as exceeding the requirements existing in their constitutions.[46]

These decisions represented state courts acting in different ways to guarantee protection when the Supreme Court chose not to occupy the field—very much what Hans Linde and William Brennan had in mind. The early twenty-first century atmosphere is one of greater comity between federal and state courts on constitutional law questions. And prominent members of the federal judiciary demonstrate more interest in state activity in the field than was once the case.

Judge Jeffrey Sutton of the Sixth Circuit lifted up the value of thoughtful exchange by state and federal courts in his 2018 book, 51 Imperfect Solutions: States and the Making of American Constitutional Law.[47] Says Sutton: "For too long, we have lived in a top-down constitutional world, in which the U.S. Supreme Court announced a ruling, and the state supreme courts move in lockstep in construing the counterpart guarantees of their own constitutions. Why not do the reverse?" Sutton notes that in multiple other areas of law, state courts are regularly "the first one to decide whether to embrace or reject innovative legal claims."

## WADING INTO DEEPER WATER

The momentum of state constitutionalism renaissance has, if anything, pushed forward to new fields that have brought state constitutional activity more prominently into general public discourse and sometimes into conflict with other branches of state government.

### Same-Sex Marriage

Close to the front of this story were the decisions of state high courts that their state charter required equal rights for gay couples. Late in 1999, the Vermont

Supreme Court heard the case of three same-sex couples, each of which had lived together in relatively long relationships. These couples had requested marriage licenses. When their requests were denied, they filed suit contending that Vermont's statutes about marriage violated the state constitution's provision declaring that "government is, or ought to be, instituted for the common benefit, protection, and security," and not for the advantage of single persons or sets of persons.[48] Looking back at the social and political moment of adoption, 1777, and examining Vermont history and similar provisions in the immediate past colonial history, the court discerned that the American Revolution had unleashed a powerful movement toward "social equivalence." It observed that Vermont's impulse in this regard produced perhaps the most radical constitution of the Revolution. The justices concluded that exclusions from the "common benefit" of marriage were not warranted under any of the arguments advanced by the government and held that same-sex couples were entitled to something akin to marriage, domestic partnership, or registered partnership, leaving it to the legislature to craft a new law.[49]

As in Vermont, several same-sex couples in Massachusetts with lengthy relationships challenged the refusal to issue them marriage licenses. The Massachusetts courts had held at least since 1810 that marriage was a union between a man and a woman as husband and wife. In 2003, the Supreme Judicial Court of Massachusetts cited general due process and equal protection, without quoting the actual provisions of the state constitution or elaborating on history. It declared that limiting the benefits to opposite-sex couples "violates the basic premises of individual liberty and equality under law protected by the Massachusetts Constitution."[50] Asked later by the state senate whether pending legislation to authorize civil unions carrying all the legal rights of marriage might suffice, the court said that using a term different than *marriage* would consign same-sex couples to an inferior and discriminating status.[51]

The gay marriage statute subsequently adopted in Massachusetts turned out to be not altogether transportable. Asked by a same-sex couple married in Massachusetts to entertain their request for a divorce, the Texas Supreme Court held that its state court did not even have subject matter jurisdiction. The court said it would "not extend comity to the laws of other states if doing so would result in a violation of Texas public policy."[52]

In New Jersey, the state supreme court ruled unanimously that gay couples were entitled to legal recognition of their union, disagreeing only on whether the legislature should be allowed to use a word other than *marriage*. It decided by a vote of 4–3 to allow the legislature to decide what word to use. Lest one imagine that these were developments singular to the East Coast, the Iowa Supreme Court invalidated a statute that prohibited same-sex marriage, relying on the Iowa Constitution. It held that same-sex couples were similarly situated to heterosexual relationships: both are based in committed and loving relationships.

The statute "provides an institutional basis for defining their fundamental relational rights and responsibilities."[53] Likewise, the New Mexico court held that a statute prohibiting same-sex marriage violated the state's constitution.[54] Of course, other state high courts reached the opposite conclusion. The Montana Supreme Court examined a claim brought by a group of same-sex plaintiffs under the state constitution and declared that it exceeded the "bounds of a justiciable controversy," adding that it was not the role of courts to declare social status.[55] Of course, these issues took a very different turn after the US Supreme Court declared in 2015 that the Fourteenth Amendment required every state to recognize same-sex marriage.[56]

## Redrawing Legislative Districts

The opportunity for a citizen to participate in choosing elected officials is a right protected by both state and federal constitutions. Judicial enforcement of this right when voting systems or electoral districts work to restrict the role of minority voters has been a regular occurrence for half a century. More recent debate and litigation have focused on whether there may be some judicial role—say, under the state or federal versions of equal protection—in assuring fairness in defining districts drawn through the ancient American practice of gerrymandering.

Just at the moment when the US Supreme Court backed away from intervening in state redistricting, at least one state plowed ahead, with its state high court deciding to draw its own lines for congressional seats. As a national effort against gerrymandering seemed to grow apace, led by Common Cause, the Democratic Party, and the League of Women Voters, the US Supreme Court rejected a challenge arising in Wisconsin. The plaintiffs claimed a violation of the First and Fourteenth Amendments because their votes had been diluted by the redistricting plan's district boundaries by putting them in districts that either wasted their votes or made them "destined to lose by closer margins." The Court rejected the plaintiffs' claim that their injury extended to a statewide harm of their "collective representation in the legislature."[57]

By contrast, the Pennsylvania Supreme Court invalidated congressional districts drawn by the state legislature nearly a decade earlier, noting that while Republicans had tended to win no more than 55 percent of the votes statewide, they tended to win almost three-quarters of the congressional races. The court held that this trend violated a provision of the constitution called the free and equal elections clause. The court gave the legislature and the governor an opportunity to submit plans for the court's approval. When they did not do so, the court itself drew new districts.[58]

The potential for other state courts to take similar actions under their own constitutions increased after the US Supreme Court in 2019 held that gerrymandering raised a "political question" not litigable in federal courts.[59] A few months later, a case from North Carolina proved the point when a three-panel trial court rejected legislatively drawn boundaries for the Ninth Congressional District boundaries under the state constitution's free elections clause, noting that "it is the carefully crafted maps, and not the will of the voters, that dictate the election outcomes." Thirteen states have a similar clause in their constitutions.[60]

## How Much to Spend on Education

Many state constitutions contain citizen guarantees in places other than the bill of rights. Wyoming's constitution, for example, requires a "complete and uniform system of public instruction." Colorado's calls for "a thorough and uniform system of free public schools throughout the state." Several dozen state constitutions establish universities or direct that the legislature support higher education.[61]

Such guarantees have been the topic of especially contentious litigation in the twenty-first century, even though the constitutional provision on education is not structured as part of the Bill of Rights. In effect, this litigation asks the judiciary to supervise legislative fealty to the education guarantee.

A leading and highly visible effort in this field was the decision of the Kentucky Supreme Court in *Rose v. Council for Better Education*, decided in 1989.[62] Litigants seeking increased school funding based their case on the state constitution's guarantee of "an efficient system of common schools." The court declared it "crystal clear" that the legislature had failed in its obligation under this provision, and it proceeded to explain what an "efficient system" was. Altogether, the court's opinion contained twenty-one characteristics of an efficient system, including requirements such as assuring that a student had "knowledge of his or her mental and physical wellness."

The Kentucky legislature considered whether to explore a way to fight the decision but ultimately decided to use the court's order as a form of political capital to support enlarging the budget for public schools.

Other legislators chose to push back. When the Washington Supreme Court declared the legislature had failed in its duty even after the court told them that the system was unconstitutional, the court held the "state" in contempt and imposed a fine of $100,000 a day. When the case finally ended in 2018, the court declared that the higher budget was adequate and said that the accumulated contempt fines could be used toward financing the increase.[63]

## Legislative Choices

The potential for courts to issue decisions in the name of state constitutional rights that look much like supervision of substantive policy choices consigned to the other two branches of government is highlighted by a number of recent court declarations. Ongoing litigation involving education and gerrymandering has led to a broader view of whether the judiciary may pass judgment on internal legislative processes. Some novel court actions have provoked debate about the appropriate role of the three branches in democracy.

The longest saga has been the virtual blood match between the Kansas Supreme Court and the legislature. The Kansas Constitution directs that the "legislature shall make suitable provision for finance of the educational interests of the state," and in 2014 the court held that the legislature had failed to do so. It adopted many of the Kentucky elements for an adequate system, and ordered the legislature to do more.[64]

Thereafter, education funding and structure have produced back-and-forth legislative and court decisions nearly every year. By 2018, after the legislature had provided nearly $1 billion in new spending, the court again declared that it was in violation. The next year, the court held that the legislature's newest budget was constitutional but announced it would retain jurisdiction over the five-year case, in effect setting the stage for annual appropriation reviews. This litigation demonstrated that there are indeed fifty state constitutions and multiple possible outcomes.

In contrast to the foregoing examples, the Iowa Supreme Court declared that the challenge before it was not really a funding case but rather a quality case, and it said it had serious doubts that a court could realistically assess educational standards.[65] Likewise, in 2019, the Florida Supreme Court brought an end to ten years of school funding litigation, noting that the plaintiffs had not provided "any manageable standard by which to avoid judicial intrusion into the powers of the Legislature." It added that the facts presented to the trial court lacked evidence of a causal relationship between additional financial resources and improved student outcomes.[66]

### Is Legislative Process Subject to Court Review?

State courts reject out of hand contentions by litigants that a particular statute that passed both houses and was signed by the governor is somehow unconstitutional because the processes followed by one or the other was out of line with constitutional requirements. This is usually called the enrolled act doctrine, and it means that courts will not intervene if the chief officers of the other branches have signed their names.

Modern state constitutional jurisprudence sometimes finds courts willing to do otherwise. In *Bevin v. Commonwealth of Kentucky*, litigants who opposed a substantial reform in state pensions challenged the enactment on grounds that the legislature had violated the very common "three readings" rule.[67] Such requirements were originally adopted in constitutions because many elected representatives could not read, and requiring bills to be read in open session assured that they had a chance to know what they were about to vote on.

In the newest Kentucky case, the pension reforms were inserted into another bill, and they had not been read three times. The Kentucky court struck down this law on grounds that the process had violated the state constitution. This decision led Kentucky's governor to denounce the court for overreaching. Multiple legislative leaders joined in criticizing the justices, and the smell of retribution was in the air. Predictions were that the next legislative session would feature bills to prevent lawsuits involving the state from being heard by the trial judge who heard the pension case as well as bills to change the selection method for the Kentucky Supreme Court.

Debate about just how much authority judges should have was likewise prompted by a Wisconsin case. After two-term governor Scott Walker lost a bid for reelection, the legislature convened a special session to adopt bills limiting the powers of the new governor and confirming scores of gubernatorial appointments made by Walker. Calling a special session through this method had occurred at least two dozen times since 1980 with support from both political parties.

In a matter of weeks, a trial judge declared that this lame-duck session had not been properly convened by the legislature and invalidated much of its product. The Wisconsin Supreme Court promptly took jurisdiction over the appeal of this ruling and others issued by a different trial judge, allowing the litigants to bypass the state's intermediate court, and set the orders aside within a few weeks. The trial court's ruling in the Wisconsin case and the Kentucky decision can be fairly viewed as quite muscular. Whether such judicial actions become more widespread remains to be seen.

## CITIZENS ARE SAFER WITH DUAL SOVEREIGNS

Can there really be any doubt that Americans have benefited enormously throughout the nation's history from the decision of the founders to embrace Montesquieu's idea that a society could find stability and prosperity through dispersing power among competing centers of authority? Surely the country is a better place, a place of greater liberty, because we have so long embraced federalism and separation of powers and the notion that we are a nation of dual sovereigns, national and state. This structure has almost always been near the center of long and contentious debate. It was central to the struggle about slavery and the ensuing Civil War.

In more recent times, difficult moments have often involved the federal government's expanded role in society. Citizens experience more contact with federal statutes and regulations in their daily lives. The regular experiences in living under both a state government and a national government produce both positive results and results that citizens or groups of citizens find unpleasant or unfair. Still, we teach each new generation that we are a country of independent states that have delegated certain roles to a national government, and we tell students it is one of the nation's strengths.

Surely the renaissance in state constitutional law is partly the product of exhortations by Brennan and Linde. It was sustained by the influence of William Rehnquist on the federal judiciary and by the similar approach of his successor John Roberts. At the end of the day, it seems certain to find sustaining power in the efforts of scholars and lawyers and state judges to do what lies within them to make their own communities safe, prosperous, and decent places.

### NOTES

1. Bernard Schwartz, *The Bill of Rights: A Documentary History*, 2 vols. (New York: Chelsea House, 1971), 2:1053. Thus, the First Amendment commences, "*Congress* shall make no law." See *Duncan v. Louisiana*, 391 U.S. 145, 173 (1968): "Every member of the Court for at least the last 135 years has agreed that our Founders did not consider the requirements of the Bill of Rights so fundamental that they should operate against the states" (Harlan, J., dissenting). People had little fear that governments close to home in state capitals would deprive them of their freedoms. See Learned Hand, *The Spirit of Liberty: Papers and Addresses of Learned Hand* (New York: Knopf, 1952), together with Learned Hand, *The Bill of Rights: The Oliver Wendell Holmes Lectures, 1958* (Birmingham, UK: Legal Classics Library 1989), 32–33.

2. *Barron v. Baltimore*, 32 U.S. (7 Pet.) 243, 247 (1833).

3. *Barron v. Baltimore*, 250.

4. 83 U.S. (16 Wall.) 36 (1873).

5. 110 U.S. 516, 535 (1884).

6. Blackf. 60, 62 (Ind. 1820). State constitutions frequently enumerate what modern dialogue calls human rights in provisions located outside the Bill of Rights. So it was with Indiana's slavery provisions. Another common example of rights in the body of state constitutions is the right to a free public education, enumerated in Article VIII of the Maryland Constitution of 1867, for instance.

7. *Case of Mary Clark*, 1 Blackf. 122 (Ind. 1821); *Donnell v. State*, 3 Ind. 480 (1852). As straightforward as such decisions on slavery and servitude might seem to the modern mind, it was not everywhere so. Working with the same Northwest Ordinance and similar state constitutional prohibitions, Illinois followed an approach called "gradual emancipation." It ultimately ended slavery altogether in *Jarrot v. Jarrot*, 7 Ill. 1 (1845).

8. *Carpenter v. Dane*, 9 Wis. 274 (1859).

9. *Webb v. Baird*, 6 Ind. 13 (1854); *Hall v. Washington County*, 2 Greene 473 (Iowa 1850). The Indiana case and other advancements in criminal law are detailed in Susan K. Carpenter, "'Conspicuously Enlightened Policy': Criminal Justice in Indiana," in *The History of Indiana Law*, ed. David J. Bodenhamer and Randall T. Shepard (Athens: Ohio University Press, 2006).

10. Stat. 27 (1866) (codified at 42 U.S.C. Sec. 1982 [1988]).

11. *Cong. Globe*, 39th Cong., 1st Sess. 1083 (1866).

12. 100 U.S. 339 (1880).

13. 118 U.S. 356, 374 (1886).

14. 166 U.S. 226 (1897) (Fourteenth Amendment due process applied to state court proceeding on taking of land).

15. 268 U.S. 652 (1925).

16. *Boykin v. Alabama*, 395 U.S. 238 (1969); *Powell v. Alabama*, 287 U.S. 47 (1932); *NAACP v. Alabama*, 377 U.S. 288 (1964). Indeed, as G. Alan Tarr and Mary Cornelia Aldis Porter wrote in *State Supreme Courts in State and Nation* (rev. ed.; New Haven: Yale University Press, 2009, 89), the Supreme Court of Alabama in the days of the segregated South may have "provided a particularly singular catalyst for the fashioning of federal constitutional principles" (citing *Powell*, 287 U.S. 47 [right to assistance of counsel in preparing for trial]); see also *Boykin* (rights for determining voluntariness of guilty plea); *NAACP* (right of association); *Norris v. Alabama*, 294 U.S. 587 (1935) (right to an unbiased jury).

17. The need for close supervision of state governments by federal judges under the incorporation doctrine has greatly diminished. The diversification of the bench in the South, for instance, featured African Americans on the supreme courts in Alabama, Arkansas, Florida, and North Carolina by the early 1980s.

18. An early proponent, Justice Thomas Hayes of the Vermont Supreme Court, complained about the rote repetition of "federal buzz words memorized like baseball cards" and said of state constitutions, "One longs to hear once again of legal concepts, their meaning and their origin." *State v. Jewett*, 146 Vt. 221, 500 A.2d 233 (1985).

19. William J. Brennan Jr., "State Constitutions and the Protections of Individual Rights," *Harvard Law Review* 90 (1977): 489.

20. David Schuman, "The Right to a Remedy," *Temple Law Review* 65 (1992): 1197n1 (noting that at least one influential commentator laid the groundwork almost a decade earlier, citing Hans A. Linde, "Without 'Due Process': Unconstitutional Law in Oregon," *Oregon Law Review* 49 [1970]: 125).

21. Cathleen C. Herasimchuk, "The New Federalism: Judicial Legislation by the Texas Court of Criminal Appeals?" *Texas Law Review* 68 (1990): 1481, 1492.

22. This was the view of Glenn Harlan Reynolds, "The Right to Keep and Bear Arms Under the Tennessee Constitution: A Case Study in Civic Republican Thought," *Tennessee Law Review* 61 (1994): 647, citing Brennan's *Harvard Law Review* article and Hans A. Linde, "First Things First: Rediscovering the States' Bills of Rights," *University of Baltimore Law Review* 9 (1980): 379.

23. Robert F. Utter, "Swimming in the Jaws of the Crocodile: State Courts Comment on Federal Constitutional Issues When Disposing of Cases on State Constitutional Grounds," *Texas Law Review* 63 (1985): 1025; Robert F. Utter, "Freedom and Diversity in a Federal System: Perspectives on State Constitutions and the Washington Declaration of Rights," in *Developments in State Constitutional Law*, ed. Bradley D. McGraw (St. Paul, MN: West, 1985), 239.

24. 423 U.S. 96 (1975).

25. 423 U.S. 96, 120.

26. This discussion relies on statistics reported each fall in the *Harvard Law Review*.

27. Robert Force, "State 'Bills of Rights': A Case of Neglect and the Need for a Renaissance," *Valparaiso University Law Review* 3 (1969): 125. See also Vern Countryman, "Why a State Bill of Rights?" *Washington Law Review* 45 (1970): 454; Jerome B. Falk Jr., "The State Constitution: A More Than 'Adequate' Nonfederal Ground," *California Law Review* 61 (1973): 273; "Project Report: Toward an Activist Role for State Bills of Right," *Harvard Civil Rights–Civil Liberties Law Review* 8 (1973): 271; Lawrence M. Newman, "Rediscovering the California Declaration of Rights," *Hastings Law Journal* 26 (1974): 481.

28. See, for example, *Landes v. Town of N. Hempstead*, 231 N.E.2d 120 (N.Y. 1967) (protection against disenfranchisement).

29. See, for example, *Simonson v. Cahn*, 261 N.E.2d 246 (N.Y. 1970) (right to grand jury); *Commonwealth v. Davis*, 343 N.E.2d 847 (Mass. 1976) (right to keep and bear arms). The Massachusetts Supreme Judicial Court noted tersely with a string of case citations that the Second Amendment was not relevant to the case, even if it should be incorporated into the Fourteenth Amendment at some future time. *Commonwealth v. Davis*, 850–51.

30. *McDonald v. City of Chicago*, 561 U.S. 742 (2010).

31. *Timbs v. Indiana*, 586 U.S. ___ (2019).

32. See, for example, *State v. Moore*, 483 P.2d 630 (Wash. 1971) (protection against self-incrimination).

33. See, for example, *State v. Burkhart*, 541 S.W.2d 365 (Tenn. 1976) (right to counsel).

34. 125 S.E.2d 207 (Ga. 1962).

35. 125 S.E.2d 207, 212 (quoting Georgia Constitution, Article I, Section 1 [1945]).

36. James A. Gardner, "The Failed Discourse of State Constitutionalism," *Michigan Law Review* 90 (1992): 761.

37. Gardner, "Failed Discourse," 816.

38. Richard Boldt and Dan Friedman, "Constitutional Incorporation: A Consideration of the Judicial Function in State and Federal Constitutional Interpretation," *Maryland Law Review* 76 (2017).

39. *Elkins v. United States*, 364 U.S. 206 (1960).

40. 943 F.2d 758 (7th Cir. 1991).

41. *Missouri v. Jenkins*, 495 U.S. 33 (1990). See also Randall Shepard, "In a Federal Case, Is the State Constitution Something Important or Just Another Piece of Paper?" *William and Mary Law Review* 46 (2005): 1437.

42. *Wickard v. Filburn*, 317 U.S. 111 (1942).

43. 514. U.S. 549 (1995).

44. 545. U.S. 469 (2005).

45. See, for example, *City of Norwood v. Horney*, 853 N.E.2d 1115 (Ohio 2006); *Bd. of County Commissioners v. Lowery*, 136 P.3d 639 (Okla. 2006). See also *County of Wayne v. Hathcock*, 684 N.W.2d 765 (Mich. 2004).

46. *Reading Area Water Authority v. Schuylkill River Greenway Ass'n*, 100 A.3d 572 (Penn. 2014); *State ex rel. Jackson v. Dolan*, 398 S.W.3d 472 (Mo. 2013).

47. Jeffrey S. Sutton, *51 Imperfect Solutions: States and the Making of American Constitutional Law* (New York: Oxford University Press 2018).

48. Vermont Constitution, Chapter 1, Article 7.

49. *Baker v. State*, 170 Vt. 194, 744 A.2d 864 (1999).

50. *Goodridge v. Dept. of Public Health*, 440 Mass. 309, 798 N.E.2d 941 (2003).

51. Opinions of the Justices to the Senate, 440 Mass. 1201, 802 N.E.2d 565 (2004).

52. *In re Marriage of J.B. and H.B.*, 326 S.W.2d 654 (Texas 2016).

53. *Varnum v. Brien*, 763 N.W.2d 862 (Iowa 2009).

54. *Griego v. Oliver*, 316 P.3d 865 (N.M. 2013).

55. *Donaldson v. State*, 292 P.2d 364 (Mont. 2012). Litigating license applicants lost cases in New York and Indiana. *Hernandez v. Robles*, 7 N.Y.3d 33, 855 N.E.2d 1 (2006); *Morrison v. Sadler*, 821 N.E.2d 15 (Ind. Ct. App. 2005). Opponents of same-sex marriage initiated ballot questions that would amend state constitutions to prevent future court decisions authorizing gay unions. Voters in eleven states adopted such proposals in November 2014, just six months after the new Massachusetts same-sex marriage law took effect. Socially conservative states like Mississippi and liberal states like Oregon were among the eleven. When Iowa's voters went to the polls after the *Varnum* decision, for example, they turned out of office all three justices who were on the ballot. It was a first.

56. *Obergefell v. Hodges*, 135 S. Ct. 2584 (2015).

57. *Gill v. Whitford*, 138 S. Ct. 1916, 1930–31 (2018).

58. *League of Women Voters v. Commonwealth*, 178 A.3d 737 (Pa. 2018); *League of Women Voters of Pennsylvania v. Commonwealth*, 181 A.3d 1083 (Pa. 2018) (adopting remediation plan based on the record developed in the Commonwealth Court).

59. *Rucho v. Common Cause* and *Lamone v. Benisek*, 588 U.S. ____ (2019).

60. "Redistricting in North Carolina," Ballotpedia, accessed September 4, 2019, https://ballotpedia.org/Redistricting_in_North_Carolina#State_court_challenges.

61. In 1973, the Supreme Court held that there was not a fundamental right to an education under the US Constitution. *San Antonio Independent School District v. Rodrigues*, 411 U.S. 1 (1973).

62. 790 S.W.2d 186 (Ky. 1989).

63. *McCleary v. State*, 269 P.3d 477 (Wash. 2012).

64. *Gannon v. State*, 319 P.3d 1196 (Kan. 2014).

65. *King v. State*, 818 N.W.2d 1 (Iowa 2012).

66. *Citizens for Strong Schools, Inc., v. Florida State Board of Education*, 2019 WL 98253.

67. 563 S.W.3d 74.

# SUGGESTIONS FOR FURTHER READING

### RIGHTS CONSCIOUSNESS IN AMERICAN HISTORY

The history of rights consciousness in the United States is more expansive, complex, and unpredictable than the standard law school casebooks tend to recognize in their stories of the progressive realization of certain founding ideals. Aspects of that longer history can be traced in Eric Foner, *The Story of American Freedom* (New York, 1998), which stresses democratic pressure from below and outside the seats of power; Richard A. Primus, *The American Language of Rights* (Cambridge, UK, 1999), which stresses the force of new circumstances and adversities; Peter N. Stearns, *Human Rights in World History* (New York, 2012), on the global context of rights construction; the essays by Hendrik Hartog and others in "The Constitution and American Life: A Special Issue," *Journal of American History* 74, no. 3 (September 1987); and Daniel T. Rodgers, *Contested Truths: Keywords in American Politics since Independence* (New York, 1987), where the arguments of this chapter were originally outlined.

The place of natural rights language in the American Revolution is explored in Bernard Bailyn, *The Ideological Origins of the American Revolution* (Cambridge, MA, 1967); Eric Foner, *Tom Paine and Revolutionary America* (New York, 1976); Garry Wills, *Inventing America: Jefferson's Declaration of Independence* (Garden City, NY, 1978); Pauline Maier, *American Scripture: Making the Declaration of Independence* (New York, 1997); T. H. Breen, *The Lockean Moment: The Language of Rights on the Eve of the American Revolution* (Oxford, 2001); Barry Alan Shain, ed., *The Nature of Rights at the American Founding and Beyond* (Charlottesville, VA, 2007); Lynn Hunt, *Inventing Human Rights: A History* (New York, 2007); and Dan Edelstein, *On the Spirit of Rights* (Chicago, 2019).

On the background to the Bill of Rights, see Gordon S. Wood, *The Creation of the American Republic, 1776–1787* (Chapel Hill, NC, 1969); Helen E. Veit et al., eds., *Creating the Bill of Rights: The Documentary Record from the First Federal Congress* (Baltimore, 1991); Jack N. Rakove, *Original Meanings: Politics and Ideas in the Making of the Constitution* (New York, 1996); Akhil Reed Amar, *The Bill of Rights: Creation and Reconstruction* (New Haven, CT, 1998); Pauline Maier, *Ratification: The People Debate the Constitution, 1787–1788* (New York, 2010); and Carol Berkin, *The Bill of Rights: The Fight to Secure America's Liberties* (New York, 2015).

On the second wave of natural rights invention, see Mark Hulliung, *The Social Contract in America: From the Revolution to the Present Age* (Lawrence, KS, 2007); Richard D. Brown, *Self-Evident Truths: Contesting Equal Rights from the Revolution to the Civil War* (New Haven, CT, 2017); Sean Wilentz, *Chants Democratic: New York City and the Rise of the American Working Class, 1788–1850* (New York, 1984); Ellen Carol DuBois, *Feminism and Suffrage: The Emergence of an Independent Women's Movement in America, 1848–1869* (Ithaca, NY, 1978); Nancy Isenberg, *Sex and Citizenship in Antebellum America* (Chapel Hill, NC, 1998); Sally G. Mc-Millen, *Seneca Falls and the Origins of the Women's Rights Movement* (New York, 2008); David Brion Davis, *The Problem of Slavery in the Age of Revolution, 1770–1823* (Ithaca, NY, 1975); Manisha Sinha, *The Slave's Cause: A History of Abolition* (New Haven, CT, 2016); and Steven Hahn, *A Nation under Our Feet: Black Political Struggles in the Rural South from Slavery to the Great Migration* (Cambridge, MA, 2003).

The rise of judicial activism is analyzed in Morton J. Horwitz, *The Transformation of American Law* (Cambridge, MA, 1977, 1992); William E. Nelson, "The Impact of the Antislavery Movement upon Styles of Judicial Reasoning in Nineteenth-Century America," *Harvard Law Review* 87 (1974): 513–66; Robert W. Gordon, "Legal Thought and Legal Practice in the Age of American Enterprise, 1870–1920," in *Professions and Professional Ideologies in America*, ed. Gerald L. Geison (Chapel Hill, NC, 1983); William E. Forbath, *Law and the Shaping of the American Labor Movement* (Cambridge, MA, 1991); and James Gray Pope, "Labor's Constitution of Freedom," *Yale Law Journal* 106 (1997): 941–1031.

The clearest guide to the anti-rights animus of progressive and New Deal reformers is found in their own writings. Among the best are Herbert Croly, *The Promise of American Life* (New York, 1909); Frank J. Goodnow, *Social Reform and the Constitution* (New York, 1911); Jerome Frank, *Law and the Modern Mind* (New York, 1930); and Thurman W. Arnold, *The Symbols of Government* (New Haven, CT, 1935).

The shifting ideological mood after 1940 is captured in Gerard N. Magliocca, *The Heart of the Constitution: How the Bill of Rights Became the Bill of Rights* (New York, 2018); Edward A. Purcell Jr., *The Crisis of Democratic Theory* (Lexington, KY,

1973); Benjamin L. Alpers, *Dictators, Democracy, and American Political Culture* (Chapel Hill, NC, 2003); Laura M. Weinrib, *The Taming of Free Speech: America's Civil Liberties Compromise* (Cambridge, MA, 2016); Elizabeth Borgwardt, *A New Deal for the World: America's Vision for Human Rights* (Cambridge, MA, 2005); Mary Ann Glendon, *A World Made New: Eleanor Roosevelt and the Universal Declaration of Human Rights* (New York, 2001); Carol Anderson, *Eyes Off the Prize: The United Nations and the African American Struggle for Human Rights, 1944–1955* (New York, 2003); Mark V. Tushnet, *Making Civil Rights Law: Thurgood Marshall and the Supreme Court, 1936–61* (New York, 1994); Michael J. Klarman, *From Jim Crow to Civil Rights: The Supreme Court and the Struggle for Racial Equality* (New York, 2004); and Risa L. Goluboff, *The Lost Promise of Civil Rights* (Cambridge, MA, 2007).

On the modern revival of rights consciousness: Sally Engle Merry, *Getting Justice and Getting Even: Legal Consciousness among Working-Class Americans* (Chicago, 1990); Samuel Walker, *In Defense of American Liberties: A History of the ACLU* (New York, 1990); Michael W. McCann, *Rights at Work: Pay Equity Reform and the Politics of Legal Mobilization* (Chicago, 1994); John D. Skrentny, *The Minority Rights Revolution* (Cambridge, MA, 2002); Felicia Kornbluh, *The Battle for Welfare Rights: Politics and Poverty in Modern America* (Philadelphia, 2007); Steven M. Teles, *The Rise of the Conservative Legal Movement: The Battle for Control of the Law* (Princeton, NJ, 2008); Jefferson Decker, *The Other Rights Revolution: Conservative Lawyers and the Remaking of American Government* (New York, 2016); Emily Zackin, *Looking for Rights in All the Wrong Places: Why State Constitutions Contain America's Positive Rights* (Princeton, NJ, 2013). For critiques of rights-based politics: Mary Ann Glendon, *Rights Talk: The Impoverishment of Political Discourse* (New York, 1991); John Gilliom, *Overseers of the Poor: Surveillance, Resistance, and the Limits of Privacy* (Chicago, 2001); Gerard N. Rosenberg, *The Hollow Hope: Can Courts Bring about Social Change?* 2nd ed. (Chicago, 2008); Michael Ignatieff, *Human Rights as Politics and Idolatry* (Princeton, NJ, 2011); Samuel Moyn, *Not Enough: Human Rights in an Unequal World* (Cambridge, MA, 2018).

### THE FIRST AMENDMENT AND THE FREEDOM TO DIFFER

The literature on free speech is vast and increasing. Because there are so many different doctrinal areas encompassed within free speech, many scholars focus on only one or two. Readers might want to begin with the following general works: Lee C. Bollinger, *The Tolerant Society: Freedom of Speech and Extremist Speech in America* (1986); Michael Kent Curtis, *Free Speech, "The People's Darling Privilege": Struggles for Freedom of Expression in American History* (2000); Murray Dry, *Civil Peace and the Quest for Truth: The First Amendment Freedoms in Political Philosophy and American Constitutionalism* (2004); Daniel A. Farber, *The First Amendment* (1998); Alexander Meiklejohn, *Political Freedom: The Constitutional Powers of the People* (1960); Paul L. Murphy, *The Meaning of Freedom of Speech: First Amendment Freedoms from Wilson to FDR* (1972); Frederick F. Schauer, *Free Speech: A Philosophical Enquiry* (1982); and Geoffrey R. Stone, *Perilous Times: Free Speech in Wartime from the Sedition Act of 1798 to the War on Terrorism* (2004).

For more on the history of free speech before World War I, see David M. Rabban, *Free Speech in Its Forgotten Years* (1997), and Zechariah Chafee Jr., "Freedom of Speech in Wartime," *Harvard Law Review* 32 (1919): 932. Chafee's influential body of work also includes *Free Speech in the United States* (1941). Chafee famously criticized the views of another well-known First Amendment scholar, Alexander Meiklejohn, while defending the clear and present danger doctrine. In addition to Meiklejohn's *Political Freedom* (mentioned above), important works by Meiklejohn include *Free Speech and Its Relation to Self-Government* (1948) and "The First Amendment Is an Absolute," *Supreme Court Review* (1961): 245.

The First Amendment jurisprudence of Justice Holmes is discussed in G. Edward White, "Justice Holmes and the Modernization of Free Speech Jurisprudence: The Human Dimension," *California Law Review* 80 (1992): 391, and Yosal Rogat and James M. O'Fallon, "Mr. Justice Holmes: A Dissenting Opinion—The Speech Cases," *Stanford Law Review* 36 (1984): 1349. The clear and present danger test is surveyed in Frank R. Strong, "Fifty Years of 'Clear and Present Danger': From *Schenck* to *Brandenburg*—and Beyond," *Supreme Court Review* (1969): 41; Hans A. Linde, "'Clear and Present Danger' Reexamined: Dissonance in the *Brandenburg* Concerto," *Stanford Law Review* 22 (1970): 1163; and David R. Dow and R. Scott Shieldes, "Rethinking the Clear and Present Danger Test," *Indiana Law Journal* 73 (1998): 1217.

Good starting points for consideration of First Amendment treatment of symbolic speech are Melville B. Nimmer, "The Meaning of Symbolic Speech under the First Amendment," *UCLA Law Review* 21 (1973): 29, and John Hart Ely, "Flag Desecration: A Case Study in the Roles of Categorization and Balancing in First Amendment Analysis," *Harvard Law Review* 88 (1975): 1482. For more on the flag-burning cases, consult Kent Greenawalt, "O'er the Land of the Free: Flag Burning as Speech," *UCLA Law Review* 37 (1990): 925; Frank Michelman, "Saving Old Glory: On Constitutional Iconography," *Stanford Law Review* 42 (1990): 1337; Geoffrey R. Stone, "Flag Burning and the Constitution," *Iowa Law Review* 75 (1989): 111; Mark V. Tushnet, "The Flag-Burning Episode: An Essay on the Constitution," *University of Colorado Law Review* 61 (1990): 39; and Arnold H. Loewy, "The Flag-Burning Case: Freedom of Speech When We Need It Most," *North Carolina Law Review* 68 (1989): 165. The *O'Brien* case is examined in Dean Alfange Jr., "Free Speech and Symbolic Conduct: The Draft-Card Burning

Case," *Supreme Court Review* (1968): 1, and in Lawrence R. Velvel, "Freedom of Speech and the Draft Card Burning Cases," *University of Kansas Law Review* 16 (1968): 149. Content-neutral restrictions are discussed in Daniel A. Farber, "Content Regulation and the First Amendment: A Revisionist View," *Georgetown Law Journal* 68 (1980): 727; Martin H. Redish, "The Content Distinction in First Amendment Analysis," *Stanford Law Review* 34 (1981): 113; and Susan H. Williams, "Content Discrimination and the First Amendment," *University of Pennsylvania Law Review* 139 (1991): 615.

Literature discussing compelled speech under the First Amendment comprises a relatively smaller body of work. Commentary on compelled speech includes Abner S. Greene, "The Pledge of Allegiance Problem," *Fordham Law Review* 64 (1995): 451, and David B. Gaebler, "First Amendment Protection against Government Compelled Expression and Association," *Boston College Law Review* 23 (1982): 995.

For a lively, opinionated overview of the history of First Amendment commercial speech development, see Alex Kozinski and Stuart Banner, "The Anti-History and Pre-History of Commercial Speech," *Texas Law Review* 71 (1993): 747. The value of commercial speech is considered in Thomas H. Jackson and John Calvin Jeffries Jr., "Commercial Speech: Economic Due Process and the First Amendment," *Virginia Law Review* 65 (1979): 1; C. Edwin Baker, "Commercial Speech: A Problem in the Theory of Freedom," *Iowa Law Review* 62 (1976): 1; Martin H. Redish, "The First Amendment in the Marketplace: Commercial Speech and the Values of Free Expression," *George Washington Law Review* 39 (1971): 429; and Alex Kozinski and Stuart Banner, "Who's Afraid of Commercial Speech?" *Virginia Law Review* 76 (1990): 627. An argument that there is no justification for not protecting commercial speech is made in Rodney A. Smolla, "Information, Imagery, and the First Amendment: A Case for Expansive Protection of Commercial Speech," *Texas Law Review* 71 (1993): 777, and in Burt Neuborne, "A Rationale for Protecting and Regulating Commercial Speech," *Brooklyn Law Review* 46 (1980): 437. Other noteworthy articles on commercial speech and the First Amendment are Steven Shiffrin, "The First Amendment and Economic Regulation: Away from a General Theory of the First Amendment," *Northwestern University Law Review* 78 (1983): 1212; Daniel A. Farber, "Commercial Speech and First Amendment Theory," *Northwestern University Law Review* 74 (1979): 372; and Ronald Rotunda, "The Commercial Speech Doctrine in the Supreme Court," *University of Illinois Law Review* (1976): 1080.

The notion of value applied to different types of speech is discussed in Martin H. Redish, "The Value of Free Speech," *University of Pennsylvania Law Review* 130 (1982): 591; Larry Alexander, "Low Value Speech," *Northwestern University Law Review* 83 (1989): 547; and Cass Sunstein, "Low Value Speech Revisited,"

*Northwestern University Law Review* 83 (1989): 555. Frederick F. Schauer's *The Law of Obscenity* (1976) provides a view of the unsettled, confused state of the law up to the point of the *Miller* decision. See also Frederick F. Schauer, "Speech and 'Speech'—Obscenity and 'Obscenity': An Exercise in the Interpretation of Constitutional Language," *Georgetown Law Journal* 67 (1979): 899. For more recent treatments of obscenity and pornography under the First Amendment, see Arnold H. Loewy, "Obscenity, Pornography and First Amendment Theory," *William and Mary Bill of Rights Journal* 2 (1993): 471, and Suzanna Sherry, "Hard Cases Make Good Judges," *Northwestern University Law Review* 99 (2004): 3.

The expanding body of literature on campaign finance reform and its treatment under the First Amendment includes Martin H. Redish and Kirk J. Kaludis, "The Right of Expressive Access in First Amendment Theory: Redistributive Values and the Democratic Dilemma," *Northwestern University Law Review* 93 (1999): 1083; Jeffrey M. Blum, "The Divisible First Amendment: A Critical Functionalist Approach to Freedom of Speech and Electoral Campaign Spending," *New York University Law Review* 58 (1983): 1273; Lillian R. BeVier, "Money and Politics: A Perspective on the First Amendment and Campaign Finance Reform," *California Law Review* 73 (1985): 1045; and C. Edwin Baker, "Campaign Expenditures and Free Speech," *Harvard Civil Rights–Civil Liberties Law Review* 33 (1998): 1.

Issues related to government-funded speech are explored in Steven Shiffrin, "Government Speech," *UCLA Law Review* 27 (1980): 565; David Cole, "Beyond Unconstitutional Conditions: Charting Spheres of Neutrality in Government-Funded Speech," *New York University Law Review* 67 (1992): 675; Martin Redish and Daryl I. Kessler, "Government Subsidies and Free Expression," *Minnesota Law Review* 80 (1996): 543; and Daniel A. Farber, "Another View of the Quagmire: Unconstitutional Conditions and Contract Theory," *Florida State University Law Review* 33 (2006): 913.

### CHURCH AND STATE

Leonard W. Levy, *The Establishment Clause and the First Amendment* (New York, 1986), remains the best single overview of this subject, but it is written from a definite absolutist position. An excellent study of the complex issues surrounding church and state in early America is Thomas J. Curry, *The First Freedoms: Church and State in America to the Passage of the First Amendment* (New York, 1986), which raises serious doubts about whether there was any "original intent" of the framers regarding the meaning of the establishment clause. Another balanced look is William Lee Miller, *The First Liberty: Religion and the American Republic* (New York, 1986).

A good general volume, which espouses a more accommodationist view, is John T. Noonan, *The Lustre of Our Country: The American Experience of Religious*

*Freedom* (Berkeley, CA, 1998). See also Michael W. McConnell, John H. Garvey, and Thomas C. Berg, *Religion and the Constitution*, 2nd ed. (New York, 2006), and McConnell, "The Origins and Historical Understanding of Free Exercise of Religion," *Harvard Law Review* 103 (1990): 1409–1517. An older but still useful overview of the issues is Mark D. Howe, *The Garden and the Wilderness* (Chicago, 1965). Also see Edwin S. Gaustad, *Church and State in America*, 2nd ed. (New York, 2003).

For good overviews of the material, Paul Finkelman, ed., *Religion and American Law: An Encyclopedia* (New York, 2000), is probably the best single volume for well-written, scholarly essays on a number of issues touching the religion clauses. Two other good sources are Philip Hamburger, *Separation of Church and State* (Cambridge, MA, 2002), and James Hitchcock, *The Supreme Court and Religion in American Life*, 2 vols. (Princeton, NJ, 2004).

One of the best ways to understand how the religion clauses work in the real world is to read case studies, and there have been some excellent ones over the years. See David Manwaring, *Render unto Caesar: The Flag Salute Controversy* (Chicago, 1962); Wayne R. Swanson, *The Christ Child Goes to Court* (Philadelphia, 1989), an examination of *Lynch v. Donnelly*; Bruce J. Dierenfield, *The Battle over School Prayer* (Lawrence, KS, 2007), on *Engel v. Vitale* and its aftereffects; David M. O'Brien, *Animal Sacrifice and Religious Freedom* (Lawrence, KS, 2004); Garrett Epps, *To an Unknown God* (New York, 2001), on *Oregon v. Smith*; and Shawn Francis Peters, *The Yoder Case* (Lawrence, KS, 2003). For a sociological view of how religious pluralism works in practice, see Robert Wurthnow, *America and the Challenges of Religious Diversity* (Princeton, NJ, 2005).

## PUBLIC SAFETY AND THE RIGHT TO BEAR ARMS

As might be expected, the *Heller* and *McDonald* cases produced a flood of literature analyzing, criticizing, and supporting the Supreme Court decisions. Some scholars disagreeing with the Scalia opinion in *Heller* have argued that the opinion—purportedly grounded in an originalist methodology—essentially got the history wrong. Proponents of this view have included historian Saul Cornell in "Heller, New Originalism and Law Office History: 'Meet the New Boss, Same as the Old Boss,'" *UCLA Law Review* 56 (2009) 1095–125, and legal historian William G. Merkel in "The District of Columbia v. Heller and Antonin Scalia's Perverse Sense of Originalism," *Lewis and Clark Law Review* 13 (2009): 349–81. In "The Second Amendment, Heller and Originalist Jurisprudence, *UCLA Law Review* 56 (2009): 1343–76, political scientist and legal scholar Nelson Lund, a supporter of the individual rights view of the Second Amendment, has argued that the Scalia opinion, while defensible on originalist grounds, departed from strict originalism on several key points. In an article written immediately after the *Heller* decision, legal scholar Reva B. Siegel put forward the view that the decision in *Heller* reflected less the vindication of originalism and more the triumph of popular constitutionalism and the victory of a social movement. See Reva Siegel, "Dead or Alive: Originalism as Popular Constitutionalism in *Heller, Harvard Law Review* 122 (2008): 191–245.

The *Heller* and *McDonald* opinions helped broaden the discussion on the Second Amendment beyond the traditional individual versus collective rights precincts. The Supreme Court declared that the right to keep and bear arms was a right of the individual, which meant that the courts would no longer be concerned with purely historical questions, such as what the drafters and ratifiers of the Second and Fourteenth Amendments might have understood or intended. Instead, courts and legal scholars and advocates would have to concern themselves with questions of how far the newly declared right might extend. Legal Scholar Darrell A. H. Miller has argued that while the courts should treat the right as fairly robust when dealing with firearms ownership in the home, they should permit government a wide degree of latitude in terms of regulating the right to carry outside the home. See Darrell A. H. Miller, "Guns as Smut: Defending the Home-Bound Second Amendment," *Columbia Law* Review 109 (2009): 1278–356. Jonathan Meltzer, looking at *Heller* and the history of firearms regulation in the nineteenth century, has argued that the Constitution should be read as protecting a right to openly carry firearms but not a right to carry concealed firearms. See Jonathan Meltzer, "Open Carry for All: Heller and Our Nineteenth-Century Second Amendment," *Yale Law Journal* 123 (2014): 1486–530. Some of the modern writing concerned with the Second Amendment and its implications for courts and legislatures addresses the application of the constitutional provision to new technologies; see, for example, Josh Blackman, "The First Amendment, the Second Amendment and 3D Printed Guns," *Tennessee Law Review* 81 (2014): 479–538. Other writings target specific pieces of legislation that might be problematic under an individualist reading of the Second Amendment; see Stephen P. Halbrook, "New York's Not So Safe Act: The Second Amendment in an Alice and Wonderland World Where Words Have No Meaning," *Albany Law Review* 78 (2015): 789–817. Legal scholars Joseph Blocher and Darrell A. H. Miller have produced a book-length study, *The Positive Second Amendment, Rights, Regulation and the Future of Heller* (2018), arguing for a reading of the Second Amendment that both protects the right of individuals to own arms as well as the ability of government to regulate the use and ownership of arms.

The outpouring of literature on the Second Amendment since the two Supreme Court cases has been voluminous, and it continues to grow. We have attempted only a small sample of the post-*Heller* literature. It is easy to forget that the amendment and the subject of the right to keep and bear arms was once something of an academic orphan. In 1965, Robert Sprecher, who would later become a judge on the Seventh Circuit Court of Appeals, authored an essay titled "The Lost Amendment" in the *American Bar Association Journal* 51 (1965): 554–57, 665–69, arguing that the Second Amendment deserved more attention from the legal profession. Although the essay won the ABA's prize for the year it was published, the legal profession at the time largely ignored the topic. The Second Amendment had also largely escaped the attention of scholars in the legal academy until the 1989 publication of Sanford Levinson's "The Embarrassing Second Amendment," *Yale Law Journal* 99 (1989): 637–59.

Prior to Levinson, important legal scholarship on the Second Amendment had been written by practicing attorneys. One of the more important of these was Don B. Kates Jr., "Handgun Prohibition and the Original Meaning of the Second Amendment," *Michigan Law Review* 82 (1983): 204–73; it was among the earliest to convince legal scholars that the Second Amendment deserved closer examination. Also important was the work of Stephen P. Halbrook, whose book *That Every Man Be Armed: The Evolution of a Constitutional Right* (Albuquerque, NM, 1984) explored the right to bear arms within the tradition of classical republican political philosophy.

After the publication of Levinson's essay, which had urged the legal academy to treat the Second Amendment as a subject worthy of serious study, an increasing number of legal scholars began publishing on the subject. The prevailing view in the legal academy throughout the 1990s and into the twenty-first century was generally supportive of the individual rights view, albeit with varying degrees of disagreement on the modern importance of the right and the vigor with which courts should enforce the amendment's mandate. Constitutional scholar Akhil Amar explored the Second Amendment within the broader framework of the Bill of Rights and its transformations brought about by the Fourteenth Amendment in *The Bill of Rights: Creation and Reconstruction* (New Haven, CT, 1998). Other legal scholars who have written articles largely supportive of the individual rights view have included William Van Alstyne, "The Second Amendment and the Personal Right to Arms," *Duke Law Journal* 43 (1994): 1236–51; Eugene Volokh, "The Commonplace Second Amendment," *New York University Law Review* 73 (1998): 793–821; Robert J. Cottrol and Raymond T. Diamond, "The Second Amendment: Toward an Afro-Americanist Reconsideration," *Georgetown Law Journal* 80 (1991): 309–61; and Nelson Lund, *A Primer on the Constitutional Right to Keep and Bear Arms* (Potomac Falls, VA, 2002). Carl T. Bogus is among the scholars who have written in support of the state or collective rights view. See, for example, Carl T. Bogus, "What Does the Second Amendment Restrict? A Collective Rights Analysis," *Constitutional Commentary* 18 (2001): 485–514. The scholarship supporting the individual rights view was strong enough to persuade constitutional scholar Laurence H. Tribe to endorse the view in the third edition of his treatise *American Constitutional Law*, vol. 1 (New York, 2000), 899–903. Tribe's endorsement of the individual rights view was a reversal of his earlier support for the collective or states' rights view expressed in previous editions.

Historians had started to look at the Second Amendment as a field worthy of academic consideration somewhat earlier than their colleagues in the legal academy. In the 1980s, historians Robert Shalhope and Lawrence Delbert Cress had debated the relative merits of the individual and collective rights views of the amendment in the pages of the *Journal of American History*. See Robert E. Shalhope, "The Ideological Origins of the Second Amendment," *Journal of American History* 69 (1982): 599–614, and Lawrence Delbert Cress, "An Armed Community: The Origins and Meaning of the Right to Bear Arms," *Journal of American History* 71 (1984): 22–42. Historian Joyce Lee Malcolm, building on earlier work done in the 1980s, provided the first book-length treatment exploring the English origins of the right to bear arms in *To Keep and Bear Arms: The Origins of an Anglo-American Right* (Cambridge, MA, 1994).

Second Amendment scholarship had produced in the two decades before *Heller* a vigorous academic debate and a high-profile academic scandal. The publication in 2000 of Michael A. Bellesiles, *Arming America: The Origins of a National Gun Culture* (New York, 2000), seemed at first likely to take the Second Amendment debate in new directions. Bellesiles, a specialist in early American history, argued that gun ownership was rare in Colonial America and through the Revolutionary period and the early decades of the nineteenth century. This rarity of firearms ownership coupled, he claimed, with often stringent regulation of firearms on the local level argued for a Second Amendment that was not meant to be protective of the individual's right to have arms. Bellesiles's thesis initially created great excitement among American historians and those who studied the Second Amendment and gun control issues more generally. The belief that Bellesiles's work would have a significant impact on the debate over the right to bear arms began to unravel as scholars took a closer look at the author's sources and found that his claims did not stand up to close scrutiny. Among the scholars who found Bellesiles's representation of the historical record problematic were independent scholar Clayton Cramer, "Gun Scarcity in the Early Republic?" http://www.claytoncramer.com/unpublished/GunScarcity.pdf; legal scholar and sociologist James Lindgren, "Fall from Grace: Arming America and the Bellesiles Scandal," review of *Arming America*, by Michael Bellesiles, *Yale Law Journal* 111 (2002): 2195–249; and historian Robert H. Churchill, "Gun Ownership in Early America: A Survey of Manuscript Militia Returns," *William and Mary Quarterly* 60 (2003): 615–42.

A later addition to the Second Amendment debate came from scholars who contended that the right to bear arms was an individual right but one that could only be used for the defense of the community in the form of the militia; since the militia as an organized and trained body has essentially ceased to exist, the right has become largely meaningless in the modern era. Among the scholars arguing this point were David C. Williams, *The Mythic Meanings of the Second Amendment: Taming Political Violence in a Constitutional Republic* (New Haven, CT, 2003), and Richard H. Uviller and William G. Merkel, *The Militia and the Right to Arms or How the Second Amendment Fell Silent* (Durham, NC, 2002). Historian Saul Cornell's study *A Well-Regulated Militia: The Founding Fathers and the Origins of Gun Control in America* (New York, 2006) represents the most ambitious effort along these lines attempting to explain the histories of both the Second and Fourteenth Amendments within this framework. The view that the Second Amendment was intended as an individual right but one that could only be exercised in the context of an organized militia had an important influence on Justice Stevens's dissenting opinion in *Heller*.

## THE ENIGMATIC PLACE OF PROPERTY RIGHTS
## IN MODERN CONSTITUTIONAL THOUGHT

The scholarly literature dealing with the rights of property owners has grown substantially in the past several decades. Stuart Banner insightfully explores what constitutes property in *American Property: A History of How, Why, and What We Own* (Cambridge, MA, 2011). Perhaps the best survey of property rights over the course of American history is James W. Ely Jr., *The Guardian of Every Other Right: A Constitutional History of Property Rights*, 3rd ed. (New York, 2008). For a monumental work that stresses that private property has curtailed governmental power and nurtured democratic institutions, see Richard Pipes, *Property and Freedom* (New York, 1999). In the same vein, Walter Dellinger, "The Indivisibility of Economic Rights and Personal Liberty," *2003–2004 Cato Supreme Court Review* 9 (200), 9–22, examines the intertwined nature of economic liberty and personal freedom. For a comprehensive study of constitutional and legal history that addresses issues relating to property rights, see Kermit L. Hall and Peter Karsten, *The Magic Mirror: Law in American History*, 2nd ed. (New York, 2009). Another important work, Kermit L. Hall, James W. Ely Jr., and Joel Grossman, eds. *The Oxford Companion to the Supreme Court of the United States*, 2nd ed. (New York, 2005), contains several articles on the Supreme Court and economic liberty.

A number of fine essay collections offer a good introduction to thinking about property rights. James W. Ely Jr., ed., *Property Rights in American History*, 6 vols. (New York, 1997); Ellen Frankle Paul and Howard Dickman, eds., *Liberty, Property, and Government: Constitutional Interpretation before the New Deal* (Albany,

NY, 1989); *Liberty, Property, and the Future of Constitutional Development* (Albany, NY, 1990). In "Property as the Keystone Right," *Notre Dame Law Review* 71 (1996): 329–66, Carol M. Rose provides a thoughtful assessment of property as a constitutional norm.

Many excellent studies examine particular subjects pertaining to the constitutional protection of property rights. James W. Ely Jr., "Economic Liberties and the Original Meaning of the Constitution," *San Diego Law Review* 45 (2008): 673–708, surveys the importance of land ownership and the rise of a market economy in the colonial and Revolutionary eras. For the significance of private property in Revolutionary thought, see John Phillip Reid, *Constitutional History of the American Revolution: The Authority of Rights* (Madison, WI, 1986). Several works explore the vital role of property rights in the constitution-drafting process. See Will Paul Adams, *The First American Constitutions: Republican Ideology and the Making of the State Constitutions in the Revolutionary Era*, expanded ed. (Lanham, MD, 2001); Stuart Bruchey, "The Impact of Concern for the Security of Property Rights on the Legal System of the Early American Republic," *Wisconsin Law Review* 1980 (1980): 1135–58; and James W. Ely Jr., "'That Due Satisfaction May Be Made:' The Fifth Amendment and the Origins of the Compensation Principle," *American Journal of Legal History* 36 (1992): 1–18. The history and development of contract clause jurisprudence is examined in James W. Ely Jr., *The Contract Clause: A Constitutional History* (Lawrence, KS, 2016). Valuable insights regarding the concept of economic due process are provided in Michael Les Benedict, "Laissez-Faire and Liberty: A Re-Evaluation of the Meaning and Origins of Laissez-Faire Constitutionalism," *Law and History Review* 3 (1985): 292–331; Herbert Hovenkamp, *Enterprise and American Law, 1836–1937* (Cambridge, MA, 1991); and Michael J. Phillips, *The Lochner Court, Myth and Reality: Substantive Due Process from the 1890s to the 1930s* (Westport, CT, 2001). David E. Bernstein's *Rehabilitating* Lochner: *Defending Individual Rights against Progressive Reform* (Chicago, 2011) offers a compelling revisionist account of a famous Supreme Court decision affirming the liberty of contract doctrine. For another rewarding account, see Paul Kens, *Judicial Power and Reform Politics: The Anatomy of Lochner v. New York* (Lawrence, KS, 1980).

For a good introduction to the complex topic of taking property and the Fifth Amendment protection afforded property owners, see David A. Dana and Thomas W. Merrill, *Property: Takings* (New York, 2002). For regulatory takings, see William A. Fischel, *Regulatory Takings: Law, Economics, and Politics* (Cambridge, MA, 1995). Lynda Butler thoughtfully explores issues pertaining to the physical taking of property in "The Governmental Function of Constitutional Property," *UC Davis Law Review* 48 (2015): 1687–778. In *The Grasping Hand: Kelo v. City of New London and the Limits of Eminent Domain* (Chicago, 2015),

Ilya Somin provides a sharp critique of the Supreme Court's broad interpretation of public use to facilitate the aggressive exercise of eminent domain power to acquire private property.

For the subordination of property rights by the Progressive movement and the New Deal, readers should consult Richard A. Epstein, *How Progressives Rewrote the Constitution* (Washington, DC, 2006); James W. Ely Jr., "The Progressive Era Assault on Individualism and Property Rights," *Social Philosophy and Policy* 29 (2012): 255–82; and Geoffrey P. Miller, "The True Story of Carolene Products," *Supreme Court Review* 1987 (1988): 397–428.

Calls for reinvigorated constitutional protection of economic interests have fueled the current debate. See Bernard H. Siegan, *Economic Liberties and the Constitution*, 2nd ed. (New Brunswick, NJ, 2006); Richard A. Epstein, *Takings: Private Property and the Power of Eminent Domain* (Cambridge, MA, 1985); and Steven J. Eagle, "The Development of Property Rights in America and the Property Rights Movement," *Georgetown Journal of Law and Public Policy* 1 (2002): 77–129. Other scholars have been critical of the renewed interest in property rights. See Bernard Schwartz, *The New Right and the Constitution: Turning Back the Legal Clock* (1990). Gregory S. Alexander, *Commodity and Propriety: Competing Visions of Property in American Legal Thought, 1776–1970* (Chicago, 1997) is a wide-ranging account of thinking about the role of private property in American society.

## EQUAL PROTECTION AND AFFIRMATIVE ACTION

The two preeminent historians of affirmative action are Herman Belz and Hugh Davis Graham. Their principal works (Belz's *Equality Transformed: A Quarter-Century of Affirmative Action* [New Brunswick, NJ: Transaction, 1991] and Graham's *The Civil Rights Era: Origins and Development of National Policy, 1960–72* [New York: Oxford University Press, 1990) were published just before major changes in civil rights laws. Graham later wrote on the relationship between affirmative action and immigration policies in *Collision Course: The Strange Conversion of Affirmative Action and Immigration Policy in America* (New York: Oxford University Press, 2002). John David Skrentny, *The Ironies of Affirmative Action: Politics, Culture and Justice in America* (Chicago: University of Chicago Press, 1996), should also be consulted, as well as Skrentny's later work, *The Minority Rights Revolution* (Cambridge, MA: Harvard University Press, 2002). Anthony Chen, *The Fifth Freedom: Jobs, Politics and Civil Rights in the United States, 1941–72* (Princeton, NJ: Princeton University Press, 2009), is a valuable additional work. Samuel Leiter and William M. Leiter provide a handy overview of civil rights laws in *Affirmative Action in Antidiscrimination Law and Policy: An Overview and Synthesis*, 2nd ed. (Albany: SUNY Press, 2011).

Two excellent accounts of presidential administrations and civil rights are Dean Kotlowski, *Nixon's Civil Rights* (New York: Cambridge University Press, 2001), and Raymond Wolters, *Right Turn: William Bradford Reynolds, the Reagan Administration, and Black Civil Rights* (New Brunswick, NJ: Transaction, 1996).

Useful works on the background of the issues of color-blindness and race-consciousness are Andrew Kull, *The Color-Blind Constitution* (Cambridge, MA: Harvard University Press, 1992), and Stephan and Abigail Thernstrom, *America in Black and White: One Nation, Indivisible* (New York: Simon & Schuster, 1997).

Alfred W. Blumrosen, one of the architects of affirmative action, provides valuable firsthand accounts in *Black Employment and the Law* (New Brunswick, NJ: Rutgers University Press, 1971) and in *Modern Law: The Law Transmission System and Equal Employment Opportunity* (Madison: University of Wisconsin Press, 1993). Law professor Randall Kennedy defends affirmative action in *For Discrimination: Race, Affirmative Action, and the Law* (New York: Pantheon, 2013). Richard Epstein offers a theoretical attack on antidiscrimination in *Forbidden Grounds: The Case against Employment Discrimination Laws* (Cambridge, MA: Harvard University Press, 1992).

On race and education, see J. Harvie Wilkinson III, *From Brown to Bakke: The Supreme Court and School Integration, 1945–78* (New York: Oxford University Press, 1979), and Raymond Wolters, *The Burden of Brown: Thirty Years of School Desegregation* (Knoxville: University of Tennessee Press, 1984). The essential work on voting rights is Abigail Thernstrom, *Whose Votes Count? Affirmative Action and Minority Voting Rights* (Cambridge, MA: Harvard University Press, 1987).

### REVERSING THE REVOLUTION

Readers who seek a survey of the due process revolution as it affected criminal defendants should begin with David J. Bodenhamer, *Fair Trial: Rights of the Accused in American History* (New York, 1992), especially chapters 5–7, a work that may be supplemented by Melvin I. Urofsky, *The Continuity of Change: The Supreme Court and Individual Liberties, 1953–1986* (New York, 1989). Samuel Walker, *Popular Justice: A History of American Criminal Law* (New York, 1980), offers a useful survey of the American criminal justice system, as does Lawrence M. Friedman, *Crime and Punishment in American History* (New York, 1993). Michael Willrich, "Criminal Justice in the United States," in *The Cambridge History of Law in America*, vol. 3, *The Twentieth Century and After*, ed. Michael Grossberg and Christopher Tomlins (New York, 2008), 195–231, is a useful overview of developments into the current century.

The story of how the guarantees of the Bill of Rights came to be incorporated into the Fourteenth Amendment as a restriction on state criminal process is found in Richard C. Cortner, *The Supreme Court and the Second Bill of Rights: The Fourteenth Amendment and the Nationalization of Civil Liberties* (Madison, WI, 1981). David Fellman, *The Defendant's Rights Today* (Madison, WI, 1975), serves as a useful guide to changes in the 1960s and early 1970s, while several essays in Herman Schwartz, ed., *The Burger Years: Rights and Wrongs in the Supreme Court, 1969–1986* (New York, 1987), and Craig Bradley, ed., *The Rehnquist Legacy* (New York, 2006), extend the discussion from the 1980s to the first decade of the twenty-first century.

Judicial biographies often serve as a good introduction to issues before the Supreme Court. James Simon, *The Antagonists: Hugo Black, Felix Frankfurter, and Civil Liberties in Modern America* (New York, 1989), details the momentous clash of these two personalities over the meaning and extent of federal due process. Two able biographies of Earl Warren, under whose leadership the due process revolution occurred, are G. Edward White, *Earl Warren: A Public Life* (New York, 1982), and Ed Cray's more journalistic *Chief Justice: A Biography of Earl Warren* (New York, 1997). Sue Davis, *Justice Rehnquist and the Constitution* (Princeton, NJ, 1989), provides a good introduction to the late chief justice's legal philosophy. An assessment of Rehnquist's legacy and his leadership are expressed by Mark Tushnet, *A Court Divided: The Rehnquist Court and the Future of Constitutional Law* (New York, 2005). Michael R. Gizzi and R. Craig Curtis wrestle with the implications of digital surveillance for Fourth Amendment protections in *The Fourth Amendment in Flux: The Roberts Court, Crime Control, and Digital Privacy* (Lawrence, KS, 2016). Michelle Alexander, *The New Jim Crow: Mass Incarceration in the Age of Colorblindness* (New York, 2010), and Bryan Stevenson, *Just Mercy: A Story of Justice and Redemption* (New York, 2014), speak forcefully and eloquently to the continuing racism in American criminal justice.

Studies of landmark cases offer another fruitful way to learn about rights of the accused during these transitional decades. Among the more useful works are Dan T. Carter, *Scottsboro: A Tragedy of the American South*, rev. ed. (Baton Rouge, LA, 1979), a study of *Powell v. Alabama* (1932); Anthony Lewis, *Gideon's Trumpet* (New York, 1964), the story of *Gideon v. Wainwright* (1963), the right to counsel case; Liva Baker, *Miranda: Crime, Law, and Politics* (New York, 1983), which provides a detailed look at *Miranda v. Arizona* (1966); and Carolyn M. Long, *Mapp v. Ohio: Guarding against Unreasonable Searches and Seizures* (Lawrence, KS, 2006). David Oshinsky offers a good, brief overview of the modern death penalty in *Capital Punishment on Trial: Furman v. Georgia and the Death Penalty in Modern America* (Lawrence, KS, 2010). Carol S. Steiker and Jordan M. Steiker provide a critical analysis of recent death-penalty jurisprudence, citing both its intended and unintended consequences, in *Courting Death: The Supreme Court and Capital Punishment* (Cambridge, MA, 2016).

## POLICE PRACTICES AND THE BILL OF RIGHTS

For an excellent discussion of the Supreme Court and the Constitution, generally, including the right to privacy, see Laurence Tribe and Joshua Matz, *Uncertain Justice: The Roberts Court and the Constitution* (New York, 2014), chap. 7. The best introduction to the constitutional law of police practices during the early part of the Rehnquist Court era is Shelvin Singer and Marshall J. Hartman, *Constitutional Criminal Procedure Handbook* (New York, 1986). Chapters 8–10 and 12 of this book provide an extremely readable analysis of the major Supreme Court cases on the Fourth and Fifth Amendments during this period. More theoretical are Herbert L. Packer's "Two Models of the Criminal Process," *University of Pennsylvania Law Review* 113 (1964): 1–68, and *The Limits of the Criminal Sanction* (Stanford, CA, 1968), which outline contrasting philosophical approaches to criminal procedure and explain why it matters whether a given criminal justice system places greater emphasis on crime control or on due process. Students interested in the history of those Bill of Rights provisions that regulate police practices should begin their reading with David Bodenhamer, *Fair Trial: The Rights of the Accused in American History* (New York, 1991). For development of the attitudes underlying these and other constitutional limitations on governmental power, see Edward S. Corwin, *Liberty against Government: The Rise, Flowering and Decline of a Famous Judicial Concept* (Baton Rouge, LA, 1948). Those interested in exploring the impact that the war on terror has had on constitutional rights should see David Cole and James Dempsey, *Terrorism and the Constitution* (New York, 2002); Sanford Levinson, ed., *Torture: A Collection* (New York, 2002); and Karen Greenberg and Joshua Dratel, eds., *The Torture Papers* (New York, 2005). For a thorough examination of the Warren Court era, see Michal R. Belknap, *The Supreme Court under Earl Warren, 1953–1969* (Columbia, SC, 2005). For a good anthology of articles dealing with the impact of Chief Justice Rehnquist on constitutional rights, see Craig Bradley, ed., *The Rehnquist Legacy* (New York, 2005).

The most readable historical work on the privilege against self-incrimination is Leonard W. Levy's Pulitzer Prize–winning classic, *Origins of the Fifth Amendment: The Right against Self-Incrimination* (New York, 1968). See also R. H. Helmholz et al., *The Privilege against Self-Incrimination: Its Origins and Development* (Chicago, 1997). An insightful examination of how the law concerning police interrogations developed is found in Yale Kamisar's *Police Interrogation and Confessions* (Ann Arbor, MI, 1980). Liva Baker's *Miranda: Crime, Law and Politics* (New York, 1985) examines the intersection of politics, law, and public opinion, explaining why *Miranda* was seen as both necessary and controversial.

Laurence A. Benner, "Requiem for Miranda: The Rehnquist Court's Voluntariness Doctrine in Historical Perspective," *Washington University Law Quarterly* 67 (1989): 59–163, critiques the Rehnquist Court rulings undermining the *Miranda* decision. In "Reconsidering *Miranda*," *University of Chicago Law Review* 54 (1987): 435–61, Stephen J. Schulhoffer provides an excellent analysis of the Supreme Court's ruling and summarizes a number of studies that assess its impact on law enforcement. For further information on the latter subject, see Otis H. Stephens Jr., *The Supreme Court and Confessions of Guilt* (Lexington, KY, 1973); Richard A. Leo, "Inside the Interrogation Room," *Journal of Criminal Law and Criminology* 86 (1996): 266–303; Paul G. Cassell and Bret Hayman, "Police Interrogation in the 1990s: An Empirical Assessment of the Effects of *Miranda*," *UCLA Law Review* 43 (1996): 839–931; and George C. Thomas, "Stories about Miranda," *Michigan Law Review* 102 (2004): 1959–97. For a discussion of the impact of *Chavez v. Martinez*, see John T. Parry, "Constitutional Interpretation, Coercive Interrogation and Civil Rights Litigation after *Chavez v. Martinez*," *Georgia Law Review* 39 (2005): 733–838. For additional studies documenting the failure of *Miranda* to protect the innocent from pressure to falsely confess to crimes they did not commit, see Welsh S. White, "False Confessions and the Constitution: Safeguards against Untrustworthy Confessions," *Harvard Civil Rights–Civil Liberties Law Review* 32 (1997): 105–57; Stephen A. Drizin and Richard A. Leo, "The Problem of False Confessions in the Post-DNA World," *North Carolina Law Review* 82 (2004): 891–1006; and Richard A. Leo, Steven A. Drizin, Peter J. Neufeld, et al., "Bringing Reliability Back In: False Confessions and Legal Safeguards in the Twenty-first Century," *Wisconsin Law Review* (2006): 479–539.

Readers interested in the Fourth Amendment should consult Anthony G. Amsterdam's "Perspectives on the Fourth Amendment," *Minnesota Law Review* 58 (1974): 349–477, regarded as a classic in the literature on that subject. For a comprehensive analytical explanation of how the Fourth Amendment applies to everyday police practices, see Judge Charles E. Moylan Jr.'s *Introduction to The Fourth Amendment Handbook*, 4th ed., ed. Laurence A. Benner (American Bar Association, 2019). This handbook also contains a concise summary of all Fourth Amendment decisions by the Supreme Court since 1914. For historical analysis, see Nelson Lasson's *The History and Development of the Fourth Amendment* (Baltimore, 1937), which while dated, remains useful because it details the historical origins of the concepts embodied in the Fourth Amendment from Roman times through the American Revolution and also analyzes early judicial interpretation of the amendment. For those seeking insights into the values protected by the Fourth Amendment, a good place to start is Ferdinand D. Schoeman, *Philosophical Dimensions of Privacy: An Anthology* (Cambridge, UK, 1984), a collection of essays by political scientists, lawyers, philosophers, and anthropologists representative of the diversity of attitudes on privacy, each introduced with a thoughtful interpretive essay critiquing the literature on the subject. Laurence A. Benner's "Diminishing Expectations of Privacy in the Rehnquist Court," *John Marshall Law Review* 22 (1989): 825–76, focuses on Supreme Court rulings that have employed the concept of a reasonable expectation of privacy to restrict the protection afforded by the Fourth Amendment. Daniel Solove's "Fourth Amendment Codification and Professor Kerr's Misguided Call for Judicial Deference," *Fordham Law Review* 74 (2005): 747–77, describes the rise of statutory protection for privacy in the face of diminished Fourth Amendment protection. For an assessment of how Fourth Amendment doctrine has resulted in minimizing the role of the courts in monitoring government surveillance, see Susan N. Herman, "The USA Patriot Act and the Submajoritarian Fourth Amendment," *Harvard Civil Rights–Civil Liberties Law Review* 41 (2006): 67–132. For a video explaining the threat to privacy created by the merging of artificial intelligence and facial recognition technology, see Joss Fong, "What Facial Recognition Steals from Us," December 10, 2019, https://www.youtube.com/watch?v=ccodqW2HCRc.

The controversial exclusionary rule, which the Court uses to enforce constitutional limitations on police practices, has received the attention of several scholars. Particularly useful are two detailed studies by Peter F. Nardulli of the rule's impact on conviction rates, "Societal Cost of the Exclusionary Rule: An Empirical Assessment," *American Bar Foundation Research Journal* (1983): 585–609, and "The Societal Costs of the Exclusionary Rule Revisited," *University of Illinois Law Review* (1987): 223–39. Also informative is Thomas Y. Davies, "A Hard Look at What We Know (and Still Need to Learn) about the 'Costs' of the Exclusionary Rule: The NIJ Study and Other Studies of Lost Arrests," *American Bar Foundation Research Journal* (1983): 611–90, which critiques previous research on the subject and reports the findings of a California study. Steven F. Schlesinger presents a vigorous critique of the rule in *Exclusionary Injustice: The Problem of Illegally Obtained Evidence* (New York, 1977). For a fascinating history of *Mapp v. Ohio*, which applied the Fourth Amendment exclusionary rule to the states, see Carolyn N. Long, *Mapp v. Ohio: Guarding against Unreasonable Searches and Seizures* (Lawrence, KS, 2006).

For an alternative approach to the protection of constitutional rights that goes beyond the rights/remedy paradigm to suggest a proactive approach to curb the racially disparate impact of unconstitutional searches and seizures by employing the privileges or immunities clause of the Fourteenth Amendment rather than the due process clause, see Laurence A. Benner, "Protecting Constitutional Rights in an Age of Anxiety: A New Approach," *Human Rights Magazine* 29 (Spring 2002), https://www.americanbar.org/groups/crsj/publications/human_rights_maga zine_home/human_rights_vol29_2002/spring2002/hr_spring02_benner/. See also Philip B. Kurland, "The Privileges or Immunities Clause: 'Its Hour Come Round at Last'?" 172 *Washington University Law Quarterly* 405 (1972).

## PRIVACY RIGHTS IN MODERN AMERICA

The history and analysis of privacy has been taken up by scholars across disciplines. For a general overview of privacy theories, issues, and disputes, see Alan Westin, *Privacy and Freedom* (New York: Atheneum, 1967); Barrington Moore's wider treatment in *Privacy: Studies in Social and Cultural History* (New York: M. E. Sharpe, 1984); and Phillippe Aries and Georges Duby's edited collection *A History of Private Life*, 4 vols. (Cambridge, MA: Harvard University Press, 1988–91).

Philosophical treatments of privacy have also been offered. For general philosophical accounts of privacy, along with analysis of privacy issues and disputes, see Anita Allen, *Uneasy Access: Privacy for Women in a Free Society* (Lanham, MD: Rowman & Littlefield, 1988); Ferdinand Schoeman, *Privacy and Social Freedom* (New York: Cambridge University Press, 1992); Julie Inness, *Privacy, Intimacy, and Isolation* (Oxford: Oxford University Press, 1992); Judith W. DeCew, *In Pursuit of Privacy: Law, Ethics, and the Rise of Technology* (Ithaca, NY: Cornell University Press, 1997); Adam D. Moore, *Privacy Rights: Moral and Legal Foundations* (University Park: Pennsylvania State University Press, 2010); and Anita Allen, *Unpopular Privacy: What Must We Hide?* (Oxford: Oxford University Press, 2011).

For philosophical views about how to define privacy and the value of privacy, see Judith Jarvis Thomson, "The Right to Privacy," *Philosophy and Public Affairs* 4 (1975): 295–314; James Rachels, "Why Privacy Is Important," *Philosophy and Public Affairs* 4 (1975): 323–33; Jeffrey Reiman, "Privacy, Intimacy, and Personhood," *Philosophy and Public Affairs* 6 (1976): 26–44; William Parent, "Privacy, Morality, and the Law," *Philosophy and Public Affairs* 12 (1983): 269–88; Thomas Scanlon, "Thomson on Privacy," *Philosophy and Public Affairs* 4 (1975): 315–22; Judith Wagner DeCew, "The Scope of Privacy in Law and Ethics," *Law and Philosophy* 5 (1986): 145–73; Adam D. Moore, "Privacy: Its Meaning and Value," *American Philosophical Quarterly* 40 (2003): 215–27; Helen Nissenbaum, "Privacy as Contextual Integrity," *Washington Law Review* 79 (2004): 119–57; and Beate Rossler, *The Value of Privacy*, trans. Rupert D. V. Glasgow (Cambridge, UK: Polity, 2005).

A general introduction of privacy law can be found in Ellen Alderman and Caroline Kennedy's *The Right to Privacy* (New York: Alfred A. Knopf, 1995) and in Daniel J. Solove's *Understanding Privacy* (Cambridge, MA: Harvard University Press, 2010). Legal conceptions of privacy in the US tradition start with Judge Thomas Cooley, *A Treatise on the Law of Torts* (Chicago: Callaghan, 1880), and Samuel Warren and Louis D. Brandeis, "The Right to Privacy," *Harvard Law Review* 4 (1890): 194, 193–220. Dean William Prosser's "Privacy," *California Law Review* 48 (1960): 383–89, helped to codify the privacy torts, which were then adopted by the states. Edward Bloustein responded to Prosser's views in "Privacy and an Aspect of Human Dignity: An Answer to Dean Prosser," *New York University Law Review* 39 (1964): 962–1007. Ken Gormley, "One Hundred Years of Privacy," *Wisconsin Law Review* (1992): 1335–441, provides a detailed historical overview of US privacy law from 1890 to 1990. Daniel Solove and Neil Richards, "Privacy's Other Path: Recovering the Law of Confidentiality," *Georgetown Law Journal* 96 (2007): 123–82, offers a comparison of US privacy law and how privacy is viewed in Europe. Other important work on legal conceptions of privacy include Richard Parker, "A Definition of Privacy," *Rutgers Law Review* 27 (1974): 275–96; Louis Henkin, "Privacy and Autonomy," *Columbia Law Review* 74 (1974): 1410–33; Ruth Gavison, "Privacy and the Limits of Law," *Yale Law Journal* 89 (1980): 421–71; Daniel Solove, "Conceptualizing Privacy," *California Law Review* 90 (2002): 1088–155; and Christopher Slobogin, "Subpoenas and Privacy," *DePaul Law Review* 54 (2005): 805–46.

Many scholars have challenged the worth of privacy and its continued importance given advancements in technology. For feminist critiques of privacy, see Jean Elshtain, *Public Man, Private Woman: Women in Social and Political Thought* (Princeton, NJ: Princeton University Press, 1981); Carol Gilligan, *In a Different Voice: Psychological Theory and Women's Development* (Cambridge, MA: Harvard University Press, 1982); Deborah Rhode, *Justice and Gender: Sex Discrimination and the Law* (Cambridge, MA: Harvard University Press, 1989); and Catharine MacKinnon, *Toward a Feminist Theory of the State* (Cambridge, MA: Harvard University Press, 2002). For communitarian critiques of privacy, see Amitai Etzioni, *The Limits of Privacy* (New York: Basic Books, 1999), and Helena Rubinstein, "If I Am Only for Myself, What Am I? A Communitarian Look at the Privacy Stalemate," *American Journal of Law and Medicine* 25 (1999): 203–31. Welcome or not, some have noted the demise of privacy and the ascendency of surveillance culture. See Richard Spinello, "The End of Privacy," *America* 176 (1997): 9–13; Charles Skyes, *The End of Privacy* (New York: St. Martin's, 1999); Jeffrey Rosen, *The Unwanted Gaze: The Destruction of Privacy in America* (New York: Random House, 2000); Michael Froomkin, "The Death of Privacy," *Stanford Law Review* 52 (2000): 1461–543; and Adam D. Moore, "Privacy, Security, and Government Surveillance: WikiLeaks and the New Accountability," *Public Affairs Quarterly* 25 (2011): 141–56.

## THE RIGHTS OF NONCITIZENS

The historiography devoted to immigration and citizenship law is immense. What follows is less a discussion of the field than a survey of essential texts. The field tends to be divided into scholarship on the law of citizenship, on the one hand, and scholarship on the law of immigration, on the other.

The leading history of the ideas, laws, and politics that went into the making of US citizenship remains James H. Kettner's *The Development of American Citizenship, 1608–1870* (Chapel Hill: University of North Carolina Press, 1978). Rogers Smith's massive *Civic Ideals: Conflicting Visions of Citizenship in U.S. History* (New Haven, CT: Yale University Press, 1997) explores the intertwining of liberal ideals of citizenship with entrenched commitments to gender, racial, ethnic, and religious hierarchies until the end of the nineteenth century. William J. Novak's wonderful essay, "The Legal Transformation of Citizenship in Nineteenth-Century America," in *The Democratic Experiment: New Directions in American Political History*, ed. Meg Jacobs, William J. Novak, and Julian Zelizer (Princeton, NJ: Princeton University Press, 2003), traces how citizenship displaced a range of other legal categories over the course of the nineteenth century. Martha Jones's *Birthright Citizens: A History of Race and Rights in Antebellum America* (New York: Cambridge University Press, 2018) deals with the free Black experience of, and struggle for, citizenship in the decades leading up to the Civil War. Lucy Salyer's *Under the Starry Flag: How a Band of Irish Americans Joined the Fenian Revolt and Sparked a Crisis over Citizenship* (Cambridge, MA: Harvard University Press, 2018) maps the politics of voluntary expatriation during the second half of the nineteenth century. On race and naturalization, the reader should consult Ian Haney López, *White by Law: The Legal Construction of Race* (New York: New York University Press, 1995). Patrick Weil's *The Sovereign Citizen: Denaturalization and the Origins of the American Republic* (Philadelphia: University of Pennsylvania Press, 2012) is an important study of how the United States stripped thousands of Americans of citizenship over the course of the twentieth century. For work on citizenship and globalization, Peter Spiro's *Beyond Citizenship: American Identity after Globalization* (New York: Oxford University Press, 2008) is a good introduction.

The literature on immigration law can be overwhelming. The single most impressive overview is Aristide Zollberg's *A Nation by Design: Immigration Policy in the Fashioning of America* (New York: Russell Sage Foundation, 2006). Daniel Kanstroom's *Deportation Nation: Outsiders in American History* (Cambridge, MA: Harvard University Press, 2007) traces the history of the impulse to expel and remove individuals and populations over the long span of American history. Roger Daniels's *Guarding the Golden Door: American Immigration Policy and Immigrants since 1882* (New York: Hill & Wang, 2004) and *Coming to America: A History of Immigration and Ethnicity in American Life* (New York: HarperCollins, 1990) are classic accounts of immigration history, strongest on the nineteenth and twentieth centuries.

For immigration in the seventeenth and eighteenth centuries, see Marilyn C. Baseler, *"Asylum for Mankind": America, 1607–1800* (Ithaca, NY: Cornell

University Press, 1998); Aaron S. Fogleman, *Hopeful Journeys: German Immigration, Settlement, and Political Culture in Colonial America 1717–1775* (Philadelphia: University of Pennsylvania Press, 1996); Alison Games, *Migration and the Origins of the English Atlantic World* (Cambridge, MA: Harvard University Press, 1999); and Marianne Wokeck, *Trade in Strangers: The Beginnings of Mass Migration to North America* (University Park: Pennsylvania State University Press, 1999).

For antebellum immigration, especially on state-level immigration regimes, the modern scholarship traces its origin to Gerald Neuman's immensely important article, "The Lost Century of American Immigration Law, 1776–1875," *Columbia Law Review* 93 (1993): 1833–901. Hidetaka Hirota's *Expelling the Poor: Atlantic Seaboard States and the Nineteenth-Century Origins of American Immigration Policy* (New York: Oxford University Press, 2017) is a detailed archival exploration of the intertwining of poor laws and immigration law in the antebellum period. Michael Schoeppner's *Moral Contagion: Black Sailors, Citizenship, and Diplomacy in Antebellum America* (New York: Cambridge University Press, 2019) explores the dilemmas surrounding the movement of Black sailors in the antebellum period.

The most studied period when it comes to the history of immigration law is the late nineteenth and twentieth centuries. Lucy Salyer's *Laws Harsh as Tigers: Chinese Immigrants and the Shaping of Modern Immigration Law* (Chapel Hill: University of North Carolina Press, 1995) is an excellent introduction to the law and politics of Chinese exclusion. A more recent work on the subject is Beth Lew-Williams, *The Chinese Must Go: Violence, Exclusion, and the Making of the Alien in America* (Cambridge, MA: Harvard University Press, 2018). For the twentieth century, the indispensable academic monograph is Mae Ngai, *Impossible Subjects: Illegal Aliens and the Making of Modern America* (Princeton, NJ: Princeton University Press, 2004). Ngai's book covers a breathtaking range of topics, ranging from the institution of national origins quotas to the emergence of the figure of the undocumented alien to Japanese internment to the Cold War persecution of Chinese immigrants. More recent work on these issues includes Katharine Benton-Cohen, *Inventing the Immigration Problem: The Dillingham Commission and Its Legacy* (Cambridge, MA: Harvard University Press, 2018) (on early twentieth-century immigration politics); Maddalena Marinari, Madeline Hsu, and María Cristina García, *A Nation of Immigrants Reconsidered: U.S. Society in the Age of Restriction, 1924–1965* (Urbana: University of Illinois Press, 2018) (on the crucial middle decades of the twentieth century); and Ana Raquel Minian, *Undocumented Lives: The Untold Story of Mexican Migration* (Cambridge, MA: Harvard University Press, 2018) (on undocumented migration from Mexico analyzed as a combination of push-pull factors).

A crucial study of the plenary power doctrine is T. Alexander Aleinikoff, *Semblances of Sovereignty: The Constitution, the State, and American Citizenship*

(Cambridge, MA: Harvard University Press, 2002). Leading legal scholar Hiroshi Motomura has drawn attention to the split between substance and procedure in modern immigration law in "The Curious Evolution of Immigration Law: Procedural Surrogates for Substantive Constitutional Rights," *Columbia Law Review* 92 (1992): 1625–704. For important big-picture studies of the trends in American immigration and citizenship law, see Hiroshi Motomura, *Americans in Waiting: The Lost Story of Immigration and Citizenship in the United States* (New York: Oxford University Press, 2007), and *Immigration Outside the Law* (New York: Oxford University Press, 2017).

As the reader of Kunal Parker's chapter in this volume will have discerned, the split between scholarship on citizenship, on the one hand, and scholarship on immigration, on the other, is one that the author (among others) rejects. For the author's own effort to blur the boundaries between the two areas, and one that explores in much greater detail the argument set forth here, the reader is directed to Kunal M. Parker, *Making Foreigners: Immigration and Citizenship Law in America, 1600–2000* (New York: Cambridge University Press, 2015).

## THE COMING OUT OF AMERICAN LAW

The study of LGBTQ rights is a burgeoning field that spans multiple disciplines, with scholarship from historians, political scientists, and sociologists deepening and supporting legal analysis and conclusions.

Much of the early work on LGBTQ rights involved studying the movement's history, which is particularly well documented and analyzed in William N. Eskridge Jr., *Dishonorable Passions: Sodomy Laws in America, 1861–2003* (New York: Viking, 2008); George Chauncey, *Gay New York: Gender, Urban Culture, and the Making of the Gay Male World 1890–1940* (New York: Basic Books, 1994); John D'Emilio, *Sexual, Politics, Sexual Communities: The Making of a Homosexual Minority in the United States, 1940–1970* (Chicago: University of Chicago Press, 1983). Several excellent monographs examine federal government regulations in the mid-twentieth century, including Margot Canaday, *The Straight State: Sexuality and Citizenship in Twentieth-Century America* (Princeton, NJ: Princeton University Press, 2009); David K. Johnson, *The Lavender Scare: The Cold War Persecution of Gays and Lesbians in the Federal Government* (Chicago: University of Chicago Press, 2004); and Allan Bérubé, *Coming Out Under Fire: The History of Gay Men and Women in World War II*, 20th anniversary ed. (Chapel Hill: University of North Carolina Press, 2010).

Most LGBTQ legal regulations are enacted and enforced at the state and local levels. Although those policies are more diffuse and difficult to capture, several authors have done so exceedingly well, writing on topics that range from family law to antidiscrimination protections to prison regulations. These include Anna Lvovsky, *Vice Patrol: Cops, Courts, and the Struggle over Urban Gay Life*

*Before Stonewall* (Chicago: University of Chicago Press, 2021); Daniel Winunwe Rivers, *Radical Relations: Lesbian Mothers, Gay Fathers, and Their Children in the United States since World War II* (Chapel Hill: University of North Carolina Press, 2013); Amy L. Stone, *Gay Rights at the Ballot Box* (Minneapolis: University of Minnesota Press, 2012); and Russell K. Robinson, "Masculinity as Prison: Sexual Identity, Race, and Incarceration," *California Law Review* 99, no. 5 (2011): 1309–408. Political scientists have repeatedly demonstrated that interpersonal contact produces social change essential to LGBTQ rights. See David Broockman and Joshua Kalla, "Durably Reducing Transphobia: A Field Experiment on Door-to-Door Canvassing," *Science*, April 8, 2016, 220–24, and Jay Barth, L. Marvin Overby, and Scott H. Huffmon, "Community Context, Personal Contact, and Support for an Anti-Gay Rights Referendum, *Political Research Quarterly* 62, no. 2 (2009).

The LGBTQ movement's advocacy efforts and gains have not been uniformly beneficial for all of the coalition's members. For discussions of this, see Marie-Amélie George, "Expressive Ends: Understanding Conversion Therapy Bans," *Alabama Law Review* 68, no. 3 (2017): 793–853; Gabriel Arkles, Pooja Gehi, and Elana Redfield, "The Role of Lawyers in Trans Liberation: Building a Transformative Movement for Social Change," *Seattle Journal for Social Justice* 8, no. 2 (2010): 579–641.

Of the LGBTQ rights–related issues, marriage equality has perhaps received the most sustained scholarly attention. For discussion of the movement's strategic decisions, see Michael J. Klarman, *From the Closet to the Altar: Courts, Backlash, and the Struggle for Same-Sex Marriage* (New York: Oxford University Press, 2013); Daniel R. Pinello, *America's Struggle for Same-Sex Marriage* (New York: Cambridge University Press, 2006); and Douglas NeJaime, "Marriage Equality and the New Parenthood," *Harvard Law Review* 129, no. 5 (2016). Numerous scholars have noted marriage equality's limits, including Nancy D. Polikoff, *Beyond (Straight and Gay) Marriage: Valuing All Families under the Law* (Boston: Beacon Press, 2008), and Melissa Murray, "*Obergefell v. Hodges* and Nonmarriage Inequality," *California Law Review* 104, no. 5 (2016): 1207–58.

The question of how courts and legislators should balance LGBTQ rights and those of religious individuals who object to them often arises in the context of marriage equality, although it extends to other areas as well. For work that emphasizes the needs of religious citizens, see Thomas C. Berg, "Religious Freedom and Nondiscrimination," *Loyola University Chicago Law Journal* 50, no. 1 (2018): 181–209; Douglas Laycock, "Religious Liberty and the Culture Wars," *University of Illinois Law Review* 2014, no. 3 (2014): 839–80. For scholarship that critiques expansive religious accommodations, see Jordan Blair Woods, "Religious Exemptions and LGBTQ Child Welfare," *Minnesota Law Review* 123 (2019):

2343–2422; Douglas NeJaime and Reva B. Siegel, "Conscience Wars: Complicity-Based Conscience Claims in Religious and Politics," *Yale Law Journal* 124, no. 7 (2015): 2202–679.

The LGBTQ movement is a relatively recent coalition that developed out of the gay and lesbian rights movement. For a discussion of how and why that happened, see Marie-Amélie George, "The LGBT Disconnect: Politics and Perils of Legal Movement Formation," *Wisconsin Law Review* 2018, no. 3 (2018): 503–91. Although the movement includes bisexual rights, several scholars have analyzed why it is that bisexuals receive short shrift in advocacy, including Elizabeth M. Glazer, "Sexual Reorientation," *Georgetown Law Journal* 100, no. 4 (2012), and Kenji Yoshino, "The Epistemic Contract of Bisexual Erasure," *Stanford Law Review* 52, no. 2 (2000): 353–461.

The LGBTQ movement is a growing coalition that is increasingly turning to nonbinary rights. Related concerns include the rights of intersex, asexual, and other sexual minorities, as well as their place within the larger LGBTQ movement. Analyses of these issues are available in Marie-Amélie George, "Expanding LGBT," *Florida Law Review* 243 (2021): 243–319; Jessica Clarke, "They, Them, and Theirs," *Harvard Law Review* 132, no. 1 (2019): 894–991; Maayan Sudai, "Revisiting the Limits of Professional Autonomy: The Intersex Rights Movement's Path to De-Medicalization," *Harvard Journal of Law and Gender* 41 (2018): 1–54; Elizabeth F. Emens, "Compulsory Sexuality," *Stanford Law Review* 66, no. 2 (2014): 303–86; Margo Kaplan, "Sex-Positive Law," *New York University Law Review* 89, no. 1 (2014): 89–164; Gregg Strauss, "Is Polygamy Inherently Unequal?" *Ethics* 122, no. 3 (2012): 516–44; and Adrienne D. Davis, "Regulating Polygamy: Intimacy, Default Rules, and Bargaining for Equality," *Columbia Law Review* 110, no. 8 (2010): 1955–2046.

## SECOND WIND FOR STATE BILLS OF RIGHTS

The leading recent works on the role of state constitutions are G. Alan Tarr, *Understanding State Constitutions* (Princeton, NJ, 2000), and James A. Gardner, *Interpreting State Constitutions: A Jurisprudence of Function in a Federal System* (Chicago, 2005). Tarr is a professor of political science who has long studied both the law and politics of state constitutions. Gardner is a law professor with valuable thoughts about the jurisprudence of state constitutions. These works follow on from earlier entries in the legal and historical literature. The broad outline of state constitutional development was treated in Kermit L. Hall, *The Magic Mirror: Law in American History* (New York, 1989), and in J. Willard Hurst, *The Growth of American Law: The Law Makers* (Boston, 1950).

The best general collection of materials is Robert F. Williams, ed., *State Constitutional Law: Cases and Materials* (Washington, DC, 1988). Williams has assembled materials that shed light not only on legal developments but on the history and political science underlying state constitutions. Phyllis S. Bamberger, ed., *Recent Developments in State Constitutional Law* (New York, 1985), contains additional valuable material. The documents themselves, including their bills of rights, can be found in William F. Swindler, ed., *Sources and Documents of U.S. Constitutions*, 11 vols. (Dobbs Ferry, NY, 1973–79).

Students of state-based rights should likewise find value in the work of Donald Lutz, who has helped link the state and federal documents. In addition to *Origins of American Constitutionalism* (Baton Rouge, LA, 1988), Lutz has published two widely influential essays: "The Purposes of American State Constitutions," *Publius: The Journal of Federalism* 12 (Winter 1982): 27–40, and "The United States Constitution as an Incomplete Document," *Annals of the American Academy of Political and Social Science* 496 (March 1988): 21–32. The best study of the impact of the state documents on the federal Constitution is Willi Paul Adams, *The First American Constitutions: Republican Ideology and the Making of the State Constitutions of the Revolutionary Era* (Chapel Hill, NC, 1980). A good modern exploration of the interplay between federal and state rights provisions is the record from the College of William and Mary School of Law Symposium on "Dual Enforcement of Constitutional Norms," *William and Mary Law Review* 46 (February 2005): 1219–531.

The nineteenth- and twentieth-century developments are treated in broad compass by Kermit L. Hall, "'Mostly Anchor and Little Sail': State Constitutions in American History," in *Toward a Usable Past: Liberty under State Constitutions*, ed. Paul L. Finkelman and Steven Gottlieb (Athens, GA, 1991), 221–45. This book contains several excellent essays on various aspects of state-based liberty. Valuable as an overview is Daniel J. Alazar, "State Constitutional Design in the United States and Other Systems," *Publius: A Journal of Federalism* 12 (Winter 1982): 1–10. Frank P. Grad, "The State Constitution: Its Function and Form for Our Time," *Virginia Law Review* 54 (June 1968): 928–73, is also a valuable introduction to problems in state constitutional rights.

The leading text exploring the institutional roles of the courts that build state constitutional law is G. Alan Tarr and Mary C. A. Porter, *State Supreme Courts in State and Nation* (New Haven, CT, 1988). The recent surge of interest in state bills of rights has begun to generate an extensive body of writing. In addition to the literature cited in the notes, readers should consult Hans A. Linde, "Without 'Due Process' of Law: Unconstitutional Law in Oregon," *Oregon Law Review* 49 (February 1970): 133–56, which applauds the possibilities of an activist state judiciary broadly interpreting state bills of rights, and Earl Maltz, "The Dark Side of State Court Activism," *Texas Law Review* 63 (March/April 1985): 995–1023, which raises substantial doubts about such activism. That there may not be quite the revolution in state constitutional law that many commentators believed is the subject of Barry Latzer, "The Hidden Conservatism of the State Court 'Revolution,'" *Judicature: The Journal of the American Judicature Society* 74 (December 1990–January 1991): 190–97.

Two law schools sponsor ongoing scholarship focused on the development of state constitutions. The Rutgers School of Law at Camden publishes an annual issue of its law journal dedicated to state constitutions, exploring rights-based matters and other topics. See, for example, G. Alan Tarr and Robert F. Williams, "Twenty-Fifth Issue on State Constitutional Law: Introduction," *Rutgers Law Journal* 44 (Summer 2014): 877–1864. Rutgers likewise operates the Center for State Constitutional Studies, which conducts research on US state constitutions and other subnational charters, provides consulting services, and presents public education programs in the field.

The Albany Law School regularly publishes an annual issue of its law journal on the topic of state constitutions, and it conducts occasional symposia. See, for example, Vincent Martin Bonventre, "Introduction," *Albany Law Review* 69 (2006): vii; "State Constitutional Commentary," *Albany Law Review* 92 (2019): 1325; Loretta H. Rush and Marie Forney Miller, "A Constellation of Constitutions: Discovering and Embracing State Constitutions as Guardians of Civil Liberties," *Albany Law Review* 92 (2019): 1353. An intriguing feature of its annual state constitutional commentary is studies of individual state activities, such as Seth Forrest Gilbertson, "New Hampshire: 'Live Free or Die,' but in the Meantime . . . ," *Albany Law Review* 69 (2006): 591.

A recent and impressive volume is *51 Imperfect Solutions: States and the Making of American Constitutional Law* (New York: Oxford University Press, 2018). The author is Judge Jeffrey Sutton of the Sixth Circuit. Sutton has recently authored *Who Decides? States as Laboratories of Constitutional Experimentation* (New York: Oxford University Press, 2021).

# CONTRIBUTORS

MICHAL R. BELKNAP is Professor of Law Emeritus at California Western School of Law. A historian-turned-lawyer, he has written numerous books and countless articles on American legal history, including *The Warren Court and the Revolution in Criminal Procedure* (2010) and *The Supreme Court under Earl Warren* (2005).

LAURENCE A. BENNER is Professor of Law Emeritus at California Western School of Law. The former Managing Director of California Western's Criminal Justice Programs, Benner's scholarship has been cited in the US Supreme Court as well as leading criminal justice textbooks and treatises on criminal procedure.

DAVID J. BODENHAMER is Professor of History and Informatics and Executive Director of the Polis Center at Indiana University–Purdue University Indianapolis. Among his most recent books on American constitutional history are *The Revolutionary Constitution* (2012) and *The U.S. Constitution: A Very Short Introduction* (2018).

ROBERT J. COTTROL is Harold Paul Green Research Professor of Law at George Washington University. He has written widely on race relations, slavery, and gun control, including *Gun Control and the Constitution: Sources and Explorations on the Second Amendment* (1993) and *The Long, Lingering Shadow: Slavery, Race and Law in the American Hemisphere* (2013).

RAYMOND T. DIAMOND is Professor of Law and Director of the Pugh Institute for Justice at Louisiana State University. He has written widely on constitutional law, race relations, and legal history, including a work in progress on recent Second Amendment jurisprudence.

JAMES W. ELY Jr., is Milton R. Underwood Professor of Law and Professor of History Emeritus at Vanderbilt University. He is author or editor of numerous works in constitutional and legal history, including *The Guardian of Every Other Right: A Constitutional History of Property Rights* (3rd ed., 2007) and *The Contract Clause: A Constitutional History* (2016).

MARIE-AMÉLIE GEORGE is Assistant Professor of Law at Wake Forest University Law School. A PhD historian, she specializes in LGBTQ rights and teaches courses on civil procedure and family law. She has published widely in academic journals has a book in progress, *Deviant Justice: The Transformation of Gay and Lesbian Rights in America.*

ADAM D. MOORE is Professor in the Information School at the University of Washington and examines the ethical, legal, and policy issues surrounding privacy, freedom of speech, and accountability. A PhD in philosophy, he is author and editor of numerous books and articles, including *Privacy, Security, and Accountability* (2015) and *Privacy Rights: Moral and Legal Foundations* (2010).

PAUL MORENO is William and Berniece Grewcock Chair in Constitutional History, Professor of History, and Dean of Social Sciences at Hillsdale College. He earned his PhD from the University of Maryland and has written on affirmative action and other constitutional topics for academic journals and mass circulation magazines.

KUNAL M. PARKER is Professor of Law and Dean's Distinguished Scholar, University of Miami School of Law. He is author of *Making Foreigners: Immigration and Citizenship Law in America* (2015) and *Common Law, History, and Democracy in America, 1790– 1900: Legal Thought before Modernism* (2011).

DANIEL T. RODGERS is Professor of History Emeritus at Princeton University. His most recent book is *As a City on a Hill: The Story of America's Most Famous Lay Sermon* (2020). Among his other books is *Contested Truths: Keywords in American Politics since Independence* (1987).

RANDALL T. SHEPARD is former Chief Justice of the Indiana Supreme Court (1987–2012). He also served as Chair of the ABA Appellate Judges Conference and as President of the National Conference of Chief Justices (2005 and 2006). He is the author of more than sixty-five articles in law reviews and chapters in books on law and legal history.

SUZANNA SHERRY is Herman O. Loewenstein Professor of Law at Vanderbilt University Law School. An expert in constitutional law, she is author of *Judgment Calls: Principle and Politics in Constitutional Law* (2009, with Daniel Farber), among numerous other books and articles.

MELVIN I. UROFSKY is Professor of History Emeritus at Virginia Commonwealth University. Among his books are *The Affirmative Action Puzzle: A Living History from Reconstruction to Today* (2020) and *Louis D. Brandeis: A Life* (2009). He also is editor of the *Journal of Supreme Court History*.

# INDEX

CPSIA information can be obtained
at www.ICGtesting.com
Printed in the USA
JSHW051001200422
25100JS00002BA/107